CRITICAL ISSUES
IN
WELFARE LAW

CRITICAL ISSUES

IN

WELFARE LAW

CURRENT LEGAL PROBLEMS

Edited by

M. D. A. Freeman

Professor of English Law
University College London

London
Stevens & Sons
1990

Published in 1990
by Stevens & Sons Ltd.
South Quay Plaza, 183 Marsh Wall,
London E14 9FT
Laserset by
P.B. Computer Typesetting, N. Yorks.
Printed by
Thomson Litho, Scotland

British Library Cataloguing in Publication Data

Freeman, M. D. A. (Michael David Alan) *1943–*
    Critical issues in welfare law. — (Current
    legal problems)
    1.   Great Britain.   Welfare services.   Law
    I.   Title
    244.1043

ISBN 0–420–48340–3

CONTENTS

	Page
Table of Cases	vii
Table of Statutes	x
Introduction— Welfare Law after Ten Years of Thatcher M.D.A. Freeman	1
Legal Foundations of the Welfare State: 10 Years On Ross Cranston	9
The Legal Structure of the Social Fund John Mesher	35
Rethinking British Housing Law: The Failure of the Housing Act 1988 Martin Partington	59
Homelessness Law: First Aid in Need of Intensive Care? David Hoath	81
The Politics of Child Care M.D.A. Freeman	103
Unprofessional Standards David Carson	123
Index	137

TABLE OF CASES

[Figures in bold refer to extended references in the text]

A. *v.* Liverpool C.C. [1982] A.C. 363; [1981] 2 W.L.R. 948 .... 8, 112, 115
A.G. Securities *v.* Vaughan [1988] 3 W.L.R. 1205, 1212; reversing [1988] 2
    W.L.R. 689; [1988] 2 All E.R. 173 31
Antoniades *v.* Villiers [1988] 3 W.L.R. 139; [1988] 2 All E.R. 309 31
Associated Provincial Picture Houses Ltd. *v.* Wednesbury Corp. [1948] 1
    K.B. 223, 227–231 (C.A.) 100
A.G. *ex rel* Tilley *v.* Wandsworth L.B.C. [1981] 1 W.L.R. 854 120
Avon C.C. *v.* Buscott [1988] Q.B. 656 33

B. and G., *Re* [1985] F.L.R. 493 106
Birmingham D.C. *v.* McMahon (1987) 151 J.P. 709, 713 .... **27**
Blawdziewicz *v.* Diadon Establishment (1988) 35 E.G. 83 31

C., *Re*, *The Independent*, September 1, 1989 120
Campden Hill Towers *v.* Gardner [1977] Q.B. 823 31
Carroll, *Re* [1931] 1 K.B. 317, 336 120
Cartlidge *v.* Chief Adjudication Officer [1986] Q.B. 360 32
Charles *v.* Charles, April 21, 1983 (unreported) 87, **88**
Cocks *v.* Thanet D.C. [1983] A.C. 286 (H.L.) 100
Council of Civil Service Unions *v.* Minister for the Civil Service [1985] A.C.
    374 .... 120, 121

D., *Re* [1976] Fam. 185 121
——, *Re* [1977] Fam. 158 .... 8, 121
—— *v.* Berkshire C.C. [1987] A.C. 317 121
Davis *v.* Johnson [1979] A.C. 264, 340 (H.L.) 96
De Falco *v.* Crawley B.C. [1980] Q.B. 460 (C.A.) 4, 89, 101, 102
Delahaye *v.* Oswestry B.C., *The Times*, July 29, 1980 98
Derrivière (1969) 53 Cr.App.R. 637 105
Din *v.* Wandsworth L.B.C. [1983] 1 A.C. 657, 930 (H.L.) 97, 100

Essex C.C. *v.* T.L.R. and K.B.R. (1978) 9 Fam.Law 15 121

F. *v.* Suffolk C.C. (1981) 2 F.L.R. 208 121

Gillick *v.* West Norfolk A.H.A. [1986] A.C. 112 107
Goddard *v.* Torridge D.C. [1982] L.A.G. Bull. 9 99

Hewison *v.* Hewison (1977) 7 Fam.Law 207 106

Islam *v.* Hillingdon L.B.C. [1981] 3 All E.R. 901, 911 (H.L.) 89, 91, **99**

J. *v.* C. [1970] A.C. 668 121
J.T., *Re* [1986] 2 F.L.R. 107 120

Jane *v*. Jane [1983] 4 F.L.R. 712 120

Lambert *v*. Ealing L.B.C. [1982] 1 W.L.R. 550 (C.A.) 4, 98, 99

M., *Re* [1967] 1 W.L.R. 1479 120
—— *v*. Westminster C.C. [1985] F.L.R. 325 121
McCall *v*. Abelesz [1976] Q.B. 585 12
Mohamed *v*. Knott [1969] 1 Q.B. 1 120
Moran *v*. Secretary of State for Social Services, *The Times*, March 14, 1987;
    The Independent, March 18, 1987 33

Otter *v*. Norman [1988] 3 W.L.R. 321; [1988] 2 All E.R. 897 17

Palmer *v*. Sandwell M.B.C. (1987) 284 E.G. 1487, *The Times*, October 12,
    1987 .... 30, 33
Practice Direction [1967] 1 All E.R. 828 121
Puhlhofer *v*. Hillingdon L.B.C. [1986] A.C. 484; [1986] 1 All E.R. 467,
    474 .... 4, 24, 85, 92, 93, 94, 96, 100

Quick *v*. Taff Ely B.C. [1986] Q.B. 809 30

R. *v*. Adesanya, *The Times*, July 16, 17, 1974 .... **105**
—— *v*. Bedfordshire C.C., *ex p*. C. [1987] 1 F.L.R. 239 121
—— *v*. Bolton M.B.C., *ex p*. B. [1985] F.L.R. 343 120
—— *v*. Broxbourne B.C., *ex p*. Willmoth, *The Times*, April 18, 1989 99
—— *v*. Camden L.B.C., *ex p*. Gillan (1988) 21 H.L.R. 114 97
—— *v*. ——, *ex p*. Wait (1986) 18 H.L.R. 434 .... 97, 101
—— *v*. Croydon L.B.C., *ex p*. Toth (1987) 20 H.L.R. 576 (C.A.) 99
—— *v*. Ealing L.B.C., *ex p*. Sidhu (1982) 80 L.G.R. 534 97
—— *v*. East Hertfordshire D.C., *ex p*. Hunt (1985) 18 H.L.R. 51 97
—— *v*. East Northamptonshire D.C., *ex p*. Spruce (1988) 20 H.L.R. 508 99
—— *v*. Eastleigh B.C., *ex p*. Beattie (No. 1) (1983) 10 H.L.R. 134, 141 99
—— *v*. —— (No. 2) (1984) 17 H.L.R. 168 .... 98, 99
—— *v*. ——, *ex p*. Evans (1984) 17 H.L.R. 515, 524 99
—— *v*. Gravesham B.C., *ex p*. Winchester (1986) 18 H.L.R. 207, 215 100
—— *v*. Hammersmith & Fulham L.B.C., *ex p*. Duro-Rama (1983) 9 H.L.R.
    71 .... 89, 99
—— *v*. Harrow L.B.C. [1989] 2 F.L.R. 51 .... 121, 122
—— *v*. Hillingdon L.B.C., *ex p*. H. (1988) 20 H.L.R. 554; *The Times*, May
    17, 1988 .... 33, 99
—— *v*. ——, *ex p*. Wilson (1984) 12 H.L.R. 61 100
—— *v*. Hopley (1860) 2 F. & F. 202 119
—— *v*. Kensington & Chelsea L.B.C., *ex p*. Cunha (1988) 21 H.L.R. 16 89
—— *v*. ——, *ex p*. Hammell (1988) 20 H.L.R. 666 (C.A.) 99
—— *v*. London Rent Assessment Panel, *ex p*. Trustees of Henry Smith's
    Charity, *The Times*, November 5, 1987; (1988) 20 H.L.R. 103 31
—— *v*. Mole Valley D.C., *ex p*. Minnett (1984) 12 H.L.R. 48 100
—— *v*. Norfolk C.C., *ex p*. M. [1989] 3 W.L.R. 502 122
—— *v*. North Devon D.C., *ex p*. Lewis [1981] 1 W.L.R. 328, 333 ...... 98, 99, 99
—— *v*. Penwith D.C., *ex p*. Trevena (1984) 17 H.L.R. 526 .... 98, 99
—— *v*. Peterborough C.C., *ex p*. McKernan, July 17, 1987 (unreported) 99
—— *v*. Plymouth Juvenile Court, *ex p*. F. and F. [1987] 1 F.L.R. 169 122
—— *v*. Portsmouth C.C., *ex p*. Knight [1984] L.G.R. 184 100
—— *v*. Preseli D.C., *ex p*. Fisher (1984) 17 H.L.R. 147 97

R. *v.* Preston Supplementary Benefits Appeal Tribunal, *ex p.* Moore
[1975] 1 W.L.R. 624 .... 5, 8
—— *v.* Reigate & Banstead B.C., *ex p.* Henry, December 16, 1982 (unre-
ported) 99
—— *v.* ——, *ex p.* Paris (1984) 17 H.L.R. 103 101
—— *v.* Secretary of State for the Home Department, *ex p.* Swati [1986] 1
W.L.R. 477 8
—— *v.* Secretary of State for Social Services, *ex p.* Child Poverty Action
Group, *The Times*, August 8, 1985; *The Times*, August 16, 1984 33
—— *v.* ——, *ex p.* Child Poverty Action Group, *The Times*, February 15,
1988 25
—— *v.* Slough B.C., *ex p.* Ealing L.B.C. [1981] 2 W.L.R. 399, 403–404
(C.A.) 97
—— *v.* South Hams D.C., *ex p.* Proctor, September 24, 1985 (unreported) ... **90, 91**
—— *v.* Surrey Heath B.C., *ex p.* Li (1984) 16 H.L.R. 79 100
—— *v.* Swansea C.C., *ex p.* John (1982) 9 H.L.R. 58 101
—— *v.* Thurrock B.C., *ex p.* Williams (1982) 1 H.L.R. 128 97
—— *v.* Tower Hamlets L.B.C., *ex p.* Monaf (1988) 20 H.L.R. 529, 541
(C.A.); (1987) 19 H.L.R. 577, 586, *The Times*, April 28, 1988 .... 33, 91,
98, 99, 100, 101
—— *v.* Wandsworth L.B.C., *ex p.* Lindsay (1986) 18 H.L.R. 502 .... 92, 93
—— *v.* ——, *ex p.* Nimako-Boateng (1984) 11 H.L.R. 95 99
—— *v.* Waveney D.C., *ex p.* Bowers [1983] Q.B. 238, 245 (C.A.) 100
—— *v.* Welwyn & Hatfield D.C., *ex p.* Holmes, February 1, 1988 (unre-
ported) 101
—— *v.* West Dorset D.C., *ex p.* Phillips (1984) 17 H.L.R. 336 .... 97, 98, 99
—— *v.* Westminster C.C., *ex p.* Tansey (1988) 20 H.L.R. 520 (D.C.); (1988)
21 H.L.R. 57 (C.A.) 93, 97
—— *v.* Wimbourne D.C., *ex p.* Curtis (1985) 18 H.L.R. 79 86
—— *v.* Woodspring D.C., *ex p.* Walters (1984) 16 H.L.R. 73 97
—— *v.* Wycombe D.C., *ex p.* Mahsood (1988) 20 H.L.R. 683, 686 100
Reid *v.* Andreou [1987] 9 C.L. 175 31
Roughead *v.* Falkirk D.C. (1979) S.C.O.L.A.G. 188 .... 7, 96
Ryan *v.* Fildes [1938] 3 All E.R. 517 119

S. *v.* S. (1978) 1 F.L.R. 143 120
Schon *v.* Campden L.B.C. (1986) 84 L.G.R. 830 31
South Northamptonshire D.C. *v.* Power [1988] 1 W.L.R. 319 33
Stourton *v.* Stourton (1857) 8 De G.M. and G. 760 120
Street *v.* Mountford [1985] A.C. 809 17

Thurley *v.* Smith (1985) 15 Fam.Law 31 (C.A.) 98, 99
Tilley *v.* Wandsworth L.B.C. [1981] 1 All E.R. 1162 (C.A.) 98, 99

W., *Re* (1982) 3 F.L.R. 129 8
—— *v.* Hertfordshire C.C. [1985] A.C. 791 .... 8, 115
Wandsworth L.B.C. *v.* Winder [1985] A.C. 461 33
West Glamorgan C.C. *v.* Rafferty [1987] 1 W.L.R. 457 33
Wooton *v.* Wooton (1985) 15 Fam.Law 31 (C.A.) 98, 99

Y., *Re* [1988] 1 F.L.R. 299 121

TABLE OF STATUTES

1933 Children and Young Per-
    sons Act (c. 12)—
    s. 1 (7) 104
1934 Unemployment Act (c.
    29) 36
1936 Housing Act (c. 51)—
    s. 99 .... 26, 27, 33
1948 National Assistance Act
    (c. 29) 36
    s. 21 (1) (*b*) 96
1957 Housing Act (c. 56)—
    s. 6 12
1961 Housing Act (c. 65)—
    s. 32 12
1966 Supplementary Benefit
    Act (c. 20)— 36
    s. 7 36
    Sched. 2,
        para. 4 (1) (*b*) 56
        para. 6 56
1968 Caravan Sites Act (c.
    52) 26
1974 Legal Aid Act (c. 4)—
    s. 28 (6A) 122
1975 Social Security Act (c.
    14)—
    s. 19 32
    s. 20 32
    s. 104 53
    Children Act (c. 72) .. 106, 107,
                      116, 121
1976 Domestic Violence and
    Matrimonial Pro-
    ceedings Act (c. 50) .. 81, 99
    Supplementary Benefits
    Act (c. 71) 38
    s. 3 38
    Race Relations Act (c.
    74)—
    s. 71 71
    s. 77 71
1977 Rent Act (c. 42) .. 64, 65, 66, 67
    Sched. 2 .... 15, 31
    Protection from Eviction
    Act (c. 43) 69
    s. 1 69

1977 Housing (Homeless Per-
    sons) Act (c. 48) 24, 81
1978 Domestic Proceedings
    and Magistrates'
    Courts Act (c. 22) 99
1979 Wages Council Act (c.
    12) 15
1980 Child Care Act (c. 5)—
    s. 1 .... 85, 98, 99
    s. 10 (3) 120
    s. 18 107
    Social Security Act (c.
    30) 38
    Housing Act (c. 51) 23, 66,
                        67, 75
1981 Supreme Court Act (c.
    54)—
    s. 31 94
1983 Matrimonial Homes Act
    (c. 19) 99
    s. 1 97
1984 Registered Homes Act (c.
    23) 127, 129
1985 Prohibition of Female
    Circumcision Act (c.
    38) 120
    Social Security Act (c.
    53)—
    s. 32 .... **19, 20**
    s. 33 .... **19, 20**
        (10) 20, 32
    s. 34 .... 20, 32
    Housing Act (c. 68)—
    s. 58 .... 83, 85
        (2A) 97
        (2B) 97
        (2) (*a*) 97
           (*c*) 97
        (3) (*a*) 97
           (*b*) 97
    s. 59 (1) 98, 99
    s. 60 .... 79, **84**, 85, 86, 87,
                         88, 90
        (1) 89, 90, 91, 99, 100
        (4) 90
    s. 62 97

1985 Housing Act—*cont.*
s. 64 (4) 102
s. 65 (2) 97
(3) 97, 98, 99
s. 69 93
(1) 82, 92
s. 71 94
s. 75 87
s. 189 (1A) 79
s. 198A 79
Pt. III 81, 83, 92, 93, 95,
98, 99, 102
Pt. V 33, 96
Housing Association Act
(c. 69)—
s. 4 78
s. 35A 78
Landlord and Tenant Act
(c. 70)—
s. 8 12
s. 11 12
1986 Children and Young Persons (Amendment)
Act (c. 28) 121
Wages Act (c. 48) 7
s. 12 (3) 16, 31
s. 13 .... 16, 31
s. 14 (1) 16, 31
Pt. II 15
Social Security Act (c.
50) 10, 18, 19, 21, 22,
25, 35, 43
s. 19 (1A) (b) 21, 32
(c) 21, 32
ss. 20–23 32
ss. 32–35 43
s. 32 32
(2) (a) 43
(8) 44
(10) 46
(11) 46, 52
(8A) 50
(8C) 50
(8D) 50
s. 33 (2) 44
(3) 46
(4) 45
(9) **44, 45**, 51
(c) 45
(d) 45
(e) 22, 32, 50
(10) 45, 46
(1A) 46
(4A)–(7) 46

1986 Social Security Act—
cont.
s. 33—*cont.*
(10A) 46
s. 34 51
(1) (b) 52, 53
(3) 52
(6) 52
(7) 52
s. 35 (2) 52
(3)–(6) 52
s. 63 32
Sched. 2, Pts. II–IV 19, 32
Housing and Planning Act
(c. 63) 92, 95
1987 Landlord and Tenant Act
(c. 26) 13
1988 Social Security Act (c.
7) 21, 26, 43
s. 1 .... 26, 33
s. 4 .... 21, 32
Sched. 3 32
Employment Act (c.
19)—
s. 27 32
Legal Aid Act (c. 34) 7,
14, 73
s. 4 (4) 14, 31
s. 16 (3) 14, 31
Housing Act (c. 50) 17, 59,
61, 83, 95
s. 13 78
(1) 78
s. 20 .... 15, 31
(4) 78
s. 21 78
s. 22 78
s. 27 13
s. 28 .... 13, 79
s. 29 31
s. 30 .... 31, 79
s. 31 .... 31, 79
ss. 34–36 .... 15, 31
s. 39 .... 15, 31, 78
(7) 78
s. 46 78
s. 47 78
s. 48 78
s. 49 78
s. 59 78
ss. 60–92 78
s. 61 (4) 78
s. 62 (3) 78
(4) 78

1988 Housing Act—*cont.*
  s. 63 (1) 78
     (2) 78
  ss. 65–73 78
  s. 79 78
  ss. 93–114 78
  s. 100 78
  s. 103 (2) 78
  s. 116 .... 12, 79
  s. 121 78
  ss. 122–128 78
  s. 130 (2) 78
  s. 137 .... 13, 79

1988 Housing Act—*cont.*
  Pt. I 65
  Chap. IV 68
  Pt. III 82
  Pt. IV 63, 82
  Sched. 1 66
  Sched. 2 .... 17, 31, 78
  Sched. 4 .... 15, 31
  Sched. 6 78
  Scheds. 7–11 78
  Sched. 12 78
  Sched. 15, para. 1 (2) ... 79
     para. 8 79
  Sched. 17, para. 22 78

Introduction

Welfare Law After Ten Years of Thatcher

M.D.A. FREEMAN

Inequality of distribution of income has increased substantially since 1979. The real increase for the top 1 per cent., was 55 per cent. The poorest 40 per cent. by contrast suffered an actual decline in real incomes (the bottom 10 per cent. lost 8 per cent. of their 1979 income).[1] Poverty in Britain has sharply increased since 1979, and a growing proportion are long-time poor. By 1985 (the latest available figures), 9.4 million people, including two-and-a-quarter million children, were living at or below the official poverty line. This amounts to 17 per cent. of the population, an increase of 55 per cent. since 1979. The number of children in poverty nearly doubled.[2] Two-thirds of disabled people (about 4 million) live at or below the poverty line.[3] In 1985, over 15 million people (or 28 per cent. of the population) were living in poverty or on its margins (defined as up to 40 per cent. above the Supplementary Benefit scale). This number includes 5.6 million pensioners and 3.55 million children. The number of households in England accepted as homeless (and, as Hoath shows,[4] tests are restrictive) doubled from 56,750 in 1979 to 112,400 in 1987. Single homeless are not included in official figures.[5] The cost to local authorities of temporary accommodation often in "bed and breakfast" accommodation reminiscent of shanty towns,[6] is £135 million a year. The number of all new houses completed in Great Britain fell by 17 per cent. The number completed by local authorities fell by 75 per cent.; their housing investment budget was cut from £5,200 million in 1978/9 to £1,100 million in 1988/9 (at 1988/9 prices). Over one million public-sector homes were sold. Meanwhile, between 1983 and 1987 waiting lists rose by 170 per cent., from 741,000 to 1,289,000.[7] Between 1979 and 1986, 286 National Health Service hospitals were closed (a further 126

1

were partially closed). The number of hospital beds was cut by more than 50,000, a loss of 14 per cent. Hospital waiting lists are up (628,000 in 1979, over 700,000 in 1987). Inequalities in health and in life expectancy between manual and non-manual workers have increased. Prescription charges have risen by 577 per cent. in real terms (1,200 per cent. in cash terms).[8]

This profile of contemporary Britain leaves out much.[9] There is no reference to unemployment,[10] to our appalling training programme,[11] to wealth,[12] taxation[13] or law and order.[14] But it provides a context for the study of welfare law, broadly defined, which is examined in this Special Issue of *Current Legal Problems*. The '80s have been a period of welfare reform. We can no longer even theorise about an expansive welfare state grounded in universal and non-stigmatised services. To-day's welfare state may have more in common with conservative nineteenth century social philosophy than with the welfare statism that was the goal of Marshall[15] or Beveridge[16] or Tawney.[17]

The Thatcher Government is committed to market-place principles, to consumerism and choice,[18] though, as Carson shows,[19] in practice the implications of an emphasis on contract and consumer perspective are not always carried through. It is committed also to seeing off a dependency culture. Its social security policies stop short, though not by much, of the workfare policies being implemented in the United States as a result of the Family Support Act of 1988. The objective of that Act is to encourage self-sufficiency amongst welfare recipients. To carry out that goal, states are required to develop workfare programmes that compel women on welfare who have children under three (at the option of states, the age of one) to participate in a work and training programme.[20]

In Britain cutting back on welfare means targeting, a phasing out of the Rent Acts (new forms of tenancy, described by Partington,[21] which give some security of tenure but little control over rents), an end to wages councils[22] and minimum wage regulation. It means a cut back on the provision of legal aid,[23] the coverage of which has been reduced by the failure of government to maintain the value of eligibility limits. It means "rolling back the state," moving responsibility from the state to the private sector.[24] This has happened in the housing field, with pensions and with sickness and maternity payments as well as in the provision of substitute care. It means the tightening of means tests.[25] This has happened in many areas, including legal aid provision, but has struck most deeply with the stipulation that all housing benefit recipients now have to pay 20 per cent.

of their rates and those whose income is above the level lose housing benefits at a faster rate than was the case previously. It means severe budgetary restraints with those needing additional funds beyond income support bearing the brunt, as Mesher describes in his account of the new "social fund."[26]

The essays in this collection tackle some of the legal problems which result from a plethora of reforms in the last decade. The legislation and the case law are complex. Homelessness legislation has been described as a "semantic nightmare"[27]: applicants are said to have to run an "obstacle race."[28] Housing legislation is equally complex, the result, Partington believes,[29] of the political compromise it represents. The new "social fund" also reflects some sort of compromise as policy objectives were trimmed in the pre-legislative and legislative processes to meet some realities. But, as Mesher remarks,[30] embodying the "rather subtle" policies of the Social Fund in legislation and in administrative rule-making (of which there are several versions) has proved a difficult problem. The combination of different levels of rule-making within one scheme only accentuates the problem. In the child care area, as Freeman notes,[31] the complexity of the legislation has been such that those charged with carrying out duties under it (in the main, social workers) have often not grasped the powers they have, and, indeed, those they do not possess. The law suffers not just from complexity but also from lack of clarity (what is "intentional" homelessness,[32] when is a need "urgent,"[33] who is a "similar child,"[34] what is "board,"[35] where is the line between licences and leases to be drawn, etc.?[36]).

All the more necessary then, given the substantive inequalities embedded in the economic structure and the laws, that the basic value of equality before the law be upheld. But, as Cranston demonstrates,[37] inability to pay, together with ignorance of what assistance is available (to which may be added fatalism) deprive the consumers of welfare legislation of legal competence, the ability to pursue claims and challenge decisions.[38] The problem is aggravated by cutbacks in legal aid provision, the undermining of the local legal centre movement and it may be even by Government plans to reorganise the legal profession[39] which is thought likely to strengthen the city solicitor whilst weakening the high street and provincial firm.[40] But, of course, the legal profession has anyway long been organised to service business and property interests, so that only a small minority of lawyers is equipped to advise on many of the matters discussed in this collection. Reich,[41] a quarter of a century ago, argued that the legal frame of reference was such that such interests as rights to welfare benefits will only be adequately protected when lawyers come to see them as property rights. Such an interpretation retains validity to-day.

The essays in this collection pursue many fundamental and urgent questions: the relationship between public, private and procedural law,[42] the relationship between policy ("the political") and legislation ("the legal"),[43] the failure of legislation adequately to implement policy objectives,[44] the use of rules and discretion,[45] the limits of judicial review,[46] the role of law in social work[47] (is it a constraint, a framework or a resource?), the use of social welfare provisions for social control purposes,[48] the role of group actions[49] and advocacy schemes,[50] the centralisation of decision-making,[51] the contradictions in government policy (for example, a failure to put its emphasis on market, on consumerism, on choice into practice in some of the vital areas discussed in these essays),[52] a mismatch sometimes between governmental objectives and judicial interpretation (an example being the encouragement of mobility to seek employment and the ruling that a person who gets "on his bike" may be intentionally homeless).[53] Each of these, and many other themes, could be described in detail in this introduction. They can, however, be picked up by the reader as he or she peruses the essays.

One theme does stand out and does, I think, require a sustained comment and that is the provision of appeal and review systems. It is integral to the rule of law that there should be controls on administrative decision-making to ensure its compliance with procedural and substantive proprieties.[54] The courts have long evinced reluctance to interfere with welfare decision-making. The *De Falco* decision,[55] discussed by Hoath,[56] the *Lambert* case in 1982,[57] the *Puhlhofer* litigation[58] are examples where courts have held that the housing of homeless persons is largely a matter for local authorities, whose discretion should be looked upon benevolently, because of the difficulties with which they are faced.[59] In *Puhlhofer* Lord Brightman thought that "great restraint" should be exercised in giving leave to proceed by judicial review.[60] In immigration,[61] social security[62] and child care cases[63] courts have come to similar conclusions. The refusal of courts to allow wardship to be used to attack local authority decision-making relating to children,[64] whilst at the same time encouraging the authorities to use it as supplement and back-stop[65] (though the latter policy is now to be partially reversed)[66] has been frequently condemned, not least by Lord Justice Butler-Sloss in the *Cleveland* report.[67] Limitations on the appeal process are commented upon in several of the contributions to this volume. Thus, the legal structure of the "Social Fund," with decision-making constrained by budgetary limitations, allows for no appeal to a Social Security Appeal Tribunal. There is the possibility of judicial review (though *Moore*'s case[68] cannot fill applicants with confidence of success and Cranston describes it as no more than a theoretical possibility[69]) and there is, somewhat anomalously, a Social Fund Commissioner. This, Mesher explains, is an "extra tier" and is intended to inject an "independent element" as compensation for deficiences in rights of appeal.[70] But is this a satisfactory solution for the dissatisfied consumer who may see this as little more than an internal, bureaucratic review? The legal framework for regulating the private and voluntary sector of residential and nursing homes seems, by contrast, unnecessarily unwieldy and badly-focussed. Carson favours greater reliance on the mechanism of contract ("legalising consumerism," as he puts it).[71] This would, of course, be perfectly consistent with the Government's own ideological commitment, now found even in its plans for the Health Service,[72] to inject market principles. The future for loans under the Social Funds cannot lie in this direction, though a shift in the direction of "entitlements" as with "cold weather heating" payments or maternity or funeral expenses could lead via "rights" to a more tightly-controlled appeal system. At present, as both Cranston and Mesher indicate, the concentration is on management rather than external review. If this leads to better decision-making, it is not necessarily a bad thing. The achievement of good decisions, the upholding of good practices, as Freeman suggests,[73] must remain an important goal. But this requires better training and ultimately more resources. Students of the current British welfare system cannot repose much confidence in government directing its attention to either of these matters.

The Thatcher administration has posed a threat to the welfare state but also a challenge to those who wish to analyse it. To what extent can it live with the market? Can it, as Novak recently put it, "exist as an island of socialism in a sea of capitalism?"[74] Where are the boundaries between the public and the private to be drawn? Can the language of the market (contract, consumerism, choice) live with the imperatives of social welfare principles? We are in a process of redefining welfare. The challenge has to be taken up by lawyers[75] as well as sociologists and social administrators,[76] and philosophers,[77] economists and others.[78] This special issue of *Current Legal Problems* provides a distinctive legal contribution to this contemporary debate.

Notes

[1] See the Family Expenditure Survey and T. Stark, *The New A-Z of Income and Wealth*. Fabian Society 1988. But John Moore M.P. (then) Secretary of State for Social Security said in a speech on May 11, 1989 that this was "quite bizarre."

[2] See House of Commons Social Services Committee, 1987–1988, No. 565; Social Security Statistics 1987; Low Pay Unit/Child Poverty Action Group, *An Abundance of Poverty*, 1988.

[3] See, *per* Office of Population, Censuses and Surveys, as quoted in *The Observer*, November 6, 1988.

[4] *Post*, p. 84.

[5] D.O.E., *Homelessness Statistics*; A.M.A. *Housing Facts*, 1988.

[6] So described by Lord Scarman (*The Times*, October 6, 1987).

[7] Housing and Construction Statistics (GB), 1976–1986, H.M.S.O. Table 61. See further, N. Ginsburg, *Critical Social Policy* no. 25, 1989, p. 56.

[8] Health and Personal Social Services Statistics, 1987 and 1988 (England), D.H.S.S. See also M. Whitehead, "The Health Divide" in *Inequalities In Health*, Penguin, 1988.

[9] For more, see *Poverty* (the Journal of the Child Poverty Action Group) and G. Wright, *ABC of Thatcherism*, Fabian Society, 1989.

[10] The proportion of those unemployed for more than one year rose from 25 per cent. in 1979 to 41 per cent. in 1988 (official figures).

[11] Training initiatives are being handed over to employers, yet in 1986–1987 they spent only 0.6 per cent. of the Gross National Product on training. As compared with West Germany, more than three times our workforce have no occupational qualifications (66 per cent. compared with 21 per cent).

[12] Inequalities of wealth were decreasing in the years 1966–1980: since then the trend to greater equality has stopped.

[13] Under the current administration the *tax cut* for the top 1 per cent. is greater than the *income* of 95 per cent. of taxpayers. See, further, J. Hills, *Changing Tax*, CPAG, 1989.

[14] An increase in the law-under-order budget (30 per cent. in real terms) but a decline in the clear-up rate and a large growth in the prison population (now the highest of any EEC country, both relatively and in absolute terms—but Turkey is keen to join the EEC!). See also M. D. A. Freeman, "Law and Order in 1984," (1984) 37 Current Legal Problems 175.

[15] T. H. Marshall, *Citizenship and Social Class*, 1950. See now D. Harris, *Justifying State Welfare*, 1987.

[16] Sir William Beveridge, *Social Insurance and Allied Services*, 1944. *cf.* Bill Jordan, *Rethinking Welfare*, 1987, Chap. 6.

[17] R. H. Tawney, *Equality*, 1964. On the ideology of inequality, see P. Green, *The Pursuit of Inequality*, 1981.

[18] On the economic theory of this see B. Fine and L. Harris in *Socialist Register 1987*, 1987, p. 365. On Thatcherism and the Welfare State, see I. Gough in (eds.) S. Hall and M. Jacques, *The Politics of Thatcherism*, 1983, p. 148. See also J. Clarke, A. Cochrane and C. Smart, *Ideologies of Welfare: from Dreams to Disillusion*, Hutchinson, 1987.

[19] *Post*, p. 123.

[20] See D. P. Moynihan, *Came The Revolution*, 1988 and H. J. Karger and D. Stoez, in Tikkun, Vol. 4, No. 2 (1989), p. 23.

[21] *Post*, pp. 66–68. See also Cranston, *post*, p. 15.

[22] Not yet abolished but, under the Wages Act 1986, no new ones can be established, and the Secretary of State has wide powers to vary or abolish existing ones. It is likely that in the foreseeable future they will be abolished.

[23] See Legal Aid Act 1988 (and Cranston, *post*, p. 14).

[24] P. Taylor-Gooby, Sociology, Vol. 20, No. 2 (1986), p. 228 found that commercial provision was seen by people as superior to State services on almost every count, though levels of satisfaction with State services were high and dissatisfaction was expressed more in terms of inadequate resources than lack of consumer control. Respondents favoured more spending on State services as well as more scope for private welfare provision.

[25] On which see B. Davies, *Universality, Selectivity and Effectiveness in Social Policy*, 1978.

[26] *Post*, p. 49.

[27] *Per* Sheriff Sinclair in *Roughead* v. *Falkirk D.C.* (1979) S.C.O.L.A.G. 188.

[28] By P. Robson and P. Watchman in [1981] J.S.W.L. 1, 65.

[29] *Post*, p. 76.

[30] *Post*, p. 43.

[31] *Post*, p. 109.

[32] *Post*, p. 84.

[33] *Post*, p. 39.

[34] *Post*, p. 105.

[35] *Post*, p. 17.

[36] *Post*, p. 17.

[37] *Post*, p. 9.

[38] See M. D. A. Freeman, *The Legal Structure*, 1974, pp. 164–171.

[39] *Legal Services: A Framework for the Future* Cm. 740 (July 1989).

[40] See C. Glasser, 86 Law Soc. Gaz. No. 13, p. 9 (April 5, 1989).

[41] 73 Yale L.J. 733 (1964).

[42] See Partington, *post*, 73.

[43] See Mesher, *post*, p. 55 and Partington, *post*, pp. 71–72.

[44] See Hoath, *post*, p. 91, Partington, *post*, p. 71, Mesher, *post*, p. 44.

[45] See Cranston, *post*, p. 19, Mesher, *post*, p. 54, Freeman, *post*, p. 108.

[46] See Cranston, *post*, p. 26, Mesher, *post*, p. 52, Hoath, *post*, p. 94, Freeman, *post*, p. 113.

[47] See Freeman, *post*, p. 108, Carson, *post*, p. 127.

[48] See Cranston, *post*, p. 21.

[49] See Cranston, *post*, p. 25.

[50] See Carson, *post*, p. 135.

[51] See Cranston, *post*, p. 25, Mesher, *post*, p. 45, Freeman, *post*, p. 116.

[52] See Carson, *post*, p. 127.

[53] See Hoath, *post*, pp. 90–91.

[54] See L. L. Fuller, *The Morality of Law*, 1964; J. Raz (1977) 93 L.Q.R. 195.

[55] [1980] Q.B. 460.

[56] *Post*, p. 89.

8 *Introduction*

57 [1982] 1 W.L.R. 550.
58 [1986] 1 All E.R. 467.
59 It would be difficult to imagine courts adopting this attitude to (say) the Inland Revenue.
60 [1986] 1 All E.R. at p. 474.
61 *R.* v. *Secretary of State for the Home Department ex parte Swati* [1986] 1 W.L.R. 477.
62 See *R.* v. *Preston Supplementary Benefits Appeal Tribunal, ex parte Moore* [1975] 1 W.L.R. 624.
63 See *W.* v. *Shropshire C.C.* [1986] 1 F.L.R. 359.
64 *A.* v. *Liverpool C.C.* [1982] A.C. 363; *W.* v. *Hertfordshire C.C.* [1985] A.C. 791.
65 *Re D* [1977] Fam. 158; *Re W* (1982) 3 F.L.R. 129.
66 See Children Bill 1989, clause 71.
67 Para. 16.37.
68 [1975] 1 W.L.R. 624.
69 *Post*, p. 20. But see J. Luba in *Welfare Rights Bulletin* 90 (1989) p. 4 and see now the description in *Welfare Rights Bulletin* 91 (1989) of two cases (p. 13). See also *Legal Action*, May 1988.
70 *Post*, p. 52.
71 *Post*, p. 134.
72 See Department of Health, *Working For Patients*, 1989.
73 *Post*, p. 118.
74 T. Novak, *Poverty and the State: An Historical Sociology* 1988, p. 175.
75 See P. Alcock in Special Number of Journal of Law and Society, "Thatcher's Law," (16 J.S.L. 97 (1989)).
76 The journal *Critical Social Policy* contains numerous articles. See also M. Loney *et al*, *The State or The Market: Politics and Welfare in Contemporary Britain*, 1987, P. Lee and C. Raban, *Welfare Theory and Social Policy*, 1988, E. Papadakis and P. Taylor-Gooby, *The Private Provision of Public Welfare*, 1987 and B. Jordan, *Rethinking Welfare*, 1987.
77 For example, D. Braybrooke, *Meeting Needs*, 1987, J. Keane, *Democracy and Civil Society*, 1988, M. Walzer, *Spheres of Justice, 1983*.
78 For example, from the realm of politics and political theory, the important text by D. Marquand, *The Unprincipled Society*, 1988.

The editor and publishers are grateful to the Controller of Her Majesty's Stationery Office for permission to reproduce extracts.

Legal Foundations of the Welfare State: 10 Years On

ROSS CRANSTON

What are the implications of 10 years of Conservative government for the welfare state, in particular the law of the welfare state? Answering the question demands that attention be given to the details of government policy and its implementation. Political rhetoric by itself is not a sure guide. Consequently, this chapter outlines some of the law and policy of recent years in areas such as housing, legal aid and social welfare benefits and services.[1] There follows an attempt to view these developments in a broader perspective. The framework used in the chapter is that first advanced in my *Legal Foundations of the Welfare State.*

The Individual and the Law

Equality before the law is a key legal value in the relationship of the individual to the law. Yet as in society generally, economic and social inequalities negate equality before the law. One aspect of this is in the exercise of legal rights. Inability to pay, and ignorance or failure to obtain legal aid or other legal assistance, mean that those without resources cannot take advantage of what the law permits or provides.

Research on housing for the Civil Justice Review in 1986 confirmed this. It carried out a small study of those with housing problems, including those with landlords who did not carry out repairs. Its finding was a reluctance to initiate court action, usually on the grounds of cost, and a low awareness of legal aid.[2]

The other side of the coin is the failure to defend legal proceedings, for example, when landlords and mortgagees institute possession actions for rent or mortgage arrears. Research for the Civil Justice Review in 1986 confirmed that few tenants or mortgagors used court forms to supply the court with written information about their family or financial circumstances. Nor did many attend the court hearing—three quarters of local authority tenants, half of private tenants, and two fifths of mortgage borrowers failed to do so. Only 8 per cent. of defendants were represented at the hearing, but inasmuch as conclusions can be drawn about these matters, representation seems to have had a positive effect on outcome.[3] Similarly, with debt—30 per cent. of County Court debtors surveyed in another research study for the Civil Justice Review did not return the summons form, almost a third interviewed said that they disputed the claim but did not file a defence, and only just over one-third appeared in court.[4]

To an extent, government policy, in particular macro economic policy, has probably accentuated the problem in recent times. Over a seven year period, the number of mortgage repossessions has risen nearly eightfold.[5] This seems attributable to both the encouragement since 1979 of home ownership—one example, of course, is the right to buy legislation for council tenants—and to the freer availability of credit. In 1985, the National Consumer Council identified increased "budget stretch" as new buyers put a greater proportion of their available income to buying housing.[6] The significant increase in interest rates since 1988—a key lever of government economic policy—must lead to an increase in mortgage default.

The same applies to debt generally. The amount of consumer credit outstanding doubled between 1983 and 1987 and has been accompanied by a slow but steady rise in the number of consumer debt claims before the courts.[7] As a result of the Social Security Act 1986, most payments from the social fund are by way of loan, which means that the Government will itself become a more significant creditor of the poor.

Whatever the indirect, and it would seem unintended, effects of government policy, the Civil Justice Review made various proposals to encourage a fuller participation in the courts by tenants, mortgagors, and debtors. Established by the Lord Chancellor in 1985, its brief was couched in terms not of broad principle, but of improving the machinery of civil justice, in particular to reduce delay, cost and complexity. The Review concluded that steps should be taken to encourage housing defendants to attend the hearing and to ensure that as much information as possible was before the court.

"Where the court has to exercise a discretion either to make a possession order or to suspend the operation of a possession order it should be the practice of the court to ensure that it has before it adequate information on which to make a proper evaluation and, where relevant, to set a realistic rate for repayment of arrears. *Plaintiffs* are best placed to provide a history of the letting or mortgage, details of the calculation and handling of the arrears and of efforts made to recover them including previous legal action (my emphasis)."[8]

As a result, it recommended reforms in procedure and court forms to provide the court with fuller evidence of the basis of the claim and the circumstances of the defendant. In addition, when landlords were seeking rent arrears, but not possession, it recommended a cheaper and speedier procedure. The proposal was designed to deal with rent arrears without tenants losing their homes.[9] The Government has accepted the general thrust of these proposals. Possession should be granted only when no other solution is acceptable.

Chief among the specific recommendations with regard to debt, the Civil Justice Review has proposed reform of the administration order, which allows a debtor with multiple debts to apply to discharge all his obligations by making regular payments into court which are distributed among creditors on a pro rata basis. Reform proposed includes enabling any debtor to apply for an order, even if there is no judgment debt; removing the monetary limit; limiting orders to three years, and if a debtor is unable to pay off debts within that time, making a compensation order for less than the full amount; and preventing creditors who provide a continuing service, in the nature of an essential utility, from circumventing the effect of an order by withdrawing it without leave of the court. The Review justifies reform because this "form of mini-bankruptcy has the important economic function of rehabilitating debtors in a comparatively short time and restoring them to their full economic status."[10]

While the latter may have a ring of free market economics to it, reform of the administration order along these lines has been advocated, and indeed welcomed, by groups such as the Legal Action Group. Success of the administration order depends, of course, on assistance being given to debtors, such as by money advice centres.[11] That, of course, requires financial assistance for such centres—outside the purview of the Review. Moreover, the Review did not pursue more radical suggestions for reforming debt actions advanced by bodies such as the Legal

Action Group. These include requiring utilities to obtain a court order before disconnecting a service, and forcing creditors to seek more information on debtors' means before granting credit or issuing proceedings for recovery.[12]

Inequalities in the substantive law occur primarily because the law favours certain categories, such as landlords, employers, and producers over others, such as tenants, employees, and consumers. Illustrative is the substantive law of landlord and tenant, which operates in the absence of agreement between the parties or legislative intervention. For example, at common law landlords have minimum obligations regarding habitability, and generally none regarding repairs. Legislation from 1885 made incursions on the common law position, imposing on landlords statutory covenants regarding fitness for habitation and repair. The statutory covenants were continued in the Landlord and Tenant Act 1985, a consolidating measure. Section 8 contains what was Section 6 of the Housing Act 1957, and applies a term of fitness for human habitation. However, the low rental values were not updated in 1985 in the light of inflation, and the covenant is in effect moribund.

Section 11 of the 1985 Act contains what was Section 32 of the Housing Act 1961. Its statutory covenant by the landlord to repair the structure and exterior, etc., is implied in respect of some residential lettings. Recent decisions indicate that Section 11 is not adequate to cover condensation. The section only applies if there is actual disrepair caused by condensation, such as crumbling wall plaster or damage to window frames.[13] A wider view of repair would be that it includes anything defective or inherently inefficient for living, or ineffective to provide the conditions of ordinary habitation.[14] However, tenants continue to obtain substantial damages in civil proceedings for breach of Section 11 when it applies.[15] Now the Housing Act 1988 extends the scope of Section 11 by obliging the landlord to repair common parts and installations.[16] Tenants of blocks of flats are thus in a better position to ensure that roofs, walls, foundations and communal boilers and heating systems are kept in repair.

Other measures beneficial to tenants relate to harassment, unlawful eviction and racial discrimination. The Housing Act 1988 strengthens the law of harassment, overcoming some of the problems of obtaining convictions against landlords.[17] Quite substantial damages are awarded in harassment cases.[18] The Housing Act 1988 also creates a new civil cause of action of unlawful eviction, thereby reversing the effect of the Court of Appeal decision in *McCall* v. *Abelesz*.[19] In calculating damages under it, courts have to take into account the vacant possession value and the development value of premises, *i.e.* the profit the landlord gains by obtaining vacant possession.[20] In the main, the provisions are a positive development for tenants,[21] although one interpretation may be that they are a corollary to the phasing out of the Rent Acts. In particular, the Government was able to counter criticism that the Housing Act 1988, in phasing out the Rent Acts (see below), would lead to a return of Rachmanism by pointing to these provisions. Finally, the Housing Act 1988 gives statutory force to a Code of Practice of the Commission for Racial Equality in the field of rented housing.[22]

The Landlord and Tenant Act 1987 attempts to tackle the problems of leasehold flats, in particular the increasing number with short leases (50 years or less) and the repair problems to which this gives rise. It is not a radical measure, eschews alternatives to leasehold tenure, and is largely confined to changes in procedure.[23] Initial indications are that the judiciary will respond favourably to an application to appoint a manager under the Act to carry out repairs in default of the landlord doing so.[24] The Act also extends the right of most tenants to have their landlord's name and address and to withhold certain payments if they are not supplied.[25]

Publicly funded legal services are a step to effecting in practice equality before the law. However, containing public expenditure has been the hallmark of government policy on legal aid since 1979. The most notable feature since that time has been the reduction in the coverage of legal aid because of a failure by the Government to maintain the value of the eligibility limits. As a consequence, probably under 60 per cent. of households and only just over half the population are now elibigle for legal aid, despite government claims that the figures are higher.[26] Delay in payment and the unremunerative nature of the work mean that some practitioners have withdrawn from the scheme. The Government is now contemplating a low cost extension of legal services by the introduction of a contingency fee system.[27]

Legal aid continues to be concentrated in matrimonial, negligence and criminal cases. Recent research into the green form scheme found that solicitors are not used to any extent in areas such as welfare benefits, employment, and consumer problems.[28] If dealt with, these matters are handled by advice and law centres.[29] Awareness of legal aid continues to be low, despite publicity material.

Legislatively, the Legal Aid Act 1988 has been the government's major initiative. The background to the Act is very much concerned with efficiency. The White Paper leading to the Act was preceded by an efficiency scrutiny, authored by officials from the Treasury and Lord Chancellor's department. Its proposals were designed to provide advice available under the green form scheme more cheaply, and to use the amount saved for better tribunal representation and an out of hours advisory service. Its specific recommendations in relation to advice were not taken up by the Government, although the Government's general intention is to provide advice and assistance in a more cost effective way.[30]

The Act transfers administration of the scheme from the profession to a government body, the Legal Aid Board. This is consistent with the arrangements in other countries, and relatively uncontroversial despite the wide discretion conferred on the Lord Chancellor to decide matters such as eligibility and remuneration. The major administrative change, however, is the power of the board to provide advice, assistance, and representation by means of contracts with persons and bodies such as lawyers and advice agencies.[31] The justification for "contracting out" is to streamline the work, reduce administrative costs, and exercise more control over the quality of service. Nothing has been done so far in this regard.

The Act and its attendant regulations contain some reductions in the scope of legal aid (for example, the green form is no longer available to most people in relation to wills and conveyancing). The Act contains provisions whereby those outside the free limits can be required to make a greater contribution than at present.[32] This step was said by the White Paper to be necessary to instill in legally aided litigants a better sense of the cost of litigation. There are provisions in the Act for group actions. Regulations will enable the Legal Aid Board to make special arrangements for representation in cases with large numbers of plaintiffs.

Publicly funded law centres continue—the number is likely to exceed 60 in 1989. In fact the law centre movement is almost 20 years old, the first being established in North Kensington in 1970. Casework continues to be used as a basis for "lead" cases, which seek to develop law in a particular area in favour of client groups.[33] Law centres depend heavily on local authority funding, and at a time when local authority finances are under tighter central government control it is not surprising that some have suffered a reduction in local authority support.

Social Welfare Regulation

The regulation of property and capital has been a central feature of the welfare state. It is here that the present government has been active in removing regulatory controls and opening the door to market forces.

Rent control has long been a bête noire of conservatives. Conservative party commentators have long seen a need to amend, if not repeal, the Rent Acts, in the hope of stimulating the private rented sector by giving landlords a greater return on their investment.[34] The Housing Act 1988 now refers to the "phasing out" of the Rent Acts. There are two main aspects:

First, no new protected tenancies can be created after the Act comes into force unless the tenancy is pursuant to a previous contract, is granted to an existing protected or a statutory tenant by the same landlord, or in certain cases where a possession order is obtained against a protected or statutory tenant on the ground of suitable alternative accommodation.[35] Similarly, where there is a residential landlord, for example, no new restricted contract can be created unless entered into pursuant to a contract made before the commencement of the Act.[36] The Act does not affect existing protected tenants, although there has been some reduction in the extent of succession after the death of a statutory tenant.[37]

Secondly, the Act creates new forms of tenancy. "Assured tenancies" give some security of tenure but little control over rents. The grounds for possession are wider than under the Rent Act.[38] "Assured shorthold tenancies," which are for a fixed term of not less than six months, give no security of tenure after the expiration of the period.[39] By applying to a rent assessment committee, assured shorthold tenants obtain some rent protection, but a lack of security is likely to discourage applications.

Developments since 1979 in minimum wage regulation are consistent with "rolling back the state." Under the Wages Councils Act 1979, wages councils regulated the pay and other conditions of employment of particular groups of workers. In 1985, there were still some 2,750,000 workers covered by the Act. However, the Government has made no secret of its desire to abolish wages councils on the grounds that they price workers, especially young people, out of jobs. A secondary objection has been to the administrative burden said to be imposed on employers.[40]

The first step was Part II of the Wages Act 1986. Under it, no new wages councils can be established, and the Secretary of

State has wide powers to abolish or vary the operation of existing councils.[41] Moreover, the Act removes workers under 21 from the protection of the wages councils, and restricts the power of the councils to set a single minimum hourly rate of remuneration, a single overtime rate, and a limit on deductions for living accommodation.[42] Consequently, the councils cannot set minimum holiday entitlement, unsocial hours payments, or different rates of pay for different areas (for example London), levels of skill or responsibility.

The Government is now considering abolishing wages councils altogether. In some respects, it believes that the 1986 legislation has not had the desired effect. Most wages councils have continued to operate in the traditional way, and the annual increases have been, in their view, too high. The legislative intention, it says, was that councils should set a rate which provided a safety net for a vulnerable minority, but would not have deleterious effects on employment in the least prosperous areas. Instead, the rates set have been appropriate to wealthier areas and indeed higher than the levels required to fill jobs. Overall, the Government is opposed to minimum wage regulation because:

> "it prevent[s] employers developing pay systems wholly in accordance with the best interest of their businesses. In that way [it] reduce[s] jobs and increase[s] employment—which is a far more frequent source of poverty than low pay."[43]

The efficacy of social welfare regulation depends on various factors—the way the legislation emerges, its legislative form, the behaviour of regulatory agencies, the susceptibility of institutions and the side effects of the legislation. Some of these factors can be influenced by government. For example, resources are crucial to the enforcement of regulation, as is political will. The present government's attitude to minimum wage regulation seems to be reflected in the record of enforcement, which continues to be poor. In 1986 nearly 2.5 million pounds was found to be owing by employers, and underpayment of wages was found in 8,205 different establishments. Yet only three of these were prosecuted by the wages inspectorate, although failure to pay the minimum rate is a criminal offence.[44]

In some respects, however, government policy is irrelevant to the enforcement of social welfare regulation. The courts, for instance, have a certain autonomy in the interpretation they place on social welfare regulation. Illustrative is their response to attempts to avoid the Rent Acts. One area arose in *Otter* v. *Norman*,[45] where the House of Lords sanctioned continental breakfast as board, by holding that tenants receiving it in a communal dining room from kitchen staff employed by the landlord were not protected. Another area is where a "licence" has been used instead of a lease as a means of avoiding the Rent Acts. The distinction between licences and leases was examined by the House of Lords in *Street* v. *Mountford*,[46] where it was said that generally objective, not subjective, factors determine which category applies. The decision disapproves some decisions of lower courts, which had recognised "non exclusive occupation agreements" as an effective means of avoiding rent control. While the decision offered some clarification of the distinction between leases and licences, it did not prevent subsequent conflicting decisions by differently constituted Courts of Appeal.[47] In 1988 the House of Lords considered the matter yet again.[48] Great weight was placed on the surrounding circumstances, including the relationship between the prospective occupiers, preceding negotiations and the nature and mode of occupation. Artificiality would be detected and frustrated, said the law lords, in agreements purporting to grant a licence where the true character was a tenancy. Lord Templeman added that the debate on the Rent Acts was for Parliament; the duty of the courts was to enforce the legislation.[49] For the future, the distinction will be less important, since the Housing Act 1988 permits landlords to avoid security of tenure by granting assured shorthold tenancies.

Whether legislative activity in this area has its intended effects turns on a range of social and economic factors. In recent years, for example, it has been very profitable for landlords to sell with vacant occupation for sub division of the property for sale. This is one factor in the decline of privately rented accommodation. Similarly, if in the next decade there is an increase in privately rented accommodation, it will be difficult to separate out the influence of other factors from the policy of the Government of phasing out the Rent Acts. For example, the Government is providing tax relief under the business expansion scheme for investors in companies providing assured tenancies. As well as the intended, there are the indirect and unintended effects of legislation. One likely unintended, if not unforeseen, effect of the Housing Act 1988 is said to be an increase in the number of homeless, since one of the new automatic grounds for possession under the Act is three months rent arrears.[50]

Social Welfare Benefits

Social welfare benefits have been a major focus of government activity. Several aspects are illustrative:

Retirement pensions are the most important social welfare benefit in terms of the number of recipients and expenditure. The major concern of the Conservative Government's pensions policy has been to encourage individuals to make their own provision and to reduce the substantial financial burden being handed to future generations. Government policy has thus been "a reduction in the emerging cost of the state earnings-related scheme; a significant increase in the number of people with an occupational or personal pension; and more flexibility and choice generally in pension provision for employers and employees."[51] Specifically, the Social Security Act 1986 makes the earnings-related pension formula less generous and widens the scope for contracting out from the state earnings-related pension scheme to include money purchase schemes. These give no guarantee, as previously, that the recipient will be in as good a position as under the state scheme.[52]

With income-related (means-tested) benefits, the main aims of the Government have been to contain costs, to improve administration, and to concentrate resources on those in greatest need. These aims relate directly to broader government concerns to control public expenditure and to promote individual responsibility rather than reliance on the state.[53]

Containing costs has been achieved firstly, by increasing benefits less than the rate of inflation. (Indeed, there is no legal duty to uprate income related benefits at all.[54]) Secondly, the Government has moved responsibility from the state to the private sector, as with sickness and maternity payments.[55] Thirdly, it has tightened means tests. For example, all housing benefit recipients now have to pay 20 per cent. of their rates and those whose income is above the level lose housing benefits at a faster rate than previously.[56]

Improved administration is to come from simplification. What the government calls the "false prospectus," that supplementary benefit could deal with each individual's special needs in detail, was abandoned in the Social Security Act 1986. Additional weekly payments and lump sum payments have been replaced by limited payment from the social fund in certain cases of need. Improved administration has also come from computerisation. Interestingly, computerisation has led in part to legal changes, as with the abandonment in income supplement of the complex distinction between householder and non-householder by the more easily computerised variable of age.[57]

Targeting can be seen in the way that family credit has been favoured over child benefit. Family credit replaces family income supplement, but by contrast with the latter is intended to be permanent, and more generous and extensive.[58] Another area where targeting is obvious is that the single, young unemployed are denied benefit. The assumption is that they are not in great need, because they can fall back on the assistance of their families.

What has all this meant legally? There have been changes in legislation, notably the Social Security Act 1986, which embodies in legal form these significant changes in social policy. In terms of the legal form of the legislation, however, the changes are not fundamental. Take income support, which replaced supplementary benefit in April 1988. It was designed to move away from assessing the personal circumstances of claimants, but its legal form is very similar to supplementary benefit in the rules of entitlement and the method of calculating benefit.[59] Some differences emerge in that premiums awarded on the basis of parenthood, age and disability replace the long term rate for supplementary benefit and additional requirements.[60]

Another legal dimension to social welfare benefits is their juridical nature—the discretion in the relevant legislation, the provisions for accountability through external review, and the basis of entitlement to benefit. Commentators have focused attention here on the creation of the social fund, which is designed to meet exceptional needs. Six different types of payment can be made from the social fund. Payment of the first three—for maternity, funeral and cold weather heating expenses—is governed by regulations. Appeals can be taken to a social security appeal tribunal. Payment of the other three—budgetary loans, crisis loans and community care grants—is discretionary.[61] The increase in discretion in relation to them was justified because of the complexity of the existing system, as a result of which help was said often to be dependent on the intricacies of interpretation rather than on a genuine assessment of need. There can be no doubt that the very rapid increase in supplementary benefit payments for special needs was also a major factor in change.

Legally, the discretion is wide. Sections 32 and 33 of the Social Security Act 1985 read in part:

32.—(2) Payments may be made out of that fund, in accordance
with this Part of this Act—

...

(b) to meet other needs in accordance with directions given or
guidance issued by the Secretary of State.

...

(5) The Social fund shall be maintained under the control and
management of the Secretary of State and payments out of it shall
be madé by him.

...

33.—(2) The question whether such a payment is to be awarded
and how much it is to be shall be determined by a social fund
officer.

...

(9) In determining whether to make an award to the applicant or
the amount or value to be awarded an officer shall have regard ...,
to all the circumstances of the case and, in particular—

(a) the nature, extent and urgency of the need;

(b) the existence of resources from which the need may be met;

(c) the possibility that some other person or body may wholly or
partly meet it;

(d) where the payment is rapayable, the likelihood of repayment
and the time within which repayment is likely;

...

The Government can issue directives as to how discretionary
payments shall be met, and these are binding on social fund
officers.[62] A manual has been published containing the
directives and guidance. In fact, there is a good argument that
while the system may limit the amound spent, it does not
eliminate discretion. The combination of directions and guidance produce a rule-bound system comparable to that
operating previously.

External review has been replaced by a system of management review. The justification was because external review
might not be equipped to judge whether an outcome was
sensible, since it was removed from the initial judgment in
terms of formality and time. There is no appeal to a social
security appeal tribunal from a decision of a social fund officer,
although claimants can request a review by a social fund officer
and then a social fund inspector.[63] Judicial review is a
theoretical possibility, but is unlikely to be successful in
practice. The result is that claimants and advisors cannot be
sure of what will be obtained, even in situations which are
identical.

The Government has been quite explicit about the social control functions which it expects social welfare benefit legislation to perform. (This has not invariably meant less generous benefit.) Encouraging work, or training for work, has loomed large. To qualify for benefit, claimants must still in general be available for work and must not have refused work.[64] The Social Security Act 1986 extended the maximum period of disqualification for voluntary unemployment to 13 weeks, and in 1988 the period was extended to a maximum of 26 weeks by statutory order.[65] In addition, claimants can now be disqualified if they refuse or fail to take advantage of a place on an approved training scheme or neglect to avail themselves of a reasonable opportunity of a place.[66] Moreover, the Social Security Act 1988 raises the minimum age for income support from 16 to 18 years. (Where they satisfy special conditions in regulations or persuade the Secretary of State that severe hardship will result, 16 year olds may still be able to obtain it.[67]) Since it offers every school leaver a guaranteed place on a training scheme the government claims that young people can choose—between continuing their education or training. The government perception, in its manifesto for the 1987 election, was that this step was necessary to ensure that those under 18 years who deliberately chose to remain unemployed were not eligible for benefit. The government's latest move in tightening conditions is in Section 10 of the Social Security Act 1989, which provides that those on unemployment benefit actively seek employment. In all this, the government denies moving to a workfare system, claiming instead that it is simply encouraging people into employment.

The trade dispute qualification, which prevents payment of benefit where a trade dispute is the reason for unemployment, remains.[68] The test for income support and unemployment benefit has been brought into line. Amendments in 1986 were designed to overcome hardship as a result of a Court of Appeal decision,[69] which disqualified from benefit certain claimants made redundant. The disqualification does not operate now if the employee is dismissed for redundancy during a stoppage or returns to work but later loses employment for a reason unconnected with the trade dispute.[70]

The cohabitation rule remains and seems to generate less concern than previously. The focus has now moved to what government ministers call the "dependency culture." Particular attention has been given to why young women become single parents, in particular whether there is an incentive for them to get pregnant so that they can obtain benefit.

The social context of benefit administration is important to an understanding of whether claimants obtain their legal entitlement. In particular, factors involved are the characteristics of social welfare claimants, the operating patterns of welfare bureaucracies, and the perceptions of social welfare in society. One aspect of the first of these is that many who are eligible do not claim social welfare benefits because they lack the knowledge, capacity or motivation to do so. The operation of welfare bureaucracy turns on factors such as their internal organisation, the information they make available to the public, the routines they operate and the adequacy of their financial and human resources. Societal perceptions of social welfare feed into judgments which welfare officials exercise at the point of delivery of benefits.

Government policy on targeting is supposed to obviate problems of takeup. The experience with family credit belies this, in that only about one in three of those eligible receive it. With regard to benefit administration, government policy can override legal provision. For example, the Social Security Act 1986 provides that the Secretary of State can set a budget for each local office and says that social fund officers are to have regard to these budgets.[71] Whatever the discretion which this language might otherwise confer, it is clear that in practice social fund officers must comply with the budgetary limits. A legal right to payment is not, of course, compatible with cash limits, since payment will not be made if the limit is exceeded, even though otherwise it would have been. Neither is an appeal to an independent tribunal, for a tribunal would be ill equipped to have regard to the priorities set as a result of cash limits. Mullen makes the valuable point that the consequence might be arbitrary decisions, not discretion (if discretion is a flexible approach to meeting needs).

"This in turn suggests that despite the expressed intention of the fund and the terms of the manual, discretion, in the sense of a flexible approach to the meeting of needs, cannot be expected to thrive. In offices whose allocations are far below past single payment expenditure there may have to be relatively crude local rules of thumb used to ensure that budgets are not exceeded. SFOs may not be allowed to say openly, 'no washing machines this month' but that may be the kind of approach offices have to adopt. Caution, not discretion, will be the watchword of SFOs."[72]

Delays, lost payments, and error lead to underpayment and have attracted considerable attention in recent years, especially in relation to social security offices in inner London. Some advice groups, such as the Greater London Citizen's Advice Bureaux' service, claimed in 1986 that the system for administering supplementary benefit in London had virtually collapsed.[73] Official accounts of the system have not been a great deal more sanguine.[74] No doubt the administrative culture of particular offices, and the trend of government policy, continue to cause a disjuncture between the legal entitlement of claimants and the benefits they actually obtain.[75]

The Provision of Public Services

The paradox of social welfare bureaucracies providing services is that although ostensibly they are devoted to the interests of the users of the service, in practice their behaviour can be contrary to those interests. There is a wide discretion entrusted to them in their constative legislation which is one factor in explaining this paradox, in that it permits a bureaucracy's own perceptions to determine events.[76] Legal correctives include structuring legal discretion—along with the opportunity of external review of decision making, and incorporating good practice into bureaucratic procedures. Greater participation by the users of a service is an important non-legal way of achieving the same end.

The Government would claim that its policies in relation to public housing have been directed to resolving the paradox by enhancing the choices, power and individual responsibilities of tenants. (No doubt other motives are there, such as breaking up council estates and the political base they have given the Labour Party.[77]) Certainly significant numbers of public housing tenants have benefited. Many tenants have exercised the right to buy introduced by the Housing Act 1980—two thirds had not expected to be owners before the legislation.[78] Public housing tenants have been able to obtain substantial damages in the courts for breach of tenancy agreements, mandated by the Housing Act 1980.[79] Since 1980, public sector tenants have had considerable security of tenure to which those residing with a tenant can succeed.[80] The other side of the coin is that the right to buy has been exercised mainly by better off tenants. Coupled with less new public housing, it has also placed pressure on the remaining housing stock. Moreover, public sector housing rents are being brought increasingly into line with market rents.[81]

The Housing (Homeless Persons) Act 1977 was the legal response to a social problem, in that it placed a legal duty on local authorities to provide for the homeless. The Conservative Government has not sought to subtract from that duty. Indeed, it accepted amendments to its Housing and Planning Bill 1986, based on a draft by Shelter, seeking to reverse the unfortunate effects of the House of Lords' decision in *Puhlhofer* v. *Hillingdon L.B.C.*[82] In broad terms that decision had held that overcrowding and unfitness of existing accommodation did not make a person homeless for the purpose of the legislation, and that a local authority would not normally be in breach of the Act even if the dwelling offered a homeless person was overcrowded or unfit.[83]

The decision was also unfortunate in that it contained *dicta* deprecating the amount of litigation by the homeless against local authority decisions, and indicating to lower courts that they should grant judicial review in this area in only exceptional cases. There is no evidence of a deluge of litigation by the homeless or that the cases brought had no substantial basis. Immediately following the case, however, the number of applications for judicial review halved and the number refused leave doubled.[84] Notwithstanding *Puhlhofer*, Homeless Persons applications are still successful before the courts.[85]

Although the Housing (Homeless Persons) Act remains on the statute book, the Government has not adopted proposals for its amendment by bodies such as Shelter—for example the legal standard for the temporary accommodation used for housing the homeless could be improved, and the punitive use of the intentional homelessness test could be curbed.[86] One reason may be the Government view that much homelessness is due to changes in lifestyle, causing increased demand. In fact, decreased supply seems to be the major factor.

Social Change and the Legal System

The Government has had firm views on the shape of the welfare state, and being committed to certain ends has not been easily deflected. Ogus writes:

"... it is an integral part of the new ideology that excessive attempts to reach consensus on major social and economic issues has sapped the moral fibre of the nation. Consequently, there has been much more centralisation of decision making. Consultative bodies are less important than they were and the position of interest groups has changed significantly... the fact that, hitherto, the government has had a large majority within the House of Commons has meant that parliament has been relatively muted as a participant in the debate of crucial issues... [M]uch of the reform of this period *has* evolved mainly as a consequence of ideology, notably in the shift of welfare provision from the public to the private sector... the parameters within which reform is perceived as being possible are now determined by politicians, rather than the administrators."[87]

Consequently, Fabian tactics of research, lobbying and media campaigns have had only relatively minor achievements. Amendments to the Housing and Planning Bill 1986 have already been mentioned. Another example of the amendment of legislation in its passage through parliament is the change to the social fund in the Social Security Act 1986.[88]

Organisations like Child Poverty Action Group, the National Association of Citizens' Advice Bureaux and Age Concern have all supported test cases in the courts. The standing of such organisations is still unresolved. In *R.* v. *Secretary of State for Social Services ex p. Child Poverty Action Group*,[89] the Secretary of State conceded the standing issue, so that the court did not have to resolve it. While in an earlier decision the judge at first instance had been prepared to accept that the Child Poverty Action Group had standing, the Court of Appeal avoided the issue.[90]

Bodies like Child Poverty Action Group continue to be attracted to test case litigation as a relatively cheap method of publicising an issue and putting pressure on government to take favourable action. Recent unsuccessful litigation, for example, drew attention to the failure of the Department of Social Security to trace claimants who had been underpaid through the wrongful application of the voluntary unemployment rule, and to the poor quality of service experienced by applicants at London offices of the Department. The Child Poverty Action Group's solicitor in the latter case found that decision a moral victory, in which the court "accepted the force of our arguments though it chose to come down on the side of the DSS on the wording of the statute."[91] It has been said that other indirect effects of the litigation, in which the Child Poverty Action Group was joined by the Citizens Advice Bureaux, were that:

"it helped officials to argue within Government for keeping staff numbers up. Finally, the CAB service may find, as has CPAG, that there are benefits from being known as an agency with the clout to mount a major court case of this nature . . . local bureaux may find that they have gained an extra respect from their local DHSS offices for the capacity collectively to organise a case of this kind."[92]

A major problem of successful test case litigation is that government can reverse its effects. This is what happened to a successful test case over the attendance allowance—it was reversed by the Social Security Act 1988.[93]

The expanding law of judicial review has proved a fertile ground for poverty law litigation. Thus in several cases squatters and travellers have gone on the offensive by seeking judicial review, when public bodies have instituted proceedings for possession against them. For example, squatters have claimed that local authorities were seeking possession in breach of their own policies or in doing so were acting unreasonably,[94] and travellers have argued that a local authority was in breach of its duty under the Caravan Sites Act 1968 to provide adequate accommodation for those residing in its area.[95] While squatters and travellers cannot defend proceedings for possession on these grounds, they can obtain an adjournment if there is a real possibility of obtaining leave to apply for judicial review.

The possibilities of judicial review depend largely, however, on the nature of the relevant legislation. As we have seen, social benefit legislation has reduced the opportunity for legal challenges to decisions. The trend has been to reduce discretion and the scope for human judgment. (The social fund is to the opposite effect, but its very wide discretion also reduces the possibility of legal challenge). As a result, one well known welfare rights lawyer has argued that the focus of work must move to the private sector.

" . . . the trend is towards fewer arguments with the DSS. As life beomes harder for the poor, and as Government policy continues to shed responsibility from the state, the adviser's work will shift towards dealing with the private sector. Why are the money-lending laws so rarely invoked? How will the privatised gas, water and electricity industries view their poorer customers? . . . Why has the Building Societies Association not yet developed even a code of practice to protect home owners from eviction"?[96]

Section 99 of the Public Housing Act 1936 continues to provide a fertile source of getting things done for tenants in poor housing. It enables any person aggrieved to take action against statutory nuisances, in particular those prejudicial to health. Although section 99 itself involves criminal proceedings, when a conviction is obtained the person aggrieved can apply for a compensation order. In recent years tenants have obtained quite substantial compensation orders in this way.[97] The court might also make a nuisance order requiring the landlord to do work to the premises. A recent notable example of such an order required the installation of central heating.[98]

As in other areas, however, the courts continue to be unattuned to collective action by tenants using section 99. In *Birmingham D.C. v. McMahon*,[99] the Divisional Court quashed a nuisance order made for a block of flats and maisonettes suffering condensation and mould. The evidence indicated a design fault, but the court ruled that it was the condition in each flat that was prejudicial to the health of occupiers, not the state of the block as a whole. Occupiers could not be persons aggrieved in relation to the whole block if affected by a statutory nuisance in their own flat or maisonette. (The court accepted, however, that a complete block of flats was capable of being "premises" for the purposes of the Act, and that a block of flats might be in such a state as to be a statutory nuisance itself.) That decision also revealed a reluctance by the courts to have a public authority incur substantial expenditure. Kennedy J. said:

"Generally speaking it is for a housing authority to decide when to embark on major works such as refurbishment of a large block of flats... the making of an order in relation to an entire block could heavily strain a local authority's finances and disrupt its housing department's programme for years to come."[1]

Conclusion

The advent of the welfare state was characterised by the centrality of equality before the law as a legal value (in particular, leading to changes in substantive law and facilitating the exercise of legal rights), the enactment of social welfare regulation, and the state provision of social welfare benefits and services. The policies of the Conservative Government have had an impact on each of these aspects. The significant policies here are threefold—constraining public expenditure, restoring markets to areas governed by regulation or public provision, and re-establishing "traditional" values of hard work and self reliance.

Equality before the law in its formal sense—impartiality and treating like cases alike—is unaffected in this area. What of equality before the law in its procedural sense, *i.e.* whether, in practice, rights are equally the subject of protection and duties of enforcement? Of major importance on the debit side is that the proportion of the population qualifying for legal aid has fallen. This follows directly from government policy on public expenditure, but also from the importance it attaches to other values such as enterprise and self provision. On the other side of the coin, however, is the conclusion of the Civil Justice Review that defendants in debt and housing cases should be encouraged to attend court hearings, and that courts should have as much information as possible in making decisions on these matters. Time will tell whether the steps proposed by the Civil Justice Review are implemented and effective.

Equality before the law is sometimes said to have a third, a substantive, implication. The common law can be said to be in breach of this, for example, in favouring landlords over tenants. Outside the area of the Rent Acts, intervention in the law of landlord and tenant by the Conservative Government has been limited and consistent with that of previous governments.[2] There have been some slight improvements in the statutory obligations of landlords to repair, and in the legislation on harassment, unlawful eviction and racial discrimination regarding housing—although the latter might be seen as a quid pro quo for the phasing out of the Rent Acts.

Restoring the market underlines much of what the Conservative Government has done with social welfare regulation—in phasing out the Rent Acts and in reducing the role of the Wages Councils. This has not meant the end of regulation, since phasing out of the Rent Acts, for example, does not mean the complete repeal of the legislation (at least at this stage), and there are transitional arrangements and arrangements to deal with some of the possible indirect effects of the phasing out (for example, harassment).

Constraining public expenditure has been an important feature of the Government's policy regarding social welfare benefits. In fact, enormous savings have been made in public expenditure as a result of linking retirement pensions and other long term benefits to prices rather than average earnings. In addition, a concern with fundamental values has underlain much of what the Government has done in this area. Discouraging voluntary unemployment, creating work and training incentives, and removing barriers to labour mobility have been important aspects. There has also been the attempt to foster greater individual and family responsibility, rather than reliance on the state, in times of need. Efficiency and computerisation have also led to important changes. Some commentators have seen the encouragement of private pension schemes, instead of the state earnings related scheme, or occupational pensions, as part of a political strategy to entrench capitalist philosophy.[3]

Similar motives reappear in the provision of public services. Containing public expenditure is one aspect of the measures with respect to public housing.[4] Enhancing individual responsibility, as with the right to buy, and the role of the market, as with public housing rents, are others. There are also the more directly political motives of furthering a political base and undermining that of opponents.

In all these areas, common themes emerge in relation to the law of the welfare state. In focussing on the emergence of social welfare legislation—whether it be with respect to the value of equality before the law, or relating to social welfare regulation, benefit or services—hindsight often gives a false coherence to government policy. One may disagree with Gamble's views as to the government's overall aims, yet still endorse his analysis that it "has had no detailed blueprint for policy. Like all administrations, many of its policies have been improvised, dictated by immediate circumstances and pressures."[5] Further, government legislation has taken a *form* which differs little from that of previous administrations. (An exception is with the social fund, where a system of detailed rules has been replaced by a framework for the exercise of quite wide discretion). The volume of legislation has not abated—indeed in some respects it has increased. For example, legislation has been necessary in the area of public housing to give tenants new rights, to provide transitional arrangements, and to control how local authorities implement government policy.[6] This last point reminds us that legislation is not automatically the subject of implementation or enforcement. One example is that the level of take up for family credit is less than the government expected. Finally, there are the unintended or indirect effects of legislation, as with the increased homelessness attributed to public housing policy.

Law in one respect has an autonomy from the political. As we have seen, the legal form and enforcement of much of the social welfare legislation of the Conservative Government do not differ significantly from that of previous governments. Legal tradition, institutional inertia and pragmatic factors are explanations. So too with the courts. For example, the Government has a real antipathy to the Rent Acts. However, the courts have not always anticipated legislative changes, and have deprecated attempts to avoid the effects of the Acts in several leading cases. In other respects, law has a direct relationship with the political. What can be called the ideological functions of law are the best illustration. Social welfare legislation now embodies values such as the primacy of markets, the need to work, and self provision, to a greater extent than at any time since the second world war. This must have an effect, however, subtle and difficult to detect, on the perceptions and behaviour of the administrators of the law and those of the public to whom it is addressed.

Notes

*I'm grateful for the comments of Professors Anthony Ogus and Michael Freeman.
[1] Details of the early period of Conservative government are referred to in my *Legal Foundations of the Welfare State*, London, Weidenfeld & Nicholson, 1985.
[2] Civil Justice Review, *Housing Cases*, Consultation Paper No. 5, Lord Chancellor's Department, 1987, pp. 25–27.
[3] School for Advanced Urban Studies, University of Bristol, *Study of Housing Cases*, Lord Chancellor's Department, 1987 p. 9; N. Hill & A. Mercer, "Participation in Housing Cases," [1987] J.Soc.W.L. 237, 240–241.
[4] Touche Ross Management Consultants, *Study of Debt Enforcement Procedures*, Lord Chancellor's Department, 1986, pp. 63, 65.
[5] R. Berthoud, *Credit, Debt and Poverty*, London, H.M.S.O., 1989, pp. 1, 23–24.
[6] National Consumer Council, *Behind with the Mortgage*, London, 1985.
[7] *Ordinary Justice*, London, HMSO, 1989, p. 358. While most poor people do not have debts, most of those in debt are unemployed or have low incomes (R. Berthoud, *op. cit.*, pp. 27–28.) In the Civil Justice Review research, nearly 40 per cent. of individual county court, and 27 per cent. of individual high court debtors were unemployed. 46 of individual county court, and nearly a third of individual high court debtors, were in receipt of social welfare benefits. (*Civil Justice Review*, Cm. 394, 1988, p. 110.)
[8] Civil Justice Review, *op. cit.*, p. 136.
[9] pp. 136–138.
[10] p. 119.
[11] See J. Davies, "De-legalisation of debt recovery proceedings," I. Ramsay (ed.), *Debtors and Creditors*, Oxon., Professional Books, 1986.
[12] *LAG Response to the Civil Justice Review Consultation Paper on Debt Enforcement*, London, 1987.
[13] *Quick* v. *Taff Ely B.C.* [1986] Q.B. 809. (The council saw this as a test case in relation to all its housing; the cost of steps to alleviate the condensation were estimated at some £9,000,000); *Palmer* v. *Sandwell M.B.C.* (1987) 284 E.G. 1487.
[14] The argument against this is that tenants would be at a disadvantage if, apart from the statutory covenant, a lease imposed the obligation to repair on them. But it would be unlikely for this to occur in practice, and creative legal reasoning could avoid the consequence if it did.
[15] See N. Madge, "Damages for Breach of Repairing Obligations" *L.S.Gaz.*, v. 85, July 20, 1988, p. 17.

[16] s.116, overturning the effect of *Campden Hill Towers* v. *Gardner* [1977] Q.B. 823.

[17] s.29. And see *Schon* v. *Camden L.B.C.* (1986) 84 L.G.R. 830.

[18] *e.g. Reid* v. *Andreou* [1987] 9 C.L. 175.

[19] [1976] Q.B. 585.

[20] ss.27, 28.

[21] But note that eviction without a court order is now unnecessary for limited categories, for example the occupier sharing general accommodation in the owner's home: ss.30, 31.

[22] s.137.

[23] M. Percival, "The Landlord and Tenant Act 1987" (1988) 51 M.L.R. 97.

[24] *Blawdziewicz* v. *Diadon Establishment* (1988) 35 E.G. 83.

[25] Interestingly, the Act provides for the recognition of tenants' associations: s.29; *R.* v. *London Rent Assessment Panel ex p. Trustees of Henry Smith's Charity, The Times,* Nov. 5, 1987.

[26] See C. Glasser "Legal Aid of Eligibility," *Law Soc. Gaz.*, March 9, 1988, p. 11; "Legal Services and the Green Papers" *ibid.*, April 6, 1989, p. 11.

[27] Lord Chancellor's Department, *Contingency Fees,* Cm. 571, 1989.

[28] J. Baldwin and S. Hill, "Research on the Green Form Scheme of Legal Advice and Assistance" (1986) 5 C.J.Q. 247.

[29] J. Baldwin, "The Role of Citizens Advice Bureaux and Law Centres in the Provision of Legal Advice and Assistance" (1989) 8 C.J.Q. 24.

[30] See National Consumer Council, *Ordinary Justice,* London, HMSO, 1989, p. 106.

[31] s.4(4).

[32] s.16(3).

[33] R. Campbell "The Role of Law Centres" *Legal Action,* February 1989, p. 7. See also Law Centres Federation, *The Case for Law Centres,* 3rd ed., London, 1989, pp. 4, 5–9.

[34] See most recently Society of Conservative Lawyers, *The Road to Reform— Thoughts for a Third Term,* London, Conservative Political Centre, 1987, pp. 13 *et seq.*

[35] s.34. See also s.35.

[36] s.36.

[37] s.39, Sched. 4.

[38] Sched. 2.

[39] s.20.

[40] L. Dolding, "The Wages Act 1986: An Exercise in Employment Abuse" (1986) 51 M.L.R. 84, 93.

[41] s.13.

[42] ss.12(3), 14(1).

[43] Department of Employment, *Wages Councils: 1988 Consultation Document,* London, p. 5.

[44] M. Turner and T. Kibling, "Private Prosecutions under the Wages Act 1986," *Legal Action,* October 1987, p. 12.

[45] [1988] 3 W.L.R. 321; [1988] 2 All E.R. 897. See P. Watchman, "Heartbreak Hotel" [1988] J.Soc.W.L. 147, 151 *et seq.*

[46] [1985] A.C. 809.

[47] *A.G. Securities* v. *Vaughan* [1988] 2 W.L.R. 689; [1988] 2 All E.R. 173. *cf. Antoniades* v. *Villiers* [1988] 3 W.L.R. 139; [1988] 2 All E.R. 309.

[48] *A.G. Securities* v. *Vaughan* [1988] 3 W.L.R. 1205.

[49] p. 1212.

[50] Sched. II, Ground 8.

[51] *Reform of Social Security*, Cmnd. 9691, 1985, p. 11.

[52] A. Ogus and E. Barendt, *The Law of Social Security*, 3rd ed., London, Butterworths, 1988, pp. 184, 209 *et seq.*

[53] *Reform of Social Security*, Cmnd. 9517, 1985, p. 45.

[54] See Social Security Act 1986, s.63.

[55] A. Ogus and E. Barendt, *op. cit.*, pp. 137, 229.

[56] See *ibid.*, pp. 493 *et seq.*

[57] See Harlow, "Discretion, Social Security and Computers," (1981) 44 M.L.R. 546.

[58] A. Ogus and E. Barendt, *op. cit.*, Ch. 12.

[59] Social Security Act 1986, ss.20–22; Income Support (General) Regulations 1987, S.I. No. 1967.

[60] Sched. 2, Parts II–IV.

[61] Social Security Act 1986, s.32; Social Security Act 1988, Sched. 3.

[62] Section 33(10). Guidelines can also be issued and must be taken into account, but are not binding. See Drabble & Lynes, "The Social Fund—Discretion or Control?" [1989] Pub. L. 297 — of course the cash limits on the fund limit discretion.

[63] s.34. See H. Bolderson "The Right to Appeal and the Social Fund" (1988) 15 J.Law and Soc. 279, 287.

[64] Social Security Act 1986, s.20 (income support); Social Security Act 1975, s.20 (unemployment benefit).

[65] See N. Wikeley, "Unemployment Benefit," *Legal Action* September 1988, p. 10; "Unemployment Benefit, the State, and the Labour Market" (1989) 16 *J.L. & Soc.* 291, 301–4.

[66] Employment Act 1988, s.27.

[67] s.4.

[68] Social Security Act 1986, s.23 (income support); Social Security Act 1975 s.19 (unemployment benefit). On tightening of the rule in the early eighties: J. Krieger, "Social Policy in the Age of Reagan and Thatcher" [1987] *Socialist Register* 177, 184.

[69] *Cartlidge* v. *Chief Adjudication Officer* [1986] Q.B. 360. The particular case involved a former member of the NUM, whose employment came to an end during the miner's strike of 1984–85.

[70] s.19(1A)(b)(c).

[71] s.33(9)(e).

[72] T. Mullen "The Social Fund—Cash-Limiting Social Security" (1989) 52 M.L.R. 64, 85. See also P. Alcock, " A Better Partnership Between State and Individual Provisions": Social Security in the 1990's, (1989) 16 J.Law & Soc. 97, 108.

[73] *Out of service*, quoted N. Wikeley, "Social Security" [1988] J.Soc.W.L. 269, 269.

[74] National Audit Office, *Department of Health and Social Security: Quality of Service to the Public at Local Offices*, London, HMSO, 1988.

[75] See I. Loveland, "Politics, Organisation and Environment" [1987] J.Soc.W.L. 216.

[76] For example, local authorities have wide discretion in allocating public housing. In 1988, the Commission for Racial Equality found that one London borough had practiced racial discrimination in housing allocations, and issued a non-discrimination notice requiring changes in policies and practices: Homelessness and Discrimination: *Report of a Formal Investigation in the London Borough of Tower Hamlets*, London, Commission for Racial Equality, 1988.

[77] See R. Forrest, *Selling the Welfare State: The Privatisation of Public Housing*, 1988, p. 100 ff.
[78] Housing Act 1985, Pt. V; M. Kerr, *The Right to Buy*, London HMSO, 1988, p. 3.
[79] *Palmer* v. *Sandwell M.B.C., The Times*, October 12, 1987; *The 1980 Tenants' Rights in Practice*, London, Housing Research Group, City University, 1987.
[80] *South Northamptonshire D.C.* v. *Power* [1988] 1 W.L.R. 319.
[81] See most recently Local Government and Housing Bill 1989, clause 129(3).
[82] [1986] A.C. 484.
[83] See D. Hoath "Housing" [1986] J.Soc.W.L. 305: "Homelessness Law after the Housing and Planning Act 1986; The Puhlhofer Amendments" [1988] J.Soc.W.L. 39.
[84] M. Sunkin "What is Happening to Applications for Judicial Review" (1987) 50 M.L.R. 432, 447–450; "Myths of Judicial Review" *Legal Action*, September 1987, p. 8; M. McAllister "Homelessness since Puhlhofer," *Legal Action*, May 1987, p. 11.
[85] *R.* v. *Hillingdon L.B.C. ex p. H, The Times*, May 17, 1988; *R.* v. *Tower Hamlets L.B.C. ex p. Monaf, The Times*, April 28, 1988.
[86] See L. Thompson *An Act of Compromise*, London, SHAC/Shelter, pp. 96–97.
[87] A. Ogus "Making and Implementing Social Laws—Political Aspects," *Acta Universitatis Wratislaviensis*, Number 1034, 1987, p. 49.
[88] H. Bolderson, *op. cit.*, p. 285.
[89] *The Times*, February 15, 1988.
[90] *R.* v. *Secretary of State for Social Services ex p. Child Poverty Action Group, The Times*, August 8, 1985; August 16, 1984.
[91] *Legal Action*, November 1988, p. 6.
[92] Editorial, "Test Cases: Losing or Winning?" *Legal Action*, March 1988, p. 3. A critical view of this case comes from Bob Holman "... the decision whether to take legal action was not made by claimants. If representatives of people who experience poverty had some choice, they might have chosen a different strategy to alleviate poverty. With the backing of £300,000 they might have opted to stimulate credit unions and food co-ops rather than trying to win legal points in the High Court." *The Guardian*, July 20, 1988.
[93] s.1; *Moran* v. *Secretary of State for Social Services, The Times*, March 14, 1987; *The Independent*, March 18, 1987.
[94] *Wandsworth L.B.C.* v. *Winder* [1985] A.C. 461; *West Glamorgan C.C.* v. *Rafferty* [1987] 1 W.L.R. 457.
[95] *Avon C.C.* v. *Buscott* [1988] Q.B. 656.
[96] N. Warren, "What Future for Welfare Rights?" *Legal Action*, April 1989, p. 25.
[97] N. Madge and J. Luba, "Recent Developments in Housing Law" *Legal Action*, December 1988, p. 21.
[98] J. Luba & N. Madge, "Recent Developments in Housing Law," *Legal Action*, September 1988, p. 15. One reason that s.99 may be unamended is that local, not central government, bears the brunt of actions under it.
[99] (1987) 151 J.P. 709.
[1] At p. 713.
[2] See The Law Commission, *Landlord and Tenant: Reform of the Law*, Cm. 145, 1987, pp. 3–4.
[3] H. McRae, "Lawson Opens Way to Shareholder Democracy," *The Guardian*, March 15, 1989.
[4] A. Stewart and R. Burridge, "Housing Tales of Law and Space" (1988) 16 J.Law & Soc. 65, 75.

[5] A. Gamble "Privatization, Thatcherism, and the British State" *ibid.*, 1, 6. See also A. Gamble, *The Free Economy and the Strong State*, London Macmillan, 1988.

[6] M. Loughlin "Law, Ideologies, and the Political-Administrative System" *ibid.* 21, 34–35.

The Legal Structure of the Social Fund

JOHN MESHER

The introduction of the Social Fund is one of the most controversial aspects of the reforms embodied in the Social Security Act 1986 and also one where the break with traditional methods and assumptions is the sharpest. As is well known, the social fund in its full operation from April 1988 has been subject to a fixed budget, rather than the system being "demand-led." The bulk of the available expenditure has been earmarked for loans to claimants, rather than non-repayable grants. Decision-making is outside the ordinary structure of social security adjudication, so that there is no right of appeal from unfavourable decisions. These are radical changes from previous methods of dealing with particular special needs, as opposed to the need for a regular weekly income. Quite apart from the arguments of policy, the novel legal structures adopted are of considerable interest. Although the nature of the previous legal structures formed part of the Government's case for reform, it will be argued that much of the new legal structure is determined by the outcome of independent policy decisions.

What follows is very much a personal view of the Social Fund. I have set out that view, with references mainly to official sources for the legal changes. I have not discussed other people's views and have not attempted to acknowledge the numerous sources from which my view is derived.[1] In particular, I have referred to scarcely anything out of the large literature on discretion. Nor have I attempted to chart the whole of the public debate about the policies of the Social Fund, but have picked out what seems necessary to illuminate the legal structure.

In order to describe and assess the 1988 changes it is necessary to look at the recent history of means-tested benefits. The Government's reform proposals will then be examined, before the actual legal structure is investigated.

35

The Background to Reform

The tension between the provision of a weekly income on a means-tested basis and meeting needs for particular expenses goes back at least as far as the legislative ancestor of income support and supplementary benefit. The first regulations made under the Unemployment Assistance Act 1934 contained a provision allowing an assessment to be increased "to provide for needs of an exceptional character by such amount as is reasonable."[1a] There was concern that payments under this provision should generally only cover needs not included in the weekly allowance and that things like the renewal of clothing or household equipment should be covered only in cases of obvious distress. In instructions of July 1935 which severely limited payments for renewals, officers were instructed that if they were not satisfied that applicants would make provision out of the weekly allowance for future renewals they could deduct up to two shillings in the pound from the weekly allowance in order to "liquidate the grant wholly or in part."[2] This remarkably familiar approach to policy, in exercising discretion to make exceptional needs payments, survived not only the making of new regulations in 1936, but also the upheaval of the great expansion of what became the Assistance Board's clientele during World War II and the passing of the National Assistance Act 1948. The Act gave the discretion to meet exceptional needs by way of a single payment. There was some growth in the number of ENPs up to the next milestone in 1966,[3] although not as much as in additions to weekly benefit in exceptional circumstances. The Ministry of Social Security Act 1966 (later renamed the Supplementary Benefit Act 1966) formalised some discretionary practices into statutory rules, but made few alterations in the provisions on ENPs. Section 7 authorised the Supplementary Benefits Commission (SBC) to provide benefit by way of a single payment to meet an exceptional need where it appeared reasonable in all the circumstances. The SBC developed a number of quite firm administrative rules about the circumstances in which ENPs were to be made. For instance, initially any capital in excess of £100 was regarded as available to meet exceptional needs.[4] More explicit assumptions were made about which needs were covered by the scale rates of weekly benefit and which were not, and more detailed guidance was given to officers about the circumstances in which needs covered by the scale rates (the 1930s "renewal" cases) could be met. This guidance was at first given in the secret A Code, but was published in the first edition of the Supplementary Benefits Handbook in 1970. An SBC inquiry into ENPs in 1973[5] revealed a steady growth in the number and amount of ENPs, but no particular anxiety was expressed about this trend since total ENP expenditure remained a very small proportion of that of the supplementary benefits scheme as a whole. However, it was noted that if payments became both very numerous and very large they would cease to be an exceptional element in the scheme.

This concern is more apparent in the extended discussion in the SBC's second annual report, for 1976. It was revealed that between 1968 and 1976 the numbers receiving supplementary benefit had gone up by 11 per cent. while the numbers of ENPs made had increased by 137 per cent (to 1,114,000 at an annual cost of £24,023,000).[6] The SBC attributed the increase and its apparent recent escalation partly to changes in the nature of the claiming population and in policy about the taking into account of other resources,[7] but more to welfare rights activities encouraging claims within the published policy and exploiting the formally open-ended discretion before appeal tribunals. Problems were identified in the unequal treatment of claimants within and between different offices and in the staff time taken up in dealing with ENP claims. Interestingly, among the solutions canvassed was to set a ceiling on the expenditure on discretionary payments.[8] At this time the group of civil servants which was to produce *Social Assistance, a review of the supplementary benefits scheme in Great Britain*[9] had already started work.

Social Assistance found the major problem to be that the scheme was supporting around five million people when it was designed to operate by the use of individualised discretion to tailor benefit to personal needs. It was impossible to do the latter while maintaining national consistency. In addition, over half of the staff in local offices were engaged in supplementary benefit work, paying out only 14.5 per cent. of the total social security budget. "Either the number of claimants must be reduced to the much lower level at which discretion could be properly administered on an individual basis; or the scheme must be adapted to its mass role."[10] Since, as civil servants, the authors could not propose increases in public expenditure, the solution had to be an adaptation to a mass role. This required that so far as possible policy rules should be expressed in legislation which did not involve discretionary judgments. On

ENPs it was accepted that some substantial expenses (*e.g.* for furniture, household equipment, removal expenses, maternity and funeral expenses) arose infrequently and often unexpectedly, so that it would be impracticable to raise the scale rates to a level at which they could be assumed to cover such expenses. Nor would it be reasonable to expect such expenses to be covered by credit facilities. Thus provision was to remain for such payments. For needs assumed to be covered by the scale rates, a system of fixed six-monthly payments for all claimants was suggested, subject to a residual discretionary power.[11] The possibility of imposing a cash limit on a scheme of last resort was rejected as impracticable.[12]

The broad approach of *Social Assistance* was accepted by the new Conservative Government. The aims were to produce a clear legal structure, a simplification of the scheme and a redistribution of existing resources to those most in need.[13] The simplification was intended to help claimants to understand the scheme, and along with clear legal entitlements, encourage take-up of benefits. In addition, it was intended to make administration and decision-making easier and less staff-intensive. The framework was implemented by the Social Security Act 1980, which amended the Supplementary Benefits Act 1976. The meat was in the 12 sets of regulations coming into force in November 1980. This date was apparently a year in advance of the timetable considered necessary by the DHSS's lawyers. In many cases the regulations consisted of a legalised version of the former A Code guidance. In the case of ENPs, which became single payments, there was a more fundamental legal change. Section 3 of the amended Supplementary Benefits Act 1976 provided for an entitlement to a single payment to meet an exceptional need, but only for a person entitled to weekly supplementary benefit who also satisfied prescribed conditions and only for a payment of a prescribed amount. Thus the open-ended discretion disappeared. The Single Payments Regulations laid down the conditions to be satisfied. Many categories were simply taken over from existing policy, although the attempt to encapsulate that policy in legislation led to frequent amendments. The major departures were in severely restricting the availability of payments for clothing and footwear (52 per cent. of ENPs had been for this category[14]) and the application of any residual discretion. In addition, the general discretion to adjust weekly benefit in exceptional circumstances disappeared, so that the possibility of compulsory savings was removed.

Even initially the structure of the regulations was very complex and soon became more so with an overlay of corrections, qualifications and other amendments. The notion of a simplification of the system for claimants has a very hollow ring to it, on the slightest examination of the bulk of the DHSS's compilation of the legislation in the "Yellow Book," or of the successive editions of my *CPAG's Supplementary Benefit and Family Income Supplement: the Legislation*. What might have seemed more plausible was that the change in the legal structure would simplify administration. To put it crudely, it would become easier to say No.[15] Even this hope was revealed to be hollow. Although the number of single payments initially went down to 834,000 in 1981 from a combined figure for ENPs and single payments of 1,129,000 in 1980, it rose to 1,873,000 in 1982 and 4,133,000 in 1985.[16] Quite apart from the absolute number of single payment claims, the new system did not remove the need to consider the claimant's individual circumstances. It still had to be decided whether the person had a need for the particular item (were the clothes "stolen" from the line in fact being hidden in the next-door flat?) and whether the circumstances fell within a category prescribed in the regulations (if a child kicked out the toes of a pair of shoes was that "accidental damage?"). In many ways the most significant form of discretion given to an officer in a bureaucratic system is in the finding of facts. The easiest way to deny a claim was to find that the settee, say, was still serviceable or the state of the decorating was adequate.[17] Once such a finding is written into the official records it is very difficult for a claimant to challenge it until she gets to an appeal tribunal where an alternative view of the facts can be presented. Particularly from the point of view of claimants, the extent of the difference between the pre- and post-1980 systems is often greatly exaggerated. The significance of the element of discretion will be explored later. After the usual dip in the number of claims following what was advertised as a tightening of eligibility, the pressure of need began to find its way to the points at which movement was possible.

At this point, the potted history shows a continuing tension between the need for a system specifically to cover one-off needs, in order to keep the level of regular weekly benefit paid to all claimants down, and the need not to allow this system to expand to a point at which the adequacy of the weekly rates is undermined or the administrative or benefit costs become disproportionate. Discretion has traditionally been a useful rationing device, but it crumbled under the pressures of a mass system in the late 1970s. Legal entitlements did not offer the immediate answer to financial control because the naive view that in some way rights would enforce themselves without much administrative effort was obviously false. This was the scene in the mid-1980s when the "Fowler Reviews" began.

The Green Paper and White Paper

The first mention of the Social Fund came in the Green Paper, *Reform of Social Security*, published in June 1985.[18] This described the systems of single payments and urgent needs payments as unacceptably cumbersome and expensive, depending more on the intricacies of a regulation than on genuine need. Their replacement in the Social Fund was to be discretionary so that appropriate and flexible help could be given to those in greatest need. There was the mention of an annual budget and of the aim of encouraging care in the community.[19] Other controversial aspects were mentioned in the more detailed proposals in "Programme for Change."[20] These were that while help for community care would be in the form of a grant, other assistance would be in the form of a loan, and that there was to be no right of appeal outside the DHSS. These proposals attracted a good deal of criticism, which it is not the purpose of this paper to consider. The Social Security Advisory Committee (SSAC) in its Fourth Report (1985) thought the idea to have potential merit in tackling an intractable problem, but expressed reservations about the operation of the budget, about the almost complete removal of entitlements from the scheme, about the operation of loans and about the removal of the right of appeal.[21] In particular, their view was that the acceptability of many aspects would depend on the level of weekly income support through the system of personal allowances and standardised premiums proposed to replace supplementary benefit. The inclusion of community care was described as interesting and imaginative, although several difficult issues were identified.

Despite these and many other criticisms, the White Paper, *Reform of Social Security—Programme for Action*,[22] published in December 1985, made few changes in the proposals. While the framework of regulations from 1980 was said to have worked well for entitlement to basic weekly income, the attempt to meet special but intermittent needs and difficulties within this framework had produced an extremely complicated scheme.[23] The stress was on flexibility and informality in a local context, free from the constraints of very detailed rules and precedents. Interestingly the word "discretion" was not used in the chapter on the Social Fund. The legislation was not to set out detailed rules, but the Secretary of State would be able to issue directions as to how the fund was to be administered. In para. 4.17 it was said that this power would be used in relation to maternity and funeral payments, where payments would be made outright and free of any budget constraint.[24] For more complex issues there would be guidance which would set out the purposes of provision and the factors to be taken into account, but would not attempt to prescribe answers to all situations.[25] The budget was presented as necessary for effective monitoring and control of expenditure, an objective sought in all benefit systems.[26] The size and distribution of the budget was to be determined after an analysis of local needs. The intention was to reduce the disparity in expenditures among local offices, but recognising that the reduction would have to be gradual.

More details were given on the intended operation of loans. The major use was to be to assist in budgeting for those on income support, by spreading expenditure through interest-free loans. What was to be spent on individual items would not need to be assessed, but a general judgment of the reasonableness of the expenditure and the practicability of recovery would be made. Some guidance would be provided on minimum and maximum loans. Recovery would normally be by direct deduction from income-replacement benefits. Loans would also be available to those, whether entitled to income support or not, facing a financial crisis who had no resources to draw on. Although the standard examples of fire, flood or theft were given, the emphasis was on flexibility to replace the rigidity of regulations. Scarcely any progress had been made on community care grants. Indeed para. 4.37 said that the Government would "continue to welcome ideas on the details of the help that might be provided."

The flexibility of decisions made in the exercise of judgment was used as the major reason for keeping the Social Fund outside the ordinary system of social security adjudication. Review would also have to be quick and be based on knowledge of local conditions. The initial response if an applicant disagreed with a decision would be for the Social Fund officer who made the decision to look at it again. If the applicant remained

dissatisfied there would be a review by senior management in
the local office.

From White Paper to Act

As might have been expected, those who had criticised the
original Social Fund proposal did not have their views altered by
the White Paper. The SSAC, for instance, in their Fifth Report,
for 1986/7, repeated the concerns expressed in their Fourth
Report and made the case that there was a range of capital
expenses which claimants could not be expected to meet out of
their weekly benefit and that some entitlements should remain.
There was also a powerful and unusual report from the Council
on Tribunals in January 1986 describing the proposal for review
by the local office as "highly retrograde" and urging that a right
of independent appeal be retained.[27]

A further significant development was that on February 24,
1986 the Secretary of State referred to the SSAC draft
regulations making fundamental amendments to the Single
Payments Regulations. The aim was to restore expenditure to
about the level of 1984, when there were 2,849,000 single
payments at a cost of £229 million in 1985 prices. Expenditure
in 1985 was £308 million and on a rising trend.[28] The proposals
were to remove some of the most difficult areas of decision-
making (for instance, on furniture and household equipment,
bedding, clothing and footwear and the assessment of the care
of existing items) and replace them by much more routine
criteria. There was to be much more use of national price lists
and fixed time-limits for claims, rather than an assessment of
individual needs. These proposals addressed the same defects in
the single payments scheme as had been identified in the Social
Fund proposals, but of course retained the right of appeal to
social security appeal tribunals and the absence of any cash
limit. Although the proposals were quite severely criticised by
the SSAC they were put into effect with some minor changes on
August 11, 1986. They did succeed in restraining single-payment
expenditure, indeed to below the 1984 level.[29] The cynic might
argue that this restriction enabled the Social Fund budget to be
set at a lower level, but it did show that control could be
exercised by limiting the eligibility criteria. However, the large
volume of appeals to the SSATs continued, although initial
decision-making had been simplified.

The Social Security Act 1986

The framework of the Social Fund was set out in sections 32 to 35 of the 1986 Act. The major change from the proposals was that an extra tier of review had to be added in response to the strong movement to retain a right of appeal to an independent tribunal, including the insertion of a clause to this effect (subsequently removed) in the House of Lords. Review is considered in more detail below. Section 32(2)(*a*) provided for regulations to define the circumstances in which payments were to be made for maternity and funeral expenses, rather than the directions referred to in the White Paper. This part of the Social Fund came into operation on April 6, 1987. The Regulations[30] provide entitlements equivalent to those to single payments with decisions being made by adjudication officers (AOs) and SSATs. A standard amount is paid for maternity expenses, while the actual costs of the basic elements of a funeral are met. No more needs to be said about the details in the context of legal structures. The Social Security Act 1988 added provision for cold weather payments, depending entirely on regulations.[31]

The Social Fund proper was due to come into effect on the same date as income support, on April 11, 1988. Before this date several amendments had to be made by the 1988 Act in order to allow the fund, in particular the budget, to operate. The discussion below will be on the basis of the final form of the legislation. A draft of the Social Fund Manual, containing the directions and guidance from the Secretary of State, was published in 1987 and provoked much discussion. The SSAC in their report on the draft Manual suggested that the emphasis on the budget went beyond what was authorised by the legislation. In a letter to the Minister for Social Security dated October 15, 1987 the Chairman of the SSAC wrote that the "decision to proceed with the social fund substantially as planned is without our support." The SSAC also suggested that single-payment expenditure for 1985–86 (£335 million) adjusted for inflation would give the minimum finance for the sort of Social Fund they wished to see.[32] In the event, the national budget for the first year of operation in 1988–89 was set at £203 million.

The Legal Structure of the Fund

How to express the rather subtle policies of the Social Fund in legislation and in administrative rule-making is obviously a very difficult problem. I shall suggest that the structure adopted is not entirely appropriate to the policy intentions, and in particular that there is very much less flexibility than advertised in the Green and White Papers. The general structure of the fund as a whole will be considered under the following headings: applications; the factors to be taken into account in making decisions; directions and guidance; the budget; and reviews. Some details of the separate parts of the fund will be considered in the section on directions and guidance.

Applications

The way in which applications must be made, having initially been controlled by directions of the Secretary of State, is now dealt with by regulation. The Social Fund (Applications) Regulations 1988[33] require applications to be made in writing on the right form, which must be properly completed (reg. 2). The Secretary of State may accept a written application not on the proper form, but the new system is stricter than that for single payments. There was no special form for single payment claims and the Secretary of State could accept oral claims.[34]

Factors for Decision

Decisions on applications must be made by Social Fund officers (SFOs) appointed by the Secretary of State (1986 Act, ss.32(8) and 33(2)). The SFO is apparently given great flexibility by section 33(9), which provides that the SFO must have regard to all the circumstances and in particular:

"(a) the nature, extent and urgency of the need;
(b) the existence of resources from which the need may be met;
(c) the possibility that some other person or body may wholly or partly meet it;
(d) where the payment is repayable, the likelihood of repayment and the time within which repayment is likely;
(e) any relevant allocation under section 32(8A) to (8D) above."

The "having regard" formula means that the SFO must consider the factors mentioned but is not precluded from considering any other relevant factor (R(SB) 25/83, R(SB) 15/86, R(SB) 6/88). The result is that no one factor can be conclusive. How this approach can work in relation to the "relevant allocation" mentioned in paragraph (e), *i.e.* the share of the budget allocated to each local office, is dealt with below in the section on the budget.

The apparent general flexibility is immediately constrained because section 33(9) is subject to section 33(10). This provides that a SFO must determine any question under section 33 in accordance with general directions issued by the Secretary of State and must take account of any general guidance issued by the Secretary of State. Both directions and guidance are contained in the Social Fund Manual. Thus, in effect, the guidance parts of the Manual can be added to the list of factors in section 33(9) to which regard must be had. But overriding the whole is the requirement to follow the directions. It has already been seen that the main area picked out in the White Paper for control by directions, that of maternity and funeral expenses, is in fact dealt with by regulation, as are several other areas. The legislation allows the Secretary of State, by the issue of directions which need no parliamentary sanction, to exercise as much or as little control as he wishes over the judgment of SFOs.[34a] The extent of the control actually imposed is dealt with in the following section. Here it can noted, for instance, that the division of the fund proper into budgeting loans, crisis loans and community care grants is not expressed in legislation, but in directions 2, 3 and 4. Section 33(4) merely provides that a SFO *may* determine that an award is to be repayable. It is direction 5 which requires budgeting and crisis loans to be in the form of a loan.

For the most part, the factors specifically mentioned in section 33(9) are not dealt with in the directions. Those directions constrain the outcome of the balancing of all factors. The exception is that directions 11 and 22 provide that no budgeting or crisis loan is to be awarded in excess of the amount which the applicant is likely to be able to repay. Thus, section 33(9)(*d*) might as well not be there, for it does not apply at all in community care grant cases and the obligation it imposes is to do no more than have regard to that factor. Section 33(9)(*c*) caused great worry to charities and voluntary and social work organisations, who feared that its effect would be that applicants would routinely be referred to them for assistance before any payment would be made out of the Social Fund. Para. 1015 of the Social Fund Manual makes it clear that this factor is intended primarily to apply to crisis loan applications. This is repeated in the guidance on community care grants (para. 6009) but not in that on budgeting loans (para. 3003). Nonetheless, the SFO must have regard to the factor in all cases and a decision which indicated that the SFO had not done so would be defective. This perhaps illustrates the clumsiness and confusion caused when four different levels of rule-making (primary and secondary legislation, directions and guidance) are combined in the same scheme.

The SFO has wide powers to determine how an award is to be paid, for instance in instalments (s.33(3)) or to a third party (s.33(1A)). Although it is for the SFO to determine that an award is repayable, it is for the Secretary of State to notify the applicant of the terms and conditions of repayment and to carry out the recovery (s.33(4A)–(7)). Decisions of the Secretary of State are outside even the review provisions of the 1986 Act. The only method of challenging such a decision will be by judicial review.

Directions and Guidance

The Secretary of State's primary power to issue binding directions comes from section 33(10) of the 1986 Act. Without limiting that power, section 33(10A) mentions some specific matters. Most of these appear to be included out of caution (apart perhaps from that authorising a direction that a SFO is not to determine an application in certain circumstances), but they do cover the establishment of the outer limits of the scheme. The power to issue guidance (including the power to give guidance on things to which directions also relate) comes from the same sections. In addition the Secretary of State may nominate a SFO for an area who can give local guidance which must be taken into account by SFOs, so long as it is not inconsistent with national directions or guidance (s.32(10) & (11)). This power has been exercised.

The framework established by directions is much more extensive than the White Paper implied. Direction 7 prevents any application being determined if it is made within 26 weeks of an application for assistance with the same item or service on which a decision (either positive or negative) has been given. The only exceptions are where there has been a change in the applicant's circumstances or, in the case of a budgeting loan, the applicant had not been in receipt of income support for long enough at the date of the earlier application. The SFO has no flexibility to lift this condition, no matter how deserving or needy the applicant is. Direction 5 requires that a budgeting or crisis loan must be in the form of a loan. The SFO has no flexibility to make an award in the form of a grant, no matter how deserving or needy the applicant is, unless the conditions for a community care grant are met.

These directions apply generally. The rest apply to particular kinds of awards. For budgeting loans, eligibility is defined by direction 8. The applicant must be in receipt of income support at the date of the award and she or her partner must have been in receipt of income support for a more or less continuous period of 26 weeks. Neither applicant nor partner must be caught by the trade dispute rule. If the capital of the applicant and partner exceeds £500, a loan will be made only to the extent that its amount is higher than the excess over £500 (direction 9). This is the old single payment rule. The minimum amount of a loan is £30 and the maximum debt is £1,000 (direction 10). A loan may not exceed the amount which the applicant is likely to repay (direction 11). Direction 12 contains a long list of expenses for which loans may not be made, many of which are taken over from regulation 6 of the Single Payments Regulations,[35] some of which, like investments and most housing costs, are new. The framework is thus quite rigid, and there is no legal reason why these directions could not have been expressed in regulations.

Some issues need to be fleshed out by guidance. The main one is the calculation of the amount which the applicant is likely to be able to repay. The guidance in Chapter 5 of the Social Fund Manual is very specific about the maximum repayment period (normally 78 weeks) and the proportions of benefit income which is to be regarded as available for repayments at different levels of existing commitments. This guidance, which may lead to applicants in the most desperate situations being denied loans because they have no margin to cover repayments, is likely to be applied quite rigidly. Again, there seems no reason why the rules could not have been put into regulations. The area which has been left open is that of establishing priorities for different kinds of need. This is necessary because of the existence of a budget (split between loans of all kinds and grants) for each local office. The setting of priorities is to assist in maintaining consistency of decision-making throughout the year. The highest priority needs should be met whenever they arise (para. 2023). Para. 3017 says that high priority must be given where the refusal of a loan could cause hardship or damage or risk to the health or safety of the applicant and her family. Some examples are given in later paragraphs of what might be of high, medium and low priority and the sorts of circumstances which might shift an item from one category to another. However, the overall discretion is stressed (para. 3012) as is the necessity to consider the state of the local budget (para. 3023). If the item or service is one for which it is appropriate to provide a loan, the precise prices need not be examined, providing that they are within the range of reasonableness (para. 3143). This area is one which could only be administered by a fairly open-ended discretion.

The directions on crisis loans are even more restrictive. The expenses must relate to an emergency or disaster and (except for some rent in advance for those coming out of institutional care) a loan must be the only means to prevent serious damage or a serious risk to health or safety (direction 3). Then, although there is no test of receipt of any kind of benefit, the applicant must be without sufficient resources to meet the immediate short-term needs of the family (direction 14). There is a more extensive list of ineligible persons than for budgeting loans (direction 15), mainly people in circumstances where their support would be expected to be taken care of, and a more extensive list of excluded needs (direction 23). The provision of maximum loans is complicated because awards to cover living expenses may be covered (directions 18 to 21). Even in a crisis an award must not exceed what the applicant is likely to be able to repay (direction 22). The statutory requirement to have regard to the possibility that some other person may meet the need or some of it, is covered only by guidance, suggesting that only realistic expectations that help would be available, and in time, would be relevant (para. 4060). Again, it is arguable that a decision which failed to consider mere possibilities of help from third parties would be defective. Much of this framework is taken from the old Urgent Cases Regulations.[36] Although a number of specific categories of need under those Regulations are only mentioned as examples of crisis loan situations under the general test, there is no reason why most of the rules could not have been expressed in regulations. Budget considerations are mentioned (para. 4023) and the budget is shared with budgeting loans, but if the conditions for a crisis loan are met, the situation almost by definition will be of high priority.

The directions are least specific about community care grants, which is, in terms of the definition of need, the most novel part of the Social Fund. Direction 4 specifies awards to assist a person to re-establish herself in the community after leaving institutional care, or to remain in the community rather than enter such care, to ease exceptional pressures on families and to cover limited travel expenses. Eligibility is limited to those in receipt of income support or who will receive it on discharge from an institution (direction 25). The £500 capital rule applies (direction 27) and most of the budgeting loan exclusions are also applied (direction 29). Guidance identifies a number of groups which should have priority, which include the elderly, the mentally handicapped, the mentally ill, the chronically sick and disabled, alcohol and drug misusers, ex-offenders and those without a settled way of life, families under stress and young people leaving care. The kind of grant to be considered varies according to the group into which the applicant falls. For instance, a start-up grant for household expenses may be considered for those leaving institutions. For families under stress, grants might cover removal expenses on the breakdown of a relationship or a reconciliation, or extra expenses caused by a child who is disabled or has behavioural problems. Discretion and flexibility are particularly stressed (para. 6033) along with the need to check the budget and to meet high priorities first (paras. 6034 & 6035). Although many of the priority groups and some of the needs to be met mirror those previously covered by the single payments scheme, the community care area is one where policy is still being developed. Relatively open discretion may therefore be appropriate as experience grows, when more formal rules can emerge. It is therefore arguable that the new structure is not imposed simply because of the existence of a budget, but also because of the nature of the area.

The disadvantage of such a structure is that potential recipients of grants have little idea in the early stages of the kind of claim which will be successful. This is particularly important when the title of "community care grant" gives a rather limited impression of the scope of the area. There is considerable freedom to develop the category of families under stress to cover a much wider range of needs than those mentioned in the Social Fund Manual. It is easier to identify potentially successful claims from a regulated structure than from the vagueness of a large document like the Manual.

The Budget

Since the imposition of a budget on social security benefit is such a new departure it is perhaps not surprising that the incorporation of the budget into the legal structure has caused considerable difficulties and left considerable confusion. At the national level the amounts allocated by the Secretary of State under section 32(8A) for 1988–89 were £141 million for budgeting and crisis loans, £60 million for community care grants and £2 million as a contingency reserve.[37] Readers may make their own comparison with the previous levels of single payment expenditure and the figure recommended by the SSAC. The Government has been at pains to stress that in the first year of operation the national figure is not a formal cash limit but is a budget, in the sense of a statement of the probable expenditure for the year.[38] This is repeated in para. 9 of Annex 2 to the Social Fund Manual. In view of the pattern of expenditure in the first nine months of 1988–89 the exact implications of this are unlikely to be faced at the national level. The allocation for 1989–90 is to be the same as for 1988–89 and is to constitute a cash limit. Since the number of income support recipients is predicted to go down, this is asserted not to amount to a cut in real terms.

The Secretary of State has power to make allocations to local offices, or even to individual SFOs, for different purposes (1986 Act, section 32(8C)). Allocations were made to local offices split between loans and grants.[39] The amounts were said to reflect levels of single-payment expenditure for the latter part of 1986–87 and the relative levels of need, based on the number and type of benefit recipients in each office.[40] There was considerable variation in the proportions of 1986–87 single payment expenditure included in the allocation, from 166 per cent. for Bognor Regis to 34 per cent. for Bathgate.[41] The inference in Parliament was that the budget did not constitute a cash limit for local offices. It was stressed that, especially in the first year, steps would be taken to prevent a local office from running out of money. The Secretary of State has the power to reallocate amounts (1986 Act, section 32(8D)), but it appears that a local office manager will have to apply to the Secretary of State before his budget can be adjusted. Section 33(9)(*e*) backs up this view of the local budget. Since the SFO must have regard to the budget as one factor among all the circumstances of the case, the budget cannot properly be treated as an overriding consideration. The directions currently say nothing about the budget, but it is not known whether this will change for 1989–90. It is relatively easy to see how a SFO may have regard to the budget in setting priorities before the budget limit is reached. Although the annual budget is divided over the months of the year according to the expected profile of expenditure, the monthly figure can be exceeded. One would expect SFOs to be exceptionally cautious in the earlier months of the year, in order to avoid an overspend or too restricted a balance in the later months. This seems to be borne out by the pattern of expenditure, so far as the published figures can be relied on.[42] The crunch might come at the end of the year. Guidance in the Social Fund Manual states very firmly that the local office's annual allocation must not be exceeded (see paras. 2016 and 2054). It is hard to envisage a SFO exceeding the annual budget, even though it may be a breach of section 33(9) not to do so.

The imposition of the budget or cash limit ensures control of benefit expenditures. It necessitates that there cannot be entitlements to benefits because the demand might break the budget. This has the additional advantage that the Government does not have to define the limits of the entitlements it is prepared to tolerate, but can, by stressing discretion and flexibility, give the impression of having created a system which will identify genuine need. There are, however, costs to this approach. The operation of a budget within a local office area is difficult enough and there will inevitably be differences in treatment between people in the same circumstnces at different times of the year. More extreme differences can be expected between people living in different areas because of the state of the budget in different local offices. This is inequitable. It also means that potential applicants cannot have a clear idea of what assistance might be available, which will tend to discourage applications. It is hard to assess how far the underspend of the budget over most of the first year of the Social Fund is due to such an effect, to an overreaction to bad publicity about the severity of the new rules, or to an absence of genuine need. One further political cost of the budget mechanism is that every M.P. knows how much his constituency has been allocated.

Review

A complex system of review is set up by a combination of legislation and directions from the Secretary of State. Section 34 of the 1986 Act authorises an SFO to review his own or another SFO's decision. An application for review must be in writing and be made within the time-limits laid down in the Social Fund

(Application for Review) Regulations 1988,[43] but these limits are perhaps not crucial since the SFO may review a decision in any circumstances he thinks fit (1986 Act, section 34(1)(*b*)). Beyond the SFO, but only on a valid application, is a review by a Social Fund inspector (SFI) (section 34(3)). SFIs are appointed from Department of Social Security personnel by the Social Fund Commissioner (sections 35(3) and (4)). The Social Fund Commissioner is appointed by the Secretary of State with the duties to train SFIs and to monitor the quality of their decisions and to produce an annual report (sections 35(2), (5) and (6)). The first appointee is a senior partner in a London firm of solicitors. This extra tier, outside the local DSS management structure, is intended to inject an independent element to compensate for the lack of a right of appeal to an SSAT. The remedy, if an applicant is dissatisfied with the decision of an SFI, is judicial review.[44] It is assumed that a SFO carrying out a review has the powers given to SFOs generally. SFIs have the power to confirm an SFO's decision, to refer the matter to a SFO or to make any determination which a SFO could make. Anyone carrying out a review must have regard to the same factors and pay the same attention to directions and guidance as a SFO making an initial decision (sections 34(6) and (7) and 32(11)).

More details are given in the directions issued by the Secretary of State about reviews. The first stage is a paper review by the SFO. If that stage does not result in a revision entirely in the applicant's favour, then the applicant must be offered an interview with the SFO before a determination is made (direction 33). At the interview the applicant can be accompanied by a friend or representative and may produce new evidence and make representations (direction 34), which must be recorded (direction 35). The initial letter of refusal should have given reasons, but at the interview the applicant must be given an explanation of the reasons. If at this stage (either after the interview or where the applicant does not take the opportunity of an interview) the SFO does not revise the decision wholly in the applicant's favour, the papers must be passed to a higher executive officer (direction 36). It is following the decision of this officer that the review by the SFI can take place. The inclusion of the interview is important, since it gives the applicant the opportunity of presenting an alternative or corrected view of the facts. Many applicants will also be able to present their case more easily in person than in writing on the application form. But since the interview will normally be with the SFO who made the original decision, there will not be the clear sense of an independent rehearing that there is on an appeal to a SSAT.

Some of the remaining directions on review are very difficult to interpret and seem to waver between review being like a review under section 104 of the Social Security Act 1975, and review being like an appeal. Review under section 104, for most of the social security system, is a two-stage process. If the conditions for review (ignorance of or mistake as to material fact, change of circumstnces or error of law) are satisfied then it should be considered whether the original decision should be revised. Some of the language of the directions hints at a two-stage process. Thus direction 39 refers to matters which on review the SFO "must have full regard to initially." These include errors of law, whether a fair procedure was followed and whether the conclusion was one which a reasonable SFO could make. This gives the impression that it is not enough in itself that the reviewing SFO might have come to a different conclusion on the facts. Then direction 32 applies after the initial review under direction 39, and requires the SFO on further review to have full regard to all the circumstances at the date of the original decision, any new evidence and any change of circumstances. In the parallel directions to SFI's in Annex 11 to the Social Fund Manual it is made clear that this second stage is to be reached if a determination has not already been impugned in the first stage. The intention seems to be for the same to apply to review by the SFO (which would be in line with section 34(1)(b) of the 1986 Act), so that a fresh view of all the facts can be taken. Thus the process is nearer to an appeal, with limited opportunities for new evidence to be presented, but the directions are unnecessarily convoluted.

The unsatisfactory nature of the review procedure may help to explain the limited use made of it so far. In the first year only 2499 decisions had been reviewed by the 40 SFIs, of which 96 were altered and 1109 were referred back to the SFO.[45]

Discretion and Justiciability

I have suggested above that the difference between the pre-1980 supplementary benefits system and the reformed system is often exaggerated, particularly in relation to single payments.

Although the pre-1980 system rested formally on discretionary powers, the reality in a mass system was that rules were made administratively for the officers who made the first-instance decisions to follow. To a large extent, the effect of the 1980 reforms was to shift the rules from the secret sphere of the SBC Codes into the public sphere of statutory regulations. Although before 1980 an officer could theoretically go outside the SBC guidance relying on his legal discretion, I suggest that the most potent way of securing this result was by manipulation of the finding and recording of facts, and that the scope for this manipulation was scarcely reduced in 1980. Indeed, the lack of difference between the systems in this respect is part of the explanation for the failure of the 1980 reforms to control the costs, particularly the administrative costs, of single payments.

If the limitation of discretion in 1980 is exaggerated, does this mean that its expansion under the Social Fund is also exaggerated? I suggest that this is to some extent true, but it is also clearly the case that the position under the Social Fund is by no means the equivalent of pre-1980 supplementary benefit. The structure of the legislation and directions within which the Social Fund operates establish quite firm limiting rules, although no applicant has an entitlement to an award within those limits. Those limits and some of the non-binding guidance which will probably be routinely applied by SFOs could perfectly easily have been expressed as rules in regulations. The operation of a loan system as such could be accommodated within such a system. It is the budget, soon to be a formal cash limit, which makes the crucial difference. The necessity is not just to abandon a demand-led system, but is also to avoid a system where a discretionary judgment as to the merits or deservingness of an application supplies the test of whether an award should be made. The decision not to make an award because the money has run out or for fear that other more deserving applicants may have no money available for them in the future is of a different kind from a decision that a claimant is not in exceptional need.

It is the same factor of the budget which seems decisive in the replacement of the right of appeal by review. The arguments in the Green and White Papers against the operation of the appeal process are very thin. Certainly, speed, informality and local knowledge could be secured by a properly funded system of tribunals. Many of the issues which arise under the Social Fund, including the question of how large a loan a person is capable of repaying, are quite suitable for tribunals. But it would be very difficult to avoid an appeal to an independent tribunal in effect importing a demand-led element. It is this which apparently makes it worthwhile to lose the important legitimating effect of the existence of a right of appeal and which pushes the review process towards a review of proper procedures rather than a complete rehearing.

The Future of the Social Fund

Any predictions about the future of the Social Fund must be speculative in the extreme. I have suggested that the present legal structure was reached in the search for certainty of control over benefit and administrative costs. However, the 1986 amendments to the single payments scheme indicated that benefit expenditure at least could be brought under control by the restriction of entitlements. Thus, cash limiting and its political costs may not be necessary for financial control, as the leaked doubts of Mr. John Moore before the implementation of the scheme tend to confirm. The budget has not come under pressure at the time of writing. The pressures of deferred needs and a change in the mildness of the winter of 1988–89 could easily alter that. The Social Fund as implemented is already much more regulated than originally intended. The new cold weather payments scheme has been implemented on the basis of entitlements contained in regulations. If the political costs of the budget become too great, more areas may be picked out where deserving groups are granted entitlements. If this could be expanded in the way indicated by the SSAC in their Fifth Report, the provision of interest-free loans could play a valuable part in assisting with capital expenses. As was shown earlier, limited provisions for taking the cost of some items out of weekly benefit have been part of the benefit system for many years. Given an adequate level of weekly benefit and a suitable system of grants for unpredictable capital expenses, many claimants would welcome the availability of interest-free loans.

Notes

[1] Since this chapter was written several studies have appeared, in particular R. Drabble & T. Lynes, The Social Fund — Discretion or Control? [1989] Pub. L. 297 and T. Mullen, The Social Fund — Cash-Limiting Social Security 52 M.L.R. 64 (1989).

[1a] The Unemployment Assistance (Determination of Need and Assessment of Needs) Regulations 1934 (S.R. & O. 1934, No. 1424, reg. VI(3). The formulation and administration of these regulations and their successors are described in Appendix C to the Supplementary Benefits Commission Annual Report 1976 (Cmnd. 6910), based on research by Tony Lynes.

[2] Supplementary Benefits Commission Annual Report 1976 (Cmnd. 6910), Appendix C, para. 13.

[3] A threefold growth to 345,000 p.a. in 1965: *ibid.* para. 7.3

[4] The statutory authority for taking capital and disregarded income into account was given by para. 6 of Sched. 2 to the 1966 Act.

[5] *Exceptional Needs Payments* (Supplementary Benefits Administration Paper No. 4), 1973.

[6] *Loc. cit.* n. 2, paras. 7.8 and 7.17.

[7] The 1975 Annual Report (Cmnd. 6615) had revealed that the practice of using the discretionary power to reduce weekly benefit in exceptional circumstances (1966 Act, Sched. 2, para. 4(1)(*b*)) to impose compulsory savings for future needs or in extreme circumstances to "pay off" a grant continued to be used (para. 8.15). It appears that the use was very much a last resort and had no significant effect on the increase in ENPs.

[8] 1976 Annual Report, para. 7.50.

[9] DHSS, 1978.

[10] *Ibid.* para. 1.12.

[11] *Ibid.* paras. 9.38–9.48.

[12] *Ibid.* para. 9.50.

[13] See First Report of the Social Security Advisory Committee, para. 4.3, and the White Paper (Cmnd. 7773).

[14] *Social Assistance*, para. 9.7.

[15] An approach summed up in the title of the CPAG report on the 1980 reforms, *We don't give clothing grants any more* (1984).

[16] Statement by the Secretary of State for Social Services on the Supplementary Benefit (Miscellaneous Amendments) Regulations 1986 and the Supplementary Benefit (Single Payments) Amendment Regulations 1984 (Cmnd. 9836), para. 19.

[17] See the excellent descriptions of the approaches of officers in Cooper, *Observations in Supplementary Benefit Offices* (Working Paper C of the Policy Studies Institute's report on the reform of Supplementary Benefit) (1985) and in Hill, "The Exercise of Discretion in the National Assistance Board," 47 *Public Administration* 75 (1969).

[18] Cmnd. 9517.

[19] *Ibid.* paras. 9.8–9.9. Para. 10.7 proposed that help with maternity and funeral costs should come from the Social Fund.

[20] Cmnd. 9518.

[21] Fourth Report, paras. 3.42–3.80.

[22] Cmnd. 9691.

[23] *Ibid.* paras. 4.4–4.5.

[24] *Ibid.* para. 4.39.

[25] *Ibid.* para. 4.42.

[26] *Ibid.* para. 4.38. The size of the budget was to be determined later after analysis of local needs, taking account of the need to be gradual in the shift from the existing pattern of single-payment expenditures.

[27] *Social Security—Abolition of Independent appeals under the proposed Social Fund*, Special Report by the Council on Tribunals (Cmnd. 9722).

[28] *Loc. cit.* n. 16, paras. 19 and 20.

[29] Expenditure for 1987–88 was said to be likely to be £200 million: H.L.Deb., Vol. 493, col. 368 (February 11, 1988).

[30] The Social Fund Maternity and Funeral Expenses (General) Regulations 1987 (S.I. 1987 No. 481).

[31] The Social Fund Cold Weather Payments (General) Regulations 1988 (S.I. 1988 No. 1724) came into force on November 7, 1988. The provisions are very similar to the old single payments ones.

[32] The Draft Social Fund Manual: Report by the SSAC, para. 10.

[33] S.I. 1988 No. 524.

[34] Supplementary Benefit (Claims and Payments) Regulations 1981 (S.I. 1981 No. 1525), regs. 3(1)(*b*), (5)(*a*).

[34a] The accuracy of this statement may be undermined by one of the first judicial review cases, due to be heard in 1990. The argument is that since s.32(2)(*b*) refers to payments "to meet other needs in accordance with directions...", the Secretary of State has no power to limit the range of needs which can be considered for a payment out of the Social Fund, only to deal with the way in which such needs might be considered.

[35] The Supplementary Benefit (Single Payments) Regulations 1981 (S.I. 1981 No. 1528).

[36] The Supplementary Benefit (Urgent Cases) Regulations 1981 (S.I. 1981 No. 1529).

[37] H.C.Deb., Vol. 121, col. 562 (November 2, 1987).

[38] See in particular Lord Skelmersdale, H.L.Deb., Vol. 494, col. 869 (March 10, 1988).

[39] H.C.Deb., Vol. 121, cols. 764–771 (November 4, 1987).

[40] H.C.Deb., Vol. 122, col. 443 (November 16, 1987); Social Fund Manual, Annex 2, para. 11, Annual Report by the Secretary of State for Social Security on the Social Fund 1988–89 (Cm. 748), Annex 3.

[41] This is according to the calculations of Robin Cook M.P., *The Guardian*, December 17, 1987.

[42] See, *e.g.* Lynes, "Welfare Watch," *New Statesman and Society*, November 11, 1988. At the end of December 1988 expenditure on loans by the four local offices in Sheffield had reached £1,767,253. The expected expenditure according to the profile was £2,100,927. The expenditure on grants had reached £544,887. The expected expenditure was £893,950. By contrast, at the end of September 1989, 51.2% of the annual budget for 1989/90 had been spent, although 61% of applications for community care grants had been refused. These figures were kindly supplied by Martin Fitch, Senior Welfare Rights Adviser, Sheffield City Council.

[43] S.I. 1988 No. 34.

[44] See Luba, "Challenging Social Fund Decisions," *Legal Action* May 1988, 9. The Social Fund Commissioner has no decision-making role in the review process, but can receive complaints as part of her monitoring duty.

[45] Annual Report of the Social Fund Commissioner for 1988–89, Appendix 10. Applications to the SFI were made in 4% of potential cases (*ibid.*, para. 2.2).

Rethinking British Housing Law: the Failure of the Housing Act 1988

MARTIN PARTINGTON

Introduction

The Housing Act 1988 received the Royal Assent on November 15, 1988, after 12 months of controversial debate during its passage through Parliament. Although there has been a number of Housing Acts since the Conservative administration came to power in 1979, there is little doubt that the latest Act was widely perceived as being of major significance in the development of British housing law. Whether or not one approves of the policies which the legislation seeks to implement and whether or not one anticipates that the law will actually enable the stated policy objectives to be achieved, it cannot be denied that legislation which provides a completely new basis for the regulation of the private rented sector (into which is now drawn the housing association sector of the housing market), that enables private sector bodies to buy up areas of Council housing, that establishes a new Housing Corporation in Wales and gives both it and the original Housing Corporation substantial new powers in relation to housing, is important.

Despite this, however, it will be argued here that the Act represents a missed opportunity for a rather more radical reconsideration of British housing law. It will be suggested that British housing law is in need of a new approach, essential for the social and economic conditions of the late twentieth century, but which, if undertaken, could assist governments in the achievement of their social policy objectives in relation to housing.

The argument to be advanced in this paper will fall into three main sections. First, a definition of housing law will be presented; secondly, since this essay forms part of a collection

of papers analysing recent social legislation, a brief overview of
the main features of the Housing Act will be set down relating
these to the stated policy objectives of the Government;
thirdly, in the light of the analysis of the Act, the argument for
the more radical reconceptualisation of housing law suggested
above will be developed.

1. The Definition of Housing Law

Before proceeding further it is necessary to provide a
definition of "housing law" for the purpose of this paper. Until
recently, many people would have regarded "housing law" as
that body of public law which relates to the provision of local
authority housing plus, perhaps, that body of law which seeks
to regulate housing standards.

In my view, this is much too narrow. Housing law should be
seen to comprise the whole of that body of law which
underpins and regulates the operation of the housing market in
Great Britain.[1] (It is thus much wider and more complex than
a single Housing Act, or even the series of Housing Acts
passed over the last 100 years or so, taken together.) More
particularly, it may be seen that housing law, in this sense,
comprises three main elements: private law, public law and
procedural law.

(a) *The private law of housing* is those areas of common law
and equity that have created the fundamental legal concepts
(estates in land, third-party rights, etc.) on which rights to own
and occupy land, and by extension, dwellings, depend.

(b) *The public law of housing* comprises both what may be
termed "macro" public law, *i.e.* those rules of law which create
broad powers in relation to housing, such as the powers given
to local authorities and housing associations to provide housing
or to central government to provide finance for housing
purposes, and also areas of "micro" public law, which create
individual statutory rights in relation to housing and have given
public bodies powers to act in relation to the issues and
disputes involving housing which directly affect the individual.

(c) *The procedural law of housing* comprises the areas of law which establish the procedures whereby those housing disputes, which are susceptible to resolution in the courts or in other dispute-resolution forums, can actually be resolved.

To anticipate the argument for a moment, it may be suggested here that any fundamental rethinking of British housing law must address all three aspects of housing law, as thus defined.

2. The Housing Act 1988

Before turning to these broader issues, it will be helpful to provide an overview of the main provisions of the Housing Act. This is preceded by a summary of the principal policy objectives which were stated by the Government as underlying the new Act.

A. The Policy Objectives

In 1987, the White Paper, *Housing: the Government's Proposals*[2] listed four main policy objectives which would be the basis for future housing legislation:

(a) *The spread of home ownership.* In relation to this there was stated to be a continuing commitment to tax relief on mortgage interest; there would be further emphasis on the right of public sector tenants to buy their dwellings; it was noted that the planning system would need to ensure an adequate supply of land for housing; and assistance would be given to owners of housing, but with limited means, to keep their property in good condition.

(b) *New life for the "independent" rented sector.* This policy was to comprise two elements: first making the renting by private landlords of dwellings an economic proposition; and, secondly, an expansion of the housing association movement so that associations would have more houses available for rent. Associated with these broad objectives were further more detailed proposals to enable private sector finance to be brought in to assist in the provision of housing association dwellings. Finally, there was a continuing commitment to helping tenants on low incomes to meet costs through housing benefits.

(c) *Encouraging local authorities to change their housing role.* Under this head, it was stated that direct provision of housing by local authorities should diminish, whilst "alternative forms of tenure" and tenant choice should increase. This objective clearly envisaged the possibility of local authority tenants opting out of local authority control.

(d) *Better use of scarce public money to give tenants a better deal.* This would include in particular the creation of Housing Action Trusts, modelled on the concept of the Urban Development Corporation.

It should be stressed that, for all the objectives it does encompass, the Housing Act 1988 did not seek to address all these policy headings.[3] In addition, other matters have been included in the legislation which seem to be important in policy terms, but which were not, surprisingly, addressed in the White Paper.[4]

B. The Housing Act 1988: Main Features

In terms of the definition of housing law set out in Part 1 of this Paper, the 141 sections of and 18 Schedules to the Housing Act 1988, had nothing to say in relation either to the private law or the procedural law relating to housing. Its provisions are a mixture of "macro" and "micro" public law. The main features under these two headings may be summarised as follows:

(1) The "Macro" Provisions

The most significant of the "macro" provisions relate to:

    (a)   public sector tenants' "choice";
    (b)   housing action trusts;
    (c)   the Housing Corporation, Housing for Wales and housing associations;
    (d)   Rent Officers.

(a) Public sector tenants' "choice."[5] Part IV of the Act
(somewhat misleadingly described in debate and the press as the
"tenants' choice" scheme) actually lays down a procedure
whereby private sector landlords who have been "approved"
within the meaning of the Act may make a bid to take over
local authority housing estates or parts thereof. No tenants'
choice arises initially; some other private body must make the
first moves.

These particular "macro" provisions are nonetheless comple-
mented by a number of "micro" provisions. It is these which
give rights to individual tenants to choose whether or not to
accept a new landlord. This may arise in one of two ways: any
individual tenant who elects to stay with his/her local authority
landlord is entitled so to do[6]; in addition, the transfer of an
estate can only take place if a majority of tenants[7] approves of
the take-over.

(b) Housing Action Trusts.[8] These provisions permit the
creation by the Secretary of State of housing action trusts[9]
which will, in relation to the areas over which they are given
powers, effectively take over all the functions of local
authorities.[10] In particular, they will have, as objectives:
repairing or improving housing; securing the proper and
effective management of housing; encouraging "diversity in the
interests by virtue of which housing accommodation in the area
is occupied and diversity in the identity of landlords"; and
generally securing or facilitating the improvement of housing
conditions in that area together with social conditions and the
general environment.[11] They may also provide and maintain
housing and facilitate the provision of shops, advice centres and
other community facilities.[12] However, no housing action trust
may come into being in any given area if a majority of tenants
living in the area vote against the idea.[13]

*(c) The Housing Corporation, Housing for Wales and housing
associations.* Under this head fall a number of somewhat diffuse
provisions.
(i) Perhaps most dramatic, since it was not envisaged in the
original White Paper is the creation of a new body—Housing for
Wales—which is, in effect, a Housing Corporation for Wales.[14]
(ii) More generally, housing associations are granted a wider
range of permissible purposes or objects.[15]

(iii) Most interesting, however, is that the Housing Corporation (together with Housing for Wales and, where relevant, Scottish Homes) has been given a number of additional regulatory powers, not only in relation to the ways in which housing associations themselves let accommodation[16] (including making recommendations as to the terms of tenancies and principles for determining rents) but also in relation to the setting of criteria and determining of procedures in relation to the bodies which may be approved to make bids to take over local authority dwellings.[17]

These developments may turn out ultimately to be the most significant in the whole Act since they give very wide powers to the Housing Corporation and Housing for Wales not only to determine the terms of lettings but also to make rules— with quasi-statutory force—which will regulate which persons or bodies can be landlords of particular classes of tenancy.

(d) Rent Officers. In the past, Rent Officers have—under the Rent Act 1977—had powers to determine fair rents in relation to particular dwellings either on application by landlords or tenants or, in certain circumstances, on application by local authorities.[18] With the replacement of "fair rents" under the Rent Acts with market rents under the Housing Act 1988 (see below), the Government clearly faced a problem in relation to housing benefit.

An important feature of the housing benefit scheme, as it emerged in 1982, was that there was no automatic statutory upper limit on the amount of eligible rent that might be paid by way of housing benefit. In the case of public sector dwellings, most local housing authorities attempt to set rents at reasonable levels. Naturally this has the *indirect* effect of limiting levels of housing benefit expenditure. In the case of private sector dwellings, where a fair rent was determined under the Rent Acts, this became the maximum "eligible" rent. Local authorities did have a power (infrequently exercised and now abolished) of referring rents to rent officers where they sought to take advantage of this restriction. In addition, the Housing Benefit Regulations provided for two sets of—carefully defined—circumstances in which a contractual rent would not be met in full by housing benefit: crudely paraphrased they were where the dwelling was larger than necessary for the occupier, or where the dwelling was in too "expensive" an area. However only a minority of private sector dwellings that might have been fair rented were actually fair rented.[19]

The abandonment of fair rents, however, has posed a more general problem for housing benefit expenditure. If the housing benefit scheme continued to permit poor tenants, who satisfied the relevant means-test, to continue to receive 100 per cent. of contractual rents, as housing benefit, there would be an obvious temptation for landlords to set whatever rent levels they liked, in the knowledge that this would be fully funded by housing benefit. This would provide as great an incentive to distort genuine market rents as fair rents were alleged to have done.

In order to prevent this, therefore, Rent Officers have been given new powers,[20] not *directly* to set fair rents, but rather to determine the maximum levels of rent which it seems appropriate for the housing benefit scheme to meet in particular areas of the country. Notwithstanding the overall policy commitment contained in the legislation to move towards market rents, it would seem that, at least so far as those landlords who are willing to provide accommodation for those on low incomes (who will be receiving housing benefit), rent regulation of a kind may have, in effect, been reintroduced indirectly through these new powers. Of course, until the levels determined by Rent Officers have been set, the precise relationship between housing benefit rent levels and market rent levels will be unclear; but it is likely that there will be pressures for housing benefit levels to be somewhat lower than market rent levels and that the gap between the two will increase over time.

(2) The "Micro" Provisions

Part 1 of the Housing Act 1988 contains the bulk of the "micro" public law provisions (those directly affecting the rights of individual occupiers of dwellings). In addition there is a number of specific alterations to the "right to buy" scheme,[21] to the law on repairs and in relation to discrimination. They will be considered under the following heads:

(a) Position of tenants already protected under Rent Act 1977
(b) The "new" assured tenancy
(c) The assured shorthold tenancy
(d) Unlawful eviction and harassment
(e) Repairs
(f) Anti-discrimination measures in relation to housing.

(a) Position of tenants already protected under Rent Act 1977. In general, private sector tenants protected under the Rent Act 1977 retain their statutory rights. There are detailed alterations to the "right of succession"[22] which come into immediate effect. And there is a number of other detailed exceptions in the case of protected shorthold tenancies and restricted contracts. But, in general, the old Rent Act law will continue to apply to existing lettings after the main provisions of the new Act came into force on January 15, 1989.

(b) The assured tenancy. This is the key concept which will in future be the basis for the regulation of the private rented sector. By itself, the concept confers no rights; it defines the circumstances in which specific rights regarding rents and security of tenure arise.[23] The "assured tenancy" is not in fact a wholly new legal concept since a version of it was developed under the Housing Act 1980. However the Mark II "assured tenancy" in the 1988 Act is so different in character that it is probably best regarded as a new concept.

Notwithstanding this point, however, the "assured tenancy" does not represent as dramatic a break with the past as might have been anticipated from the initial publicity surrounding the publication of the White Paper and the accompanying consultation documents. When they first appeared, it seemed to be suggested that there would be a wholly new legal regime put in place to replace the Rent Acts. What has emerged however is, to the lawyer's eye at any rate, not dissimilar to what was in the Rent Acts. To be an "assured tenancy" there must be "a" "dwelling-house" "let" "as" a "separate dwelling." The tenant must be an individual; the tenant must occupy the dwelling as his "only or principal home." And Schedule 1 to the Act sets out a long list of provisions excluding particular categories of letting from the status of assured tenancy: these include lettings above certain rateable value levels; lettings for holidays; lettings by defined institutions to students. Many of these key definitional concepts are precisely the same as or very similar to those which existed under the Rent Act. (In addition, there is, as already noted, the underlying principle that existing tenants protected under the Rent Acts should retain protection so long as existing tenancies continue to occupy the dwelling). Thus the transition from the old regulatory regime to the new one will be by no means as dramatic as might have been expected.

Indeed it does seem extraordinary that more thought was not
given to these initial questions of status-definition in order to
see whether or not a single regulatory regime for all short/
medium-term lettings could not have been created.

Security of Tenure

The "assurance" referred to in the concept of the assured
tenancy derives from the not inconsiderable restrictions surrounding the circumstances in which a landlord may obtain
possession of a dwelling let under an assured tenancy. These are
substantial measures of tenant's protection, similar in many
respects to provisions in the Rent Acts relating to security of
tenure.

As with the Rent Acts, the grounds for possession which a
court may use to order possession are divided into mandatory
and discretionary grounds. As between these two categories,
there *are* important differences as between the former Rent
Acts and the new Housing Act designed to make lettings more
commercially attractive to private investors.[24] But, despite
claims by Government to the contrary, the list of grounds for
possession is still long and complex.

Rent Levels

The fundamental difference between the assured tenancy and
the Rent Act protected tenancy is, as already noted in passing,
that rent levels of the former are to be at market levels, *i.e.*
those determined by the contract not by the Rent Officer or
rent assessment committee. There is a theoretical possibility, in
defined circumstances, of referring increases in rents of assured
tenancies to a rent assessment committee, but since this may be
easily contracted out of,[25] it is anticipated that this will not
result in much effective rent regulation.

(c) The assured shorthold tenancy. The "assured shorthold
tenancy" is a new concept developed from the protected
shorthold tenancy introduced into the Rent Act 1977 by the
Housing Act 1980. The 1988 Act provides that, so long as a
proper notice is served,[26] and that a tenancy for a minimum

period of six months is granted, and that all the other criteria for the assured tenancy are satisfied, then an assured shorthold tenancy may come into existence.

Security of Tenure

Once created it may be determined on any of the 16 grounds available for assured tenancies plus, in addition, the crucial provision that there is to be a mandatory ground for possession on the giving of two months' notice.[27] Thus a tenant who holds over after the initial contractual period will be liable to eviction on two months' notice at any time thereafter, irrespective of any default or misbehaviour on the part of the tenant and irrespective of any commercial or other need for the dwelling on the part of the landlord. Thus, despite the "assured" label, the assured shorthold tenancy does not, in fact, offer any substantial security of tenure.

Rents

As regards rent levels, the principle again is that market rents should be permitted. There is a one-off opportunity for referring rents that are alleged to be "significantly" higher than the market rent for assured tenancies (whether shorthold or not) in the locality, to the rent assessment committee.[28] Apart from this, however, rents may not be referred to a rent assessment committee unless there is no contractual rent review clause in the tenancy agreement.[29]

It should be stressed that both these two new concepts—of the assured tenancy and the assured shorthold tenancy—will apply not only to private sector dwellings but also to housing association tenancies. The position prior to the coming into force of the 1988 Housing Act, whereby (broadly) housing association tenancies came under the Rent Acts for the purpose of rent regulation, and under the Housing Acts for the purpose of security of tenure, is now changed. Housing association tenancies and private sector tenancies are brought together under the single legislative assured tenancy code for the "independent" sector.

(d) Harassment and unlawful eviction. Chapter IV of Part 1 of the Housing Act contains some important amendments to the

law on unlawful eviction and harassment and also to the related statute law to be found in the Protection from Eviction Act 1977.[30]

(i) Recognising the fact that past experience with attempts to relax measures of rent control had been accompanied by a rise in unacceptable behaviour on the part of certain landlords, the Government has sought to incorporate into the 1988 Act certain additional protections for tenants. The most important measure (though it was watered down somewhat as the Bill processed through Parliament) is the creation of a new action in tort whereby tenants could seek damages for unlawful eviction. Most significantly, given the low level of damages that has tended to be awarded in such cases, the basis for the assessment of damages is also prescribed in the legislation. In essence, this is to be the difference in value of the dwelling with the occupier continuing to occupy the premises, and the value with the occupier out of the premises.[31]

There are at least two issues of possible difficulty arising from this formulation:

(a) the value of a dwelling will be diminished considerably less by an occupier who is a licensee or a shortholder (*i.e.* with very limited security of tenure) than by an occupier who has full assured or Rent Act protected security. Thus, if it can be assumed that the kinds of landlord who are most likely to resort to unlawful eviction are also those who will have sought to give the least rights of security to their residential occupiers, the protective value of this new measure may not be as great as at first anticipated;

(b) the legislation does not permit the possibility of a court ordering reinstatement of the unlawfully evicted occupier into the dwelling. Although making such an order on the part of the court might frequently prove unrealistic, nonetheless it may be suggested that the possibility that it might on occasion be done could have increased the deterrent value of those provisions.

(ii) Proof of the criminal offences of unlawful eviction and harassment is made somewhat easier by amendments to the statutory definitions of those crimes to be found in Section 1 of the Protection from Eviction Act 1977. In particular it will, in future, only be necessary to prove that acts are "likely" to cause an occupier to leave the premises, rather than "are calculated" to do so. The new formulation requires the court to adopt a more objective approach to the facts surrounding the commission of these offences. It will not be necessary to prove intent on the part of the accused.[32]

(iii) The principle that occupiers should not be turned out on to the streets without a court order is extended to include those who reside under valid licence agreements, as well as true tenancies.[33]

(iv) However, certain categories of tenancy and licence are to be wholly excluded from (iii) above.[34] These include: cases where the occupier shares accommodation with a landlord or licensor which is part of the latter's principal home; holiday licensees or tenants; certain hostel dwellers; and gratuitous licensees. These exclusions may not cause many difficulties in practice, but, at least in the context of the holiday tenancy/ licence exclusion, it may be asked whether this will not cause problems. It certainly used to be the case that, in order to avoid the Rent Acts, "holiday lets" were often to be discovered in extremely implausible locations. The exclusion of the category from the potential of being considered by the court in possession proceedings may mean that this particular kind of sham letting will be even less easy to challenge in the future than was the case in the past.[35]

(e) Repairs. One of the (possibly optimistic) objectives noted in the White Paper was that, by enabling landlords to receive a better return on their investment, they would, in turn, spend more of the profits on their properties by way of repairs and improvements in order to maintain and enhance the capital value of the building. One may be sceptical as to the extent to which this is likely to occur. Nonetheless, in order to reinforce these policy objectives, the Housing Act 1988 does contain a number of important provisions relating to repair and improvement.

(i) First, the statutory repairing covenant imposed on land-lords is extended to include a liability in relation to the common parts of buildings which have been let as flats.[36]

(ii) Secondly, and related to the last point, the definition of "unfitness for human habitation" is amended so that a flat may be unfit, where the unfitness relates to common parts, outside the flat, rather than in the flat itself.[37]

(iii) Local authority powers in relation to the enforcement of repairs notices have been substantially enhanced. Indeed, it is now a criminal offence to fail to execute repairs in compliance with a repairs notice.[38]

(f) Anti-discrimination measures. Two measures aimed at discrimination on racial grounds are to be found in the Act.

First, the Housing Corporation, and Housing for Wales, now have section 71[39] of the Race Relations Act 1976 applied to them, as it is already applied to local authorities.

Secondly, the Race Relations Act 1976, section 77 has, itself, been amended to give the Commission for Racial Equality specific powers to develop anti-discrimination codes of practice in relation to rented housing.[40]

3. Rethinking British Housing Law

Having considered the main provisions of the Housing Act 1988, it is not proposed in this essay to offer any predictions as to the likelihood or otherwise of the Government's policy objectives being achieved as a result of the passing of the Act. That will be a matter for empirical analysis at a later date.

It can however be remarked that while there are respects in which past housing legislation has made significant contributions to the ways in which the housing market in Britain is structured and operates, there are other respects in which it has signally failed to operate as apparently intended by government.[41] Indeed, in some cases new laws have been counter-productive in policy terms.

Sociologists of law will not find this surprising; the phenomenon of the "gap" between law in the books and law in practice is now very familiar. (Indeed there are some who regard it as surprising that any of the prescribed objectives of legislation are ever actually achieved.)

However, the fact that the gap has been observed in the past should not prevent the question from being asked as to whether it *needs* to exist. Put slightly differently, a broader question may be raised, namely: what is the relationship between housing policy and housing legislation?

Policy-makers and legislators tend, it may be suggested, to characterise legislation in rather "mechanistic" terms. On this view, law becomes the means by which policy initiatives are turned into some kind of operational reality. Law will set the context within which government officials may act; it will provide legitimation for their acts. Law will attempt to regulate relationships between parties (or between the individual and the state) and provide procedures for the resolution of disputes.

But if this view of the law does not actually reflect what happens in social reality, if the law does not in fact work in the ways in which it is assumed to work by policy-makers and politicians, then should the question at least not be asked whether the legal techniques being adopted to advance particular policy measures are actually likely to be able to assist in the achievement of specific policy goals? In other words, should we not be encouraging the policy-makers to stop thinking of law as simply being a means to an end and to start asking whether the very nature of the legal techniques being employed are themselves part of the reason why specific policy objectives are or are not being met.

It will be argued here that British housing law suffers from two, possibly three, crucial defects which will only be resolved by careful thought and the expenditure of considerable intellectual energy. The rest of this essay offers some preliminary thoughts on these defects and argues the case that if British housing law is to make more easy the achievement of stated policy goals, steps should be taken to address these defects.

The perceived defects are:

    (i)   the lack of coherence of British housing law;
   (ii) the lack of a "consumer perspective" in British housing law;
  (iii) (possibly) the complexity of British housing law.

Each of these heads will be discussed in turn.

(i) The Lack of Coherence

In Part 1 of this paper, a definition of "housing law" was offered as the basis for the present discussion. It will be realised that the three elements identified (the private, the public and the procedural law of housing) are in fact brought together from a wide range of sources.

For example, the "private law" part is, in effect, those rules of property law which have been created in the courts of common law and equity over many decades, centuries even; the "procedural law" aspects of housing law are part of the wider body of law relating to the procedures of courts and tribunals and the structure of the legal system for which the Lord Chancellor's Department will be primarily responsible; the "public law" of housing will be the more "political" parts of housing law and policy in which the Department of the Environment will be the dominant actor.

It is significant to note, however, that the Housing Act 1988 hardly contains any provisions devoted to the question of how rights, created under the Act, are to be enforced. One of the consequences of the new Legal Aid Act 1988 and the establishment of the Legal Aid Board is that there may now be some prospect of the creation of new forms of legal services which might incidentally relate to the resolution of housing disputes. But the Housing Act did not address in any direct way the question of the provision of advice and assistance on housing law matters, essential if the legislation is to have its full impact.

Similarly, the Civil Justice Review and the research that preceded its publication considered the question of the enforcement of housing rights in the courts[42] and noted that, possession proceedings apart, very few matters were being brought before the courts, despite overwhelming evidence that the kinds of circumstance which housing legislation was seeking to do something about (in particular the enhancement of housing conditions) were not actually being litigated in the courts. It may be that new procedures will be developed as a result of this initiative. However, again there was no consideration of these matters in the Housing Act itself.

Some consideration is currently being given by the Law Commission to a number of matters relating to questions of whether our existing categories of estates in land are adequate for the modern age. Particular attention has been given to the question of the purchase of flats.[43] But despite these initiatives there does not appear to be any move towards any consideration of more fundamental questions, as to whether the present overall system of ownership and other rights in property is still an appropriate base on which to build entitlement to rights of residential occupation in the late twentieth century. Certainly these issues were not considered in the Housing Act.

It is probably too simplistic to suggest that there should be a single government department responsible for all aspects of housing policy, and for developing a coherent legal framework within which to set it. Too many established interests would probably be put at risk were that to happen. But at present it does appear that, in this area of policy-making, our governmental structure itself lacks coherence and is not adequately geared to creating the kinds of inter-departmental linkages needed for a more coherent legal framework.[44]

(ii) The Lack of a "Consumer Perspective"

A second defect of British housing law which I regard as a fatal flaw (and which could be addressed in the overall review of the law suggested in (i) above) is the lack of any "consumer perspective."[45]

Rights to occupy housing are based on two of the most potent symbols of our law: contract and property. The freedom of parties to contract as they wish, the freedom of parties to use their property as they wish are both very powerful. Much social legislation in relation to housing has been the subject of criticism for interfering with contractual and property rights. But, as is obvious, "freedom of contract" may disguise an inequality of bargaining power between two contracting parties; and this imbalance may be compounded when the rights of the owner of property are set alongside the lack of rights of the person who has no property.

In most other sectors of the economy, it is now widely accepted—on both sides of the political divide—that there is a consumer interest that needs protection from those who may be tempted to abuse their position in the market place. Thus the consumers of a wide range of goods and services are able to utilise (at least in theory) a wide range of statutory protections against, *e.g.* faulty workmanship or poor service delivery. No doubt the providers of those services and those manufacturers would prefer not to have constraints imposed on them by legislation. Nonetheless this is accepted as part of the price to be paid for participating in the market place.

By contrast, housing policy and housing law, although purporting to create rights for tenants as well as landlords, do not project an analogous consumer perspective. To do so would not require as major a recasting of approaches to this area of the law as might be envisaged. For example, the "tenants' charter" provisions of the Housing Act 1980 might be said to provide a basic model for a code of housing consumer practice which could be expanded to encompass the private sector as well. The complex law on the control of service charges and other detailed developments in relation to, *inter alia*, rights of pre-emption, again indicate the willingness of government to give measures of consumer protection to tenants, in this case long-term tenants. The non-statutory tenancy relations officers employed by many local authorities could be seen as being in an analogous position to trading standards officers. And, in what may eventually turn out to be the most fundamental change in the Housing Act 1988, the new powers given to the Housing Corporation may in the longer term come to be seen as the first steps towards the creation of an "Office of Fair Housing."

If housing law came to be regarded as being as firmly within the range of consumer protection measures now common in the other sectors of the economy, this would offer at least three major advantages:

First, it could encourage the development of the more coherent approach to housing law, a lack of which has already been noted.

Secondly, it could provide the basis for a more politically neutral approach to housing policy. This would not imply, as some commentators wish to do, that "politics should be taken out of housing." This is simply not possible. But if housing policy (and thus housing law) is *too* politically controversial, so that it is *inevitable* that there will be the prospect of further amending legislation when there is a change of government, which in turn may affect the legal rights of tenants or landlords, this is bound to affect the impact of housing legislation. Unlike other consumer products, housing takes a long time to produce and, once produced, should last for a considerable period of time. No matter how secure the political party which is in government may appear to be at any particular moment in time, the reality is that during the lifetime of a house or a block of flats there are likely to be changes of government. If the policies of the contending political parties would clearly dramatically affect the value of buildings that have been erected or converted, it is also inevitable that cautious or merely prudent investors will need to assess the likelihood of their investments turning sour.

Thirdly, a consumer approach to housing might encourage the recognition of the provision of housing services as another

branch of the service sector of the economy. Were this to
happen this might also encourage the development of "associations of housing producers," again analogous to other trade
associations, organised for the purpose of establishing standards
of good practice in the industry, disciplining members who do
not conform to those standards and offering at least a measure
of protection to tenants who fall foul of malpractice. (One might
anticipate similar developments amongst housing consumers as
well[46]). A fundamental weakness of the housing market,
particularly in the private rented sector, is that it is an area of
economic activity frequently portrayed as characterised by sharp
practice and shady dealings; proper encouragement should be
given to the industry to establish mechanisms of self-regulation
as well as state regulation, aimed at improving this poor image.

(iii) The Complexity of British Housing Law

A common criticism of British housing law is that it is too
complex. Certainly an area of law which is designed to affect
literally everyone in the country who owns and/or occupies
residential accommodation but which can only be encompassed
in four large loose-leaf volumes,[47] or analysed in a text of well
over 1,000 pages[48] might appear, on the face of it, to be too
complex.

I would not dissent from the view that much of the law is
unnecessarily complex. Indeed the Housing Act 1988 has added
to that complexity. But those who complain of complexity too
often fail to recognise the causes of that complexity. All social
legislation, even from a government that projects a rather
single-minded ideological image, on closer analysis is seen to
contain political compromise. Detailed exceptions to general
principles are conceded to reflect the range of interests that will
inevitably be affected where new law is made. It is more than
likely that a body of law that seeks to be sensitive to a variety
of demands and pressures will have, to a greater or less extent,
to be complex. Housing law is particularly susceptible to such
conflicting pressures.

Were there to be the more coherent body of law,
underpinned by the more consumer approach considered in
outline above, it might well follow that some of the complexity
would disappear and this would be welcome. But it may be
more sensible to accept that there will be a substantial measure

of complexity. Instead of complaining about this and rather optimistically asserting that the law can be made simpler (as Ministers, in particular, are wont to do), it might be better to recognise that there will be a need for the educational programmes, the advisers and lawyers, the courts and tribunals that are able to cope with these complexities in the interests of the consumers of "housing products."

Conclusion

The remarks in Part 3 of the essay have been critical of the lack of a sense of vision in the Housing Act 1988. That Act was, of course, a highly "political" measure, in the sense that it was aimed at delivering a set of promises contained in the Conservative Party's election manifesto of 1987.

I have not sought to criticise directly the measures contained in the 1988 Act though, at least so far as housing policy in relation to the most disadvantaged in our society is concerned, it seems highly likely that their place in the housing market is not going to be substantially enhanced.[49] For example, the policies of allowing rents to rise to market levels while also setting maximum levels of housing benefit do appear, candidly, to be in fundamental conflict.

The ultimate objective of housing policy, of whatever government is in power, must surely be to ensure that there is enough accommodation available, of an appropriate standard, at a price which people can afford to pay, in which people may live with a sense of security. These seem to be the eessential preconditions if all citizens are to be given equality of opportunity and a good start in life. While there are crucial *political* decisions (not least over levels of public sector investment and public subsidies, and the extent of the involvement of the private sector in housing provision) which are of central importance, this paper seeks to argue that there may also be important questions about the legal framework within which housing policy is sought to be delivered which need to be thought about much more seriously. The Housing Act 1988 has not done this; it is in this sense, if no other, that it must be regarded as a failure.

Notes

[1] This was certainly the approach adopted by Andrew Arden and myself in our *Housing Law* (Sweet and Maxwell, London, 1983).

[2] Cm. 214, 1987, paras. 1.13–1.17.

[3] Indeed it was acknowledged in the White Paper that further legislation would be required: *ibid.* para. 7.7. (Already a new Housing and Local Government Bill 1989 has been presented to Parliament to continue what the Government itself recognises to be unfinished business).

[4] Important developments in the role and funding of the Housing Corporation and Housing for Wales may be mentioned specifically in this context. This was hinted at in one of the Consultation Papers that was published at the same time as the White Paper. But, a reading of the Parliamentary Debates surrounding the passage of the Bill suggests that further significant policy steps in relation to the Housing Corporation and Housing for Wales were adopted as the Bill progressed through Parliament.

[5] ss.93–114 and Sched. 12.

[6] *Ibid.* s.100.

[7] As curiously defined; *ibid.* s.103(2).

[8] *Ibid.* ss.60–92 and Scheds. 7–11.

[9] *Ibid.* ss.65–73.

[10] The bodies so created are actually statutory corporations, *ibid.* ss.62(3) and 63(4), not "trusts" in the most commonly understood sense of the term.

[11] *Ibid.* s.63(1).

[12] *Ibid.* s.63(2).

[13] *Ibid.* s.61(4).

[14] *Ibid.* ss.46, 47 and 59 and Sched. 6.

[15] *Ibid.* s.48, amending Housing Associations Act 1985, s.4.

[16] *Ibid.* s.49, introducing a new s.35A in the Housing Associations Act 1985.

[17] *Ibid.* s.94. Similar procedures are also to be used by the Corporation to determine "approved persons" to whom housing action trusts may dispose of properties in their areas: *ibid.* s.79.

[18] This power is abolished, with effect from January 15, 1989: Housing Act 1988, Sched. 17, para. 22.

[19] See Doling and Davies, *Public Control of Privately Rented housing* (1984).

[20] See Housing Act, 1988, s.121; the details of the Rent Officers' powers are to be found in regulations.

[21] See ss.122–128. These will not be considered further in this paper.

[22] A "member of the family" claiming a right to succession will after January 15, 1989 have to have resided in the dwelling for two years rather than the former six months; only one right of succession, not two, is permitted; and successors will succeed to an assured tenancy, not a Rent Act protected or statutory tenancy: Housing Act 1988, s.39.

[23] There is no longer any control of premiums in relation to the granting of an assured tenancy as there was with tenancies protected under the Rent Acts.

[24] For example, there are new mandatory grounds giving the possibility of the landlord obtaining possession where he/she wishes to redevelop; or where there are three months' arrears of rent. The full details of the 16 grounds of possession are set out in Sched. 2 to the Act.

[25] So long as the tenancy contains a specific provision whereby the rent level may be altered, the Rent Assessment Committee will have no jurisdiction: *ibid.* s.13(1).

[26] There is a small number of detailed exceptions to this general proposition: *ibid.* s.20(4), s.39(7).

[27] *Ibid.* s.21.

[28] *Ibid.* s.22.

[29] *Ibid.* s.13.

[30] See generally, Arden and Partington, *Quiet Enjoyment* (2nd ed. 1985) (Legal Action Group, London).

[31] Housing Act 1988 s.28.

[32] *Ibid.* s.29.

[33] *Ibid.* s.30.

[34] *Ibid.* s.31.

[35] It might in theory be possible to ask the court for a declaration as to the status of an occupier where this was in doubt, but it is unlikely to be a practical option in many cases.

[36] See Housing Act 1988, s.116.

[37] *Ibid.* s.130(2), amending Housing Act 1985, s.604 and see Housing Act 1985, s.189(1A) introduced by Housing Act 1988, Sched. 15 para. 1(2).

[38] Housing Act 1985, s.198A introduced by Housing Act 1988, Sched. 15, para. 8.

[39] This creates a rather general duty to eliminate racial discrimination and promote equality of opportunity.

[40] See Housing Act 1988, s.137.

[41] There is substantial literature on this: see, *e.g.* my "Landlord and Tenant: The British Experience" Chap. 10 in *Law and Social Control* (ed. Kamenka and Tay) (Edward Arnold, London, 1980).

[42] See Cm. 394, *Report of the Review Body on Civil Justice* (HMSO, London, 1988) at pp. 121–142.

[43] See, *Commonhold: Freehold flats and Freehold ownership of other interdependent dwellings.* (Cm. 179) (HMSO, London, 1987).

[44] This is not to suggest that there are no interdepartmental links at all; rather that they are not very effective in producing an overall policy. One example may be considered in this context. The Children's Bill currently before Parliament appears to be the outcome of a structured programme of thought and legislative drafting between the Law Commission, the Lord Chancellor's Department and the Department of Health. Clearly the scandals which have affected children in recent years have influenced this radical rethink and given it political impetus which has not, perhaps, occurred in the housing field. Nonetheless it is trite to observe that housing (or lack of it) affects everyone; perhaps there would be a case for taking a closer look at our housing law with a view to raising the political pressure needed to put in place the administrative and policy-making infrastructure essential to give this area of law a more coherent structure.

[45] This theme is developed further in A. Murie *et al, The Consumer Implications of the Housing Act, 1988*, (Working Paper 77, School for Advanced Urban Studies, University of Bristol, 1988).

[46] See my "Collective-Bargaining in the Landlord-Tenant relationship" in (ed.) Neal, *Law and the Weaker Party* (Professional Books, Abingdon, 1981).

[47] *Encyclopedia of Housing Law* (Sweet and Maxwell, London).

[48] Above, n. 1.

[49] Already there are clear indications that landlords are taking substantial advantage of the new assured shorthold tenancy arrangements. What will happen in the months leading up to the next general election, particularly if there are signs that the party in government might change and the Conservatives be replaced by a party that could, for example, give shorthold tenants greater security of tenure, must be a cause of concern, not least to local housing authorities to whom the evicted tenants may turn as being homeless.

Homelessness Law: First Aid in Need of Intensive Care?

DAVID HOATH

Introduction

The Domestic Violence and Matrimonial Proceedings Act 1976 has been called "first aid" legislation.[1] Another very important piece of 1970s social welfare legislation, providing "first aid" of a different sort, was the Housing (Homeless Persons) Act 1977 (now consolidated in Part III of the Housing Act 1985). The Housing (Homeless Persons) Act imposed duties on local housing authorities in relation to the homeless, and, according to Lord Brightman, its aim was "to provide for the homeless a lifeline of last resort."[2] The 1977 Act was undoubtedly an improvement on the highly confusing homelessness legislation which it replaced,[3] but its loose drafting has given rise to considerable difficulties, so that the "lifeline" is in places now distinctly frayed; indeed, one M.P. thought that the Act (when in Bill form) was so "sloppy" and "ill-prepared" that it "could have been drafted on the back of an envelope in an evening, while watching television,"[4] while a Scottish judge condemned it as a "semantic nightmare."[5]

It is not possible in this paper to cover all the difficulties arising from the present state of homelessness law[6]; an attempt will however be made to examine a few of the more acute legal problems, to set them in their practical context, and to produce some modest proposals for reform.

The Extent of the Homelessness Problem

Homelessness is regrettably a growth area, both worldwide and nationally. It was estimated in April 1988 that one billion

81

people, a fifth of the world's population, were then homeless or living in slums, and that the number was likely to rise to three billion within 12 years unless governments made a number of fundamental changes in their current approach to the problem.[7] In England, the number of *applications* for help under the homelessness legislation reached a record figure of 250,000 in 1986, and the number of homeless households actually *accepted* for rehousing in that year was 103,000 (whereas in 1978 the number of acceptances had only been 53,100).[8] It has been alleged that, among the developed countries, the problem of homelessness in Britain is second only to that in the United States[9]; and that there are more homeless people sleeping rough on the streets of London than in any other capital in Europe, except Istanbul.[10]

Councils have had to face an escalating homelessness problem at a time when their resources have been drastically cut back. Few councils have been able to embark on ambitious building programmes in recent years, and a considerable amount of better-quality housing has been lost to the public sector through the exercise by sitting tenants of their statutory "right to buy."[11] The schemes for privatisation of council estates contained in Parts III and IV of the Housing Act 1988 (the "Housing Action Trust Areas" and "Change of Landlord" provisions) will further hamper the ability of councils to accommodate the homeless. Indeed, the Government envisages that some councils will lose their entire housing stock, although they will retain statutory liability for the homeless.[12]

It is not difficult to appreciate that a council without any council housing could have rather a problem in accommodating the homeless. However, under section 69(1) of the Housing Act 1985 a housing duty owed to a homeless person can be discharged either by the council providing its own suitable accommodation, or by the council arranging for the homeless person to obtain suitable accommodation from some other person; the Government contemplates that a council which has disposed of all its stock should be able to enter into agreements with the block purchasers of its estates, giving the council access to the transferred accommodation in order for it to discharge its homelessness responsibilities.[13]

Faced with such problems, many councils have resorted to placing the homeless in private sector bed and breakfast institutions (which have been described[14] as "equivalent to the shanty towns of the Third World"). The enormous cost of such provision, and the misery caused to many of the occupants, has been widely documented.[15] However, the use of bed and breakfast may diminish in the future, since in July 1988 the Government blocked all further subsidies in relation to the leasing by councils of accommodation in bed and breakfast hotels; instead, councils were encouraged to provide alternative forms of housing for the homeless, for example through the allocation by central government of additional grant-aid for the refurbishment of empty council dwellings.[16]

Although the 1987 White Paper on Housing[17] did not contain any specific references to homelessness, there seems little doubt that the package of reforms to the law governing the public and private rented sectors which was introduced by the Housing Act 1988 will have an effect on the homelessness crisis; whether that effect will be to diminish the crisis, or to increase it, remains to be seen.

The Conditions Precedent to Rehousing

Under Part III of the Housing Act 1985, a person who is "homeless" within the definition in section 58 is only entitled to be rehoused if he has a "priority need" for accommodation.[18] If the council is satisfied that he is in priority need, and it is not satisfied that he became homeless intentionally, then the applicant is entitled to be rehoused indefinitely.[19] If, however, the council is satisfied that, although he is in priority need, his homelessness was intentional, then its only obligations are (a) to furnish him with advice and appropriate assistance in relation to his attempts to find accommodation, and (b) to offer him *temporary* accommodation, for such period as it considers will give him a reasonable opportunity of finding his own accommodation.[20]

The council must make the necessary inquiries on these matters[21] (and must do so promptly, so that temporary closure of its homelessness section, even though due to staffing and financial difficulties, will clearly be unlawful[22]). The council must "satisfy" itself on the relevant issues, so that it has the burden of pursuing the appropriate inquiries[23]; in particular, as regards "intentional" homelessness, if the council remains in any doubt on the issue, the applicant is entitled to the benefit of that doubt,[24] and should therefore be found unintentionally homeless.

Nevertheless, in practice many councils have felt it necessary to adopt a hard line in dealing with homelessness applications;

the reasons for this include lack of resources and antipathy towards the legislation on political grounds. Consequently, the legislation has been described as operating in practice as a "homeless persons' obstacle race,"[25] and it has spawned a volume of cases which has been described as "remarkable, having regard to the short time it has been in force, the extent of the discretion it confers and the absence of an ordinary right of appeal."[26] In view of the fact that a roof over one's head is a rather fundamental human need, however, the persistence of applicants in challenging the homelessness decisions of councils by way of judicial review is not wholly surprising.

Some Problems Concerning Intentional Homelessness

Most of the cases have been fought over the issue of intentional homelessness. It is proposed here to consider the ways in which the "intentionality" cases have dealt with two areas of particular practical importance, namely family disputes and job-related moves. Before doing so, however, it may be helpful to set out the relevant statutory provisions defining intentional homelessness.

The Definition of Intentional Homelessness

Section 60 of the Housing Act 1985 states:

"60.—(1) A person becomes homeless intentionally if he deliberately does or fails to do anything in consequence of which he ceases to occupy accommodation which is available for his occupation and which it would have been reasonable for him to continue to occupy.

...(3) For the purposes of subsection (1) ... an act or omission in good faith on the part of a person who was unaware of any relevant fact shall not be treated as deliberate.

(4) Regard may be had, in determining whether it would have been reasonable for a person to continue to occupy accommodation, to the general circumstances prevailing in relation to housing in the district of the local housing authority to whom he applied for accommodation or for assistance in obtaining accommodation."

As regards the "reasonableness" criterion in section 60(1) and (4), the position has been somewhat obscured by virtue of the introduction of this criterion (and of the relevance thereto of the general housing circumstances in the council's area) into the definition of "homelessness" itself, contained in section 58.[27] This reform, achieved by the Housing and Planning Act 1986 in response to the harsh decision of the House of Lords in *Puhlhofer* v. *Hillingdon L.B.C.*,[28] has the effect of deeming a person to be statutorily "homeless" if, although he has accommodation, it is not accommodation which it would be reasonable for him to continue to occupy. Thus, where an applicant has left accommodation which it would not have been reasonable for him to continue to occupy, the true analysis appears to be that he is not "intentionally homeless" because he was legally "homeless" *even before he left*, so that his departure is logically irrelevant to the intentionality issue.[29] This reasoning merely achieves the same result (*un*intentional homelessness) by the section 58 route rather than the section 60 route.

Allegations of Intentional Homelessness Arising from Family Disputes[30]

(i) The effects of a finding of intentional homelessness. Where a relationship breakdown causes a family member to leave home, then although he or she may well be legally "homeless"[31] even in the absence of any locking-out or violence by the other partner,[32] and although he or she will often be in "priority need,"[33] there is nevertheless a danger that the council may find that the homelessness was intentional, so that it will only be obliged to offer housing on a temporary basis.[34] When the applicant is eventually forced to leave this temporary accommodation, no further application can be made to the same housing authority until the material circumstances have changed[35] (for example, by the applicant breaking the "chain of intentionality" by obtaining his or her own settled accommodation[36]); and, even if children are involved, there is no automatic duty on the social services authority to offer "first aid" housing to the applicant under section 1 of the Child Care Act 1980 in order to avoid the children being taken into care.[37]

(ii) The "infectious intentionality" hurdle. Sometimes a family dispute can result in homelessness, not because one family member decides to leave, but because the strained relationship has caused other difficulties (typically, financial) which have led to homelessness as a result of the action of a third party (typically, repossession by a landlord or mortgagee for rent or mortgage arrears). Where the deliberate actions or inactions of one partner have indirectly caused the other partner's homelessness in this way, some councils have sought to adopt a policy of, in effect, "infectious intentionality," so that the "innocent" partner has been "tarred with the same brush" as the "guilty" partner.[38]

It is clear from the more recent cases, however, that the claims of the applicant must be considered by the council on their own merits, and that he or she can only be found to have acquiesced in the conduct of a "guilty" family member if there is some reasonable evidence pointing to such acquiescence.[39] Further, even where the family home which has been repossessed due to rent or mortgage arrears was in the joint names of the partners, each partner is entitled to separate consideration when the council is deciding whether there is the necessary element of wilful default to justify a finding of intentional homelessness, provided the facts raise the possibility of non-acquiescence.[40]

(iii) The "moral turpitude" hurdle. Although councils have frequently been urged not to adopt "moralistic" attitudes towards applicants such as unmarried mothers and cohabitees when allocating their housing,[41] applicants who are homeless due (directly or indirectly) to domestic disputes may still sometimes find that moral overtones affect the council's decision on the question of whether the homelessness is intentional.[42]

It seems clear that homelessness caused by a domestic dispute arising from the woman's pregnancy cannot properly be regarded as intentional, even if the pregnancy was intended and the child is not that of the man with whom she was living; for the pregnancy would not be a relevant "deliberate act" for the purposes of section 60 of the Housing Act 1985.[43]

A case which well illustrates the need for an authority to eschew moral judgments in this area is *R. v. Wimbourne D.C., ex p. Curtis*.[44] Here, following marriage breakdown, the spouses entered into a separation agreement whereby a house was made available for the wife's use, but under the trust deed the power of sale was to be triggered if she cohabited or remarried. After the wife moved into the house, her boyfriend joined her, and she later had his child. Not surprisingly, the husband exercised the power of sale, as a result of which the wife became homeless. Equally unsurprisingly, the council found her intentionally homeless. However, it will be recalled that one of the elements of the definition of intentional homelessness in section 60 of the 1985 Act (set out above) is that the applicant must have left accommodation which was "available" for his or her occupation. Under section 75, accommodation is only "available" for these purposes if it is available for occupation *both* by him or her *and* by any other person who "might reasonably be expected to reside" with him or her. The wife succeeded in persuading the court to quash the council's finding of intentionality, through a somewhat devious argument based on this "availability" criterion: she had not left "available" accommodation, because the accommodation was not available for occupation by her boyfriend (due to the non-cohabitation clause in the trust deed), and it was *reasonable* to expect the boyfriend to reside with her. The council was found to have failed to consider this point properly.

(iv) The "failure to apply for domestic relief" hurdle.[45] In an appropriate case, an authority may find that the omission of a homeless spouse or cohabitee to take court action[46] against the other partner, in order to preserve the former's right to peaceful residence, renders the homelessness intentional.[47] The reasoning of the authority in such a case would be that although the *act of departure* might not of itself cause the homelessness to be intentional (because, for example, the applicant was driven out by violence), the *refusal to take relevant court action* was a deliberate *failure* to act, as a result of which there has been a cessation of occupation of accommodation which it would have been reasonable for the applicant to continue to occupy had he or she taken such action.[48]

In this context, a distinction appears to have been drawn between violent and non-violent domestic disputes. The Code of Guidance, in a passage[49] which has received judicial approval,[50] states uncompromisingly[51] that "a battered woman who has fled the marital home should *never* be regarded as having become homeless intentionally because it would *clearly not be reasonable* for her to remain."

It is a sad fact of life that no court order can guarantee a woman's safety if her former partner is determined to continue assaulting her.[52] In *Charles* v. *Charles*,[53] the Court of Appeal refused to give a battered wife an ouster injunction against her husband, who had a history of serious violence towards her, because such an injunction would have exposed her to further risk when she returned to the matrimonial home (since the husband would know where to find her), and an injunction would in effect have forced the wife into this dangerous situation, because if she had applied to the council as a homeless person, the existence of the injunction would probably have caused the council to find her intentionally homeless. Although the case directly involved only the spouses *inter se*, so that the council was not a party to the action, Dunn L.J. said, in a significant passage[54]:

> "...it was reasonable...for this lady to leave...because of the husband's violence...it appears that this lady...is homeless...and could not be held to be intentionally homeless."

It therefore follows that, where occupation of the family home will expose the applicant to the sort of risks envisaged in *Charles* v. *Charles*, neither the applicant's departure nor the failure to seek relief through court action should give rise to a finding of intentional homelessness.[55]

(v) The "grin and bear it" hurdle. Where the applicant has not been exposed to the risk of physical assault, then the cases appear to require him or her to show a considerable degree of fortitude in the face of unpleasant or anti-social behaviour by the other occupiers: he or she may be expected to remain in occupation (and take advantage of relevant legal remedies), so that departure may lead to a finding of intentional homelessness.[56]

There is a wide spectrum of behaviour, short of violence, in which spouses or cohabitees can indulge, much of which may make life intolerable for their partners. It is therefore arguable that the line which the courts appear to be drawing between violent and non-violent domestic disputes for section 60 purposes is undesirably rigid, particularly because (as we have seen) the applicant is entitled to the benefit of the doubt on intentionality issues. The most recent trend in the "reasonableness" case law, however, is to take an even harder line in cases of *non-domestic* violence: here, although the authority must consider the violence as a relevant "reasonableness" issue notwithstanding its non-domestic nature,[57] the applicant may apparently be expected to stay put and run serious risks[58] (even, indeed, where effective police protection is not available[59]), for want of which he or she may be found intentionally homeless.

Allegations of Intentional Homelessness Arising from Job-related Moves[60]

Another area in which the "reasonableness" element of intentional homelessness has given rise to difficulties is that of job-related moves. In the era of "on yer bike" employment policies, it might be thought that it should not be regarded as "reasonable for [the applicant] to continue to occupy"[61] accommodation which he has vacated in order to seek or take up employment elsewhere.

The Code of Guidance asks councils to "exercise care in dealing with loss of accommodation arising from a move to seek work."[62] Further, there have been some indications that the courts are prepared to be sympathetic to the plight of the applicant in such cases. In *Islam* v. *Hillingdon L.B.C.*[63] Lord Lowry thought that "[t]here will be, of course, and in the interests of the mobility of labour ought to be, cases where the housing authority will under s[60(1)] accept that it would not have been reasonable in the circumstances for the applicant to continue to occupy the accommodation which he has left." Subsequently, in *R.* v. *L.B. of Hammersmith & Fulham, ex p. Duro-Rama*[64] the council was found to have failed to take relevant circumstances into account when it had omitted to consider whether it was reasonable for the applicant to continue to occupy accommodation which he had left due to lack of employment prospects in the area. Most recently, in *R.* v. *Kensington & Chelsea L.B.C., ex p. Cunha*,[65] Otton J. recognised that where an applicant has come from overseas, his difficulty in obtaining employment in the country from which he has come is a relevant fact for the authority to consider in determining the intentionality issue (although on the facts in *Cunha* the council's finding of intentionality was upheld, because the court decided it would have been an "unwarranted burden" for the council to have had to inquire into the local employment conditions in Brazil).

There is however a separate set of cases taking a much harder line,[66] in upholding councils' decisions that moves for the purpose of looking for or taking up work elsewhere can be regarded as constituting intentional homelessness, because it would have been reasonable for the applicant to stay put. In *De Falco* v. *Crawley B.C.*,[67] for example, an Italian family had left Italy and arrived in England; there had been "nothing in the answers received [by the council during the initial interview with the applicants] to indicate ... that there was any reason for leaving [Italy] *except the wish to come and work in England.*"[68] This "job-search" factor cut no ice with the Court of Appeal, which found the family intentionally homeless.

A particularly clear example of the courts' refusal to accept employment mobility as a justification for leaving settled accommodation is the decision of McNeill J. in *R. v. South Hams D.C., ex p. Proctor.*[69] Here the applicant left his council house in Chesterfield because of unemployment, and moved to temporary and overcrowded accommodation with his brother-in-law in Devon in order to explore a job opportunity, which indeed materialised into employment; the applicant's wife then gave up the tenancy of the council house in Chesterfield and moved[70] with the children into her brother's already over-crowded accommodation in Devon. The judge upheld the council's finding of intentional homelessness, saying:

> "It does not seem to me that I am entitled under this statute to consider whether it would have been reasonable for the applicants to continue to occupy that accommodation [in Chesterfield] when there was no work for the first applicant in Chesterfield, but there was work for him in Devonshire. As I read it, it would require Parliamentary intervention to enable a court to say that the availability of work in one place rather than another bears on reasonableness under section [60(1)] ... No doubt with the best of intentions, and he is to be complimented on his effort to find work, the first applicant left what was secure accommodation. He left it to go into what can only be described as temporary and inadequate accommodation with his brother-in-law. ... "

One wonders why the judge considered that it was not possible to regard job mobility as a reasonableness issue under section 60(1) in the absence of any precise reference to this factor in the statute. The only specific guidance in the statute on the section 60(1) reasonableness issue is contained in section 60(4), which states (as noted above) that regard may be had "to the general circumstances prevailing in relation to housing" in the district of the local authority to which the application is made. The courts have emphasised that this reference is not exhaustive, and indeed was only included because, if it had been omitted, the courts would have regarded it as irrelevant.[71] Thus the courts have had no difficulty in regarding the following factors (*inter alia*) as relevant to the issue of whether it was reasonable to continue to occupy the vacated accommodation, notwithstanding that section 60 makes no express reference to them: domestic violence[72]; the impact of immigration rules[73];

the "custom and lifestyle" of the applicant's local community[74]; and the lack of security of tenure.[75] It therefore seems very strange to single out job mobility as an issue which the courts must ignore until Parliament chooses specifically to include it.

McNeill J. in *Proctor* did not consider any of the relevant cases on intentionality, save for the reference made by Lord Lowry in *Islam* to the significance of labour mobility,[76] a reference which was dismissed in a somewhat cavalier fashion:

> "I do not think that the sentence there relied upon justifies me in entering into a debate as to whether the presence of work in one place and the absence of work in the other where secure accommodation is available is a relevant consideration under section [60(1)]. . . . "

Two very different approaches therefore emerge from the cases regarding the relevance or otherwise of job mobility to a decision as to whether the applicant's homelessness is intentional. The approach taken by Lord Lowry in *Islam* is flexible, and treats the issue as relevant in an appropriate case. By contrast, the approach taken by McNeill J. in *Proctor* goes to the other extreme, and treats the issue as completely irrelevant in all cases, however laudable the applicant's attempts to seek work may have been. A third approach involves simply "sitting on the fence": in *R. v. L.B. of Tower Hamlets, ex p. Monaf*,[77] Lloyd L.J. stated, in relation to the argument that the council had disregarded the poor employment prospects in the area which the applicant left, that this would not ground an application for judicial review unless it was a factor which the council was obliged to consider, but in any event he did not accept that this factor had been disregarded by the council; none of the relevant case law on job mobility was discussed.

In view of the current emphasis on encouraging mobility of labour as a means of assisting economic regeneration, it is submitted that it is very undesirable for authorities to be able to close their minds to this issue when deliberating upon intentional homelessness. If it really does now require legislation (as McNeill J. suggests) for Lord Lowry's approach to be adopted, then there is a strong case for Parliament giving this matter urgent attention. It is not of course suggested that homelessness resulting from moves prompted by considerations of job mobility ought *never* to be regarded as intentional, but merely that authorities should give careful attention to these considerations where they are relevant.

Problems Concerning the Standard of Accommodation Offered to the Homeless

It was noted earlier in this paper that where a council owes a housing duty to an applicant, then under section 69(1) of the Housing Act 1985 the council can secure the necessary accommodation either by providing its own housing or by arranging accommodation for him from "some other person." Section 69(1) further requires that the accommodation must be "suitable," having regard to the provisions in the Housing Act relating to slum clearance, overcrowding, and multiple occupation.

This "suitability" requirement was introduced into section 69 by the Housing and Planning Act 1986, in order to reverse the effects of certain dicta of Lord Brightman in *Puhlhofer* v. *Hillingdon L.B.C.*,[78] where he stated that no qualifying adjective was to be implied when construing the word "accommodation" in Part III of the 1985 Act, and that in particular the statutory fitness and overcrowding criteria were not to be imported "for any purpose." These dicta had been applied, in the specific context of the discharge of the council's rehousing responsibilities, by Simon Brown J. in *R.* v. *L.B. of Wandsworth, ex p. Lindsay*[79]: here a mother with two very young children was found unintentionally homeless, but the council made her a single offer of a maisonette, on the ninth floor of a tower block, which had a balcony which was particularly dangerous for small children. The judge refused to interfere with this offer, saying that, in the light of *Puhlhofer*, the accommodation offered to the homeless "need only be premises properly so describable even if . . . unfit, inadequate or otherwise unsuitable."[80] Thus, even after clearing all the hurdles presented by the Act (*i.e.* the legal definition of homelessness, the priority need categories, and the "intentionality" trap), the applicant could end up in thoroughly unsatisfactory accommodation. This result was in marked contrast to the advice given to councils by the Housing Services Advisory Group in 1978[81]:

> " . . . it is essential that people should not be penalised in terms of quality by the urgency of their need: every applicant, from whatever allocation group, should be offered the best available property consistent with his degree of priority, and not the poorest that he is likely to accept because of his desperation."

To what extent does the new statutory "suitability" requirement redress the balance in favour of the Housing Services

Advisory Group's approach, and away from the harsh line taken in *Puhlhofer* and *Lindsay*? Largely due to the constraints of the courts' role under the judicial review procedure (discussed below), the homeless can unfortunately expect little improvement in the quality of the accommodation which is offered to them. For example, in *R. v. Westminster C.C., ex p. Tansey*[82] the applicant, who was found to be in priority need and unintentionally homeless, sought to challenge the council's decision to place him in hostel or hotel accommodation, arguing that such accommodation was not "suitable" within the amended section 69, since it conferred no security of tenure, had no cooking facilities, offered no protection against intrusion, and was not affordable. He was refused leave to apply for judicial review, initially[83] on the grounds that accommodation, even for an unintentionally homeless person,[84] did not have to attract security of tenure in order to be "suitable," and the council was entitled, in considering what accommodation initially to offer an applicant, to bear in mind the security of tenure or lack of it experienced by the applicant in his or her previous accommodation.

Although it must be acknowledged that councils should retain a broad discretion regarding the type of accommodation to be provided for each individual applicant, it is suggested that more specific guidance on the "quality" issue should at least be given in the Code, the relevant provisions of which are currently rather vague.[85]

Problems Concerning the Procedure for Challenging the Council's Decision

Many of the difficulties caused by the present state of the case law on Part III of the Housing Act 1985 arise from the inherent constraints of the judicial review procedure. Although the Act itself confers no specific remedy on the applicant for challenging the council's homelessness decision, the courts have been prepared to intervene; however, it is now clear that as regards most of the key issues (concerning, for example, the council's "decision-making" functions in respect of the definition of homelessness, the assessment of priority need, findings of intentional homelessness, and even, apparently, the quality of the accommodation offered), the appropriate remedy is by way of judicial review in the Divisional Court of the Queen's Bench

Division, under Order 53 of the Rules of the Supreme Court and section 31 of the Supreme Court Act 1981.[86]

This procedure[87] involves a two-stage process (*ex parte* application for leave, followed, if successful, by the substantive application itself), and it has considerable drawbacks from the applicant's viewpoint, among which are the following. First, there is no right of appeal on the merits: the judge is restricted by the well-known administrative law "Wednesbury principles"[88] to an examination of the manner in which the council's decision has been reached, and cannot upset the decision merely because he disagrees with it, however "harsh" it may appear[89]; and, in the particular context of the Ministerial Code of Guidance, although under section 71 of the Housing Act 1985 councils must "have regard" to its advice, the courts have made it clear that the Code is of no direct statutory force, and councils are not bound to follow it in any particular case provided they at least *consider* it.[90] Secondly, the House of Lords in *Puhlhofer* v. *Hillingdon L.B.C.*,[91] troubled by the supposedly prolific use of judicial review in homelessness cases,[92] insisted that leave to apply should only be granted where the case is "exceptional." Thirdly, the courts have sometimes been prepared to redraft the stated (and prima facie defective) reasons[93] of the council in order to make them comply with the law.[94] Fourthly, the procedure is usually lengthy,[95] although an interim injunction may be obtained *ex parte* in an appropriate case securing accommodation pending the court's decision.[96] Fifthly, there are often difficulties in obtaining legal aid[97]; in particular, a successful application for leave to bring judicial review proceedings is often necessary before the application for legal aid can succeed.[98] Sixthly, a "victory" for the applicant in judicial review proceedings can prove pyrrhic if the council, on being required by the court to reconsider the case in accordance with the proper "Wednesbury principles," then reaches exactly the same (adverse) decision but manages to achieve a suitably sophisticated set of reasons in the new decision letter.[99]

Not surprisingly, the application of this procedure to homelessness cases has been heavily criticised; and there have been many calls for a simple, swift, independent and locally-based appeal system for these crucial and difficult cases, enabling the merits of a particular decision to be carefully examined.[1]

Conclusions

It is submitted that the current state of homelessness law is not fit for the purpose of dealing effectively with this escalating social problem. The relevant legislation was drafted in vague terms, and the amendments introduced by the Housing and Planning Act 1986 do not appear to have achieved any real improvement. This paper has sought to show that the judges cannot be relied on to "sort out" Part III of the Housing Act 1985; indeed, the case law has largely reflected the lack of clarity in the legislation itself. Emphasis has been placed here, by way of example, on "intentional homelessness" decisions in the separate areas of family disputes and mobility of labour. We have seen that, as regards these two important areas, there have been some welcome developments (such as the restraints imposed on findings of "infectious intentionality.") However, several less desirable trends have emerged, which were not warranted by the legislation, such as the artificial and inflexible distinctions between violent and non-violent domestic disputes, and between domestic and non-domestic violence. There has also been much inconsistency between the various court decisions, for example on the key issue of whether the fact that homelessness was caused by a job-related move can be taken into account in considering intentionality.

Ultimately, the homelessness problem is only likely to be solved by a marked increase in resources, and it does not seem that the wide-ranging reforms in the private and public rented sectors implemented by the Housing Act 1988 will contribute much towards alleviation of the problem. However, Part III of the Housing Act 1985 could be improved in several respects. If the concept of intentional homelessness is to be retained, there needs to be clarification of the matters which may and may not be taken into account by the council in reaching a decision on the issue. More precise rules need to be laid down concerning the "suitability" of the accommodation offered to the homeless. The Ministerial Code of Guidance (which is so often in practice ignored) could be given "teeth" if councils were clearly subjected to the burden of justifying a refusal to follow the Code's provisions. As regards challenges to the homelessness decisions of councils, a more effective mechanism than judicial review needs to be introduced, perhaps by way of recourse to the county court or an independent local tribunal.

At the time of writing, however, it must be admitted that this "first aid" legislation is unlikely to receive in the near future the intensive care which it deserves. Indeed, it is rumoured that the Government intends to amend the 1985 Act with the purpose (*inter alia*) of defining homelessness more strictly, in terms of "rooflessness," and so as to provide that, even where the "full" duty is owed to an applicant, the council need only offer housing on a temporary basis.[2] This would be akin to using a chain-saw on a patient whose complaint requires much more careful and constructive treatment. Two years after the International Year of Shelter for the Homeless, we should surely be seeking to clarify and extend the rights of homeless people, rather than to restrict them.

Notes

[1] *Davis* v. *Johnson* [1979] A.C. 264, 340 (H.L.), *per* Lord Salmon.

[2] *Puhlhofer* v. *Hillingdon L.B.C.* [1986] A.C. 484, 517 (H.L.).

[3] *i.e.* the National Assistance Act 1948, s.21(1)(*b*); see further, *e.g.* D. Hoath, *Homelessness* (1983), pp. 2–6.

[4] Mr. G. Cunningham, *Hansard*, H.C.Deb., Vol. 934, cols. 1723–1724 (July 8, 1977).

[5] *Per* Sheriff Sinclair in *Roughead* v. *Falkirk D.C.* [1979] S.C.O.L.A.G. 188.

[6] For more general treatments, see, *e.g.*: A. Arden, *Homeless Persons—The Housing Act 1985 Part III* (3rd ed., 1988); P. Watchman and P. Robson, *Homelessness and the Law in Britain* (1989); D. Hoath, *op. cit.*; D. Hoath, *Public Housing Law* (1989), Chaps. 4–6; L. Thompson, *An Act of Compromise* (1988).

[7] Conference of the UN Commission on Human Settlements, Delhi, reported in *The Times*, April 7, 1988.

[8] *Hansard*, H.C.Deb., Vol. 109, col. 985 (February 4, 1987); H.C.Deb., Vol. 115, col. 721 (May 6, 1987); see also: *Housing the Homeless: The Local Authority Role*, Audit Commission, 1989, para. 22; A. Evans and S. Duncan, *Responding to homelessness: Local authority policy and practice*, D.O.E. (1988), para. 2.8 and Fig. 5.

[9] R. Hackney, President-elect of the Royal Institute of British Architects, reported in *The Times*, January 5, 1987.

[10] *Hansard*, H.C.Deb., Vol. 136, col. 1189 (July 7, 1988): Mr. Paul Boateng.

[11] See the Housing Act 1985, Pt. V; around 800,000 dwellings have been sold under the right to buy: D.O.E., *Tenants' Choice: The Government's Proposals for Legislation* (1987), para. 3.

[12] D.O.E., *Large Scale Voluntary Transfers of Local Authority Housing to Private Bodies* (1988), paras. 1, 4, 10–12; D.O.E., *Housing Action Trusts: A Consultation Document* (1987), paras. 25–26; by way of example, in October 1988 Gloucester City Council decided to sell its entire housing stock to a single private landlord: [1988] November *Legal Action* 32.

[13] D.O.E., *Large Scale Voluntary Transfers, op. cit.* para. 10; D.O.E., *Housing Action Trusts, op. cit.* para. 26.

[14] By Lord Scarman, in his capacity as British president of the International Year of Shelter for the Homeless, 1987 (see *The Times*, October 6, 1987).

[15] See, *e.g.*: P. Q. Watchman, [1988] J.S.W.L. 147–50; J. Conway (ed.), *Prescription for Poor Health: the Crisis for Homeless Families* (1988); *Hansard*, H.C. Written Ans. Vol. 125, col. 826 (January 21, 1988); B. Toman, "Room at the Inn," *Wall Street Journal*, May 1988 (reprinted in *The Sunday Times*, May 29, 1988); *The Sunday Times*, November 13, 1988; Chartered Institute of Public Finance and Accountancy, *Homelessness Statistics* (1988); Audit Commission, *op. cit.* para. 59.

[16] *Hansard*, H.C. Written Ans. Vol. 125, cols. 553–556 (January 18, 1988); H.C. Written Ans. Vol. 136, col. 606 (July 6, 1988).

[17] *Housing: The Government's Proposals*, Cm. 214.

[18] H.A. 1985, s.65(2)–(3).

[19] *Ibid.* s.65(2), as interpreted in *R. v. L.B. of Camden, ex p. Wait* (1986) 18 H.L.R. 434; however, the council is entitled to provide such accommodation in stages, the first stage of which may be the customary purgatorial stint in bed and breakfast or hostel accommodation: *R. v. East Hertfordshire D.C., ex p. Hunt* (1985) 18 H.L.R. 51; *R. v. Westminster C.C., ex p. Tansey*, March 6, 1987 (unreported).

[20] H.A. 1985, s.65(3); see, *e.g. R. v. Slough B.C., ex p. Ealing L.B.C.* [1981] 2 W.L.R. 399, 403–404 (C.A.).

[21] H.A. 1985, s.62.

[22] *R. v. Camden L.B.C., ex p. Gillan* (1988) 21 H.L.R. 114.

[23] *R. v. Woodspring D.C., ex p. Walters* (1984) 16 H.L.R. 73.

[24] See, *e.g.*: *R. v. Thurrock B.C., ex p. Williams* (1982) 1 H.L.R. 128; *R. v. Preseli D.C., ex p. Fisher* (1984) 17 H.L.R. 147; *R. v. West Dorset D.C., ex p. Phillips* (1984) 17 H.L.R. 336.

[25] P. W. Robson and P. Watchman, [1981] J.S.W.L. 1, 65.

[26] *Per* Lord Lowry in *Din v. Wandsworth L.B.C.* [1983] 1 A.C. 657, 930 (H.L.).

[27] H.A. 1985, s.58(2A)–(2B).

[28] [1986] A.C. 484 (H.L.).

[29] See further D. Hoath, [1988] J.S.W.L. 39, 44–45.

[30] For a general treatment of homelessness problems created by family disputes, see, *e.g.*: F. Logan, *Homelessness and Relationship Breakdown* (Brunel Socio-Legal Working Paper, 1987); R. Thornton, [1989] J.S.W.L. 67.

[31] For example, because he or she is a cohabitant or spouse with no entitlement to occupy by virtue of an interest (H.A. 1985, s.58(2)(*a*)); a spouse who has rights of occupation under the Matrimonial Homes Act 1983, s.1, and no legal or equitable proprietary interest, will rank as homeless despite the 1983 Act rights, because, having left the family home, he or she no longer "occupies" it "as a residence" (H.A. 1985, s.58(2)(*c*)). The securing of temporary "crisis"-type shelter in a refuge will not prevent the applicant being statutorily "homeless": *R. v. Ealing L.B.C., ex p. Sidhu* (1982) 80 L.G.R. 534.

[32] If the applicant is locked out of the family home or it is probable that occupation of it will lead to violence or threats of violence from the other partner, then the applicant is treated as "homeless" in any event, regardless of any entitlement to occupy which he or she may have: H.A. 1985, s.58(3)(*a*)–(*b*).

[33] For example, because of pregnancy, or because there are dependent children, or because of "vulnerability" (particularly if the applicant is at risk of violence from the other partner): H.A. 1985, s.59(1); *Housing (Homeless Persons) Act 1977 Code of Guidance (England & Wales)*, H.M.S.O. (2nd ed., 1983), para. 2.12c(iii); the fact that one partner, if made homeless, would be in

priority need and therefore entitled to housing under Pt. III of the Housing
Act, whereas the other partner would not be so entitled (typically, a man
who is not in priority need because he does not have the children with
him), may influence a court in deciding whether to grant an ouster order
under the family jurisdiction: *cf., e.g. Wooton* v. *Wooton* (1985) 15 Fam.
Law 31 (C.A.) with *Thurley* v. *Smith* (1985) 15 Fam. Law 31 (C.A.),
discussed further by D. Pearl in *Essays in Family Law 1985* (1986) (ed. M.
D. A. Freeman), at pp. 28–29.

[34] *i.e.* under H.A. 1985, s.65(3) (discussed above).

[35] See, *e.g. Delahaye* v. *Oswestry B.C., The Times*, July 29, 1980.

[36] See, *e.g. Lambert* v. *Ealing L.B.C.* [1982] 1 W.L.R. 550 (C.A.), where,
however, the chain of intentionality had not on the facts been broken.

[37] The broad discretion of social services authorities in these cases of
intentional homelessness was emphasised in *R.* v. *Tower Hamlets L.B.C.,
ex p. Monaf* (1987) 19 H.L.R. 577 (D.C.), (1988) 20 H.L.R. 529 (C.A.);
however, a council cannot completely remove the discretion of its social
services department by resolving that the department will *never* provide
assistance under s.1 of the Child Care Act for families which the housing
department has judged to be intentionally homeless: *Tilley* v. *Wandsworth
L.B.C.* [1981] 1 All E.R. 1162 (C.A.).

[38] See, *e.g. R.* v. *North Devon D.C., ex p. Lewis* [1981] 1 W.L.R. 328, 333.

[39] See, *e.g.: R.* v. *Eastleigh B.C., ex p. Beattie (No. 2)* (1984) 17 H.L.R. 168
(mortgage arrears); *R.* v. *West Dorset D.C., ex p. Phillips* (1984) 17
H.L.R. 336 (rent arrears); *R.* v. *Penwith D.C., ex p. Trevena* (1984) 17
H.L.R. 526 (surrender of tenancy).

[40] *R.* v. *East Northamptonshire D.C., ex p. Spruce* (1988) 20 H.L.R. 508 (a
case which also decides that *awareness* of arrears built up by one's partner
is not of itself to be equated with acquiescence).

[41] See, *e.g.* Central Housing Advisory Committee, *Council Housing Purposes,
Procedures and Priorities* (1969), para. 96.

[42] See, *e.g. Roof*, January 1980, p. 9 (authority decided that a young
pregnant woman was intentionally homeless on the grounds that she
"became pregnant and married without arranging for suitable accommodation in which to live.")

[43] See *Code of Guidance, op. cit.* para. 2.16 (" ... nor would it be appropriate
that a homeless pregnant woman be treated as intentionally homeless
simply because she is pregnant"); see also, *per* Woolf J. in *R.* v. *Eastleigh
B.C., ex p. Beattie (No. 1)* (1983) 10 H.L.R. 134, 141: "[I]t cannot be said
that a family fall within s.[60(1)] because they have chosen to have
additional children."

[44] (1985) 18 H.L.R. 79.

[45] For a more detailed discussion of the relationship between the homelessness legislation and the domestic violence legislation, see, *e.g.*: M. Bryan,
[1984] J.S.W.L. 195; R. Thornton, [1989] J.S.W.L. 67.

[46] Under, *e.g.* the Domestic Violence and Matrimonial Proceedings Act 1976,
the Domestic Proceedings and Magistrates' Courts Act 1978, or the
Matrimonial Homes Act 1983.

[47] See, *e.g.* A. Arden, *op. cit.* paras. 6.27–6.32, 6.108.

[48] See the wording of H.A. 1985, s.60(1), discussed above.

[49] *Op. cit.* para. 2.16 (italics supplied).

[50] *R.* v. *Eastleigh B.C., ex p. Evans* (1984) 17 H.L.R. 515, 524.

[51] But *cf.* Pearl, *op. cit.* p. 30.

⁵² See, *e.g.* a leader in *The Times*, January 7, 1987, discussing a briefing paper published by the London Strategic Policy Unit's Police Monitoring Group entitled *Police Responses to Domestic Violence*, and referring to "the limited protection afforded by the power of injunction to prevent a man from attacking a woman and entering her home," "cases in which the police might take preventative action when they do not," and "judges who appear to dismiss the seriousness of domestic attacks on women."

⁵³ April 21, 1983, unreported, but noted by A. Halpern, [1984] *Legal Action* 81.

⁵⁴ This extract is taken from the transcript.

⁵⁵ See also: *R. v. Kensington & Chelsea R.L.B.C., ex p. Hammell* (1988) 20 H.L.R. 666 (C.A.); *R. v. Broxbourne B.C., ex p. Willmoth, The Times*, April 18, 1989.

⁵⁶ See, *e.g.*: *R. v. Reigate & Banstead B.C., ex p. Henry*, December 16, 1982 (unreported) (husband a heavy drinker, but did not subject applicant to violence); *R. v. Wandsworth L.B.C., ex p. Nimako-Boateng* (1984) 11 H.L.R. 95 (husband had been staying away from home, sometimes for several days at a time, without giving applicant any explanation, but did not subject her to violence); *R. v. Eastleigh B.C., ex p. Evans*, above (general matrimonial difficulties, but no violence).

⁵⁷ *R. v. L.B. of Hillingdon, ex p. H* (1988) 20 H.L.R. 554; *R. v. Broxbourne B.C., ex p. Willmoth, The Times*, April 18, 1989.

⁵⁸ See, *e.g. R. v. L.B. of Croydon, ex p. Toth* (1987) 20 H.L.R. 576 (C.A.) (applicant threatened with violence by husband's creditors).

⁵⁹ See, *e.g. R. v. Peterborough C.C., ex p. McKernan*, July 17, 1987 (unreported), where the applicant had fled from sectarian intimidation and violence in Northern Ireland.

⁶⁰ See generally, J. Conway and E. Ramsay, *A Job To Move* (S.H.A.C., 1986).

⁶¹ For the purposes of the definition of intentional homelessness in H.A. 1985, s.60(1) (set out above).

⁶² *Op. cit.* para. 2.18.

⁶³ [1981] 3 All E.R. 901, 911 (H.L.).

⁶⁴ (1983) 9 H.L.R. 71.

⁶⁵ (1988) 21 H.L.R. 16.

⁶⁶ A similarly hard-line approach on intentionality has been taken regarding job-related homelessness where the applicant has been forced to leave settled accommodation for reasons connected with his contract of employment: see, *e.g.*: *R. v. North Devon D.C., ex p. Lewis* [1981] 1 W.L.R. 328; *Goddard* v. *Torridge D.C.* [1982] L.A.G.Bull. 9.

⁶⁷ [1980] Q.B. 460 (C.A.).

⁶⁸ *Per* Sir David Cairns at p. 484; italics supplied.

⁶⁹ September 24, 1985, unreported; this account of the case is taken from the transcript.

⁷⁰ See, as regards the "double moves" aspect of this case, Lord Lowry's comments in *Islam* v. *Hillingdon L.B.C., loc. cit.*: "... it can properly be decided that an applicant has become homeless intentionally whether the family moves as a unit or the husband, leaving suitable accommodation, comes first and then calls on the family to follow"; this passage was however qualified by his "mobility of labour" point, discussed above.

⁷¹ *R. v. L.B. of Hammersmith & Fulham, ex p. Duro-Rama* (1983) 9 H.L.R. 71, 77–78; *R. v. L.B. of Tower Hamlets, ex p. Monaf* (1987) 19 H.L.R. 577, 585–586.

⁷² See the earlier discussion in this paper.

[73] *R.* v. *Hillingdon L.B.C., ex p. Wilson* (1984) 12 H.L.R. 61.

[74] *R.* v. *L.B. of Tower Hamlets, ex p. Monaf* (1987) 19 H.L.R. 577, 586; the Court of Appeal's decision in this case referred to the applicant's "pattern of life": (1988) 20 H.L.R. 529, 541.

[75] See, *e.g.: R.* v. *Mole Valley D.C., ex p. Minnett* (1984) 12 H.L.R. 48; *R.* v. *Portsmouth C.C., ex p. Knight* [1984] L.G.R. 184; *R.* v. *Surrey Heath B.C., ex p. Li* (1984) 16 H.L.R. 79.

[76] See n. 63 above.

[77] (1987) 19 H.L.R. 577, 586 (D.C.); the "job mobility" point was not specifically discussed when the case reached the Court of Appeal ((1988) 20 H.L.R. 529).

[78] [1986] A.C. 484, 517 (H.L.).

[79] (1986) 18 H.L.R. 502.

[80] *Ibid.* at p. 506.

[81] *The Allocation of Council Housing*, para. 4.22.

[82] March 6, 1987 (unreported).

[83] The applicant subsequently obtained leave from the Court of Appeal to bring judicial review proceedings, but the action failed again, with particular emphasis being placed by the Divisional Court on the court's limited supervisory jurisdiction: *R.* v. *Westminster C.C., ex p. Tansey* (1988) 20 H.L.R. 520; the end of the *Tansey* saga came when the Court of Appeal subsequently refused to decide whether the court's jurisdiction in the context of the suitability of accommodation was supervisory or appellate, because on the facts the applicant was only challenging a general, "in principle" resolution of the council (before it had decided any individual case), so that the issue was merely an "abstract question of law": *R.* v. *City of Westminster, ex p. Tansey* (1988) 21 H.L.R. 57 (C.A.).

[84] Although such an applicant has the right to be permanently accommodated (see *R.* v. *L.B. of Camden, ex p. Wait* (1986) 18 H.L.R. 434), the *Tansey* case makes it clear that he does not have the right to be granted security of tenure in any particular unit of accommodation in which he may from time to time be placed.

[85] *Op. cit.* paras. 4.3–4.5, A2.11–A2.14.

[86] See, *e.g.: Cocks* v. *Thanet D.C.* [1983] A.C. 286 (H.L.); *R.* v. *Westminster C.C., ex p. Tansey* (1988) 20 H.L.R. 520.

[87] See further, *e.g.* G. Aldous and J. Alder, *Applications for Judicial Review: Law and Practice* (1985).

[88] See *Associated Provincial Picture Houses Ltd.* v. *Wednesbury Corp.* [1948] 1 K.B. 223, 227–231 (C.A.).

[89] See, *e.g.: Din* v. *Wandsworth L.B.C.* [1983] 1 A.C. 657, 684 (H.L.); *Puhlhofer* v. *Hillingdon L.B.C.* [1986] A.C. 484, 517 (H.L.); *R.* v. *Gravesham B.C., ex p. Winchester* (1986) 18 H.L.R. 207, 215; *R.* v. *Wycombe D.C., ex p. Mahsood* (1988) 20 H.L.R. 683, 686.

[90] See, *e.g. De Falco* v. *Crawley B.C.* [1980] Q.B. 460 (C.A.); in practice the judges tend to treat the Code with disdain where the relevant guidance does not fit in with their own conclusions as to the correct legal position (as in *De Falco*'s case), while regarding it as "of great assistance" where the guidance accords with those conclusions (as in *R.* v. *Waveney D.C., ex p. Bowers* [1983] Q.B. 238, 245 (C.A.): *per* Waller L.J.).

[91] *Loc. cit.*

[92] Research has however shown that the numbers of judicial review applications in homelessness cases, even prior to *Puhlhofer*, had been modest: M. Sunkin, (1987) 50 M.L.R. 432, 447–450.

93 Issued pursuant to the duty in H.A. 1985, s.64(4).
94 The judges have varied in their willingness to indulge in this exercise: *cf.*, *e.g.* the interventionist approach in *De Falco* v. *Crawley B.C.* [1980] Q.B. 460 (C.A.) and *R.* v. *Swansea C.C., ex p. John* (1982) 9 H.L.R. 58, with the stricter approach in, *e.g. R.* v. *Reigate & Banstead B.C., ex p. Paris* (1984) 17 H.L.R. 103 and *R.* v. *L.B. of Tower Hamlets, ex p. Monaf* (1988) 20 H.L.R. 529 (C.A.).
95 The average time taken to obtain judicial review is over a year: R. Poynter, [1988] February *Legal Action* 9, 11.
96 As in *R.* v. *Welwyn & Hatfield D.C., ex p. Holmes*, February 1, 1988 (unreported).
97 See, *e.g.* A. McAllister, [1987] May *Legal Action* 11.
98 M. Shrimpton, [1987] October *Legal Action* 24.
99 This happened, for example, following the Court of Appeal's decision in *R.* v. *Tower Hamlets L.B.C., ex p. Monaf*, above: see *London Evening Standard*, May 10, 1988.
1 See, *e.g.*: *Annual Report of the Council on Tribunals for 1984–85*, H.C.P. 54, para. 2.15; Law Centres Federation, *The Courts and the Housing Crisis* (1985), p. 10; although no specific recommendations relating to homelessness cases were included in the 1988 *Report of the Review Body on Civil Justice* (Cm. 394), it appears that the D.O.E. is considering rights of appeal during the course of its own review of the operation of Part III of the Housing Act 1985.
2 See, *e.g.*: *Roof*, November 1988, at p. 14; J. Stearn, [1989] January *Legal Action* 10; and note in [1989] July *Legal Action* 6.

The Politics of Child Care*

M. D. A. FREEMAN

Child care has become an intensely political issue. I do not
mean by this that the issues of child care divide the political
parties. Would that they did! On the whole the area is one of
party political consensus. But political debate abounds, as the
Cleveland affair,[1] a seething volcano which erupted again in
February of 1989,[2] illustrates. The positions of those who
support Drs. Higgs and Wyatt and those who believe that
injustice was wreaked in Cleveland (the battle-lines are often
drawn on gender lines)[3] are as intractable as the warring nations
bogged down in the trenches in World War One. When what
happened in Cleveland is contrasted with the events in Brent
over Jasmine Beckford[4] or Greenwich over Kimberley Carlile[5]
or Southwark over Tyra Henry[6] (to name only three recent
instances), the most striking of political conflicts emerges. Social
workers are castigated when they do not intervene: they are
pilloried when they do. To intervene or not is but one of the
many conflicts inherent in child care decision-making.

Autonomy Versus Intervention

The conflict here mirrors one in wider political debate
between those who believe in autonomy (sometimes called
"market forces") and those who favour intervention or
regulation. In child care, leading advocates of non-intervention
are Goldstein, Freud and Solnit. They argue that:

"the law does not have the capacity to supervise the fragile, complex
inter-personal bonds between child and parent. As *parens patriae* the
state is too crude an instrument to become an adequate substitute for
flesh and blood parents. The legal system has neither the resources
nor the sensitivity to respond to a growing child's ever-changing

103

needs and demands. It does not have the capacity to deal on an individual basis with the consequences of its decisions, or to act with the deliberate speed that is required by a child's sense of time."[7]

Whether one accepts this philosophy or not (and I elsewhere have been critical of its implications),[8] it has to be accepted that parental autonomy is important, so that the case for leaving state intrusion into the family to cases of clear abuse, at least where the values of liberal democracy prevail,[9] is convincing. But what is "clear abuse?" How much autonomy should we give parents? There are clear dangers in treating the family as a private area outside the law.[10]

Hitting Children

The problem is well illustrated by the debate which I appear to have engineered over the moral propriety of hitting children.[11] To me it is self-evident that the use of hostile force against a child amounts to abuse of that child. We know that much child abuse is corporal punishment gone wrong. Parents, it is true, do not see physical punishment as (to quote Elizabeth Elmer) "even remotely related to abuse" for they are "performing their duty," acting within "the cultural heritage" of the country.[12] But our concern to control or even eliminate child abuse (albeit a recent concern) has not led to any serious reconsideration of the legitimacy of physical chastisement. An amendment to the Children Bill to undermine the practice (by removing the defence in s.1(7) of the 1933 Children and Young Persons Act to a charge of wilful assault) was lost in the House of Lords[13] (as was one to remove the sanction from foster parents)[14] but it is bound to return—and ultimately succeed. Critics of the anti-corporal punishment lobby are said to want to wield the "smack of statism,"[15] as Barbara Amiel put it in *The Times*: in other words to favour intervention, the "nanny state" or, even worse in today's climate of opinion, social workers. But to argue against corporal punishment is not necessarily to argue for more (or much more) intervention into families than now. The importance of legislation to "outlaw" spanking is of greater symbolic than instrumental importance. It would be an important declaration of public policy.

The law already outlaws physical punishment, that is provides for intervention, where the punishment is not deemed "moderate and reasonable,"[16] deemed, that is, by a judge retrospectively. It is not easy to tell a parent in advance what is acceptable and what is not. But standards shift: what was acceptable a generation ago would not be so today. And they differ from community to community. Yet social workers have to decide at present whether it constitutes "ill-treatment" and judges have to decide whether they were right. Recall the criminal case of *Derrivière*,[17] where a West Indian father was told by an English appeal court that he had to conform to the standard of behaviour acceptable in England, or the care case involving "Vietnam boat-people" in which an Appeal Court judge pontificated that "beating with sticks" was common in Chinese village society though not excusable here.[18]

Cultural Pluralism

To what extent are differing practices of child care to be tolerated? The law cannot impose a uniform standard for a multi-cultural society. It cannot even require optimum rearing, for, if it did, few of us would escape. It can outlaw particular practices: for example, child marriage[19] or female circumcision[20] (though in the latter case it probably drives it underground). A successful prosecution may have a deterrent effect. Take the issue of "scarification."[21] In *R. v. Adesanya*[22] a Nigerian mother from the Yoruba tribe, living in North London, made small incisions with a razor blade on the face of her two sons. She was following a Nigerian custom. Nevertheless, she stood trial at the Old Bailey charged with assault occasioning bodily harm and was convicted. In granting her an absolute discharge the judge proffered this general warning:

> "You and others who come to this country must realise that our laws must be obeyed... It cannot be stressed too strongly that any further offences of this kind in pursuance of tribal traditions... can only result in prosecution. Because this is a test case... I am prepared to deal with you with the utmost leniency. But let no one assume that they will be treated with mercy. Others have now been warned."[23]

It is worth pursuing this example at length because, under the Children Bill in assessing the standard of care the court (and therefore by implication the social worker) must compare what would be "reasonable to expect the parent of a similar child" to provide.[24] What is a "similar child" is set to become a long-running saga. It may be predicted that the 1991 or 1992 *Family Law Reports* will be peppered with *Re Bs, Re Cs* and *Re Ss*, full of judicial exegesis. The phrase is a legal minefield. Is a similar child a child of the same age and gender, or just age or just gender? Is social class relevant? We have long tolerated neglect by upper-class parents who regularised and institutionalised the practice of using public schools and nannies. Is income relevant? Can we tolerate poorer care by low-income families? Is a similar child one whose mother is also on income support? Is a similar child one whose neglect is partly attributable to the clawing back of a social fund loan by deductions from income support, thus placing the family below the poverty line? Is sexual orientation of the parents relevant? Is a similar child one with the same intelligence? Are different standards of care countenanced for children who are E.S.N., have Down's syndrome, are physically handicapped or blind or deaf? And what of race, religion, nationality, national origins, ethnicity? Are the children of Jehovah's Witnesses or Plymouth Brethren or Muslim Fundamentalists or Jewish Hassidim or Scientologists similar to children whose parents are WASPs? And are the Chinese children of Vietnam refugees, the sons of Yoruba mothers, children of Afro-Caribbean fathers accustomed to not "sparing the rod" to be accorded the same treatment, the same standards, as children of the indigenous population?

Grasping Religion

The law of England has never grasped the race nettle very securely. It has attempted to tackle the question of religion. For example, local authorities, who have the care of children do not acquire the power to change their religion.[25] Courts have been reluctant to allow the child's religion to be changed following custody or adoption proceedings.[26] In such proceedings they adopt the principle, somewhat rhetorically, of non-discrimination as between different religions,[27] though where they observe that the social practices which form part of the faith are detrimental to the child's welfare they may decide against a parent who professes that religion. Latey J.'s diatribe against Scientology in *Re B. and G.* is a remarkable example.[28] Exclusive Brethren (*Hewison* v. *Hewison*[29]), Jehovah's Witnesses, (*Jane* v. *Jane*)[30] and even Rastafarians (*Re J.T.*)[31] have all also suffered "discrimination" (as have, for that matter, lesbians).[32] In placing a child for adoption it is no longer possible to insist on the religion of the adopters but it is worth remembering that the provision in the Children Act of 1975 which removed this option was the most contested of provisions in the whole Act.[33]

Tackling Race

The issue of race has only become visible more recently. But the law has not yet really adapted to its presence. We know that there are a disproportionately high number of black children in care; that they spend longer in care; that they are more likely than white children to live in residential homes and, if fostered, might well be placed with white families.[34] More attention has focussed on trans-racial adoption which is, in general, deprecated.[35] But, on race, the law has set no standards. Arguably, section 18 of the Child Care Act 1980 could be interpreted to imply that matters of race should be considered when "first consideration" is given to a child's welfare and due consideration to the wishes and feelings of the child (the importance of which was enhanced by the Lords' decision in *Gillick*).[36] It may be argued also, that a local authority which does not take s.18 properly into account is acting unlawfully, so as to open itself to judicial review.[37] But does it further a black child's welfare to be removed from white foster parents because it is thought to be in black children's interests to be brought up in a black environment? A local authority has to treat cases on their merits, as individual cases rather than routinised examples. It may not fetter its discretion[38]: thus any policy adopted in blanket fashion which outlawed trans-racial placements or adoptions would open itself to challenge in the courts through the medium of judicial review. The Short committee had these issues drawn to its attention but its response was far from confident. The problems "specific to ethnic minority children" had, they said, to be "articulated but not exaggerated. That is a major challenge facing those charged with providing care for children."[39] They saw no need to recommend any changes in the law to deal with the problem. Nevertheless, the Children Bill does recognise the problem. Clause 18(5)(c) requires a local authority in making a decision about a child in care (or about to go into care) "to give due consideration ... to the child's religious persuasion, racial origin and cultural background." This is an important step, albeit a small one. The duty is only to give "due" consideration and the importance to be attached to "race" (and equally important "culture") is in no sense weighted. Is it not time for legislation to go further? Legislation in the United States is far more positive. The Federal Indian Child Welfare Act of 1978[40] (directed towards native Indians) establishes a hierarchy of placements: a non-Indian one may only be made where no other placement is available. In addition, no Indian child may be removed from his family without evidence from an expert in Indian family affairs that this is the best course of action. The new provision in the Children Bill is a step in this direction but a small one: much will be left to the discretion of individual social work departments.

The Legalistic Model of Social Work

But this presupposes that in these areas of policy and conflict the law ought to provide firm constraints for social work practice. Should it? There is a school of thought that believes it should. Indeed, which goes further than this and defines social work activity almost as a legal practice. The Blom-Cooper report on Jasmine Beckford (*A Child In Trust*) contains a clear statement of this position. It states:

> "We are strongly of the view that social work can in fact be defined *only* in terms of the functions required of it by their employment agency operating within a statutory framework."[41]

And it continues:

> "We are conscious that social workers do not always take readily, or kindly, to legal intervention in the practice of social work. But . . . the law provides the basic framework in which social workers must operate."[42]

The Report thus argues that social work as a practice and an institution can only be defined in terms of its statutory remit. As Parton explains:

> "Not only is social work secondary to the law and can only be understood within its legal framework, in effect social work activity is the functioning of one area of the law in practice."[43]

The Report rests on a particular and very narrow conception of social work—the social worker as a local government function-ary who operates in and through the framework of legislation which lays down duties and confers powers. It is very much a lawyers' view of social work which emphasises the paramountcy of lawyers and legal discourse and states baldly: "the truth is that the law is part and parcel of the functions of every department."[44]

This view is quite startling and would hardly bear consideration were it not for the influence that it has had. This was graphically portrayed in Cleveland, as the Butler-Sloss report acknowledges.[45] The ideology of legalism has begun to permeate deep into both social work techniques (note the use of contracts with clients)[46] and into the thinking behind the Children Bill. *Working Together*,[47] the recently-issued DHSS guidelines on inter-agency co-operation and responsibilities for child abuse, also emphasises the pre-eminence of the law in defining the social work role, as well as that of other agencies. So does CCETSW (The Central Council for the Employment and Training of Social Workers) in its recent report on social work training and law.[48] It would not be going too far to describe the ideology of legalism as the new consensus. But what does this amount to? A few comments on the limitations of the Blom-Cooper thinking (the ideology of legalism) are called for.

First, as Dingwall, Eekelaar and Murray have commented (though not specifically on the Beckford report) "social workers are not law-enforcement officers, permanently and selectively attuned to discovering breaches of statute. They [doctors and health visitors are included] are better characterised as problem-solving agents for whom the law exists as one possible resource for dealing with social troubles."[49]

Secondly, and despite CCETSW reports[50] urging greater legal training for social workers, social workers are not lawyers. Nor are they policemen. Their skills lie elsewhere, in guidance, counselling, therapy. They must acquire rudimentary knowledge of legal resources and limitations. It is a legitimate criticism of them that they thought (as in Cleveland) that a place of safety order entitled them to subject a child to a medical examination, or to refuse parents access to children.[51] They can be justly condemned when (as in the Carlile case) it is clear that they were unaware of powers that could be used to gain entry to a child at risk.[52] But how many lawyers know this? Until recently there were hardly any child care law specialists and even now they are thin on the ground. Social workers are invariably better lawyers than lawyers are social workers.[53] Each should acquire his own expertise, though each, of course, should understand the other's language, practices and values. Communication failures are caused as much by ignorance of respective roles and concepts as by ideological conflicts rooted in different "images of man."[54]

Thirdly, there is almost a naive simplicity about the Blom-Cooper assumption that there is some kind of close fit between the law and the appropriate course of action. It is clearly an assumption that only a lawyer working within the framework of legalism,[55] could make. It is one that may work in some areas of law, though I doubt it, but even ignoring the fact that the solution may not lie in using legal resources at all (point 2, above), the assumption that there is a discrete entity, neatly packaged, waiting to be taken down and objectively applied without using judgment or discretion is clearly fanciful. Child care law is a "patchwork quilt"[56] the pieces of which rarely fit. It is full of ambiguity and uncertainty.

Fourthly, it is worth considering what the consequences of such an approach are for the families targeted by it. The events in Cleveland offer insight into this legalism at work. The emphasis on preventive work of a pre-emptive nature, in particular the rampant use of the place of safety order usually for the maximum time-span of 28 days, rather than the utilisation of more primary prevention policies, using social work skills and invoking greater expenditure, typifies this approach. Hand-in-hand with this approach comes a belief that families can be divided into "dangerous families"[57] and low-risk families. The latter can be protected by casework: the former can only be tackled by statutory intervention, using the whole panoply of legal powers culminating in adoption (the transfer of the child into another "cereal packet" norm family). Since the emphasis is on the high-risk family, where legal action can be invoked, the amount of support that those assessed as low-risk can expect is minimal. The implications of a shift to the legalistic model are thus profound. They are not, however, unique to the child care field (there is scepticism about welfare programmes and professionals generally).[58] On a more general level the reassertion of legalism may be seen as part of the rhetoric of a government committed to "law and order" and its concomitant values.

That social workers should assume the mantle of law fits the ideology of our times. The tentacles of social control dig deeper: even the prison is now to be created outside the prison walls.[59] That there are some who would like social work to be more like work of the probation service or even more like police work should not, therefore, cause real surprise.

Law as a Framework

There is, however, an alternative way of looking at the relationship between social work and law. The law may be seen as a framework within which good social work skills and practices may develop. Such a perspective acknowledges both the power of social workers and the need to control this, as well as the professionalism of its practitioners. Professions are repositories of skills and of values. Professionals, unlike clerks, can exercise discretion.[60] I agree with Olive Stevenson that the "image of the social worker as 'agent of the law' is...partial and dangerous." For, as she notes:

"it encourages a view of professional competence which rests solely or mainly on an ability to interpret and execute legal requirements, whereas, in fact, such competence rests on far wider abilities in which that elusive but crucial element of professional judgment is central."[61]

Towards Constraint

A view of social work which sees the law as a framework is, I believe, a better way of looking at the tasks that social workers engaged in child care practice must fulfil. The Children Bill has emerged out of a long process. A realisation that the law was complex, complicated, incomplete, unjust and in urgent need of rationalisation. A concern, vocalised in the media over the many notorious incidents of abused children from Maria Colwell to Tyra Henry and on to Cleveland, that social workers and other professionals were not protecting children from abuse, physical, emotional or sexual. A belief, substantiated by the Family Rights Group, by the revelations about Cleveland, by evidence and anecdote, that parents' rights were being trampled upon. The reports of inquiries, in particular the two chaired by Louis Blom-Cooper, played their part. So, of course, did the Butler-Sloss report into child sexual abuse in Cleveland. The Law Commission's role cannot be underestimated either.[62] The Government's intentions have filtered through a *Review*[63] and a *White Paper*.[64]

The *Beckford* report is sandwiched between the two and the *White Paper* clearly bears the imprint of having been influenced by the Blom-Cooper thinking of *A Child in Trust*. A clear example is parents' abilities to challenge emergency protection orders.[65] Unlike the *Review* it is clearly about a legal framework rather than about social work with families and child protection. The Children Bill is, I believe, a continuation of this thinking. The Government, we know, has a low respect for social workers. David Mellor's angry outburst last autumn should not be seen as an aberration.[66] The Government is, however, caught in a cleft stick: it has to be seen to be doing something to tackle child abuse; it has, at the same time, to ensure that social workers whom it does not trust are so strait-jacketed that no abuse of power by them can occur. Social workers are thus seen by the Government (indeed the general public) as incompetents who do too little too late (as in *Beckford* or *Carlile*) or too much too soon (as in *Cleveland*).[67]

Let us acknowledge that abuses have occurred, that there are thoroughly bad social work practices and thoroughly bad social workers. Children who should have been protected have fallen through the safety net. Innocent parents have suffered, as have their children. There are errors of judgment in all professions. At the same time that Martin Ruddock was being pilloried for failing to protect Kimberley Carlile, a report was published to the effect that at least 1,000 patients a year die as a result of operating theatre errors by surgeons and anaesthetists.[68] How many of these doctors have lost their jobs, as Martin Ruddock did?

What, therefore, is the role of the law? What can the legal system do to encourage better decision-making by social workers? To what extent can and should it supervise or control? It can confer powers on social workers: it can also withdraw them. The end of the assumption of parental rights provision, the purely administrative action by which parental rights have been removed from parents without court intervention must therefore be welcomed. A legacy of the Poor Law, it remained a dangerous anachronism. To vest such powers in social workers, with only the veneer of local government control, was an affront to civil liberties whose passing will not be mourned.

The Bill also takes much of the sting of another oft-criticised and much-hated power away from social workers, that to regulate access to children by parents. It was this power which the Lords in *A.* v. *Liverpool City Council*[69] decided lay within the discretion of the local authority, which led to appeals to Europe, to HASSASSA (The Health and Social Services and Social Security Adjudications Act) in 1983 and the Code of Access, and which has continued to be challenged.[70] The Bill provides for a presumption of reasonable contact.[71] The decision to stop access will be transferred from local authorities to the courts. The court will be able to make an order authorising the local authority to refuse to allow the parent contact, if it is necessary to do so to safeguard the child's welfare. An authority's powers to refuse contact are most restricted: it will only able to do so in matters of urgency, for a maximum period of seven days and then only if satisfied that it is necessary to do so to safeguard the child's welfare. All will welcome the encapsulation in statute of a presumption of reasonable contact. But we must ask what the new controls amount to?

On the face of it the impression is conveyed that the courts will be in control. But this is an illusion for a number of reasons. First, only a few access decisions will be brought to them. Secondly, where they are, the court will be confronted with the authority's interpretation of "welfare." It will be possible for a court to gainsay this (courts have in the past disagreed with social work reports in custody and adoption cases, as well as on matters of access), but not easy. "Welfare" is not a justiciable issue.[72] There are different views as to what is in a particular child's best interests. It is difficult to believe that a court, whether a bench of justices or a judge, is really in a better position to determine whether a particular course of action furthers welfare or not. Most courts think this too. Different courts may adopt different policies (as happened in the late 1970s and early 1980s over the question of the propriety of step-parent adoptions)[73] and this may affect social work decision-making. They will have the capacity to stop outrageous decisions (those that no reasonable local authority would make),[74] but even in these cases firmer resolution will be required if applications are not, as has happened with place of safety applications in the past, merely to be rubber-stamped. The "place of safety" order was described in the Butler-Sloss report as a "discretionary judicial act,"[75] though there is little evidence that the justices of Cleveland saw their role in this way.

The place of safety order is to be abolished and replaced by the emergency protection order. It is generally agreed that this is an improvement. It will be limited in time to a maximum shorter period; there will be a presumption of reasonable contact; the applicant (not limited to local authority social services departments, but likely to be them in the majority of cases) will have its powers and duties relatively clearly defined. If a medical examination is thought necessary, the power to consent will be vested in the applicant who, the Bill makes clear, will have "parental responsibility." But, should any doubt remain, the court, when making an emergency protection order, may give whatever directions it considers appropriate regarding "medical or psychiatric examination of the child." This suggests that local authorities are being encouraged to seek court approval for medical examinations, and it may become the norm for a local authority to apply for such directions at the same time as seeking the emergency protection order. But the question remains as to what sort of controls are being created? Will the granting of an emergency protection order be any more a "discretionary judicial act" than its predecessor was? Applications will still usually be *ex parte* (a practice encouraged in the Carlile report).[76] It would be very surprising if many were refused. Much will depend on the willingness of magistrates to test evidence but too many will continue to grant orders on the nod, much as they granted place of safety orders and continue to grant police search warrants. It is said that no magistrate has ever refused a place of safety order or search warrant twice!

The law then can confer power. It can also take it away. One consequence of the widening of the scope of the care grounds, though hardly a necessary one, is the new restriction on recourse to wardship. A local authority which cannot acquire parental responsibility using a statutory ground will not be able to use wardship as a safety valve. With the care ground expanded to cover, for example, prognosis of harm where none has yet occurred,[77] there will, it is true, be less justification for an additional and back-up source of power. It will now be easier to accomplish the removal of a new-born baby at birth legitimately through care proceedings.[78] It will also be easier to remove the children of drug-addicted parents.[79] In other words, the new ground covers a number of recently uncovered problematic areas. It is right that the grounds for removal of a child should be stated clearly (though this goal has not been accomplished in the current Bill, as I indicated previously). There are dangers in giving social workers the type of blanket authority encompassed within a test based on "welfare," particularly when it is so difficult for a court to differ from a social worker's interpretation of this. But, nevertheless, there is concern, justifiable I believe, that clause 71 (which limits recourse to wardship) could have dangerous implications.[80]

It is somewhat ironic that persons other than social workers will be able to seek to protect children through wardship[81] when this course of action is closed to the main agency entrusted by society with the protection of children. An educational psychologist was thus able (and still would be able under the proposed law) to protect a mentally handicapped girl from being unnecessarily sterilised (I refer to the famous "Sotos Syndrome" case of the mid-1970s),[82] but in similar circumstances a social worker would be compelled to have recourse to care proceedings. It is dubious whether care is appropriate for such a case and it is also quite wrong that such a problem should not be taken immediately to a High Court judge. It is possible that under the Children Bill, it is to this forum that such a matter would be transferred, but, like with so much else, we cannot be certain until we see the detailed regulations. The removal of the wardship option from social workers is an attack on their professional judgment, a restriction on the use of social work skills, an undermining of the discretion which hitherto has been vested in them. To see it as a logical corollary of the restriction on parents, relatives and others using wardship to challenge local authority decision-making is to put a premium on symmetry. With the Butler-Sloss report[83] I deprecate the House of Lords decisions in *A.* v. *Liverpool City Council* and *W.* v. *Hertfordshire C.C.*[84] The House of Lords rulings were unwise and arguably legally wrong.[85] But there was an acknowledgment that the courts can deal with social work decisions rather better using judicial review, where their concern is with proprieties, with illegality and excess of power,[86] than they can when wardship is invoked and the court is in effect being asked to "second-guess" what is best for the child in the jurisdiction in which welfare is the "golden thread."[87]

In reformulating the care ground, the law then limits the exercise of social work discretion. It also purports to define parents' rights. It does neither of these things especially well. The language used remains vague and value-laden. Laying down substantive standards is one way the law can confront social work. It sets a threshold for intervention.

Procedural Standards

Another way in which the law can operate on social work decision-making is to impose procedural standards. Lawyers refer to the "principles of natural justice" or the duty to "act fairly" to embrace requirements that ensure that each side is able to put its case before an independent decision-maker who is able to test the evidence submitted. It is in this role that courts are particularly proficient. The English trial process is adversarial. It assumes a contest between two parties and it assumes that they are represented.[88] Disputes over children have long disturbed these assumptions. It is clear (though only comparatively recently[89] has it been clear to our policy-makers) that in cases involving children, they have interests which may conflict with those of their parents. The multi-party proceeding fits uneasily into our paradigm of the trial. The result has been that at various times (including today) the interests of parents and/or children have not been adequately taken care of by the system. Only in August 1988 were parents accorded party status and a right of appeal in care proceedings.[90] They could not even obtain legal aid in such proceedings until 1983.[91] The separate representation of children in care proceedings only emerged with the Children Act of 1975[92] after the impact of the Maria Colwell tragedy had been appreciated. Children today are often not parties in cases which intimately concern them, such as custody and access and in wardship proceedings where the child is commonly represented by the Official Solicitor. What is represented is what the Official Solicitor considers to promote the child's welfare and not the child's views as to the appropriate course of action. The episode over the proposed Office of Child Protection is instructive. This seems to have been formulated as an afterthought during the deliberations over the Cleveland inquiry report. It is not clear what its role was to be, but in part it would have scrutinised local authority applications for a care order. Although it is not clear how it would have been staffed, it emerges as yet another attempt to inject legalism into the childcare decision-making process.[93] At least, that is how the very last paragraph of the report, which floats the proposal, reads. Nevertheless, a proposal to introduce the Office was put by the Lord Chancellor's Office[94] in a hastily-prepared so-called Consultation Paper which went out in late July 1988. It did not meet with approval and, in a rare instance of humility, the Government conceded it was wrong.

That the proposal could have emerged at all remains interesting. After well over a decade in which children in care proceedings were not just separately represented by a social worker independent of the authority which had brought the case (a guardian *ad litem*) but also by a solicitor, at least where personnel were available,[95] the proposal that children should only have a guardian *ad litem*, legal services being provided by a bureaucratic monolith (the OCP), was startling. The theory was that this institution would scrutinise the local authority's case, rather like the Crown Prosecution Service does police evidence (at least that is the theory). The influence of Blom-Cooper ideology on the proposal was not far below the surface. Had it been implemented it would have left the child in care proceedings either unrepresented by a lawyer or represented by some lawyer from the Office of Child Protection which had already decided that there was substance in the local authority's case. It was not clear which of these models was envisaged, but neither is satisfactory. The first turned the clock back: the second involves forfeiture of independence.

The proposal was dropped but the Children Bill on this matter is far from satisfactory. It does not provide for automatic party status for either parents or children. Whether or not they get it will depend on the court. The courts themselves will be guided by the rules of court, which needless to say, have yet to be made. We are assured that these will provide for representation, in the case of children by a solicitor, as well as by a guardian *ad litem*. It is, however, troublesome that this is not in the Bill. There is very much less control over Rules of Court than there is over legislation, and in these days of "elected dictatorship"[96] there is precious little control over that.

It should concern us that we continue to be so lax about imposing true due process in the area of child care decision-making. It is also somewhat paradoxical that a system moving towards constraint of social workers in the substantive area should fail to take seriously the imposition of a framework for action in the procedural context. A decision which is substantively appropriate may cause justifiable grievance where justice has not been seen to be done. Sometimes it may be wondered whether those who make and administer our laws realise that there is "life after court," that social workers have to work with parents who have lost their children in situations perceived by them to constitute injustice. One of the problems, too little considered, is that the law bites, if it bites at all, only comparatively late in the decision-making process. Only very recently have attempts been made to subject decision-making at case conferences[97] and the placing of a child's name on a child protection register[98] to legal surveillance.

Limits of Court Action

There are limits to what courts can do. There are also dangers in exaggerating the competence of courts. The question must therefore be raised as to what alternatives exist for setting standards and controlling social work decision-making. To what other mechanisms can one turn? Lawyers, indeed policy-makers, have a habit of assuming that, if something cannot be achieved by legal means, it cannot be accomplished at all.

Bureaucratic controls, such as the statutory review, can prevent standards falling below that deemed absolutely essential, but are unlikely to achieve more. June Thoburn, in a thoughtful article,[99] lists some 30 mechanisms which exist at national level or locally and which may be considered as ways of ensuring efficient and effective child care and child protection services. These include many mechanisms already considered or referred to in this article as well as others I have argued for elsewhere, in particular the notion of a Children's Ombudsman.[1] Whatever the formal system of accountability, it is clear that it is the social worker who has the major influence on the decision (or non-decision).

Vernon and Fruin's study bears this out.[2] They examined the impact of some 196 reviews on the care careers of 185 children in 11 local authorities and found that they were of marginal significance when compared with either case conferences or the attitudes and actions of individual social workers. Even if effective, the impact on "little" but crucial decisions is minimal, decisions such as paying parents' fares or deciding what response to make if parents cancel a visit or whether to discuss with a grandmother whether she could care for the child. Such decisions, research by Sinclair[3] and by McDonnell and Aldgate[4] indicates, continue to be inadequately monitored. It is therefore Thoburn's view that quality in child care depends on raising and maintaining professional standards so that social work skills are relied upon. She states: "Recent research findings lead this writer to the conclusion that there will be fewer children in unplanned care if the "little" decisions and most of the "bigger" decisions are not divorced and can be *safely* left in the hands of case accountable social workers and the parents and children themselves."[5] She adds that the inadequacy of day-to-day practice documented in studies and inquiries suggests that few basic grade social workers possess the necessary skill and knowledge.

We come, therefore, to a truism that better social work practice requires *less* resources to be given to supervision, surveillance or control. Is it that the shift to what I called the Blom-Cooper ideology (the constraint of social work by the stranglehold of law) is the result of decisions that are manifestly bad? If, as I have indicated, the law can only have a limited effect on decisions, we must be looking to ways to improve decision-making. It would therefore be ironic (if it were not a decision of this Government) that at the very time the Blom-Cooper ideology seeps into legislation, a decision is also taken not to increase the length of training that social workers receive.[6] Lawyers have recognised that those who work in the child care area should be specialists.[7] Surely the time has come to accept not just the need for specialism within social work (which has gradually returned), but also the concept, which could be readily adopted from the mental health area, of the Approved Social Worker. Only social workers with a specialist qualification should be able to work with children. This requires an injection of resources far beyond the Government's wildest fears. Without it new legislation like the Children Bill will have at best limited achievement. And that, at the end of the day, is why child care is a political issue.

Notes

* This article emanates from seminars and lectures in London in December 1988 and January 1989. I am grateful to those who commented, particularly those at a Criminal Justice Associates meeting held at Kings College, Chelsea.

[1] Report of the Inquiry into Child Abuse in Cleveland 1987 (the Butler-Sloss report), London, HMSO, 1988, Cm. 412.

[2] With a letter from 11 paediatricians claiming 90 per cent. of the children were abused (see *The Guardian*, February 18, 1989).

[3] *cf.* S. Bell, *When Salem Came To the Boro*, London, Pan, 1988 with B. Campbell, *Unofficial Secrets*, London, Virago, 1988 or the special number (No. 28) of *Feminist Review*. See also L. Dominelli (1989) 19 Br.J. of Soc.Work 291.

[4] L.B. of Brent, *A Child In Trust* (the Blom-Cooper Report), London, L.B. of Brent, 1985.

[5] L.B. of Lambeth, *Whose Child?*, London, L.B. of Lambeth, 1987.

[6] L.B. of Greenwich, *A Child In Mind* (the second Blom-Cooper Report), London, L.B. of Greenwich, 1987.

[7] *Before The Best Interests of the Child*, New York, Free Press, 1979, pp. 11–12.

[8] *The Rights and Wrongs of Children*, London, Pinter, 1983 Chap. 7 and (1980) J.S.W.L. 70.

[9] See U. Bronfenbrenner, *Two Worlds of Childhood: U.S. and U.S.S.R.* New York, Simon and Schuster, 1972. See also J. Harwin (1989) 3 Int.J. of Law and Family 58.

[10] See J. Pahl, *Private Violence and Public Policy*, Tavistock, 1985.

[11] "Time to Stop Hitting Our Children," *Childright* (Oct. 1988), No. 51, pp. 5–8. See also P. Newell, *Children Are People Too*, London, Bedford Square Press, 1989.

[12] *Children in Jeopardy*, Pittsburgh, Univ. of Pittsburgh Press, 1967, p. 65.

[13] *Hansard*, H.L., January 24, 1989, cols. 542–548.

[14] *Hansard*, H.L., February 7, 1989, cols. 1443–1453.

[15] *The Times*, October 21, 1988.

[16] See *per* Chief Justice Cockburn in *R.* v. *Hopley* (1860) 2 F. & F. 202. See also *Ryan* v. *Fildes* [1938] 3 All E.R. 517.

[17] (1969) 53 Cr.App.Rep. 637.
[18] [1987] 2 F.L.R. 12.
[19] But *cf. Mohamed* v. *Knott* [1969] 1 Q.B. 1.
[20] Prohibition of Female Circumcision Act 1985.
[21] See S. Poulter, *English Law and Ethnic Minority Customs*, Butterworths, 1986, pp. 148–152.
[22] Discussed by Poulter (1975) 24 I.C.L.Q. 136.
[23] Judge Alan King-Hamilton, quoted in Poulter, *op. cit.*, note 21, p. 151.
[24] Children Bill 1989, cl. 26.
[25] Child Care Act 1980, s.10(3). See also A. Bainham, *Children, Parents and the State*, London, Sweet and Maxwell, 1988, pp. 177–182.
[26] *Stourton* v. *Stourton* (1857) 8 De G.M. and G. 760; *Re M.* [1967] 1 W.L.R. 1479.
[27] *Re Carroll* [1931] 1 K.B. 317, 336 *per* Scrutton L.J.
[28] *Re B. and G.* [1985] F.L.R. 493.
[29] (1977) 7 Fam.Law 207.
[30] [1983] 4 F.L.R. 712.
[31] [1986] 2 F.L.R. 107.
[32] *S.* v. *S.* (1978) 1 F.L.R. 143. See also Rights of Women Lesbian Custody Group, *Lesbian Mothers' Legal Handbook*, Women's Press, 1986.
[33] It was not in the original Bill, but was added by the House of Lords at Report stage (H.L. Vol. 357, cols. 1100–1107).
[34] See the concern voiced by the House of Commons Social Services Committee on *Children in Care*, Second Report, 1984. See also L. Knight, *Community Care*, June 15, 1977, (on Lambeth).
[35] And see now *Re P., The Independent*, September 1, 1989. This has caused quite a stir (see, *e.g. The Times*, August 25, 1989).
[36] [1986] A.C. 112.
[37] See *Council of Civil Service Unions* v. *Minister for the Civil Service* [1985] A.C. 374 and *R.* v. *Bolton M.B.C., ex parte B.* [1985] F.L.R. 343.
[38] *A.-G. ex rel. Tilley* v. *Wandsworth L.B.C.* [1981] 1 W.L.R. 854.
[39] House of Commons Committee on *Children in Care*, House of Commons, 1984.
[40] 25 U.S.C.A. § 1911 (a). For a recent interpretation see *Mississippi Band of Chotaw Indians* v. *Holyfield* 109 S.Ct. 1597 (1989).
[41] *Op. cit.*, note 4, p. 12.
[42] *Ibid.* p. 152.
[43] (1986) 16 Br.J. of Social Work 511, 514.
[44] *Op. cit.*, note 4, p. 153.
[45] *Op. cit.*, note 1, p. 81.
[46] J. Corden and M. Preston-Shoot, *Contracts In Social Work*, Gower, 1987. More critical is C. Rojek and S. A. Collins (1987) 17 Br.J. of Social Work 199. See also D. Nelken, (1987) 40 *Current Legal Problems* 207.
[47] DHSS *Working Together: Guidelines for Inter-Agency Co-operation for the Protection of Children*, 1988.
[48] CCETSW, *The Law Report*, 1988.
[49] *The Protection of Children*, Oxford, Blackwell, 1983, p. 148.
[50] CCETSW, *Legal Studies in Social Work Education*, Paper 4, 1974; CCETSW, *The Law Report*, Paper 4.1, 1988.
[51] A "highly interventionist policy" was in operation (see Butler-Sloss report, *op. cit.*, note 1, para. 10.7).
[52] The Blom-Cooper report (*A Child In Mind*) criticises them for this lack of knowledge.

[53] On the case for teaching lawyers social work see M. D. A. Freeman in (1978) 94 Adoption and Fostering 36.

[54] *cf.* C. Stoll (1968) 47 *Social Forces* 119.

[55] See J. Shklar, *Legalism*, Harvard Univ. Press, 1964.

[56] *Per* M. D. A. Freeman, Introduction to *The Child Care and Foster Children Acts 1980*, p. v.

[57] P. Dale *et al*, *Dangerous Families: Assessment and Treatment of Child Abuse*, Tavistock, 1986.

[58] See, *e.g.* W. Gaylin, *Doing Good: The Limits of Benevolence*, Pantheon 1978.

[59] With the introduction, *inter alia*, of electronic tagging. See A. Rutherford, *The Independent*, September 12, 1989.

[60] See M. D. A. Freeman (1980) J.S.W.L. 64.

[61] (1986) 16 Br.J. of Social Work 501, 503.

[62] Law Com. No. 172 (1988); also Working Paper No. 101 (1987).

[63] DHSS, *Review of Child Care Law*, 1985, HMSO.

[64] DHSS, White Paper on *Child Care and Family Services*, Cm. 62, HMSO, 1987.

[65] See *Hansard* H.C. Vol. 136, col. 1062 (challenge an E.P.O. after 72 hours, as proposed in the *Beckford* report, but rejected in the *Review of Child Care Law* of 1985.)

[66] Reported in *Social Work Today*, October 27, 1988, p. 3.

[67] On the social workers' role see now Margaret Adcock, in *Focus on Child Abuse* (ed. Allan Levy), Hawksmere, 1989, p. 34.

[68] *The Independent*, December 9, 1987.

[69] [1982] A.C. 363.

[70] *Re Y.* [1988] 1 F.L.R. 299.

[71] Clause 29(2).

[72] See R. Mnookin, (1975) 39 Law and Contemporary Problems 226.

[73] Well-documented by R. Rawlings (1982) 45 M.L.R. 637.

[74] *R.* v. *Bedfordshire C.C., ex parte C.* [1987] 1 F.L.R. 239. *cf. R.* v. *L.B. of Harrow*, [1989] 2 F.L.R. 51.

[75] *Op. cit.*, note 1, para. 16.5.

[76] *Op. cit.*, note 6, p. 26.

[77] The present law was couched in the present or present continuous tense and did cause problems. See *Essex C.C.* v. *T.L.R. and K.B.R.* (1978) 9 Fam. Law 15; *F.* v. *Suffolk C.C.* (1981) 2 F.L.R. 208; *M.* v. *Westminster C.C.* [1985] F.L.R. 325.

[78] See M. D. A. Freeman (1980) 10 Fam. Law 131.

[79] *cf. D.* v. *Berkshire C.C.* [1987] A.C. 317.

[80] See also S. Cretney, *The Times*, April 25, 1989.

[81] See Practice Direction [1967] 1 All E.R. 828; R.S.C., Ord. 90, r. 3(3B).

[82] *Re D.* [1976] Fam. 185.

[83] *Op. cit.*, note 1, para. 16.37.

[84] [1982] A.C. 363 and [1985] A.C. 791 respectively.

[85] By pursuing the public law rather than child welfare analogy (in *J.* v. *C.* [1970] A.C. 668).

[86] See *Council of Civil Service Unions* v. *Minister for the Civil Service* [1985] A.C. 374.

[87] *Re D.* [1977] Fam. 158.

[88] Sir Jack Jacob, *The Fabric of English Civil Justice*, Stevens, 1987, pp. 5 *et seq.*

[89] The watershed being the Children Act 1975.

[90] Children and Young Persons (Amendment) Act 1986, operative from August 1, 1988.

91 See Legal Aid Act 1974, s.28(6A).
92 See C. M. Lyon in (ed.) M. D. A. Freeman, *Essays in Family Law 1985* (1986), Sweet and Maxwell, p. 1.
93 See C. M. Lyon (1988) 18 Fam. Law 454 for a good critique of the proposal.
94 See Lord Chancellor's Department, *Improvements in the Arrangements for Care Proceedings*, 1988.
95 See *R. v. Plymouth Juvenile Court, ex parte F. and F.* [1987] 1 F.L.R. 169.
96 In Lord Hailsham's ringing phrase.
97 *R. v. L.B. of Harrow* [1989] 2 F.L.R. 51.
98 See the *Norfolk* case [1989] 3 W.L.R. 502.
99 (1986) 16 Br.J. of Social Work 543.
1 Children and Society vol. 1(4), p. 299, 315.
2 *In Care—A Study of Social Work Decision Making*, National Children's Bureau, 1986.
3 *Decision Making in Statutory Reviews on Children in Care*, Gower, 1984.
4 *Reviews of Children in Care*, Barnett House Papers, Oxford, 1984.
5 *Op. cit.*, note 99, p. 554.
6 Currently two years. Proposals to increase it to three years have been rejected.
7 With the establishment of child care specialists under the aegis of a Law Society scheme.

Unprofessional Standards

DAVID CARSON

This chapter argues that, despite an ideology of commitment to the market-place and the virtues of being a consumer rather than a mere recipient of services, including social welfare services, recent British governments have not been consistent by implementing the full implications of the values and relationships that support that approach. Whilst claiming that services and standards are best provided and met by adopting market mechanisms, the governments have not been prepared to concede market-place powers and rights to recipients of social welfare services. Hence these governments' claims to be enhancing standards cannot be supported. The chapter also suggests some legal changes that would appear to be consistent with these governments' values and goals but which have not been implemented.

Values and Ideology

The governments led by Mrs. Thatcher have been associated with major changes in and attitudes towards the welfare state and the services that constitute it. Despite the popularity of specific limbs of the welfare state, in particular the National Health Service, the extent of popular concern about issues such as child care policed by social services authorities, and the degree of dependence of large proportions of the population in periods of record levels of unemployment on services such as social security, these governments have retained a high level of popular support at elections and as measured through opinion polls. One explanation may be that these governments have occurred at a time of "national selfishness" when people have been much less concerned about the discomforts of others. It

123

was inconceivable, in the 1980s for example, that a television documentary on homelessness, and there were several, could galvanise public opinion in the way that "Cathy come home" did for an earlier generation. The extent to which the Government led or used this phenomenon, and the presentation of issues and consensus by the popular media, is an important matter for consideration elsewhere.

Another cause, it is submitted, has been the governments' harnessing of developments in management sciences which has, in turn, been linked to increased appreciation and use of information technology. Continuing developments in the National Health Service exemplify this. Consensus management by a district management team covering separate spheres of responsibility has given way to unit, district and regional managers personally accountable for the total delivery and planning of services and rewarded by forms of performance-related pay. Management, both in the public and private sectors, has largely shaken off its association with bureaucracy and administration. Managers have demonstrated methods of increasing efficency, such as by managing waiting lists and operating schedules and often, through collecting more useful information, have increased opportunities for strategic planning and choices. In doing so they have removed or undermined some of the mystique and implicit claims to professional privilege or exemption from management. For example the development of diagnosis-related groupings, whereby all hospital-based medical treatments have been grouped and categorised—originally to restrain the growth of costs in the United States' Medicare and Medicaid schemes—is being developed in Great Britain to provide an information base which permits comparison between practitioners, procedures, outcomes and costs. In the past these would have been seen as matters for the professionals involved to investigate and deal with but are now being opened up to more scientific scrutiny and accountability.

This "new managerialism" has had at least two effects upon criticisms of these governments' policies and records towards the welfare state. Increasing numbers of people working in and for the limbs of the welfare state are attracted by and involved in using the management approaches or science to achieve their goals. Secondly, the new approaches are being shown to work; for example more people are being treated in our hospitals for the same resources.

A third explanation for the absence of a strong and coherent opposition to these governments' policies has been a lack of different values to argue over. For example both the governments and their critics have espoused individuality, choice and self-determination for service users. The debate has largely been about means rather than goals. Certainly the same value can be given very different interpretations, in particular, the meaning of equality. But the same values have been espoused by "both sides" and public debate has not been so sophisticated as to draw out differences in emphasis.

Although, as has been argued, there has been limited opposition to these governments' policies, there remains a concern about standards. If such a trial and verdict were possible, it is submitted that most people would regard both these governments' commitment to and their alleged attacks upon the welfare state as "not proven." Whilst services may be more efficiently provided, in terms of more services for similar resources, there is certainly no consensus that standards, in terms of quantity or quality, have generally improved, for example that the quality of life of people in residential establishments has improved as a result of government policy. It will be argued here that this is, in part, because these governments have not been consistent or committed in their policies.

Consumerism

These governments have sought increased freedom for individuals by increasing their disposable income by reducing direct taxation. This has not helped those dependent upon social security. They have sought to ensure that more choices are available by encouraging competition. Competition has also been designed to encourage alternative models of services and to challenge orthodoxies as well as being more economically efficient. There has been an emphasis upon devolving to smaller managerial groups, partly achieved by privatising parts of larger services, although the contracts have often gone to large private firms. Individuality and responsibility have been emphasised both in terms of the accountability of managers for providing services and in the focus of services. "Consumerism" has become a catch-phrase to summarise these values. Clients should be treated like private purchasers of a product rather than as passive recipients of a service. This implies that they, rather than service providers, should be "sovereign." They are entitled to choice and control over the service they receive. They should be regarded as competent and entitled to choose or otherwise determine the services they need. Clients are to determine needs or wishes not professionals or service providers.

These changes are illustrated by *A Positive Choice*,[1] the report of the Independent Review of Residential Care, chaired by Lady Wagner which was commissioned by the Secretary of State. It reflects and seeks to lead this major change in approach. The title emphasises the committee's desire to see residential care as a positive experience.

> "Unless society at large feels the same sense of burning indignation as the Committee at the way in which the present system can devalue the lives of some of the people most in need of help and support—despite the dedicated work done by many—recommendations will remain recommendations." (p. 5)

Their recommendations embody the move to and values of consumerism:

> "We believe that giving primacy to the views and wishes of service users will, inevitably, alter the context in which residential services operate. We believe that people should be able to make a positive choice between different models of care when they can no longer cope with life unaided. . . . Given this power of choice, there will in time be a change in the fundamental dynamics of the relationship between client and professional which could lead society into a more positive understanding of the needs of its most dependent members." (p. 3)

Similar sentiments are made in *Community Care: Agenda for Action*,[2] the report by Sir Roy Griffiths, an archetypal business manager, on the future arrangement of health and social services provided in the community. (The appointment of just one person, who is a manager without professional experience of the health or social services, to analyse and report briefly, is in marked contrast to the previous practice of appointing a Royal Commission or other committee involving a delicate balance of the different interest groups.)

> "The primary function of the public services is to design and arrange the provision of care and support in line with people's needs. That care and support can be provided from a variety of sources. There is value in a multiplicity of provision, not least from the consumer's point of view, because of the widening of choice, flexibility, innovation and competition it should stimulate. The proposals are therefore aimed at stimulating the further development of the "mixed

economy" of care. It is vital that social services authorities should see themselves as the arrangers and purchasers of care services—not as monopolistic providers." (p. 5)

Sir Roy also emphasised management virtues:

"Nothing could be more radical in the public sector than to spell out responsibilities, insist on performance and accountability and to evidence that action is being taken; and even more radical, to match policy with appropriate resources and agreed timetables." (p. v)

But this emphasis on consumerism is half-hearted and involves more form than substance. It may be summarised as a move from service- or resource-led (clients had to fit into the existing services) to needs-led where the services are to fit the client and not the client to fit into the services. The developments stop well short of client-led. Implementation of the Wagner and Griffiths reports would still leave significant power in the hands of professionals and managers. Consumerism implies a contract which is associated with a rich imagery of political and legal rights. Consumers are presumed to be free and competent to make choices whether to and with whom to contract. By being able to choose whom to contract with, and on what terms, they can demonstrate and articulate their individuality, realise themselves by making positive choices and influence the demand for particular kinds of services. In contracting, the parties have power, and are not dependent recipients on others' charity or state discretion, at least to take their business elsewhere. Being a contractor involves status. Certainly there may be a considerable gap between this theory of contractual rights and what happens in practice but, it is submitted, the failure of these governments and reports to develop or significantly associate themselves with these ideas is highly significant. Indeed contracts may be regarded as a paradigm for private enterprise and responsibility and yet have not been developed by the governments most associated with those goals.

Regulation by Contract

The Registered Homes Act 1984 provides the legal framework for regulating the private and voluntary sector of residential and nursing homes. It is strong on procedure providing mechanisms to ensure that there is detailed consultation about the standards that will be required of each unit, and it makes provision for appeal to an independent tribunal. Some minimum standards, such as on qualifications of staff, are prescribed. Other specific issues are addressed, such as supply of hot water and food, but in broad language open to variations in interpretation. And there are two codes, developed by agencies concerned with standards, which provide more detail and permit local variation. Nowhere is there a requirement for contracts either between the unit's owners and the registering authority or between the owners and its residents.

There is no point, many would argue, in having a contract between the owners and the supervising authority, because the latter have statutory authority to enforce and even change registration conditions against the owners, and even withdraw registration. However the authority's decisions are subject to the Registered Homes Tribunal which is not required to consider the codes. Many of the Tribunal's decisions will require consideration of whether a deviation from pre-agreed standards justifies withdrawing registration. That would involve closing the unit with all the implications that has for those resident there. They will have to decide whether the breach has been "serious enough." Indeed the registration authorities will not enforce all their pre-stated requirements because they do not think certain breaches are "serious enough," or predict the Tribunal would so decide. More seriously they could decide not to enforce certain breaches because of the financial and logistical implications for them as health or social services authorities in having to provide the services for these clients instead of the owner. At present they can feel compelled to provide services to support the unit, not at the owner's expense, by providing support services. Owners must come to appreciate that they have a practical power to breach certain requirements.

If the relationship was based upon contract then the authority would be able to enforce breaches by seeking damages against the owners. They would be able to intervene at early stages in a potential downward spiral in standards. Since the registration authority is not experiencing loss by a breach of the agreed standards, any damages awarded are likely to appear more as a fine than compensation. However, the authority will have the costs of registering and monitoring which could be deemed its loss. This could lead to good units paying less for being monitored and reregistered than the poorer quality units. Or the authority could sue on behalf of and allocate the damages to the unit's residents on the basis that, presuming that the standards were stipulated for a purpose related to the quality of residents' experiences, they suffered loss.

At least as important would be the contract between residents and the unit's owners. This would begin, at least, to give the residents more of the respect and rights that come with having a contract. Residents will, automatically, have a contract once agreement on their stay has been reached. But, the terms and conditions will largely be implied, such as the amount of notice to be given of increases in fees or termination of contract. Many topics are likely to be ignored, such as whether the contract may be terminated if the client becomes incontinent, and whether the fees paid cover services such as physiotherapy and detailed standards of the quality of care and services to be provided. The Act could, quite easily, have specified that owners must offer residents a contract which covered a number of listed issues and gave the residents time to consider. The Wagner report encourages contracts as the "most effective means" for "upholding the individual resident's right to personal independence." But, it sees contracts as a means rather than an end in its own right and neither develops an extensive list of minimum contents nor proposes a model. Contracts, despite their ideology, are not yet perceived as an integral means of organising the delivery or quality of services. The provision of residential care, and the 1984 Act, is but one example of what might be achieved by using contracts to state and enforce standards consistent with a consumerism philosophy.

Despite its emphasis upon consumer choice the Griffiths Report also has remarkably little to say about contracts. It could have recommended otherwise but presumes that the quality of the private and voluntary sector will continue to be assured by registration procedures. It recommends that " . . . a home should be registered in relation to its stated objectives." (p. 21) That might be an improvement but it does not refer to the home's objectives for individual clients. Despite the influence of new forms of managerial thinking the report concentrates upon inputs and processes rather than outputs. The implicit assumption is still that homes should provide services rather than achieve specific results. Even if a client is going to require long-term care, where there is no prognosis of improvement, his or her care or services can be stated in terms of individualised goals that take into account his or her priorities and opinions as to what constitutes a high-quality service, for example, particular moral and religious values which might not be considered as important by the owners of the unit or service providers. Contracts can emphasise outcomes.

Avoiding Contractual Controls

The Griffiths Report recommends structures and procedures which are inimical to the development of contracts.

"At local level the role of social services authorities should be reorientated towards ensuring that the needs of individuals within the specified groups are identified, packages of care are devised and services co-ordinated: and where appropriate a specific care manager is assigned. The type of services to be provided would be derived from analysis of the individual care needs: the responsibility of the social services authorities is to ensure that these services are provided within the appropriate budgets by the public or private sector according to where they can be provided most economically and efficiently." (p. vii)

Clients are to be assessed for their needs, which being different from wishes, will be assessed by relevant professionals. This will be a relationship of dependence; the client will rely upon the professional to produce a favourable report. (It would be understandable if that statement of needs unconsciously took into account the resources likely to be made available and the philosophy, form or extent of services available locally.) That report leads to a decision about the services to be made available. That process may require the appointment of a care manager. That role is distinctly outside all existing professional relationships and allegiances. The care manager, or other decider, would then organise for someone or some agency to meet those needs.

The relationship between the care manager and the care provider will be contractual if it involves the private or voluntary sector. Care is to be privatised wherever possible. But the client does not get to make a contract with anyone. Once again, the client will be a dependent rather than a contractor. He or she will not be able to enforce either the original statement of needs or the subsequent arrangement between social services, or their care manager, and the carers who have been awarded the contract. This approach, despite appearances, will not foster the values implicit in being a "consumer." There is no contract between a client and the National Health Service or social services authority. There will be no advantages for clients to have their "needs" met by the private or voluntary sector rather than the public sector. Indeed there may be advantages in receiving care from the public authorities as they are less likely to become bankrupt. The private and voluntary sector will have to be monitored by social services with an increased problem of potential "blackmail." As the role of social services reduces, to funding and monitoring but not providing care, it will have fewer resources to enable it to step in and take over the care of people where the providers are not performing to contract. In the absence of competition to provide the care the social services authority might have to condone poorer standards. The assumption is that there will be plenty of competition but market analogies are inappropriate. Social services authorities, as both the funders and the organisation responsible for ensuring that needs are identified and met, will of necessity be trying to meet as many needs, with limited resources, as is possible. The surplus available to them for innovation, at least, is likely to be little, recalling that many providers will be seeking profits from a competitive tender.

The proposals for reform of the National Health Service in *Working for Patients*[3] continue this approach of nominally favouring patients but stopping short of passing legal power or control to patients. A major proposal is that funding should follow rather than precede the patient. General practitioners will be able to purchase services from hospitals. There will be internal markets so that hospitals can acquire additional income by being efficient and economical in particular forms of treatment. Private health care is attractive to many, not just because of its ability to avoid waiting lists, but also because private patients are contractors and can, for example, insist upon how (for example the kind of treatment and the amount of information given in advance about it), when and by whom they are treated.

Client-led

Advocating a client-led service and a contract between consumers and both service providers and funders would not involve dispensing with objective (for example by schedule of disabilities) or professional assessments of the needs of clients. But it could, for example, involve a client-led statement of personal priorities. A client might wish to emphasise his or her lack of mobility outside the home and wish to "cash in" any other needs or rights, for example to use of libraries and aids and adaptations in the home, in order to fund this priority. The client may simply wish to have the cash, not the service, to organise assistance on his or her own. The Wagner Report noted the comments of one of their correspondents:

> "We find this whole enquiry deeply hurtful and frankly very annoying. Once again eminent persons are debating and deciding what will happen in our lives." (p. 103)

However, it erroneously dismissed the implications of the comment by assuming that it had more to do with people with only physical handicaps and indicating that it was not a criticism of them—because they were in favour of maximum consumer choice and independence. But their limited step towards consumerism still emphasises needs, not wishes and professional assessment. They wish to maximise choice and independence; that is give but hold on to control. A client-led approach would allow the customers to take the money instead of the services and decide how they wish to use it. A client-led service allows its customers to take the same risks other customers can, both with their person and their funds, rather than just trying to inhibit the inhibiting of risk-taking. A client-led service would mainstream, by seeing issues of control, such as the way in which to respond to people who voluntarily make themselves a burden upon the state or when the state can interfere to protect individuals from themselves or others, as matters for general law potentially applying to everyone and not part of service design.

Vouchers could be used to enable patients and clients to become contractors, without affecting the public source of funding. Instead of care managers or general practitioners determining who is to provide the care or treatment, the client or patient might choose for him or herself. Objections would immediately be raised that unwise choices would be made but that would just demonstrate the objector's preference for maintaining professional determination of both the needs and the appropriate services. If there is a commitment to presuming consumer competence and freedom and right to determine individual preferences, then vouchers provide a means. The Wagner Report saw a case:

> "We have been much attracted by the idea of issuing Community Care Allowances to people with special needs, to be used by them to procure care services of their choice." (p. 33)

It saw the case in terms of encouraging consumer choice, being more satisfying to users, encouraging flexible provision and possibily being more economical. But it only recommended further study in terms of costs, eligibility and assessment. It does not seem to have been sufficiently committed to the values of enhancing clients' relative positions.

The New "Weak" Institutional Forms of Management

Geoff Mulgen has reached a similar conclusion, that "the Right's" understanding of how to use markets to produce choice and accountability is partial, but by a rather different approach. He has analysed the development of weak power structures associated with new forms of corporate management and development.[4] The Right, he argues, wants the market to replace administrative structures and for regulation to be swept away:

> "... though they have been pioneered in the leading sectors of capitalism, none of the soft controls and loose structures of post-Fordism have yet to make an impact on the Right's theory of how the world works.
>
> Real markets combine many kinds of control and communication. Price works alongside trust, flows of inside information and shared knowledge, authority and ethos.... Accountability would be restructured so that it flows in many directions at once, simultaneously to funding bodies, to workers and users." (pp. 30 & 31)

Mulgen cites examples such as planning laws requiring developers to get the consent of local dwellers as well as councillors. He continues:

> "Other possible examples might include publicly-funded old people's homes where managements are also accountable to those they look after; independent networks of midwives or acupuncture specialists providing services to NHS patients and regulating their own training and standards; ... the simultaneous use of parent/pupil election of school governors with voucher systems to allow for choice between schools. Each example recognises the need for multiple structures of accountability that allow the citizen to exercise control simultaneously as a voter, a customer and as a participant." (p. 31)

For Mulgen it is not a Right versus Left issue as both currently prefer "strong" systems of control. Perhaps his analysis concentrates on form over substance too much;

organisational structures may be more informal and interlocking, but individuals' positions in hierarchies and their assessment, such as by rewards, particularly in an increasingly inegalitarian society, are at least as distinct as before, and accountability, in terms of requirement to produce results or perish, is increasing even in the archetype of informal control, the universities. At times he also appears to be calling for more professionalism as when advocating, as quoted above, networks of service providers who determine their own training and standards. Excluding the customer from determining those issues is contrary to his more general thesis in which he is surely right, both descriptively and normatively, that we could have many more ways of involving people in the monitoring of the quality of the services they provide or receive.

It may also be asked whether governments, particularly those that have centralised power so much as those led by Mrs. Thatcher, would be prepared either to allow weak forms of control as described by Mulgen or follow through consistently the implications of a consumer ideology. Employees of a corporation can have, and be encouraged via a wage packet to have, an orientation towards the general goals of the company, including profit. But citizens may have very different goals, which a government may be unwilling to allow, and they are all likely to be too frightened to risk losing much of the apparatus of control. How, it might ask, are weak and loose forms of control to be implemented in the Ministry of Defence? (By setting up loose and informal relationships with all possible enemies is likely to be regarded as unfairly avoiding that question.)

Legalising Consumerism

But if the Government was willing to enhance consumers' rights and become committed to improving standards in the welfare state there are a number of initiatives it could take. Instead of requiring customers to enforce standards, and risking their reputation and finances by complaining, a multitude of reporting systems could be developed whereby automatic publicity, at least, is given when certain standards drop. The health service could lead the way by using its developing information systems so that, for example, when morbidity levels in a particular hospital for a particular treatment exceed a regularly reviewed rate, a trigger system ensures that publicity is given and the hospital concerned is given an opportunity to explain the occurrence. Opportunities for more complaints to be raised could be increased by changing the emphasis on inputs and processes to, consistent with consumerism, outcomes. Residential care, its legal regulation and funding, is dominated by beds first and then other facilities. Social security payments, for example, are to provide a client with a place to sleep. The focus ought to be on the quality of experience those resources are used to produce, how many clients experience rehabilitation, for example, how quickly and to what extent? A justification for state provision of residential accommodation is that it reduces dependence, but organisational emphasis on resources has increased dependence.

Consumerism is predicated upon choice which presumes information. Without a massive development in our information systems and facilities for making the results readily available and comprehensible to consumers, the Government's proposals to make the National Health Service more accountable and customer-orientated, by allowing patients to choose where, when and by whom to be treated, must fail.

Obtaining information is one prerequisite, being able to use it is another. Clients and patients are not changed into customers simply by providing choice and information. Years of deference to and dependence on professionals, and expectations of types of relationships with them, will not quickly disappear. The mobile, adequately educated, assertive and articulate can use markets and choice better. Consumer skills could and should be taught in schools. As assertiveness depends upon the existence of others who are not assertive, there must always be people, though not necessarily those with handicaps, who will require assistance in expressing their wishes. Advocacy schemes could and should be developed.

More information is insufficient if it cannot be trusted or tested. The information made available will largely consist of advertisements which are self-serving and subject to restrictive practices, such as agreements only to promote your product (or possibly compare it) rather than criticise your competitors, and rules such as not to advertise the safety of an aeroplane or airline. Establishing quangos to regulate consumers' interests, such as in the postal and telephone services, protects the provider from the customer. Industrial agencies or standards, such as the Press Council and advertising standards, protect those standards and do not permit participation in stating the rules. The Government could alter the law of defamation so as to require that a corporate plaintiff, who alleges defamation in the quantity or quality of services or product, must prove bad faith. Despite their protest of belief in a free press our media are very reluctant to carry any specific critical copy of services or products, largely for fear of libel actions, and certainly reluctant in comparison with critical copy of famous people who do anything embarrassing. Such a reform could increase the amount of information available to begin to let a market operate.

The Government could also assist the new managers who are keen to obtain high standards, by encouraging and protecting those employees who blow the whistle on abuse of clients or customers. Managers in manufacturing industry wish to know which component, human or material, is leading to poor quality products. Managers in human services wish to know which employees or equipment are assaulting or damaging clients and customers. And yet the risks, for example of retaliation and actions for slander, discourage many from reporting on a colleague. People may be dismissed from employment for "making waves" despite the quality of their case. The Government could add such cases to the others, such as dismissal for involvement in trade union activities, where additional protections exist in unfair dismissal law. But given that these governments have also used information as power, have acted strenuously to prevent certain information getting into the public domain and penalising those who have sought to do so, this, too, may be expecting too much. There has been insufficient commitment to the implications of their own ideology.

Notes

[1] Chaired by Lady Wagner, 1988, HMSO, London.
[2] 1988, HMSO, London.
[3] HMSO, London, 1989.
[4] "The Power of the Weak" *Marxism Today*, December 1988, pp. 24–31.

INDEX

Access, 12, 113
Accommodation,
    standard of and homelessness, 92–93
Administration order, 11
Adoption,
    trans-racial, 107
    step-parent, 113
Advocacy schemes, 4, 135
Aldgate, J., 118
Amiel, B., 13, 104
Approved social worker, 119
Assumption of parental rights, 112
Assured shorthold tenancies, 67–68
Assured tenancies, 15, 66, 67
Autonomy, 103, 104

Beckford, Jasmine, 103, 108, 111, 112
Bed and Breakfast accommodation, 1,
    82–83
Beveridge, Sir W., 2
Birth,
    removal of baby at, 114
Blom-Cooper, L., 108–109, 110, 111,
    114, 116, 118
Bureaucratic controls, 118

Carlile, Kimberley, 103, 109, 112, 114
Case conference, 117
CCETSW, 109
Challenging local authorities, 93–94
Child into care,
    preventing the taking of a, 85
Child Poverty Action Group, 25
Children's ombudsman, 118
Civil Justice Review, 9, 10–11, 28, 30, 73
Cleveland, sexual abuse in, 5, 103, 109,
    110, 111, 112, 113, 119
Cohabitation rule, 21
Colwell, Maria, 111, 116
Consumerism, 74–76, 124–127
Consumer Credit, 10
Contact, 112–113
Contract,
    avoiding controls of, 130–131
    freedom of, 74
    regulation by, 127–130

Corporal punishment, 104–105, 106
Council tenants,
    right to buy, 10
Courts,
    autonomy, 16–17
    role, 112–114, 117–119
Cultural pluralism, 105–106

Dale, P., 110
Dangerous families, 110
Decision-making,
    improving child-care, 118–119
Defamation, 136
Dingwall, R., 109
Discretion, 19–20, 36, 37, 39–40, 53–55
Drug addiction, 114
Domestic violence, 81, 87–88, 90, 98,
    100

Eekelaar, J., 109
Elmer, E., 104
Equality, 3, 9

Family credit, 22
Family disputes, homelessness and,
    85–88, 95, 97
Family Rights Group, 111
Freud, Anna, 103–104
Fruin, D., 118

Gamble, A., 29
Goldstein, J., 103–104
Griffiths, Sir R., 126–127, 129, 130
Guardian *ad litem*, 116, 117

Harassment, 12–13, 68–69
Henry, Tyra, 103, 111
Higgs, Marietta, 103
Hitting children, 104–105
Holman, B., 33
Homelessness, 1, 81–101
    family disputes and, 85–88, 95–97
    intentional, 3, 84–91, 98
    job-related moves and, 4, 89–91, 95
    problem, 3, 81–82
    rehousing, 83–84

Homelessness—*cont.*
  rent arrears and, 17
  standard of accommodation and, 24,
    92–93
Home ownership, 10, 61
Hospitals, 1–2
Housing Act 1988,
  main features, 61–71
  policy objectives, 61–62
Housing benefit, 2–3
Housing corporation, 63–64
Housing law,
  definition, 60–61
  re-thinking of, 71–77
Housing, public, 23–24

Income distribution, 1
Income support, 19, 21
Individual and the law, 9–14
Inequalities, 9–14
Intentional homelessness,
  definition, 84–85
  moral turpitude and, 86
  pregnancy and, 86, 98, 99
  reasonableness and, 89–91
Intervention, 103, 104, 120

Job-related moves,
  homelessness and, 4, 89–91, 95
Judicial review, 4, 5, 26, 94

Landlord and tenant, 28, 112–113
Law,
  as bias, 12
  as constraint, 108–110
  as framework, 4, 110–111
  and order, 2, 6, 110
  and policy, 4
Law centres, 14
Leases, 3
Legal Action Group, 11–12
Legal Aid, 2, 3, 9, 13, 14, 94, 116
Legalism, 108–110, 116
Licences, 3, 17
Loans, 41
  crisis, 48

Managerialism, 124–125, 127
Market forces, 2, 5, 103, 123, 133
Marshall, T., 2
McDonnell, P., 118
Means tests, 2, 18
Medicaid, 124
Medicare, 124

Mellor, David, 112
Minimum wage legislation, 2
Mortgage repossessions, 10
Mulgen, G., 133, 134
Mullen, T., 22
Murray, T., 109

National Consumer Council, 10
National Health Service, 1, 123, 124,
    130, 131, 133, 135
  Working for Patients, 131
Non-intervention, 103, 104
Nursing homes, 127–130

Office of Child Protection, 116–117
Ogus, A., 24–25
Ombudsman, children's, 118

Parton, N., 108
Pensions, 18
Pluralism, cultural, 105–106
Poor Law, 112
Poverty, 1
Prescription charges, 2
Privatisation, 2, 18, 82, 125
Procedural standards, 115–117
Public and private, 4
Public housing, 23–24

Race, 12, 71, 105, 107–108
Rachmanism, 13
Refuges, 97
Registers,
  child protection, 117
Regulation, 103
Reich, C., 3–4
Religion, 106–107
Rent Acts, 15
Rent Officers, 64–65
Representation of parents and children,
    116–117
Residential homes, 127–130
Rights, 3–4, 5
Rooflessness, 95–96
Ruddock, Martin, 112
Rules and discretion, 4

Scarification, 105
Security of tenure, 67, 68
Short Committee, 107
Sinclair, R., 118
Social control, 4
Social fund, 3, 5, 35–58
  budget, 49–51, 56

Social fund—*cont.*
  directions and guidance, 46–49
  legal structure, 43–46
  review, 51–53
Social work,
  legalistic model of, 4, 108–110
Social worker,
  approved, 119
Solnit, Albert, 103–104
Stevenson, Olive, 111
Stoll, Clarice, 109

Take-up, 22
Targeting, 2, 19, 22
Tawney, R., 2
Taylor-Gooby, P., 7
Taxation, 125
Test cases, 25–26
Thatcher Government, 2, 5, 123, 134
Thorburn, June, 118
Trade disputes, 21

United States,
  homelessness in, 82

United States—*cont.*
  Indian Child Welfare Act, 108
  Medicare and Medicaid, 124
  workfare policies, 2

Values and ideology, 123–125
Vernon, J., 118
Violence, domestic, 81, 87–77, 90, 98,
  100
Vouchers, 132, 133

Wages Councils, 2, 16, 28
Wagner Report, 126, 127, 129,
  132
Wardship, 4, 114–115, 116
Warren, N., 26
Welfare,
  non-justiciable, 113
Welfare State, 2, 5
Workfare policies, 2
Working Together, 109
Wyatt, Geoffrey, 103

Yoruba tribe, 115

HISPANIC CLASSICS
Golden-Age Drama

Tirso de Molina

THE TRICKSTER OF SEVILLE
and the
STONE GUEST

(El burlador de Sevilla y el convidado de piedra)

Translated with an Introduction & Commentary
by
Gwynne Edwards

ARIS & PHILLIPS

WARMINSTER

UK ISBN   085668 300 0 *cloth*
          085668 301 9 *limp*

Tirso, *de Molina*
   The trickster of Seville and the stone
   guest. -- (Hispanic texts)
   I. Title II. Edwards, Gwynne III. Series
   IV. El Burlador de Sevilla. *English &*
   Spanish
   862'.3   PQ6435.E5

Printed in England by Aris & Phillips Ltd., Teddington House, Warminster, Wiltshire
Published by Aris & Phillips Ltd, Teddington House, Warminster, Wiltshire.

CONTENTS

Introduction   vii
   I   The Spanish *Comedia*   viii
   II   The Golden-Age *Corral*   x
   III Tirso de Molina   xiii
   IV   The Trickster of Seville   xix
   V   Analysis of the Play   xxiv
   VI   The Translation   xxxviii
   Notes to the Introduction   xli

THE PLAY AND COMMENTARY   1

ACT 1 *Jornada primera*   4

ACT 2 *Jornada segunda*   74

ACT 3 *Jornada tercera*   126

To
Paul Chamberlain

INTRODUCTION

The Spanish drama of the sixteenth and seventeenth centuries has many points of contact with its Elizabethan counterpart and is for that reason immediately accessible to the English-speaking reader. During the period in question Spain achieved, of course, immense economic and political power and became during the reigns of Charles V (1517–1556) and Philip II (1556–1598) the most influential country in Europe, enjoying territorial domination of the Low Countries and Italy, not to mention its increasing role in the exploration and exploitation of the Americas. Undoubtedly, the emergence of Spain as a great political and economic power lies at the heart of the great flowering of artistic activity that took place in the seventeenth century – the age of Cervantes, Velázquez, Lope de Vega, Tirso de Molina and Calderón –, though by that time the nation's political power was fast declining. Within that outburst of creative genius, the drama occupied a prime position and achieved between about 1580 and the death of Calderón in 1681 a vigour, inventiveness and quality unequalled before or since. In this respect, as in others, Spanish drama of the Golden Age rivals Elizabethan drama, though in terms of output Shakespeare's 36 plays cut a poor figure alongside Lope de Vega's 800, Tirso de Molina's 300, and Calderón's 120. During the one hundred years in question the theatre in Spain presents a spectacle of constant and continuous development. By the end of the sixteenth century, the principal towns and cities had fixed theatres, the *corrales*, as opposed to the groups of itinerant actors who in the earlier part of the century had performed in town and village squares. By the 1630s the more elaborate Court theatres had come into being, notably in the Buen Retiro just outside Madrid, where technical innovation and ingenious stage-designers made possible the presentation of complex plays and highly elaborate stage-effects. If, in conjunction with the development of the *corrales*, or public theatres, and the more sophisticated Court theatres, account is also taken of the vigorous tradition of religious plays or *autos sacramentales* that were performed throughout this period to celebrate the festival of Corpus Christi, some idea may be formed of the richness of what on its own merits has come to be called Golden-Age drama.[1]

I. THE SPANISH *COMEDIA*

The Spanish *comedia* of the seventeenth century – *comedia* is simply used to mean 'play' – was fashioned in large part by Lope de Vega (1562-1635), building on and perfecting the experiments of a number of lesser dramatists of the late sixteenth century. During the first half of the sixteenth century, when there were no established public theatres or acting companies in Spain, drama was for the most part associated with the Court or the Church and reveals little of the truly popular character that was to distinguish its later development. Thus Juan del Encina (1468?-1530?), initially a courtier and later an archdeacon and canon, wrote both highly artificial pastoral *églogas*, or eclogues, and religious pieces. Similarly, Gil Vicente (1465?-1537?), a dramatist at the Portuguese Court from 1502 to 1536, wrote for a sophisticated bilingual court audience, producing romantic comedies, morality plays, allegorical fantasies and pastoral works, eleven of them in Spanish. The work of a third dramatist, Bartolomé de Torres Naharro (1485?-1520?), reveals both a marked Italian influence and a knowledge of classical theory which makes his contribution to the later drama quite significant. But none of these dramatists, though important in their way, suggest the emergence of the *comedia* of Lope de Vega as clearly as do the group of writers who appeared in the latter part of the sixteenth century.

Although Lope de Rueda (1509?-1565) is an influential rather than outstanding dramatist, his short comic plays or *pasos* are the clear predecessors, both in their lively, down-to-earth prose dialogue and their sharply-drawn characters and situations, of the strong comic element in the drama of the seventeenth century. This popular comic strain is to be found too in the short pieces or *entremeses* of Cervantes (1547-1616), a great admirer of Rueda. It is, though, in the serious drama of the last twenty-five years of the sixteenth century that the most significant changes are to be seen. Juan de la Cueva (1550?-1610), Cervantes, Lupercio Leonardo de Argensola (1559-1613) and others wrote plays in which the influence of classical tragedy is strong, though in some of them the subject is Spanish, thus anticipating the highly nationalistic character of the theatre of Lope and his followers. Secondly, we see a movement away from the five-act classical format to a play of four and, in some cases, three acts, the structure to be adopted by Lope himself. Again, there are numerous examples of the breaking of the classical unities of place and time and evidence too of the variety of metre and stanza-forms which Lope would advocate so strongly. And finally, all these changes were taking place at a time when theatres were themselves beginning to evolve. The stage was set for the emergence of the true seventeenth-century *comedia*.

The dramatic formula worked out by Lope in his plays and advocated in a poetic essay of 1609, the *Arte nuevo de hacer comedias en este tiempo*, may be described briefly as follows: the play has a three-act structure, corresponding to the exposition of the situation, its complication and dénouement; the strict separation of serious and comic elements is abandoned, even though the predominant mood of a given play may range from tragic, to tragic-comic, to comic; the unities of action, time and place are greatly relaxed, for the main plot is often interwoven with one or more sub-plots, the time-span of the events portrayed in a play usually extends beyond twenty four hours and in some instances covers many years, and the action, far from being limited to a single setting, ranges widely, moving not only from inside to outside, and town to town, but also from country to country; the language of the play is accommodated to the subject-matter and the status of the speaker, which, given the mixture of serious and comic elements mentioned above, means in turn a mixture of styles and language, embracing kings, noblemen, servants, soldiers and peasants; a variety of metre and stanza forms is used, corresponding to the dramatic requirements of given situations, but the backbone of the *comedia* is, in fact, the eight-syllable line with assonance in alternate lines, the traditional line of Spanish ballad poetry distinguished above all by its capacity to inject pace and vitality into the spoken word; subject-matter avoids, on the whole, classical material (Calderón is the exception here) and draws instead on Spanish history, legend and literature, as well as on Italian sources; and finally, the aim of the *comedia* is, in the tradition of classical literature, to entertain and delight and at the same time to teach – an idea encapsulated in the phrase *deleitar aprovechando* which is, curiously enough, the title of a book by Tirso de Molina.

The dramatic formula outlined above, so different from French classical theatre yet so reminiscent of Elizabethan drama, was practised by Lope in all his writing for the stage, was received enthusiastically by a theatre-going public eager for novelty and excitement, and provided the model which Lope's contemporaries and successors followed and adapted in their different ways. Lope's own drama is one of immense variety. On the one hand there are plays like *Fuente Ovejuna* or *Peribáñez* in which history and the clash of nobles and peasants provide the material for the portrayal of essentially human and individual conflicts, combining emotional impact and didactic intention. On the other, the Bible provided Lope with much material, as in the case of *La hermosa Ester*, his dramatisation of the Book of Esther. Thirdly, there are delightful comedies of intrigue, often revolving around the theme of love, such as *La discreta enamorada, Amar sin saber a quien* and *Las bizarrías de Belisa*. And finally there are much darker, more tragic plays, many of them focusing on the code of personal honour and the consequences of its loss: such is *El castigo sin venganza*, a particularly grim piece which ends in bloodshed and anguish, and is one of the finest tragedies written in the Golden Age. It has to be said, nevertheless, that the volume and variety of Lope's theatre makes any categorization impossible, as indeed is the case with many of the dramatists who followed in his footsteps: Tirso de Molina (1581?-1648), Pérez de Montalbán (1602-38), Vélez de Guevara (1579-1644), Ruiz de Alarcón (1581?-1639) Mira de Amescua (1574?-1644) and Calderón de la Barca (1600-81). The list is incomplete, but it is sufficient to give some idea of the dynamism of the theatre of seventeenth-century Spain which Lope helped so much to generate.[2]

II. THE GOLDEN AGE *CORRAL*

Although mention has been made of the Court theatres, the development of the *comedia* took place in the public theatres or *corrales* and was influenced greatly by the physical characteristics of such spaces. As the word suggests, a *corral* was in fact a courtyard, rectangular in shape and overlooked by the backs of houses. It was also therefore largely exposed to the sky. The stage, situated at one end of the rectangle, projected into it. The central area of the auditorium, the *patio*, was nothing more than a large space where the commoners stood to watch the play. A few rows of seats ran along the sides of the theatre arranged in tiers, and above these were the windows of the surrounding houses which served as boxes, *aposentos*, and which were often hired by the wealthy on an annual basis. At the back of the theatre, at ground-floor level, were the entrances, one for men and one for women, as well as the theatre bar or *fruteria*, while at first-floor level were to be found the enclosures specifically set aside for women of the lower classes and unflatteringly known as *cazuelas*, or stewpots. Finally, at second-floor level, directly above the *cazuelas*, was another enclosure, the *tertulia*, which was reserved for the clergy.

The stage itself consisted of a projecting apron, a mid-stage and back-stage area. There was no proscenium arch or curtain. Part of the back-stage was usually curtained off and its curtains could be drawn back to reveal an inner space or to disclose some dramatic 'discovery'. Above the stage was a gallery which ran round the theatre at first-floor level and which could be brought into use when the stage-action required, as, for example, the top of a mountain or the battlements of a castle. At a level higher still the balcony of a house might be used to represent Heaven, and the various levels could be linked to the stage by ladders and ramps which could be used by the actors to move from one level to another. In the floor of the stage a trapdoor might be employed to suggest a pit or even Hell itself, belching forth smoke and even flames. The more sophisticated public theatres possessed various kinds of stage-machinery such as rocks which could open, and the wealthier acting companies seem to have had an excellent stock of costumes, though it has to be said that characters of whatever period wore contemporary costume. In general, scenery was simple and, since the theatres were exposed to the skies and performances took place in daylight, audiences were obliged and were, of course, accustomed to using their imaginations. Undoubtedly, the performance of plays presented those audiences with a vigorous, swift-moving and exciting spectacle.

A typical afternoon performance in a *corral* would commence with musicians playing and singing. Then would come the *loa*, a kind of prologue recited or sung in praise of an individual, the audience, or the play, and followed by the performance of the play itself. Between the acts short farces would be presented – *entremeses* and *sainetes* –, so that there was no interval in the modern sense to interrupt the continuous flow of the action and allow a restless Spanish audience to become bored. Not without cause did Lope himself comment in his *Arte nuevo* on this aspect of Spanish theatre-goers as well as on their craving for entertainment. It was this, indeed, which meant that a run of any given play was usually of no more than two or three days.

As for the actors themselves, they were organized into companies in the cities, each company coming together during Lent and beginning the theatrical year at Easter. The theatre-going season would then last until Lent came round once more. Each acting company was headed by an *autor de comedias*, a manager, not to be confused with the dramatist who would be known as the *poeta* or *ingenio* and from whom the manager of a company would obtain his plays. An acting company would contain about four young actors, including the lead-actor or *primer galán*, two men specializing in elderly parts (*barbas*), two comedians (*graciosos*), and six actresses, including the female lead or *primera dama*. While these companies performed for most of the time in the *corrales*, they might also be called upon for performances in the Court theatres as they developed over the years, an order which they could hardly refuse to comply with but which created difficulties for the management of the *corrales* and greatly inconvenienced the theatre-going public of Madrid whose two public theatres, the Corral de la Cruz and the Corral del Príncipe, founded in 1579 and 1582 respectively, were deprived of plays for many weeks at a time.

The theatres of the Golden Age came into being as providers of income for charitable institutions, in particular hospitals, and they were indeed both the owners and the beneficiaries of Madrid's two public theatres. Initially the running of these theatres was placed in the hands of lessees, but by the seventeenth century they had become the equivalent of theatre managers whose responsibilities involved both the hiring of acting companies and the general administration of the entire organization, a part of the daily box-office takings and the cost of the lease of the theatre going to the hospitals. Later on the ownership and administration of the theatres would be taken over by the Town Council itself, and the hospitals then received an annual subsidy. The link between the theatres and the hospitals also had an important consequence in relation to the frequency with which plays were performed and the length of time for which they ran. At first plays were performed only on Sundays and holidays, but the financial needs of the hospitals meant that eventually performances were given on most days of the week. This being the case, and Madrid having a relatively small population with an enormous appetite for the theatre, a given play was unlikely to run for more than a week, a factor which in turn accounts for the vast productivity of the dramatists of the Golden Age.

Finally, it is important to draw attention to the kind of public which went to the theatre. In Madrid this evidently embraced all sections of the population. The standing area, by far the largest part of the auditorium, would have been occupied by the ordinary people, including the noisier elements – servants and soldiers – who both abused or applauded the actors and argued amongst themselves. The rows of seats along the sides of the theatre would clearly be taken by wealthier and more educated members of the public, and the balconies and rooms overlooking the stage, some of which were reserved for town offcials, would be rented by the nobility. Even the King had a 'box' at the Corral de la Cruz. The audience, in short, consisted of a great cross-section of the public, in consequence of which the dramatists were obliged to appeal to a variety of tastes ranging from the 'groundlings' to the monarch. In those circumstances it is hardly surprising that the theatre of the Golden Age should be distinguished by its variety as well as its vitality[3].

III. TIRSO DE MOLINA
<u>Life</u>

Tirso de Molina is the pseudonym of Fray Gabriel Téllez who was born in Madrid, probably in 1580. Nothing certain has been discovered about his parentage, although the theory has been advanced by Doña Blanca de los Ríos that he was the illegitimate son of the Duke of Osuna. An entry in one of the parish registers of Madrid for March 9, 1584, refers to Gabriel, son of Gracia Juliana and an unknown father, while some words added in the margin and subsequently crossed out were deciphered by Doña Blanca as '*Tz. Girón, hijo del Dq. Osuna*', i.e., Téllez Girón, son of the Duke of Osuna[4]. Most scholars have dismissed the evidence for the theory as far too flimsy, but if it is in fact correct and the Gabriel Téllez mentioned there was the child who later became Tirso de Molina, the dramatist was the son of one of the most famous noblemen and public figures of the Golden Age. The strongest contradictory evidence to the above is to be found in documents, one of which points to Tirso's birth in 1583, while the other – a personal statement – indicates that he was born in 1580.

In 1600 Tirso became a novice in the Mercedarian Order in Guadalajara and, on completion of his novitiate, became a friar of the order. Undoubtedly, he would have undergone a very thorough training in theology, though his works are certainly not cramped or inhibited in any way by the oppressive weight of dogma. 1606, 1607 and the years 1612-15 find him in the house of the Mercedarian Order in Toledo, and it seems likely that there he met Lope de Vega, then a resident of that city. At all events, documentary evidence shows that in 1612 Tirso sold three plays to an actor-manager in Toledo. Clearly, his interest in the theatre was increasing, and the years immediately following witnessed the composition of some of his very best work.

New portrait of Tirso de Molina by Anthony Stones, 1985.

In 1616 Tirso was sent with six monks of the order to the West Indian island of Santo Domingo where he remained and taught theology for two years. It was probably the expedition to the Caribbean which allowed Tirso to become acquainted with the ports of Lisbon and Seville respectively, both of which were to figure prominently in *The Trickster of Seville*. After his return from Santo Domingo, he lived in Toledo, and in 1620 moved to his birthplace, Madrid, commencing there a period of intense literary activity and participation in literary competitions which seems to have ended abruptly in 1625. On March 6 of that year, the *Junta de reformación*, a body appointed to safeguard public morality, accused Maestro Téllez, otherwise known as Tirso, of writing profane works and recommended the King, Philip IV, to banish the dramatist to a remote house of his order where, under threat of excommunication, he be forbidden to write *comedias*. Although in 1626 Tirso was made prior of a Mercedarian friary at Trujillo in Extremadura, a long way off from Madrid, it seems unlikely that this was in response to the accusation of the *Junta*. He remained at Trujillo until 1629, after which he may have moved to Toledo. At all events he was promoted in 1632 to the position of historian of the Order of Mercy. In 1634 he returned to Madrid and over the next two years, assisted by a nephew, published four volumes of his plays. In 1640 a member of his own order, Fray Marcos Salmerón, an official visitor to the friary of the Order of Mercy in Madrid, instructed that no inhabitant of the friary should have in his possession any book of profane plays or poetry or write prose or poetry which attacked or criticised the government of the day. Tirso, choosing to ignore the instruction, was banished for a time to Soria but later returned to Madrid. In 1645 he became prior of the friary of the Order of Mercy in Soria. Two years later he moved to Almanzán, also in Soria, where he died in 1648.[5]

Drama
Tirso's dramatic work can on the whole be categorized rather more easily than that of the prolific Lope, though in the last resort any attempt at classification has its dangers. Broadly speaking, Tirso can be said to have written (a) comedies, (b) historical plays, and (c) religious dramas.

The comedies are, for the most part, about love, particularly jealousy, and involve a group of lovers, a tangle of relationships, and thus a complex plot. Amongst them are some skilfully written and amusing pieces, such as *Don Gil de las calzas verdes*, but as a comic dramatist Tirso is considered by many critics to have lacked both the inventiveness and the dramatic technique of Lope de Vega and to have lapsed too often in the comedies into cliché and the mechanical working-out of a well-tried dramatic formula. On the other hand, the comedies are often distinguished by an insight into character which is a feature of Tirso's drama as a whole. Thus, *El vergonzoso en palacio* contains some interesting examples of female psychology – a sister far bolder than her bashful suitor, and another sister, averse to men, who falls in love with a portrait of herself in male costume. Other plays reveal women who are ambitious and forceful and who to that extent suggest a reversal of traditional roles. In general, though, in accordance with the formula of comedy, character is subordinated to plot, and it was left to Tirso's more serious work to develop this aspect of his art.

As far as the historical plays are concerned, there is a good deal of unevenness, but also some very fine pieces. Tirso's best-known historical play, *La prudencia en la mujer*, has as its protagonist Queen María, widow of Sancho IV of Castile and León, and deals with her struggle to retain the throne for her son, Ferdinand, in a time of political upheaval. The strength of the play lies, clearly, in the presentation of the courageous and heroic central figure surrounded by treacherous and scheming enemies, as well as in its powerful and stirring language, while the relevance of its message to the contemporary political situation – the manipulation of the young Philip IV by the powerful Count-Duke of Olivares – adds a further ring of authenticity. Another chronicle-play of considerable interest and power is *Antoña García* in which the country-girl, Antoña, takes up the cause of the Catholic Kings, Ferdinand and Isabella, in defiance of the local feudal overlord. Once more Tirso turns historical material into powerful and exciting theatre and creates in the main character an enormously vital and appealing heroine.

Tirso's religious plays consist of powerful dramas based on biblical stories and works whose themes are religious in a more general sense. Amongst the former are *La venganza de Tamar*, a dramatisation of the story of King David's warring children; *La mujer que manda en casa*, based on the story of Jezebel and Naboth; and *La mejor espigadera*, which takes its material from the Book of Ruth. Tirso, of course, brought his theological training and knowledge to bear on the dramatic treatment of the material in question, but above all these are plays which portray human conflict at crucial moments in the history of a people. Nothing illustrates the point better than *La venganza de Tamar*, generally acknowledged to be one of Tirso's very finest works. On a human level the fatal attraction of Amnon, David's son, for his half-sister, Tamar; his violation of her; his murder by her brother, the envious and ambitious Absalom: all the complexity of individual and collective motivation is convincingly and movingly set before us. On a broader level, the sense of individuals as part of a greater, unfolding pattern in which sin, guilt and punishment are closely interwoven, contributes to a feeling of universality.

Amongst the plays that deal with religious material in a more general sense, *El condenado por desconfiado* is particularly outstanding and, along with *The Trickster of Seville*, is probably Tirso's best-known play. The intellectual background to the play has to do with the theological controversy waged at the end of the sixteenth century between the Molinists and the Banezians over the extent to which Divine Grace enables a man to achieve salvation. In the controversy the Molinists held free-will to be of enormous importance, almost to the exclusion of the role of God's grace, while the Banezians clung to the totally different view that man was virtually predestined. Tirso's play embodies the different viewpoints in its two central characters: Paulo, the hermit who believes that Divine Grace is not available to the true sinner, convinces himself that confession of his sins is useless, and is doomed; and Enrico, the criminal who, for all his terrible crimes, believes in God's mercy, repents, and is saved. But if *El condenado por desconfiado* is a play of ideas, it is, more than that, a play about human conflict and dilemma, and in this respect Paulo and Enrico are two of the most memorable characters in the whole of Golden-Age drama: the former an apparently pious man beset by doubt, arrogantly rebelling against the fate which he thinks God has in store for him; the latter a passionate, instinctive monster of a man redeemed by love of his father, which leads him finally to trust in God's mercy. Undoubtedly, it can be argued that the play's religious preoccupations limit its broader appeal, particularly to an age in which religious values have declined. On the other hand, it cannot be denied that in terms of characterization, construction and emotional impact, *El condenado por desconfiado* is a very great play.[6]

Tirso and the Lopean *comedia*

As we have seen, Lope's views on the drama had been expressed in 1609 in the *Arte nuevo de hacer comedias*. His enthusiasm for a new form of drama which broke the stranglehold of Classicism led in the years that followed to an often fierce controversy in which individuals took up entrenched positions and in which Tirso himself came down very firmly on Lope's side. In 1621 he wrote, for example, a miscellany of stories, plays and poems entitled the *Cigarrales de Toledo* in which a group of well-to-do people leave Toledo for their estates and proceed to entertain themselves. The performance of Tirso's own *El vergonzoso en palacio* leads to a discussion on theatre and to a discourse by one of the characters which amounts to Tirso's defence of Lope's dramatic practice. Above all, Tirso argues, the aim of the drama should be the imitation of life. In this context any attempts to preserve the unity of time and to suggest something as complex as a love-affair in an action covering twenty-four hours is the very opposite of life-like, as indeed is the strict separation on the stage of the serious and the comic. The argument that the ancients deserve respect for their achievements is not to say that their work cannot be improved upon. Indeed, times change and taste changes accordingly, demanding a new art of which Lope is justifiably the champion:

> Lope, having established the *comedia* and endowed it with its present subtlety and perfection, is great enough to lead a school of his own; and those amongst us who regard ourselves as his followers should consider ourselves fortunate to have such a master, and should always defend his teachings against those who violently impugn them.[7]

There are, of course, essential differences between Tirso and Lope as dramatists. Firstly, Tirso clearly lacked that gift for spontaneity and sheer inventiveness which led to Lope's being known as the *monstruo de naturaleza*, a dramatist as creative as Nature itself. On the other hand, as earlier remarks have perhaps suggested, Tirso's intellect was greater than Lope's so that many of his works have a greater profundity and seriousness, and in that sense look forward to the more intellectual drama of Calderón. Again, Tirso's insight into character and the working of the human mind, sharpened no doubt by his experience as a priest, is sharper and deeper than Lope's and to that extent has been regarded by some critics as more Shakespearean.[8] In terms of dramatic technique, Tirso tends to be the more careful of the two writers in the construction of his plots and, although *The Trickster* is not a good example, reveals in many of his plays a striking ability to interweave in different proportions main and sub-plots, or two plots of equal importance, as is the case in the brilliantly constructed *El condenado por desconfiado*.

IV.   THE TRICKSTER OF SEVILLE
The two versions
Two early printed versions of the play exist: *El burlador de Sevilla y convidado de piedra* was published in a collection of plays dated 1630 and is stated there to be a '*comedia famosa del Maestro Tirso de Molina*'; another version, entitled *Tan largo me lo fiáis*, was published by itself, with no date, and carrying the words '*comedia famosa de Don Pedro Calderón*'.[9] The problems surrounding the accurate dating and priority of seventeenth-century printed texts is indeed complex, and is not the concern of this Introduction, but the general conclusions to be drawn from the available evidence are as follows: the differences between the two versions, which involve the names of some of the characters (Don Juan's father is one), certain speeches (*Tan largo* has in Act I a speech not on Lisbon but on Seville), individual scenes and the use of particular verse-forms, point on balance to *Tan largo's* being, despite all its imperfections, closer to Tirso's original. It derives in the printed form we have, which may well be as late as 1660, from earlier printings. The text of *El burlador*, on the other hand, is probably a version constructed from the memory of a number of people: possibly Tirso himself; a company of actors; or a memory-man used by a company to pirate the play of another company. In conclusion, it has to be recognized that both versions are imperfect and somewhat removed from the original play. In terms of theatre *El burlador* is often better than *Tan largo*, no doubt because it owes something to people working in the theatre, and it is the version which is generally available in modern editions.

Authorship
As the earlier discussion has shown, the name of Tirso de Molina appears on the title-page of *El burlador de Sevilla* in the collection of plays dated 1630, while *Tan largo* is attributed to Calderón. The latter possibility is not, in fact, one that has ever been taken seriously, but it is an indication of the problems that often surround both the authorship and dating of

Golden-Age plays. Indeed, an argument has been put forward for Andrés de Claramonte as the *refundidor* or reviser of the 1630 version of *El burlador*.[10] Four of the play's lines appear in one of his own plays, *Deste agua no beberé*; he was a known plagiarist; and he also had his own company of actors. A reasonable hypothesis is that Claramonte revised an earlier version of *El burlador* for a performance by his own company and was thus responsbile for some of its corruptions. Be this as it may, there is nothing to suggest that Tirso was not the original author of the play. The style is generally consistent with his work; the versification corresponds on the whole to Tirso's practice; and the suggested date of composition is clearly well within the period of his writing for the theatre. Even if the play does not form part of the *Partes* or collections of Tirso's work (each *Parte* containing twelve plays), its omission, given the circumstances surrounding the publication of such volumes, does not mean that Tirso did not write *El burlador*.

Date

The actual date of composition of the original play from which *El burlador* and *Tan largo* derive is pure supposition. Tirso was, as we have seen, in Seville in 1616 on his way to the Indies, but he was also there on his return in 1618. In 1619 Philip III visited Lisbon, which may account for the speech about Lisbon in *El burlador*. The title-page of the latter in the collection dated 1630 states that it was performed by Roque de Figueroa who, records indicate, did not have his own company until 1624, while in 1625 there is evidence of the performance in Naples of a play called *Il convitato di pietra*, probably in Spanish, by the company of Pedro Osorio. In short, it seems that the original certainly existed by 1625 and may well date back to 1616. It does not seem likely that the play was written before 1616.[11]

Sources

Attempts have been made by various scholars to discover a source for Tirso's Don Juan amongst his contemporaries. One such theory, held for quite a long time, was that he was modelled on Miguel de Mañara Vincentelo de Lesca, reputed to be an infamous libertine who subsequently changed his ways. The discovery that Mañara was born in Seville in 1626 and was therefore only a child when Tirso wrote his play is sufficient indication of the perils of flying such kites. Other historical models have also been suggested, including Mateo Vázquez de Leca, a Sevillian, nephew of Philip II's secretary, who is said

xx

to have lived a scandalous youth and who was born in 1571. The most convincing, if any are convincing, is, however, Don Pedro Téllez Girón, Marquis of Peñafiel and later to become the notorious Duke of Osuna. In his own lifetime (1579-1624) Don Pedro's adventures were indeed scandalous. During his teenage years, his father found it impossible to control him, he married early but continued to indulge in numerous affairs, he frequently broke his word, lied, obtained money under false pretences, and even killed a man in a brawl. An idea of his notoriety can be gleaned from the fact that his exploits became, not long after his death, the subject of a play, *Las mocedades del duque de Osuna*, by Cristóbal Monroy y Silva. Morevoer, Don Pedro's official residence was at Osuna, a town near Seville, and he therefore made Seville the focal point of his various activities, making his mark in a city known for its crime and general sleaziness. In addition, it seems that he had a particular liking for the sexual trick, the *burla*, so favoured by Tirso's Don Juan. And finally, as far as a personal link with Tirso is concerned, there is the intriguing possibility that, as Doña Blanca de los Ríos has suggested, Don Pedro Téllez Girón may have been his half-brother, in which case the portrayal of Don Juan and his scandalous behaviour can be seen as Tirso's reaction to and rebuke of someone who would not recognise him as a Girón.[12]

A second line of argument suggests that particular features of *The Trickster* are to be found in Italian religious drama supposedly of the fifteenth and sixteenth centuries, in particular in a play called the *Ateista fulminato*. The play deals with the seduction of Leonora by Count Aurelio and his punishment by the statues of the girl's parents who drag him down to Hell. A promising theory turns out in the end to be supported by extremely flimsy evidence, for it has now been proved that this play belongs to the end of the seventeenth century and, far from influencing *The Trickster*, is influenced by it. Another suggested dramatic source is *Leonzio, ovvero la terrible vendetta di un morto*, first performed at the Jesuit school of Inglostadt in 1615. Count Leonzio, a follower of Machiavelli, kicks a skull which he finds near a cemetery and invites it to dinner. The invitation is taken up by an enormous figure who proves to be Leonzio's grandfather, sent by God to punish the young man, who splits his skull and takes him to Hell. While this plot lacks some of the essential ingredients of the Don Juan play, in particular the return-invitation motif, it clearly reflects important elements of a legend widely known throughout Europe and in which the most probable source for *The Trickster* is to be found.

This legend, part of ancient European folklore and frequently found in ballad form, describes a young man who is in many versions on his way to church and comes across a skull or a skeleton which he kicks or insults and mockingly invites to dinner. The dead man, in the form of a ghost, skull, skeleton or even statue, appears and invites the young man to eat with him, on which occasion he is either punished by death or escapes because he is protected by a holy relic.

As far as the Hispanic versions of the tale are concerned, all but one contain the return-invitation motif and most suggest that the young man is on his way to church not to hear Mass but to look at the girls. Clearly, these elements are both prominent in *The Trickster*, the second in the character of Don Juan himself, the former leading to the play's climactic scene in the church. Of particular interest here is the work done many years ago by Marcelino Menéndez Pelayo and Ramón Menéndez Pidal in relation to popular ballads in the provinces of Burgos, León and Segovia. A ballad discovered in León in the village of Cureña contains the following elements: a young man goes to church to look at the girls; he sees a skull at the roadside, kicks it and invites it to supper; the skull arrives in time for the meal and invites the young man to eat with him in the churchyard; the young man accepts the invitation and, protected by a religious relic he is wearing, escapes with a warning. A second ballad which Menéndez Pidal says was recited to him in 1905 in Riaza in the province of Segovia, is even more interesting in relation to *The Trickster* and for this reason is given here in my own translation:[13]

> There was a young man, the story says,
> Who went to church to say his prayers.
> Once there he knelt, his prayer began,
> Close to the figure of a stone man.
> The youngster pulled the statue's beard,
> And said to him, as though he heard:
> 'You're a respectable old sod!
> Who would have thought that this young bod
> Would one day have the nerve to dare
> To tug the thin and scrawny hair
> Of your chin? Why don't you tonight
> Turn up at my place for a bite
> To eat? I know you won't agree.
> Your belly's not exactly pretty.
> On the contrary, it's long and thin.
> I doubt that you'll eat anything.'
> At that the young man took his leave;

How could he, after all, conceive
What the consequences might be
Of that outrageous affrontery?
And so it was around nightfall
The dead man came to pay his call.
The servants said: 'Who's at the door?'
Came the reply: 'Only a poor
Lost soul who's looking for a meal.
Go quick, ask your master if he'll
Accommodate the man he's asked
To come to share his evening repast.'
The servants hurried with this news.
It left the master all confused.
Within his bones he felt a chill;
With sudden fear his heart stood still.
But, even so, the master said:
'Invite him in, although he's dead.'
The servants went and lit two flares
So the stone man could climb the stairs.
They placed a chair in front of him
That, if he wished, he could sit in.
'Eat all you want', the young man said.
'The food's ready. Get yourself fed!'
'Thank you', the corpse replied. 'I'm fine.
I've only come to see you dine.
But I'd like to know if you'll agree
To share another meal with me
In the churchyard, tomorrow night'.
The young man rose when it was light,
Got quickly dressed, left his abode,
To San Francisco's church he rode
And there called for a man of God,
Confessing his sins as best he could.
The priest, granting him confession,
Gave him a cross for his protection.
So the youngster, when darkness came,
Made his way to the church again.
There he beheld a pick and spade,
And an open grave freshly made.
Nine o'clock and everything silent,
The dead man kept his grim appointment.
'Now, my fine fellow, come and eat.
For you I've prepared a real treat:
Scorpions and vipers for our dinner,
Accompanied by gall and vintage vinegar.'

The young man viewed this grisly sight,
And suddenly lost his appetite.
'You can be glad', the dead man said,
'You've just partaken of holy bread.
Otherwise I'd force you to join in,
Make you account for a life of sin.
Always remember what I've said.
Don't make fun of those that are dead.
Instead, pray that their souls find rest,
Or you'll become my permanent guest.
Take heed out there, all you sinners,
Unless you wish to come to dinner.'

While there are great similarities between both the León and the
Riaza ballads, the latter not only has a stone figure but
emphasizes the hostile relationship between him and the young
man. The date of the ballads cannot be ascertained with any
certainty, but it seems quite likely that they preceded Tirso's
play and that he knew them. As a source for *The Trickster*,
they appear to be a very likely possibility, though they cannot,
given their brevity, flesh-out the characters. It was left to
Tirso to create the character of Don Juan, and in doing that he
had many models in contemporary Spanish drama. The measure
of his success may be gauged by the extent to which Tirso's
protagonist, the first-ever Don Juan, inspired so many later
writers and musicians to produce their variations on the
original.

V. ANALYSIS OF THE PLAY
Themes
        Like its Elizabethan counterpart, the drama of the Golden
Age is both entertaining and instructive: a case, as has been
pointed out, of *deleitar aprovechando*. Its moral emphasis and
thus the importance of theme has been greatly emphasized and
probably over-stated by A.A. Parker in numerous studies over
the last forty years, but it would, of course, have been
inconceivable that the theatre of a country as fervently Catholic
as seventeenth-century Spain should not have placed due
emphasis on moral issues.[14] In this respect the action of *The
Trickster* revolves around a cluster of themes.
        The principal theme of *The Trickster* is undoubtedly the
theme of justice, embodied in the words of the statue as it
destroys Don Juan:

> His fate provides the lesson
> You should heed, for each man reaps the harvest
> Of his deeds.   (Act III, 973-75)

Whether or not Don Juan is damned is not specifically stated, but his punishment, extremely painful and without confession, is certainly a case of divine retribution for an offence which, over and above all others, is an offence against God. This consists essentially of an assumption by Don Juan that the mercy of God will be available to him, as it were, on demand, and that there is therefore no need to ask for it until the very last moment: the source of his oft-repeated 'Plenty of time for me to pay that debt!' The dangers of last-minute repentance and of taking too much for granted were, indeed, frequently emphasized by theologians and moralists in sixteenth and seventeenth-century Spain and would certainly not have been lost on a contemporary audience.

While the offence against God is Don Juan's most serious crime, divine retribution may be seen as a kind of blanket-punishment covering a range of other misdemeanours, most of them social.[15] The seductions perpetrated on Isabela, Tisbea, Aminta and other women in the past involve deception on Don Juan's part, and, as often as not, a violation of the accepted laws of hospitality and friendship, as well as honour. Thus, Tisbea and the fishermen care for and entertain Don Juan and are cruelly taken advantage of, as are Aminta and Batricio later in the play. Similarly, Don Juan uses his friendship with Mota to further his designs on Ana and violates the trust she places in him to seek entry to her house. And having done so, and murdered her father to facilitate his own escape, he has no scruples about allowing Mota to take the blame for his misdeeds. The deliberate flaunting of accepted standards of behaviour is not, though, something practised by Don Juan alone. Isabela and Ana indulge in secret and illicit affairs, scorning conventional moral attitudes and, in Ana's case, deceiving a trusting father. Don Pedro Tenorio is guilty, in protecting his wayward nephew, of disloyalty to the King of Naples, while the King himself prefers to shut his eyes to much that is going on around him. And at the other end of the social scale, Aminta's father, Gaseno, is quite prepared to forget his obligations to his proposed son-in-law, Batricio, if there is the chance of her marrying a nobleman.

Amongst the play's social themes, honour is especially important.[16] As a nobleman or *caballero*, Don Juan possesses the honour conferred on him by noble birth, as indeed do many of the other characters in the play. Yet his and their behaviour are often the opposite of what we would regard as honourable in the moral sense and point to the distinction between honour as reputation, social standing and public image, and honour as virtue, a theme much explored by Golden-Age dramatists. The two men in the play who are honourable in both senses of the word are Don Diego Tenorio, Don Juan's father, and Don Gonzalo de Ulloa. Other characters like Duke Octavio and Doña Ana fall below that standard, for their respective involvement in secret love affairs is immoral and a danger to their own and their families' good name. As for Don Juan, his 'honourable' status as a nobleman is denied by practically everything he does, from his failure to keep his promises to his defiance of the King's commands. Even the apparently honourable gesture of keeping his promise to the statue has to be weighed against Don Juan's self-interested desire of not wishing to be regarded as a coward. In short, Tirso's presentation of the theme of honour as it is embodied in Don Juan and most of the play's other characters serves to pinpoint the degree to which honour, in its true moral sense, has been devalued by a society bent on largely material pleasures, be it the pursuit of sex, status or money.

The latter is, of course, at the heart of two of the play's themes: the pursuit of pleasure and the passage of time. The traditional theme of 'enjoy life while you can', so typical of Renaissance attitudes, is embodied above all in Don Juan's breathless sexual journey through the play, but that philosophy, as the quotation indicates, is circumscribed by the inescapable fact of time running out, eloquently voiced by Catalinón in the phrase: 'Live now and pay later!' (Act II, 314). The theme of life's brevity and of the sands of time running through one's fingers is, indeed, all-pervasive in Spanish literature of the seventeenth century, the Baroque's disillusioned response to a Renaissance exuberance long disappeared as much as the austere reminder of a fervently Catholic Spain to those who would put too much faith in the fleeting pleasures of the physical and temporal world. To that extent *The Trickster*, far from being a jaunty catalogue of sexual adventures, voices the much more sombre thoughts of an age that was fully conscious of the proximity of life and death.

Characterization
Much has been written by many critics over many years about Don Juan, and a good deal about Tirso's Don Juan.[17] What we, the audience, know about him, however, is no more or less than the dramatist chooses to place before us in terms

of action and word in the space of the two hours or more that the performance of the play requires. What, then, can we say about Don Juan Tenorio as the result of that observation? What, indeed, can we say about the other characters in the play?

Don Juan

The first thing to be said is that, whatever subsequent ages have made of him, Don Juan is not a great lover. Rather, the key to his character lies in the play's title, *The Trickster of Seville*, and it is the trick, the *burla*, the deception as much as the physical enjoyment of women which fascinates him. Thus it is not only the irresistible beauty of a woman that attracts him to her or the sensual pleasure of the encounter that lingers with him afterwards – on the contrary, it is the challenge to ingenuity and the winning of the victory that provide the stimulation and the sense of triumph. To that extent Don Juan, like his friend the Marquis of Mota, is a typical, dissolute, irresponsible Sevillian nobleman who delights in fooling and deceiving women. But he enjoys too mocking and getting the better of people in general. The attempted deception of Doña Ana is, for example, tied up with the deception of Mota to whom Don Juan delivers a false version of her message. After the seduction of Isabela in Act I, he leaves his uncle, Don Pedro, with the impression that he will lie low in Milan or Sicily but confides in the audience that he will head for Spain. Banished from Seville by the King, Don Juan defiantly returns. And seeing the statue of Don Gonzalo de Ulloa in the church, he mocks it by tugging at its beard and inviting it to dinner. In short, nothing is sacred or inspires reverence in Don Juan. He is the personification of that youthful arrogance and flippancy often to be found in the aristocracy.

If, on the other hand, Don Juan were nothing more than this, he would scarcely impress himself so firmly upon our imagination or have become a source of inspiration to other writers and musicians. The truth is, clearly, that there are in *The Trickster* clues to Don Juan's character and meaning that go deeper than that superficial, stock gallant mentioned above. The first occurs, surely, when in the opening scene, in reply to Isabela's inquiry about his identity, he describes himself as 'a man who's nameless' (Act I, 15). Though flippant, the remark invests this stanger in a woman's room at night with a sense of mystery and power that is increasingly in evidence as the action unfolds. In Act III, entering Aminta's bedroom at night, Don Juan observes: 'The hours of darkness are my special hours' (208). Earlier in the play Don Pedro Tenorio describes Don Juan's escape from the palace of the King of Naples in terms which invest him with daemonic significance: 'But I am quite convinced the very devil/Had in that person taken human form' (300-01). Cradled in Tisbea's lap, he makes an almost miraculous recovery for a man who has just been dragged from the sea, and the persistent allusions to fire, though part and parcel of the conventional language of love, have the effect – both here and elsewhere – of transforming him into an elemental force, an impression heightened constantly by the dynamism of his movement through the play, the darkness which frequently surrounds him, the devastation that he so often leaves in his wake, the galloping horses that bear him away, and the sheer energy and magnetism that seem to distinguish him from ordinary mortals. It is, though, Don Juan's final confrontation with the statue, the challenge flung out to those forces and powers beyond human understanding, that transform Don Juan from a merely flippant rebel against social norms into a much more heroic embodiment of the human spirit ranged against insurmountable odds. If it can be argued that Don Juan's refusal to be cowed by the statue stems from arrogance and self-esteem, and is therefore to be viewed negatively, it cannot be denied that the spectacle of such defiance in the face of dangers whose magnitude are not lost on him – Tirso very effectively suggests Don Juan's contained terror – is inspiring. Although crimes are punished and the moral lesson is set before us, Tirso seems in the closing scenes of his play to have created a figure with whose heroic stand he is, despite himself, in sympathy. In this original Don Juan Tenorio the seeds of later, more romantic and heroic versions have already been sown.

Isabela and Ana

Of the two noblewomen we only in fact see Isabela, for Ana never appears on stage. What both women have in common is their indulgence in secret love-affairs and their evident willingness on that account to run the risk of dishonour in relation both to themselves and their families.[18] As far as Isabela is concerned, there is little evidence in the play of any real love for Duke Octavio. After her seduction by Don Juan, she is much more concerned that Octavio will marry her and thus save her reputation. Later, the arranged marriage to Don Juan is less important to her than continuing gossip about her conduct, and when she finally marries Octavio there is nothing to indicate any enthusiasm. As for Ana, her letter to Mota stems from the King's decision to marry her to Octavio and points to a genuine desperation on her part, even though Mota is presented to us as a less than desirable catch. She is, perhaps, somewhat less calculating than Isabela, but on the other hand is not averse to deceiving her father. Neither woman is shown to be particularly virtuous, for all their beauty and social standing.

Tisbea and Aminta

Tisbea is by far the most interesting and intriguing female character in the play. In one sense she is a traditional literary type modelled on the disdainful shepherdesses of sixteenth-century pastoral novels: beautiful but aloof from her many male admirers. On the other hand, it is the sense of Tisbea's individuality, of the contradictions in her character, and of the powerful passions which boil beneath the cool and beautiful exterior which are the source of her real fascination for us. Her delight in the sufferings of her suitors stems not from her indifference to passion but from her belief in her own control of the situation.[19] It is this which is tested by Don Juan's arrival and which, after a teasing but dangerous game with him, begins to crumble. Having held the upper hand over the local fishermen, Tisbea discovers that, inasmuch as she finds Don Juan difficult to resist, he has the upper hand over her. Abandoned by him, her outrage, which is far more desperate than that of her disappointed suitors, seems directed as much at herself, conscious as she is of her own part in her downfall, as against Don Juan's treachery. Greater self-knowledge has been obtained only at great expense, leaving Tisbea with the proof that men are not to be trusted but also with the more disturbing question, previously not really asked of her, of the extent to which, in given circumstances, she can trust herself.

In comparison, Aminta is far less complex, a naïve country girl who is flattered and overwhelmed by the attentions of a courtier. In general she is also intrinsically more honest and virtuous than the other women in the play. She is annoyed by the fact that the arrival of Don Juan upsets Batricio; she protests when he enters her bedroom at night; although flattered by his attentions, her good sense tells her not to trust him; and she accepts his offer of marriage only when he leads her to believe that Batricio has abandoned her. She clearly does not merit the fate which Isabela, Ana and Tisbea bring upon themselves largely as the consequence of their misdemeanours. That she suffers is a comment less upon herself than upon the malice and self-interest of other people.

Octavio and Mota

Of the two noblemen Octavio is by far the better morally, though he is certainly not without fault. His secret affair with Isabela is less than admirable, though he is genuinely distraught by the news of her misdemeanours in the palace. On the other hand, he does not seem to mind the proposed marriage to Ana and, when that does not materialize, accepts Isabela without any obvious enthusiam. In general Octavio seems to be presented as a conventional *caballero*, conscious of his honour and social standing and set-up by Tirso to be mocked and poked fun at on that account.

Mota is another Don Juan but on an altogether different level. He is given to the same *burlas* or deceptions but without the same success. Don Juan's cheeky disregard for social convention and given individuals becomes in Mota a disagreeable callousness, the deception of sophisticated noblewomen and the cheating of ignorant whores. No doubt Mota regards himself as a sharp man-about-town but is easily duped by Don Juan himself and even obliged to suffer the consequences, albeit temporarily, of the latter's murder of Don Gonzalo. There is almost nothing to be said in favour of this idle, immoral, boastful and callous rake. The only possible explanation of Ana's interest in him is that she is unaware of his true character, and it does seem most unlikely that marriage to her will change him in any fundamental way.

Batricio and Gaseno

Although a shepherd, Batricio's concept of his own honour is that of a nobleman, a fact which allows Tirso to present this rustic in a comic manner. His willingness to yield Aminta to Don Juan to safeguard his *own* honour thus removes the sympathy we might otherwise feel for this unfortunate lover and renders his manipulation by Don Juan, comic. He completely lacks the resolution of peasants in other Golden-Age plays for whom their honour is, as much as reputation and name, their own integrity.

Gaseno, Aminta's father, is a social climber, less interested in his daughter's happiness than in the enticing possibility that her marriage to Don Juan will make her a lady and enhance his own standing. His pretentiousness is equalled only by his foolishness, and his protests at the outcome of events, though morally justified in themselves, are on his lips incongruous and comic.

Don Pedro and Don Diego Tenorio

Don Pedro, who is Don Diego's brother and Don Juan's uncle, is in a sense Don Juan thirty or more years on. As a young man he must have been very like his nephew in matters of seduction, and in questions of expediency shows now the same duplicity which in earlier years must have characterized his amorous exploits. The amorous *burla* of earlier years simply becomes Don Pedro's *burla* of the King of Naples and then of Octavio, both of them conducted with the kind of *panache* revealed by Don Juan himself in his various seductions. The parallel between uncle and nephew is further reinforced in the sense that both deceive others only to be deceived themselves: Don Pedro is himself fooled by Don Juan, despite the latter's promises, and Don Juan, as we have seen, is finally and fatally deceived by the stone guest. If Don Juan is the irresponsible, devil-may-care young courtier of his day, Don Pedro is the typical courtier-politician for whom duplicity passes for diplomacy.

Don Diego could not be more different. Like his brother, he occupies an important and influential position at Court, in this case the Spanish Court, but unlike Don Pedro he is never guilty of deceiving the King. Whenever Don Diego seeks to protect Don Juan, he does so out of concern for family honour, frequently upbraids his son for his scandalous behaviour, and, having failed to convince him of the error of his ways, commends his punishment to God. His failure to control Don Juan points, perhaps, to an earlier over-indulgence of the young man for which Don Diego, to judge by the severity of his warnings, now feels responsibility.

Don Gonzalo de Ulloa

Before his death at Don Juan's hands, Don Gonzalo strikes us as an extremely conventional figure. He is certainly rather stiff – even if the long Lisbon speech found its way into the play for reasons other than characterization –, highly deferential to the King, conventionally obsessive in relation to his honour, yet apparently ignorant of his daughter's secret meetings with Mota. His death is, of course, unjustified, though it is in part due to his lack of self-control, and prompts a certain sympathy, but on the whole Tirso portrays him, as he does so many of the characters, ironically.

The King of Naples

He appears only in Act I in relation to the indiscretions of Isabela and is presented by Tirso as a ruler who, above all, is anxious to protect his good name. In order to achieve that he prefers to have others – in this instance Don Pedro Tenorio – hush up possible scandals, but in placing his trust in such people he shows himself to be less than circumspect. In the King of Naples Tirso is clearly criticising the power invested in royal favourites by seventeenth-century Spanish monarchs.

Alfonso XI of Castile

Throughout the play King Alfonso is shown to be attempting to patch up the havoc created by Don Juan and to be in that respect a patcher and a botcher – in short, far removed from the idealized monarchs of many Golden-Age plays. No sooner has he arranged the marriage of Ana to Don Juan than news of the Isabela affair forces him to change his plan, while he appeases Octavio with the offer of Ana's hand in marriage. Subsequently, Mota is wrongly arrested on his orders and, when released, is allowed to marry Ana at her request. The King's bewilderment is exemplified by the play's final scene when he is bombarded by complainants. He is rescued, moreover, not by any decisive action on his part but by news of Don Juan's death at the hands of the statue. If in the course of the play Tirso presents a nobility which is self-seeking and corrupt, he also portrays a monarch who is less than ideal.

Catalinón

Catalinón is a particularly good example of the *gracioso*, the comic character of Golden-Age drama. In *The Trickster* the fact that he is the servant of a man as reckless and as scornful of all social and even divine constraints as Don Juan serves to highlight the traditional self-interest of the *gracioso* – particularly his concern for saving his own skin. The calamitous situations in which Catalinón finds himself in this play are more extreme than those confronting most *graciosos* and thus allow for highly amusing scenes, notably in the confrontations with the stone guest. In addition, though far from being a moral man himself, the *gracioso* was often used by Golden Age dramatists to express moral sentiments, usually in relation to his master's imprudent behaviour. In some respects, indeed, Catalinón's moral outrage at Don Juan's behaviour, particularly in regard to less fortunate girls like Aminta, seems to be perfectly genuine. This, combined with moments of weakness in which self-interest silences him, makes Catalinón an interesting and credible character, and he is certainly one of the most colourful of Golden Age *graciosos*.

Language

In the *Arte nuevo de hacer comedias* Lope de Vega had recommended that the dramatist's aim should be to imitate Nature, but at the same time made his characters speak in verse. On the other hand, he argued that the language of the play should never be so obscure as to make comprehension impossible and in practice aimed to create a dramatic style which, despite its imagery and sometimes ornate poetic elaboration, was clear, direct and capable of carrying the action swiftly forward. As one of Lope's principal supporters, Tirso largely followed his example in matters of language, and *The Trickster* is indeed distinguished by its racy, cut-and-thrust dialogue. In general too, in accordance with Lope de Vega's recommendations, language matches the social status of the characters, the earthiness of Catalinón contrasting, for example, with the more refined utterances of the noblemen. The principal exception to this rule is Tisbea, a fishergirl who indulges in poetic conceits more appropriate to a lady of the Court, yet the apparent incongurity is easily explained by Tisbea's belief in her own superiority.

In any Golden-Age play imagery is, much more than a purely decorative element, a pointer to the play's themes and is, more often than not, used systematically.[20] This is particularly true of *The Trickster*, for while there is nothing very original or subtle about its imagery, it does in fact underpin the play's dominant themes. In this respect the allusions to fire are important. On the one hand the image of fire evokes passion, be it Tisbea's or Don Juan's, but it may refer just as much to ardour as to destructive force. In addition, fire, as in the chapel scene, points to hell and damnation, or, by means of allusions to Troy in flames, links present to past treachery, thereby universalizing the particular situations of the play. Similarly, daemonic imagery occurs on a number of occasions and in a variety of ways, but always in association with Don Juan. His uncle describes him as 'the very devil' (I, 300) and Batricio believes that 'the devil sent him straight to us' (II, 677). The association is deepened by Don Juan's frequent allusions to darkness, while Catalinón's descriptions of him as 'the scourge of women' (I, 895) and 'a locust to all women!' (I, 436) add to our impression of Don Juan as a destructive and evil force.

The allusive nature of the play's imagery, repeatedly transforming the particular into the universal, may be illustrated too in relation to Tisbea, notably her allusion to the peacock's tail. Using this image to describe the beauty of the ship's sails (I, 487-93) destroyed by the assault of the waves, she fails to grasp, as we do not, the relevance to herself of this traditional embodiment of beauty and pride. The effect of the image, especially for an age accustomed to emblems, would have been - and still is for the most part - to underline Tisbea's shortsighted arrogance and simultaneously to place it in the context of the folly of pride in general, as though she were the example or text around which the ensuing sermon, the play itself, is constructed.

The same effect is achieved by means of the metaphor of payment which in one form or another threads its way through the play's dialogue. Thus Don Juan is warned repeatedly of the debt that he will finally have to pay. He repays Tisbea's kindness by deceiving her. Ana pays dearly for the deception of her father, while Mota acknowledges that he will be obliged to pay for a trick gone wrong. Don Diego's warning to his erring son refers to the payment that God will ultimately demand, and the idea of the reward linked to the actions of the individual is summed up in the statue's concluding words:

> His fate provides the lesson
> You should heed, for each man reaps the harvest
> Of his deeds.   (III, 973-4)

Clearly, much of the imagery has a strong didactic purpose and must be related to the moral purpose of the play as a whole. In this context the allusive, universalizing nature of many of the images makes sense too, for their effect is to transform individual episodes and characters into general examples that have a relevance to all of us.

Staging

Many of the points made earlier in relation to the Golden Age stage can be illustrated by reference to *The Trickster*.[21] A reading of the play reveals very clearly the continuous flow of the action and its movement through both time and space: from day to night, Italy to Spain, court to seashore to countryside. The dialogue itself is used by the dramatist, given the lack of scenery and the fact that the performance would have taken place in daylight, to inform the audience of the location and time of a given episode: the opening scene in the palace at night; Tisbea on the sea-shore by day; Don Juan and Mota in the streets of Seville at night; Aminta and Batricio in the countryside by day. The uninterrupted flow of the action and the frequent entrances and exits of different characters also allow us to see the importance of the two doors situated at either side of the back-stage. Thus at the beginning of Act I

Don Juan makes his exit from the palace. Not long afterwards, when Don Pedro Tenorio arrives to arrest Octavio, he enters by one of the doors. And in Act III both doors are used in a particularly striking way when Don Juan and Catalinón leave the stage, their exit suggesting their entrance into the church, only to emerge through the other door, the stage itself now becoming the interior of the church. It is a moment which suggests very vividly the great flexibility of the Golden-Age stage and its demands upon the imagination of the audience.

The so-called 'discovery space', a curtained area of the back-stage, is used on several occasions. Thus, when in Act III Don Juan enters Aminta's bedroom, it seems likely that this inner stage would be used. Again it would clearly be the place for Don Gonzalo's tomb in the church. In the same act the trap-door in the stage would have allowed the statue to drag Don Juan down to the lower regions, to the accompaniment of much noise and, probably, thunderflashes. In contrast, there seems to be no occasion in the play when the upper levels – the gallery and the balconies – would have been used, for there is no reference to mountains or to Heaven, and when in Act I Don Juan makes his escape by means of 'this high balcony' (106), he merely exits through one of the doors, for the action is taking place on the stage itself.

As far as costumes are concerned, they would have been seventeenth-century, despite the fact that the action is set in medieval times. Of particular interest in this respect, of course, is the way in which the statue would have been presented. It is more than likely played by an actor, dressed either to suggest the polychrome statues of the period or simply in grey cloak and gloves with his face masked. Another possibility is that the actor would have worn armour. And yet another, though less likely, is that the statue would have been represented by some kind of automaton, which the better-off companies of Tirso's time would have been able to afford and which was also within the capability of current technology.[22] At all events, we can well imagine how a seventeenth-century audience would have been transfixed by the appearance of a figure from the afterlife.

Don Juan after Tirso

Don Juan is, with Hamlet, Faust and Don Quixote, one of the great figures of world literature, yet few people on hearing his name would think of Tirso's Don Juan. In part this is due to a lack of familiarity with the literature and culture of Spain in comparison to, say, a much closer acquaintance with

Mozart's opera *Don Giovanni*, but it is explained too by the fact that in the popular imagination Don Juan has come to signify much more than the character created by one man or, indeed, a group of writers taken together and extending from Tirso to Bernard Shaw. Clearly, Don Juan is the expression of something deeply embedded in human nature, be it sexual desire or the pursuit of ideal beauty, and Tirso, in creating the first Don Juan, caught something of that. The writers and composers who followed Tirso also did so in varying degrees, adapting the Don Juan figure in the light of their own or their age's particular preoccupations.[23]

Molière's *Dom Juan ou le Festin de Pierre* was written only some thirty-five years after Tirso's play, was not based directly on it, and is very different from it, above all in its presentation of Don Juan as a thinking, sophisticated, self-justifying seducer rather than as a man of action. Molière has embodied in his protagonist the libertine and religious sceptic of his age, the self-absorbed sensualist intent on justifying and continuing his way of life at all costs. He thus transformed the Don Juan character into a figure who is much more intellectual and psychologically interesting, but who at the same time lacks the drive and passion of Tirso's hero and who, since he does not believe in the supernatural forces which confront him in the form of the statue, does not suggest the same kind of reckless and heroic challenge.

Mozart's *Don Giovanni*, first performed in 1787, brings together different elements from earlier versions of the story, for Da Ponte's libretto is an extremely effective synthesis of *The Trickster* and *Dom Juan* in particular. For this reason Don Giovanni retains the passion and vitality of Tirso's character as well as the wit and sophistication of Molière's Dom Juan. Nevertheless, Mozart's protagonist is still very much the cynical realist concerned solely with his own pleasure and in that sense is closer to Molière. The eighteenth century in general was less concerned with the religious aspects of Don Juan's pursuit of pleasure than with the pursuit of pleasure itself.

In the nineteenth century, in accordance with the preoccupations of Romanticism, the Don Juan story took a different turn. Hoffman's short story, *Don Juan*, presents the character as someone in search of the ideal woman and who, in his disappointment, wreaks his vengeance on man and God. He is also shown to be irresistible as far as women are concerned. This new conception of Don Juan, personifying romantic attitudes, influenced Hoffman's successors greatly, amongst them Alfred de Mussett, Hans Bethge, Nikolaus Lenau and

Alexander Pushkin. In Spain itself José Zorrilla's *Don Juan Tenorio*, first performed in 1844, portrays its hero as a ruthless seducer in pursuit of personal pleasure and therefore returns in a sense to Tirso's Don Juan. On the other hand, the Romantic element is to be seen in the fact that Don Juan Tenorio is a religious sceptic and is saved finally by the love of a pure woman. In short, Zorilla achieved an effective synthesis of the old and the new.

A reaction against the nineteenth-century Don Juan described above is to be found in the nineteenth century itself in the criticisms of such writers as Stendhal and Georges Sand who objected, for example, to Don Juan's devaluation of love and to his victimization of women. Despite such attacks, he continued to fascinate and draw different responses from different writers, and in the twentieth century has engaged the attention of creative writers as diverse as George Bernard Shaw, Albert Camus, Jean Anouilh and Henri de Montherlant. Shaw, whose *Man and Superman* belongs to the very beginning of the century, predictably uses the figure of Don Juan as a mouthpiece to voice his own ideas. The play deals with the idea of the Life Force and the roles of Man and Woman in relation to it, but in the course of the play Shaw reveals that Man is in fact used by Woman as an instrument to achieve her function of procreation, and Don Juan, far from being the pursuer, is the pursued. It is an interpretation which virtually closes the door on any further variation of the Don Juan myth. For Camus, whose collection of essays, *Le Mythe de Sisyphe*, published in 1942, contains a study of Don Juan, he is no mystic in search of pure love but a man who is constantly aware of the absurdity of human existence in the face of death and who therefore resolves to enjoy the life he has in the way he considers best: the enjoyment of women. In this respect the protagonist of Anouilh's *Ornifle ou le Courant d'air*, performed in 1955, is very similar, though the character is certainly small-scale. De Montherlant's *Don Juan*, written three years later, has a protagonist who is sixty-six years old, a man who is therefore facing death, who is conscious of the desperate need to squeeze every drop of pleasure out of life and who is, in more ways than one, a return to Tirso's obsessive seducer. Clearly, in the twentieth century, in accordance with its complex character, the Don Juan theme has undergone and is still likely to undergo varied and diverse treatments.

VI THE TRANSLATION

In terms of metre and rhyme Golden-Age drama reveals certain marked differences from its Elizabethan counterpart. The *comedia* was not in fact tied to a single metre, and lines in a given play may be found to consist of seven, eight or eleven syllables. It is, however, the eight-syllable line which was by far the favourite of Golden-Age dramatists, and for a very good reason: it allows the dialogue to move swiftly and enabled the dramatists to create that sense of pace and movement in the play which, as we have seen, Lope de Vega felt essential if the interest of a Spanish audience was to be maintained.

As far as rhyme is concerned, Golden-Age drama is distinguished by its variety of rhyming stanza forms: eight-line *octavas*, ten-line *décimas*, five-line *quintillas*, four-line *redondillas*, three-line *tercetos*, all using the octosyllabic line. The most common and important form of all was, however, the *romance*, characterized not by full rhyme but by assonance: see, as a typical example, II. 375-516 of Act I of *The Trickster* in which alternate lines have the characteristic *romance* pattern of repeated stressed and unstressed vowels – ro̲sa̲, o̲la̲s, so̲la̲, etc. The line is again octosyllabic. In short, Golden-Age drama has a shorter line and a much greater degree of rhyme than Elizabethan drama with its normally unrhymed iambic pentameter.

In undertaking translations into English of Golden-Age plays, different translators have chosen different approaches. As far as *The Trickster* is concerned, Roy Campbell's translation of 1959 is for the most part in iambic pentameter and employs a considerable amount of rhyme.[24] The experience of those directors I have consulted is that Campbell's translation is unreadable and unactable. The explanation for this seems to me to have nothing to do with the fact that Campbell's chosen metre was iambic pentameter but much to do with his decision to use rhyme. Firstly, rhymes in English are often very difficult to find. Secondly, and more importantly, the need to use them, once the decision has been taken, imposes severe restrictions on the translator, in particular the inescapable demand to twist the syntax into a shape which allows the rhyming word to fall into the right place. Rhyme becomes thus a self-imposed straight jacket and the lines themselves acquire the kind of inversions and cumbersome 'poetic' effects which literally sinks the translation in terms of its actability. Campbell's choice of individual words and phrases which he must have considered literary and poetic but which in reality give his translation a cumbersome and old-fashioned feel is a further drawback. The following example from Act I illustrates very well the points made above:

Don Pedro   The king sent me.
Octavio   Well if the king's kind thought
Bend to me thus, I reck my life as naught
To serve my liege, and would not count the cost
If in the cause of honour it were lost.
Tell me, my lord, what planet of good cheer,
What stroke of goodly fortune, brought you here
To say I am remembered by the King? (pp.241-2)

A prose translation does, of course, avoid the problems inherent in metre and rhyme, as may be seen in Robert O'Brien's version, published three years after Campbell's.[25] Above all, prose immediately eliminates the awkward inversions often imposed by rhyme and therefore allows for a word-order which is straightforward, natural and speakable. On the other hand, a prose version lacks the pulse and the discipline of metre, two of the essential ingredients of Golden-Age and Elizabethan theatre, the framework within which, as in a piece of classical music, emotion is contained and a constant tension between content and form established. Prose dissipates all this. And it dissipates too the pleasure to be derived from listening to verse.

Although he has not translated or adapted any of Tirso's plays, Adrian Mitchell has in recent years produced versions of Calderón's *El alcalde de Zalamea, La vida es sueño* and *El gran teatro del mundo*. Working from a literal English prose version of the Spanish text, he has set himself the extremely difficult task of retaining for the most part both Spanish metres and rhyme schemes, and it would be churlish to deny the vigour and the effectiveness on stage of his versions. The following example, from Act I of *El alcalde de Zalamea*, is in octosyllables and the four-line *redondilla* - a bb a:[26]

SERGEANT   You're a minority of one
CAPTAIN   I'm wrong?
SERGEANT   No sir, let's say that I'm
Sure there's no way of killing time
Better than - doing it for fun,
With no love guff. A patch of grass,
A bottle and a loaf or two
And a ripe peasant princess who
Can't tell her elbow from her arse. (pp.6-7)

A very different passage, in which Mitchell has in fact

abandoned the assonance of the Spanish *romance* for blank-verse, but in octosyllabic lines, reveals Isabel's strong emotions at the beginning of Act III:

> I was torn with anxieties.
> My mind full of a thousand fears,
> Each fear chained to another fear.
> I could not breathe, or see, or hear.
> I wandered. I fell down. I ran
> Without a guiding star or light,
> All through the forest till I fell
> And lie, exhausted at your feet. (p.76)

The difference in quality between Mitchell's and Campbell's lines is self-evident. It is, of course, to do with language — Mitchell's is simpler, more natural — but it is also very much to do with the fact that, when as in the first of the two examples he employs rhyme, the syntax is really that of prose.

In my own attempt to produce a version of *The Trickster*, I have been very conscious of the need to maintain the syntax of prose as far as possible, for it is this which makes the lines speakable, as in Tisbea's quite poetic description in Act I of a sinking ship:

> Stranded there, it's like some lovely peacock,
> The sails in imitation of the tail,
> Their beauty and dazzling brightness commanding
> The sailors' eyes, ravishing their sight.
> The movement of the waves plucks at its feathers;
> Its loveliness and pride begin to fade,
> And all its splendour's slowly stripped away.
> (II. 487-93)

The decision to opt for iambic pentameter was taken as the result of discussions with several theatre directors, all of whom felt that this is the metre in which British actors feel most at ease. There are, of course, disadvantages, the most important of which is the need to lengthen the original line by two or more syllables and thus introduce more words. To that extent the result is not a translation but a free adaptation, and the reader should always bear this in mind. Nevertheless, the experience of participating in a workshop at Theatre Clwyd, Mold, in the autumn of 1984 proved to me the effectiveness of this version on the stage and opened the eyes of those present to the qualities of Tirso's play, previously unknown to them. For that opportunity I wish to express my gratitude to the then associate director, Paul Chamberlain, and his actors.

NOTES TO THE INTRODUCTION

1. On the general background see N.D. Shergold, *A History of the Spanish Stage from Medieval Times until the End of the Seventeenth Century* (Oxford, 1967); H.A. Rennert, *The Spanish Stage in the Time of Lope de Vega* (New York, 1909; 2nd ed., 1963); Margaret Wilson, *Spanish Drama of the Golden Age* (Oxford and London, 1969); and E.M. Wilson and D. Moir, *The Golden Age: Drama 1492-1700. A Literary History of Spain*, Vol. 3. Ed. R.O. Jones (London, 1971).

2. For the development of the *comedia* the reader is recommended to the studies mentioned above, as well as to J.P. Wickersham Crawford, *Spanish Drama before Lope de Vega* (Philadelphia, 1922; 2nd revised ed., 1937; 3rd revised ed., 1967); H.J. Chaytor (ed.), *Dramatic Theory in Spain* (Cambridge, 1925); Duncan Moir, 'The Classical Tradition in Spanish Dramatic Theory and Practice in the Seventeenth Century', in *Classical Drama and its Influence*, ed. M.J. Anderson (London, 1965), 191-228; and R. Schevill, *The Dramatic Art of Lope de Vega together with 'La dama boba'* (Berkeley, 1918).

3. The most detailed study of the Golden-Age *corrales* is that by N.D. Shergold, *A History of the Spanish Stage*. See in particular chapters 7 and 14.

4. See Blanca de los Ríos, *Tirso de Molina. Obras dramáticas completas*, vol.I (Madrid 1946), lxxv.

5. For an account of Tirso's life and career see the relevant chapter in Margaret Wilson, *Spanish Drama of the Golden Age*, and, for a more detailed history, Blanca de los Ríos, *El enigma biográfico de Tirso de Molina* (Madrid, 1928).

6. Two of Tirso's best religious plays are to appear in this present series (Aris and Phillips *Hispanic Classics*): *Tamar's Revenge* (*La venganza de Tamar*) in a translation by John Lyon (1987) and *Damned for Despair* (*El condenado por desconfiado*) in a translation by Nicholas Round (1986). In his introduction to *Tamar's Revenge* John Lyon explains the theatrical background, and the main themes and characteristics of Tirso's drama, while Nicholas Round in *Damned for Despair* describes the religious and intellectual background to the period and provides a substantial bibliography to up-date the standard reference works by Williamson, Placer and Dorst.

7. See Margaret Wilson, *Spanish Drama of the Golden Age*.

8. On Tirso's contribution to Golden-Age drama in terms of

characterization and intellectual depth, see in particular I.L. McClelland, *Tirso de Molina. Studies in Dramatic Realism* (Liverpool, 1948).

9. Detailed comparisons of the two versions have been undertaken by Gerald E. Wade and Robert J. Mayberry, *'Tan largo me lo fiáis* and *El burlador de Sevilla y el convidado de piedra'*, *Bulletin of the Comediantes*, XIV, I (1962), 1–16; María Rosa Lida de Malkiel, 'Sobre la prioridad de *¿Tan largo me lo fiáis?* Notas al *Isidro* y a *El burlador de Sevilla'*, *Bulletin of Hispanic Studies*, XLII (1965), 18–33; and Albert E. Sloman, 'The Two Versions of *El burlador de Sevilla'*, *Bulletin of Hispanic Studies*, XLII (1965), 18–33. For the text of *Tan largo*, see *Tan largo me lo fiáis*, ed. Xavier A. Fernández (Madrid, 1967).

10. There is a detailed discussion of Claramonte's rôle by Gerald E. Wade, *El burlador de Sevilla y convidado de piedra* (New York, 1969), 6–11.

11. See, for example, the arguments put forward by H.A. Rennert, *The Spanish Stage in the Time of Lope de Vega*, and Joseph C. Fucilla, *'El convidado de piedra* in Naples in 1625', *Bulletin of the Comediantes*, X, I (1958), 5–6.

12. Many critics have discussed possible contemporary models. The different views and arguments are neatly and conveniently brought together by Gerald E. Wade, *El burlador de Sevilla y convidado de piedra*. See in particular pp.29–35.

13. For the background to the literary and folkloric origins of *The Trickster*, the reader is recommended to Dorothy McKay, *The Double Invitation in the Legend of Don Juan* (Stanford and London, 1943), Leo Weinstein, *The Metamorphoses of Don Juan* (Stanford, 1959), and R. Menédez Pidal, 'Sobre los orígenes de *El convidado de piedra'*, in *Estudios literarios*, 6th ed., (Buenos Aires, Colección Austral, 1946), pp. 89–113). For the ballads discussed and translated here, see the latter, pp. 95–109.

14. One of the most influential of A.A. Parker's studies has been *The Approach to the Spanish Drama of the Golden Age*, Diamante, VI (London 1957).

15. See, in particular, J.E. Varey, 'Social Criticism in *El burlador de Sevilla'*, *Theatre Research International*, 2(1977), 197–221.

16. On the question of honour see C.A. Jones, 'Honor in Spanish Golden-Age Drama: Its Relation to Real Life and to Morals', *Bulletin of Hispanic Studies*, XXXV (1958), 199–210, and P.N. Dunn, 'Honour and the Christian Background in Calderón', *Bulletin of Hispanic Studies*,

XXXVII (1960), 75-105, reprinted in *Critical Essays on the Theatre of Calderón*, ed. B.W. Wardropper (New York, 1965), 24-60.

17. The most detailed study of the play as a whole, and in particular its characters, is that by Daniel Rogers, *Tirso de Molina. El burlador de Sevilla. Critical Guides to Spanish Texts* (London, 1977). See too Gerald E. Wade, 'The Character of Don Juan of *El burlador de Sevilla*', in *Hispanic Studies in Honor of Nicholson B. Adams*, ed. J.E. Keller and K.-L. Selig. University of North Carolina Studies in the Romance Languages and Literatures, LIX (Chapel Hill, North Carolina, 1966), 167-78.

18. See in this respect A.A. Parker, 'Los amores y noviazgos clandestinos en el mundo dramático-social de Calderón', *Hacia Calderón: Segundo coloquio anglogermano* (Berlin, New York, 1970), 79-87.

19. On this point see Melveena McKendrick, *Woman and Society in the Spanish Drama of the Golden Age: a study of the 'mujer varonil'* (Cambridge, 1974), 158-9.

20. On the play's imagery, see C.B. Morris, 'Metaphor in *El burlador de Sevilla*', *Romanic Review*, LV (1964), 248-55, and D. Rogers, *Tirso de Molina, El burlador de Sevilla...*, 55-60.

21. See D. Rogers, *Tirso de Molina. El burlador de Sevilla...*, 21-25, and J.E. Varey, 'The Staging of Night Scenes in the "Comedia"', *The American Hispanist*, II, 15 (1977), 14-16.

22. See J.E. Varey, *Historia de los títeres en España (desde sus orígenes hasta mediados del siglo XVIII)* (Madrid, 1957), 24-90.

23. The most detailed study is that by Leo Weinstein, *The Metamorphoses of Don Juan* (Stanford, 1959).

24. Roy Campbell's version is to be found in *The Classic Theatre. VOLUME III: Six Spanish Plays* ed. Eric Bentley (New York, 1959).

25. Robert O'Brien's prose version, *The Rogue of Seville*, is published in *Spanish Drama*, ed. Angel Flores (New York, 1962).

26. *The Mayor of Zalamea or The Best Garrotting Ever Done*, adapted by Adrian Mitchell (Edinburgh, 1981).

THE TRICKSTER OF SEVILLE AND THE STONE GUEST

EL BURLADOR DE SEVILLA Y EL CONVIDADO DE PIEDRA

HABLAN EN ELLA LAS PERSONAS SIGUIENTES

DON DIEGO TENORIO, *viejo*
DON JUAN TENORIO, *su hijo*
CATALINÓN, *lacayo*
EL REY DE NÁPOLES
EL DUQUE OCTAVIO
DON PEDRO TENORIO
EL MARQUÉS DE LA MOTA
DON GONZALO DE ULLOA
EL REY DE CASTILLA
DOÑA ANA DE ULLOA

FABIO, *criado*
ISABELA, *duquesa*
TISBEA, *pescadora*
BELISA, *villana*
ANFRISO, *pescador*
CORIDÓN, *pescador*
GASENO, *labrador*
BATRICIO, *labrador*
RIPIO, *criado*
AMINTA, *villana*

The Spanish text reproduced here is based on the edition of Américo Castro, originally published in 1910 in the *Clásicos Castellanos* series. See 6th edition (Madrid, 1958). Where Castro has made amendments or suggested variations on the text, these have been included.

DRAMATIS PERSONAE

DON DIEGO TENORIO, *an old man*
DON JUAN TENORIO, *his son*
CATALINÓN, *a servant*
THE KING OF NAPLES
DUKE OCTAVIO
DON PEDRO TENORIO
THE MARQUIS DE LA MOTA
DON GONZALO DE ULLOA
THE KING OF CASTILE
DOÑA ANA DE ULLOA

FABIO, *a servant*
ISABELA, *a duchess*
TISBEA, *a fishergirl*
BELISA, *a peasant-girl*
ANFRISO, *a fisherman*
CORIDÓN, *a fisherman*
GASENO, *a peasant*
BATRICIO, *a peasant*
RIPIO, *a servant*
AMINTA, *a peasant-girl*

JORNADA PRIMERA

Salen Don Juan Tenorio y Isabela, duquesa

Isabela	Duque Octavio, por aquí
	podrás salir más seguro.
D. Juan	Duquesa, de nuevo os juro
	de cumplir el dulce sí.
Isabela	¿Mis glorias serán verdades, 5
	promesas y ofrecimientos,
	regalos y cumplimientos,
	voluntades y amistades?
D. Juan	Sí, mi bien.
Isabela	Quiero sacar
	una luz. 10
D. Juan	Pues ¿para qué?
Isabela	Para que el alma dé fe
	del bien que llego a gozar.
D. Juan	Mataréte la luz yo.
Isabela	¡Ah, cielo! ¿Quién eres, hombre?
D. Juan	¿Quién soy? Un hombre sin nombre. 15

---

1   <u>Octavio</u>: Isabela believes the man who has just made love to her to be Octavio, her lover. Neither she nor we suspect that he may not be Octavio until he objects to her bringing a light.

2   <u>unseen by anyone</u>: Isabela's wish that 'Octavio' should depart without being seen arises from the fact that she fears for her reputation. Her affair with Octavio is clearly conducted in secret, a situation generally disapproved of in seventeenth-century Spain on both moral and social grounds. Should Isabela's relationship with Octavio become common knowledge, her reputation in the eyes of others will inevitably be diminished, and should Octavio subsequently abandon her, her chances of finding a husband will be slight indeed. Clandestine affairs abound in the literature of Golden-Age Spain, partly because they provided writers with highly dramatic material, but they evidently had their counterpart in real life. Clandestine marriages had been recognized by the Roman Catholic Church until 1563 when the Council of Trent prohibited them. The secret affair between individuals who meet on the understanding of marriage continued to be a favourite subject with Spanish writers, including Cervantes, Tirso de Molina and Calderón de la Barca, long after the Council of Trent. Isabela's affair with Octavio has the added complication and danger of being conducted in the Royal Palace, thereby violating palace decorum. For a discussion of clandestine relationships see A.A. Parker, 'Los amores y noviazgos clandestinos en el mundo dramático-social de Calderón', *Hacia Calderón: segundo coloquio anglogermano* (Berlin, New York, 1970), 79-87.

4   <u>My vow of marriage</u>: Isabela's insistence on marriage points to the fact that her relationship with Octavio is not merely frivolous. On the other hand, she and Octavio are social equals and there seems to be no obstacle to their marriage, a circumstance which underlines the folly and imprudence of their secret meetings. See the reaction of Octavio's

ACT I

Enter Don Juan Tenorio and Isabela, a duchess

Isabela	Quickly, Octavio, follow me through here
	And you'll escape unseen by anyone.
D. Juan	Duchess, my faithful promise I renew.
	My vow of marriage I insist is true.
Isabela	If dreams could only be reality, 5
	And promises and love's sweet flattery,
	The gifts and offerings inspired by love,
	Were really signs of a heart that's firm and true!
D. Juan	Of course they are, my love.
Isabela	Then let me bring
	A light.
D. Juan	But why on earth do you need a light? 10
Isabela	So that my soul can in the sight of you
	Find confirmation of my happiness.
D. Juan	You bring a light, I swear I'll put it out!
Isabela	Heaven help me! Tell me truthfully! Who are you?
D. Juan	I'll tell you who I am: a man who's nameless. 15

---

servant, Ripio, Act I, 227–230.

10   A light: in the public theatres, the *corrales*, of seventeenth-century Spain, where *The Trickster* would have been performed, there was no artificial lighting and plays were therefore performed in the afternoon (see the section on staging in the Introduction). Invariably, the dramatist used the dialogue to locate the time and the place of the action. As a further aid to the suspension of disbelief, the costumes and the movements of the characters would also have been important. Here Isabela probably leads 'Octavio' by the hand to the door through which he is to make his escape, their movement across the stage suggesting the uncertainty and insecurity of people in a darkened room. On this particular aspect of Golden Age plays there is an interesting article by J.E. Varey, 'The Staging of Night Scenes in the "Comedia"', *The American Hispanist*, II, 15 (1977), 14–16.

14   Who are you?: while Isabela's failure to distinguish between her lover, Octavio, and a total stranger might seem puzzling, there are a variety of explanations: the thrill and the danger of a clandestine meeting sweep aside all reason; possibly, from the moment of Don Juan's entry and initial embrace, there is no further conversation between them; it is conceivable that Isabela knows the man to be a stranger but, like the other women in the play, finds him irresistible. Ambiguity of motive and intention is certainly a feature of Tirso's presentation of his characters and adds greatly to the fascination of the play.

15   a man who's nameless: much has been made of Don Juan's reply to Isabela in terms of its symbolic suggestion, i.e., Don Juan as the male sex-force. While this is true, it is also important to realize that he is here taunting Isabela, delighting in the trick he has played on her, joking at her expense, his flippancy contrasting delightfully with her confusion.

5

Isabela	¿Que no eres el duque?
D. Juan	No.
Isabela	¡Ah, de palacio!
D. Juan	Detente:

dame, duquesa, la mano.

| Isabela | No me detengas, villano. |

¡Ah, del rey! ¡Soldados, gente!   20

*Sale el Rey de Nápoles con una vela en un
candelero*

Rey	¿Qué es esto?
Isabela	*[Ap.]* ¡El rey! ¡Ay, triste!
Rey	¿Quién eres?
D. Juan	¿Quién ha de ser?

Un hombre y una mujer.

| Rey | *[Ap.]* Esto en prudencia consiste. |

¡Ah, de mi guarda! Prendé   25
a este hombre.

| Isabela | ¡Ay, perdido honor! |

*Vase Isabela. Salen Don Pedro Tenorio, embajador
de España, y Guarda*

| D. Ped. | ¡En tu cuarto, gran señor, |

voces! ¿Quién la causa fué?

| Rey | Don Pedro Tenorio, a vos |

esta prisión os encargo.   30
Siendo corto, andad vos largo;
mirad quién son estos dos.
Y con secreto ha de ser,

20+   The King of Naples: the action of the play occurs before 1350, a time at
      which only Sicily belonged to Spain. The King of Naples at this time
      was Roberto, who ruled from 1309 to 1343 (see Pedro Salazar de
      Mendoza, *Monarquía de España*, I (Madrid, 1770), 337). Spanish
      dramatists of the Golden Age were, however, notoriously indifferent to
      historical accuracy, as will be seen later. In general terms the spirit of
      Tirso's play is much more seventeenth than fourteenth century,
      especially in relation to the picture of social manners which Tirso gives
      us and the criticism which he makes of the characters' behaviour.

23   Do you need more proof?: an addition to the original.

24   prudence might be called for here: as has been pointed out, the lovers'
      rendezvous constitutes a violation of palace decorum and, were the
      matter to become public knowledge, a slur upon the personal honour of
      the King. His immediate concern is therefore for his reputation, which
      will best be protected by the prudent action of having the matter dealt
      with quickly and, above all, secretly.

Isabela	You mean you aren't the Duke?
D. Juan	Of course I'm not!
Isabela	Assist me, guards, at once! I beg of you!
D. Juan	Oh, don't play hard to get! Give me your hand!
Isabela	I order you to set me free at once!
	Guards! Soldiers! Courtiers! I need your help! 20

The King of Naples appears, holding a candle

King	What's all this noise?
Isabela	*[Aside]* The King himself! I'm lost!
King	Who's in there? Speak!
D. Juan	Who do you think it is?
	A man and woman! Do you need more proof?
King	*[Aside]* I think that prudence might be called for here.
	Attend here quickly! Guards! Arrest this man 25
	Immediately.
Isabela	My reputation's ruined!

*Isabela leaves. Enter Pedro Tenorio, the Spanish
ambassador, with guards*

D. Ped.	My lord, it's very rare there's such commotion
	In your quarters. What's the cause of it?
King	Don Pedro, I command you see to it
	That this arrest is made with utmost speed. 30
	Force might be needed; use it if you must.
	Attempt to identify the guilty pair.
	At every step proceed with utmost caution,
	For there's cause, I think, for some suspicion,
	And if it proves to be the thing I fear, 35

26+   **Pedro Tenorio, the Spanish ambassador:** although a foreigner, Don
Pedro is portrayed very much as the King of Naples' right-hand man,
entrusted here with the execution of a very delicate matter. The
question of the monarch's reliance on those near to him, especially on
royal favourites or *privados*, was one which preoccupied greatly
Spanish dramatists of the seventeenth century and may be related to
contemporary political events. During the reigns of Philip III
(1598–1621) and Philip IV (1621–1665) the influence of royal favourites
such as the Duke of Lerma and the Count – Duke of Olivares became
very great indeed, and the moral issues posed by such developments
were reflected in many plays of the time. Notable examples are: Lope de
Vega's *Las mudanzas de fortuna*; Tirso de Molina's *Privar contra el
gusto*; Pérez de Montalbán's *Cumplir con su obligación*; Vélez de
Guevara's *El conde don Pero Vélez*; and Mira de Amescua's *La próspera
fortuna de don Álvaro de Luna* and *La adversa fortuna de don Álvaro
de Luna*. In *The Trickster* the responsibilities of the monarch and his
reliance on others are suggested in the relationship of the King of
Naples with Don Pedro and later in that of King Alfonso of Castile with
Don Diego. The fact that Pedro and Don Diego are brothers helps,
amongst other things, to spotlight this theme.

	que algún mal suceso creo,	
	porque si yo aquí lo veo	35
	no me queda más que ver.	

Vase el Rey

D. Ped.	Prendelde.	
D. Juan	¿Quién ha de osar?	
	Bien puedo perder la vida;	
	mas ha de ir tan bien vendida,	
	que a alguno le ha de pesar.	40
D. Ped.	¡Matalde!	
D. Juan	¿Quién os engaña?	
	Resuelto en morir estoy,	
	porque caballero soy	
	del embajador de España	
	Llegue; que solo ha de ser	45
	quien me rinda.	
D. Ped.	Apartad;	
	a ese cuarto os retirad	
	todos con esa mujer.	

Vanse Guarda

	Ya estamos solos los dos;	
	muestra aquí tu esfuerzo y brío.	50
D. Juan	Aunque tengo esfuerzo, tío,	
	no le tengo para vos.	
D. Ped.	¡Di quién eres!	
D. Juan	Ya lo digo:	
	tu sobrino.	
D. Ped.	*[Ap.]* ¡Ay, corazón,	
	que temo alguna traición!	55
	¿Qué es lo que has hecho, enemigo?	
	¿Cómo estás de aquesa suerte?	
	Dime presto lo que ha sido.	
	¡Desobediente, atrevido!. . .	
	Estoy por darte la muerte.	60
	Acaba.	
D. Juan	Tío y señor;	
	mozo soy y mozo fuiste;	
	y pues que de amor supiste,	
	tenga disculpa mi amor.	

---

36   turn my royal eyes elsewhere: in making no attempt to discover the truth for himself, the King of Naples reveals a lack of resolution and purpose which was certainly characteristic of both Philip III and Philip IV. It seems likely that Tirso wrote *The Trickster* between 1616 and 1625. For obvious political reasons he could not portray the King of Castile in an overtly unfavourable light. In the play, therefore, it is the King of Naples who is shown to be the more blameworthy, but this

	I'd rather turn my royal eyes elsewhere.	

The King leaves

D. Ped.	Get hold of him!	
D. Juan	Who'll be the first to dare?	
	If it's the case my own life's to be lost,	
	I'll guarantee the cost will be so high,	
	That none of you will want to pay the price.	40
D. Ped.	Finish him off!	
D. Juan	Let no one be deceived!	
	I promise you I'm not afraid to die,	
	For I'm a man of some nobility,	
	Not unrelated to the Spanish embassy.	
	Come on then, now! The fight is man to man.	45
	Whoever wins, wins single-handed.	
D. Ped.	Leave us!	
	Wait in the other chamber, all of you!	
	Ensure the woman's guarded properly.	

The guards go out

	Well, here we are, you rascal, man to man.	
	We'll have a demonstration of your spirit.	50
D. Juan	I've lots of spirit, uncle, have no doubt,	
	But your presence stops me showing it.	
D. Ped.	Who are you, man?	
D. Juan	I've said already, uncle.	
	Your nephew.	
D. Ped.	*[Aside]* Heavens above, what is he saying?	
	Might this not be an act of treachery?	55
	[Aloud] What have you been about, you wretched boy?	
	What can it be you're doing in the palace?	
	I want to know, so out with it at once!	
	You are a bold and disobedient fellow.	
	I'd like to put an end to all your tricks!	60
	Explain yourself immediately!	
D. Juan	My good lord,	
	I'm a young man, as you were also young.	
	You knew everything there was to know of passion,	
	So my obsession you will understand.	

---

would not have prevented a contemporary Spanish audience from drawing similar conclusions about their own ruler.

44   Not unrelated to the Spanish embassy: Don Juan ensures thus that his uncle, in order to avoid any scandalous gossip concerning himself, will dismiss the palace guards. It is one of the many examples in the play of his manipulation of both people and situations. At this moment his identity is concealed by the fact that he has drawn his cloak over his face, so that as yet Don Pedro does not know whom he is dealing with.

	Y, pues a decir me obligas	65
	la verdad, oye y diréla:	
	yo engañé y gocé a Isabela	
	la duquesa. . .	
D. Ped.	No prosigas,	
	tente. ¿Cómo la engañaste?	
	Habla quedo o cierra el labio.	70
D. Juan	Fingí ser el duque Octavio. . .	
D. Ped.	No digas más, calla, basta.	
	[Ap.] Perdido soy si el rey sabe	
	este caso. ¿Qué he de hacer?	
	Industria me ha de valer	75
	en un negocio tan grave.	
	Di, vil: ¿no bastó emprender	
	con ira y con fuerza extraña	
	tan gran traición en España	
	con otra noble mujer,	80
	sino en Nápoles también	
	y en el palacio real,	
	con mujer tan principal?	
	¡Castíguete el cielo, amén!	
	Tu padre desde Castilla	85
	a Nápoles te envió,	
	y en sus márgenes te dió	
	tierra la espumosa orilla	
	del mar de Italia, atendiendo	
	que el haberte recebido	90
	pagaras agradecido,	
	iy estás su honor ofendiendo,	
	y en tal principal mujer!	
	Pero en aquesta ocasión	
	nos daña la dilación;	95
	mira qué quieres hacer.	
D. Juan	No quiero daros disculpa,	
	que la habré de dar siniestra.	

---

75 Some kind of cunning: the King has ordered Don Pedro to arrest the
intruder, but the revelation of the latter's identity and its implications
for Don Pedro's reputation lead him to put self-interest before loyalty
to the King. As the action unfolds, all the characters are seen to be
less than admirable. These scenes take place, as we have seen, at
night. In the play as a whole, as in so many Golden Age plays,
darkness is not merely a cover for the subterfuges of the characters
but also a metaphor for their moral defects. On this aspect of the play
see J.E. Varey, 'Social Criticism in *El burlador de Sevilla*', *Theatre
Research International*, 2(1977), 197-221.

	But since you force me to confide in you	65
	This little episode, I will, so listen:	
	I've tricked and just seduced sweet Isabela,	
	The duchess. . .	
D. Ped.	What? Good Lord above! I'll hear	
	No more. Deceived her? How did you deceive	
	Her? Just speak quietly or hold your tongue	70
D. Juan	I just pretended I was Duke Octavio. . .	
D. Ped.	Stop. Not another word. You've said enough.	
	[Aside] I'm lost if news of this affair gets out	
	And reaches the King's ears. What can I do?	
	Some kind of cunning's the sensible thing	75
	In any matter as perilous as this.	
	[Aloud] Speak up, you rascal! Wasn't it enough	
	For you to carry out with such bravado	
	That act of unforgivable deception	
	Against a Spanish lady of distinction?	80
	Was there any need to repeat it here	
	In Naples, in the royal palace too,	
	And with a woman of such noble birth?	
	I pray that Heaven'll grant your just reward!	
	I know your father's been obliged already	85
	To pack you off to Italy from Spain,	
	But then, as soon as Italy's friendly shore	
	Extends its welcome, letting you set foot	
	Here on its foamy sand, rightly convinced	
	The guest's obligation's to his host,	90
	And that kindness will with kindness be repaid,	
	You straight away reject that solemn trust,	
	And with a woman of such high distinction!	
	But now the sticking-point's been reached, it's clear	
	Delay is but a further aggravation.	95
	Consider well, my lad, what's best for you.	
D. Juan	For me to say I'm not to blame	
	Would be a lie, so there's no point in that.	

---

84   just reward!: the first allusion in the play to divine justice. Subsequently Don Juan is warned of God's punishment by many of the characters. The play is wholly concerned with divine justice rather than divine mercy and must be seen within the religious context of seventeenth-century Spain.

90   The guest's obligation's to his host: Don Juan flouts his obligation to those who offer him shelter and hospitality on a number of occasions. It provides but one example of his disrespect for all social and moral values.

	Mi sangre es, señor, la vuestra;	
	sacalda, y pague la culpa.	100
	A esos pies estoy rendido,	
	y ésta es mi espada, señor.	
D. Ped.	Alzate y muestra valor,	
	que esa humildad me ha vencido.	
	¿Atreveráste a bajar	105
	por ese balcón?	
D. Juan	Sí atrevo,	
	que alas en tu favor llevo.	
D. Ped.	Pues yo te quiero ayudar.	
	Vete a Sicilia o Milán,	
	donde vivas encubierto.	110
D. Juan	Luego me iré.	
D. Ped.	¿Cierto?	
D. Juan	Cierto.	
D. Ped.	Mis cartas te avisarán	
	en qué para este suceso	
	triste, que causado has.	
D. Juan	[Ap.] Para mí alegre, dirás.	115
	Que tuve culpa, confieso.	
D. Ped.	Esa mocedad te engaña.	
	Baja, pues, ese balcón.	
D. Juan	[Ap.] Con tan justa pretensión	
	gozoso me parto a España.	120

Vase Don Juan y entra el Rey

D. Ped.	Ejecutando, señor,	
	lo que mandó vuestra alteza,	
	el hombre. . .	
Rey	¿Murió?	
D. Ped.	Escapóse	
	de las cuchillas soberbias.	
Rey	¿De qué forma?	

---

101   Offence: the offence to which Don Juan refers is both his seduction of
      Isabela and his compromising of his uncle's honour and reputation. In
      theory Don Pedro's killing of his nephew would cleanse any stain upon
      his reputation, but in practice would lead only to gossip and
      speculation, given the nature of life at Court. Don Juan's histrionic
      submission to his uncle's will is made in full knowledge of that fact and
      is entirely consistent with his ironic and mocking attitude to everything
      around him.

106   high balcony: in the *corrales* a gallery supported by pillars ran across
      the back of the stage and could be used for balcony-scenes. Here, on
      the other hand, Don Pedro instructs Don Juan to leap down from the
      level, i.e., the stage-level, on which they are standing. His exit would
      therefore be made, as was Octavio's, through one of the two doors at
      the back of the stage, in which case the balcony is not actually visible.

	But my blood, uncle, is the same as yours,	
	So spill it now and punish me for this	100
	Offence; I kneel here humbly at your feet.	
	Take this sword! Kill me if that's your wish!	
D. Ped.	Get up and show me you've more nerve than that!	
	Humility has overcome my anger.	
	See if your nerve will get you to the ground	105
	By means of this high balcony.	
D. Juan	I'll fly,	
	Uncle! Your faith in me has given me wings!	
D. Ped.	Well, the truth is my main concern's to help,	
	So fly to Sicily as best you can,	
	Or maybe Milan, and seek refuge there.	110
D. Juan	I'm on my way!	
D.Ped.	You promise me?	
D. Juan	I promise.	
D. Ped.	My letters will inform you of the end	
	Of this affair, this sorry tale for which	
	You, nephew, bear responsibility.	
D. Juan	[Aside] But, even so, it's turned out well for me!	115
	[Aloud] I confess, uncle, all the fault was mine.	
D.Ped.	Your youth, my boy, is leading you astray.	
	But down the balcony and on your way!	
D. Juan	[Aside] I think my uncle's gone and said it all.	
	I fancy making Spain my port of call.	120

Don Juan leaves. The King appears

D. Ped.	Your majesty, we tried our very best
	To carry out your orders. I'm afraid
	The fellow. . .
King	Is he dead?
D. Ped.	Got right away,
	Escaping the fierce thrusts of all our swords.
King	How did he manage that?

109–10 Sicily...Milan: see 20+, note. Milan did not come under Spanish rule
until 1535.

119–20 I think...call: it is important to draw attention to the dramatist's use of
the 'aside' in relation to Don Juan. The fact that the stage of the
seventeenth-century *corral* jutted out into the auditorium made
communication between actor and audience a feature of Golden-Age
plays, as was the case indeed in Elizabethan theatre, and in this
context the 'aside' came to be a particularly useful convention. In *The
Trickster* Don Juan's relationship with the audience is very important,
his 'asides' allowing him to take the audience into his confidence,
making them his accomplices in his tricks and deceptions, and thereby –
for much of the play – winning their sympathies. The audience,
privileged witnesses to the deception of others, can take as much
delight in their undoing as does Don Juan himself.

| D. Ped. | Desta forma: | 125 |

Aun no lo mandaste apenas,
cuando, sin dar más disculpa,
la espada en la mano aprieta,
revuelve la capa al brazo,
y con gallarda presteza,   130
ofendiendo a los soldados
y buscando su defensa,
viendo vecina la muerte,
por el balcón de la huerta
se arroja desesperado.   135
Siguióle con diligencia
tu gente; cuando salieron
por esa vecina puerta,
le hallaron agonizando
como enroscada culebra.   140
Levantóse, y al decir
los soldados: "¡muera, muera!",
bañado de sangre el rostro,
con tan heroica presteza
se fué, que quedé confuso.   145
La mujer, que es Isabela,
que para admirarte nombro,
retirada en esa pieza,
dice que es el duque Octavio
que, con engaño y cautela.   150
la gozó.

| Rey | ¿Qué dices? |
| D. Ped. | Digo |

lo que ella propia confiesa.

| Rey | [Ap.] ¡Ah, pobre honor! Si eres alma |

del hombre ¿por qué te dejan
en la mujer inconstante,   155
si es la misma ligereza?
¡Hola!

---

125   **Let me explain:** Don Pedro invents the story of the intruder's escape,
filling his account with lurid and melodramatic details in order to add
conviction. In performance, gesture and delivery play an important part
in this essentially histrionic performance.

149   **Octavio:** Don Pedro, far from being told this by Isabela, distorts the
information given to him by Don Juan.

153   **fragile honour:** the theme of honour in its various forms was a favourite
with most dramatists of the Golden Age and figures prominently in many
plays. Whether or not the honour situations presented on the stage
correspond closely to real life or were used by dramatists for theatrical
effect is a subject which has been much debated. See, for example,
C.A. Jones, '*Honor* in Spanish Golden-Age Drama: Its Relation to Real

D. Ped.	Let me explain:	125

No sooner had you told us to arrest him
Than he, without a word and quick as light,
Went for his sword, brandished the naked steel
Before our eyes, using his cloak to bind
His arm, and made a swift assault upon   130
Your soldiers, making thus defence attack,
Confronting us with quite unusual boldness.
But conscious then, no doubt, that death was close
At hand, he made a dash for it, and threw
Himself into the garden from a window.   135
The guards went after him as best they could,
Rushed quickly down the stairs, made their way out
Into the garden by some other door,
And found him lying there, rolling about
And twisting like a serpent facing death.   140
Then suddenly, he's up and on his feet;
Your men are closing in to make the kill;
His face is just a mask of blood, occasioned
By the fall, when, all at once, inspired by
Some superhuman agency, he's gone!   145
The woman is the Duchess Isabela
I name her to amaze you even more.
The guards have her a prisoner in this chamber.
She claims the man involved is Duke Octavio,
Who, by some cunning stratagem, has just   150
Seduced her.

King   Are you sure?
D. Ped.   All I can say
         Is what the girl's already said to me.

King   [Aside] Oh, fragile honour, source and very essence
         Of man's existence, yet your pure wholeness
         Relies entirely on fickle woman,   155
         Herself the very image of inconstancy!
         [Aloud] You there!

Life and to Morals', *Bulletin of Hispanic Studies*, XXXV (1958),
199–210. As far as the drama is concerned, Lope de Vega had drawn
attention to the popularity of honour as a dramatic subject in his *Arte
nuevo de hacer comedias (The New Art of Writing Plays)*, a poetic
essay on the writing of plays published in 1609:

            Cases of honour are by far the best.
            They move the passions of each spectator.

In the plays of the Golden Age a man's honour - honour in the sense of
reputation and good name - is often threatened or lost as a result of
the vulnerability of the female members of his family, especially wives,
sisters and daughters, to the attentions of marauding males of the Don
Juan variety.

Sale un Criado

Criado	¡Gran señor!
Rey	Traed

delante de mi presencia
esa mujer.

D. Ped.	Ya la guardia

viene, gran señor, con ella.   160

Trae la Guarda a Isabela

Isabela	[Ap.] ¿Con qué ojos veré al rey?
Rey	Idos, y guardad la puerta

de esa cuadra.   Di, mujer:
¿qué rigor, qué airada estrella
te incitó, que en mi palacio,   165
con hermosura y soberbia,
profanases sus umbrales?

Isabela	Señor . . .
Rey	Calla, que la lengua

no podrá dorar el yerro
que has cometido en mi ofensa.   170
¿Aquél era el duque Octavio?

Isabela	Señor. . .
Rey	¡Que no importan fuerzas,

guarda, criados, murallas,
fortalecidas almenas
para amor, que la de un niño   175
hasta los muros penetra!
Don Pedro Tenorio: al punto
a esa mujer llevad presa
a una torre, y con secreto
haced que al duque le prendan,   180
que quiero hacer que le cumpla
la palabra o la promesa.

Isabela	Gran señor, volvedme el rostro.
Rey	Ofensa a mi espalda hecha

es justicia y es razón   185
castigalla a espaldas vueltas.

Vase el Rey

D. Ped.	Vamos, duquesa.
Isabela	Mi culpa

no hay disculpa que la venza;

---

170   Offence: see 24, note.
175   a mere boy: Cupid.
186   My back is turned: the King of Naples both turns his back on and
closes his eyes to the truth of the matter. He is concerned only with

16

A servant enters

Servant	Your majesty!
King	I want the woman

In front of me at once, so fetch her from
The other chamber.

D. Ped.	The guards already

Have her here, my lord. Here is the lady   160

A guard enters with Isabela

Isabela	*[Aside]* Such is my shame, I daren't look at the King!
King	Leave us in private and ensure the door's

Securely guarded. Now, madam. The truth!
What cruel destiny or hostile fate
Obliges you, and in the royal palace,   165
To use your beauty and your high position
To stain my own unblemished reputation?

Isabela	Your majesty. . .
King	Silence! No words of yours

Can hope to gild the seriousness of this
Offence against my noble royal presence.   170
Can it be true Octavio was the man?

Isabela	Your highness. . .
King	Are not bolts and bars enough,

As well as servants, guards, high battlements,
Thick walls and watchtowers, all well-protected,
To keep out love, to stop a mere boy   175
From breaking through such strong and stout defences?
Don Pedro, I command two things of you:
Take the woman with you and tell the guards
To place her in the tower; then proceed
In secret and arrest the man, Octavio.   180
I'll force him to make good his word to her;
A promise is to be a promise kept.

Isabela	Your majesty, why turn your back on me?
King	Since the offence took place behind my back,

The punishment's appropriate and just: 185
My back is turned towards the one who's guilty.

The King leaves

D. Ped.	Come with me, duchess!
Isabela	My offence is such,

There's not an explanation will erase it!

---

191   hushing up any potential palace scandal.
     It's early: a good example of the way in which Golden-Age dramatists
     used the dialogue to locate the time and place of the action. See 10,
     note.

	mas no será el yerro tanto	
	si el duque Octavio lo enmienda.	190

Vanse todos y salen el Duque Octavio y Ripio, su criado

Ripio	¿Tan de mañana, señor, te levantas?	
Octav.	No hay sosiego	
	que pueda apagar el fuego	
	que enciende en mi alma amor.	
	Porque, como al fin es niño,	195
	no apetece cama blanda,	
	entre regalada holanda,	
	cubierta de blanco armiño.	
	Acuéstase, no sosiega,	
	siempre quiere madrugar	200
	por levantarse a jugar,	
	que, al fin, como niño, juega.	
	Pensamientos de Isabela	
	me tienen, amigo, en calma,	
	que como vive en el alma	205
	anda el cuerpo siempre en pena,	
	guardando ausente y presente	
	el castillo del honor.	
Ripio	Perdóname, que tu amor	
	es amor impertinente.	210
Octav.	¿Qué dices, necio?	
Ripio	Esto digo:	
	impertinencia es amar	
	como amas; ¿quies escuchar?	
Octav.	Ea, prosigue.	
Ripio	Ya prosigo.	
	¿Quiérete Isabela a ti?	215

---

193   **this raging fire**: Tirso presents us here with a delightfully ironic picture of the traditional sleepless lover. The irony of Octavio's situation stems largely from his preoccupation with Isabela's honour and our knowledge that she has none – a good example of our privileged position as spectators of the action.

195   **love's a child**: Cupid. See 175, note.

205   **she occupies my very soul**: Golden-Age literature is full of allusions to lovers whose souls have become the property of the loved one. Frequently the lover who is about to depart speaks of leaving his soul behind, i.e., with the loved one, for the latter possesses his whole being. Thus, in Lope de Vega's *El caballero de Olmedo* (*The Knight From Olmedo*), Alonso departs with these words to his beloved Inés:

| | Perhaps my error won't seem quite the same | |
| | If only Octavio will save my name. | 190 |

They leave. The Duke Octavio enters with Ripio, his servant.

Ripio   It's early, master; just the crack of dawn.
What gets you out of bed like this?

Octav.   No sleep
Can ever overcome this raging fire
That love has lit and kindled in my breast!
The explanation's simple: love's a child,   195
And for that reason he detests a bed
That's over-soft and made with linen sheets,
Or covered with an eiderdown of ermine.
He goes to bed but cannot settle down.
He's eager to be up when it's still night,   200
To play some game or have a bit of fun.
Who can stop a child acting like a child?
My thoughts are always with sweet Isabela,
The source, Ripio, of all my pain and anguish,
And since she occupies my very soul,   205
Her presence there denies my body rest,
Obliging it to be the constant guardian
Of honour's pure, chaste and sacred fortress.

Ripio   Forgive me, master, but it seems to me
Your love's a proper case of lunacy.   210

Octav.   You are the lunatic! Shut up!

Ripio   It's true,
Master. To love a woman as you do
Must be lunacy. Shall I say my bit?

Octav.   Well, only if you must.

Ripio   Then I'll say it!
How can you be sure the woman loves you?   215

Great is my sorrow. I leave for Olmedo
And leave my soul behind me in Medina.(Act III,2175-76).
For a detailed study of love in Golden-Age literature the reader is
recommended to Otis H. Green, *Spain and the Western Tradition: The
Castilian Mind in Literature from 'El Cid' to Calderón* (Madison, London,
1968), I, 72-300.

213   Shall I say my bit?: in the drama of the Golden Age the common sense
of servants often contrasts with the imprudence of those they serve and
allows the dramatist to underline the moral dimension of the play. It
does not follow from this, however, that the servants are themselves
particularly moral characters, for they are usually susceptible to the
same temptations that they condemn in their masters.

Octav.	¿Eso, necio, has de dudar?	
Ripio	No; mas quiero preguntar:	
	¿y tú, no la quieres?	
Octav.	Sí.	
Ripio	Pues ¿no seré majadero,	
	y de solar conocido,	220
	si pierdo yo mi sentido	
	por quien me quiere y la quiero?	
	Si ella a ti no te quisiera,	
	fuera bien el porfialla,	
	regalalla y adoralla,	225
	y aguardar que se rindiera;	
	mas si los dos os queréis	
	con una mesma igualdad,	
	dime: ¿hay más dificultad	
	de que luego os desposéis?	230
Octav.	Eso fuera, necio, a ser	
	de lacayo o lavandera	
	la boda.	
Ripio	Pues, ¿es quienquiera	
	una lavandriz mujer,	
	lavando y fregatrizando,	235
	defendiendo y ofendiendo,	
	los paños suyos tendiendo,	
	regalando y remedando?	
	Dando dije, porque al dar	
	no hay cosa que se le iguale,	240
	y si no a Isabela dale,	
	a ver si sabe tomar.	

Sale un Criado

Criado	El embajador de España	
	en este punto se apea	
	en el zaguán, y desea,	245
	con ira y fiereza extraña,	
	hablarte, y si no entendí	
	yo mal, entiendo es prisión.	
Octav.	¡Prisión! Pues ¿por qué ocasión?	
	Decid que entre.	

216-17 The literal translation of these lines is:
OCTAVIO: Can you be in any doubt, you fool?
RIPIO: No; but I want to ask you a question.
231-42 I have translated these lines fairly freely but in a way which attempts
to capture the down-to-earth vulgarity of the *gracioso*.
233 <u>Let them get married!</u>: Duke Octavio implies that, unlike commoners,

Octav.	As it's a fact that you're a fool, it's true.	
Ripio	No need to get narked! Answer me this truly!	
	Are you sure that you love her?	
Octav.	Most surely!	
Ripio	Then tell me this: aren't I a proper fool,	
	A first-class chump of the very best school,	220
	If I persist in knocking my brains out,	
	When of her love I've not the slightest doubt?	
	Now if her love for you was not the case,	
	You would be wise to set out on the chase,	
	To give her gifts and praise her to the skies,	225
	To press your case until you win first prize.	
	But if the two of you are so in love,	
	And both of you are like two cooing doves,	
	I've got to say that I can't see the problem.	
	For God's sake make of her an honest woman!	230
Octav.	The argument, fool, might just be relevant	
	To a lackey or to some female servant.	
	Let them get married!	
Ripio	It's plain audacity	
	To call a washer-woman a nobody.	
	I tell you, master, she's superbly clean;	235
	She's always full of energy and steam,	
	Eager to put her linen on display,	
	Anxious to give her all in every way.	
	Her generosity's a precious gift,	
	There's nothing else can ever equal it.	240
	The moral is give it to Isabel.	
	If she rejects it she can go to Hell.	

A servant enters

Servant	The ambassador of Spain's arrived, my lord.	
	He's there outside, dismounted in the courtyard.	
	I don't know what's the cause, but he's insisting	245
	On speaking with you in an angry tone	
	Of voice; and if I heard him right, I'm sure	
	The word prison was one that passed his lips.	
Octav.	Why would he speak of prison? There's no reason.	
	Ask him to enter.	

---

people of quality should not rush into marriage but ensure first that
the proposed partner is suitable in all senses. While there is no doubt
that he and Isabela love each other and intend to be married, their
delay in so doing points less to any practical reason than to a
self-indulgent delight in the risks and pleasures of a pre-marital
relationship.

D. Ped.	Quien así	250
	con tanto descuido duerme,	
	limpia tiene la conciencia.	
Octav.	Cuando viene vuexcelencia	
	a honrarme y favorecerme	
	no es justo que duerma yo;	255
	velaré toda mi vida.	
	¿A qué y por qué es la venida?	
D. Ped.	Porque aquí el rey me envió.	
Octav.	Si el rey, mi señor, se acuerda	
	de mí en aquesta ocasión,	260
	será justicia y razón	
	que por él la vida pierda.	
	Decidme, señor, ¿qué dicha	
	o qué estrella me ha guiado,	
	que de mí el rey se ha acordado?	265
D. Ped.	Fué, duque, vuestra desdicha.	
	Embajador del rey soy;	
	dél os traigo una embajada.	
Octav.	Marqués, no me inquieta nada;	
	decid, que aguardando estoy.	270
D. Ped.	A prenderos me ha enviado	
	el rey; no os alborotéis.	
Octav.	¡Vos por el rey me prendéis!	
	Pues ¿en qué he sido culpado?	
D. Ped.	Mejor lo sabéis que yo;	275
	mas, por si acaso me engaño,	
	escuchad el desengaño,	
	y a lo que el rey me envió.	
	Cuando los negros gigantes,	
	plegando funestos toldos,	280
	ya del crepúsculo huyen,	
	tropezando unos con otros,	
	estando yo con su alteza	
	tratando ciertos negocios,	
	porque antipodas del sol	285

---

250   Well, I'd say the man: from the outset Don Pedro, knowing Octavio to be innocent, treats him as though he were guilty. The scene between them is another bravura acting performance on Don Pedro's part, in the course of which he employs sarcasm, the weight of his authority, and a superbly embroidered account of Isabela's seduction to bludgeon Octavio into submission. Once again, though, our privileged position as spectators of the action allows us to observe both Don Pedro's self-interested motives and his disloyalty to the king.

Enter Don Pedro Tenorio, with guards

D. Ped.   Well, I'd say the man   250
Who sleeps so soundly, evidently free
From care, must surely sleep with easy conscience.

Octav.   When you decide to call on me, my lord,
Granting me honour and favour by your visit,
For me to favour sleep would be an insult;   225
I'd rather spend my entire life awake.
But tell me: what's the reason for your visit?

D. Ped. I come, my lord, commanded by the King.

Octav.   The King? Why should the King concern himself
With me, sending you as his emissary?   260
If this is true, it's only fair and just
That I for him should sacrifice my life.
But you can tell me, sir, what kindly fate
Or friendly constellation smiles on me,
That I should occupy the King's thoughts now. 265

D. Ped. The King's preoccupation is your misfortune.
I come, sir, as ambassador to the King,
Entrusted by him with this special mission.

Octav.   But, Marquis, I've done nothing wrong to merit
This, so you had better tell me why you've come. 270

D. Ped. The purpose of my visit's to arrest you.
The King's orders! It's best you don't resist!

Octav.   Is this some foolish joke? To arrest me?
You'd better tell me what's the accusation.

D. Ped. You'll know the cause of it as well as I.   275
But if there's some mistake or explanation
Needed, this is the story I've been told;
You'll see the action of the King's well-founded.
When those dark messengers of gloomy night
Unfurled black canopies across the sky,   280
And banished swiftly evening's friendly light,
Their sudden haste the cause of their confusion,
I was in conversation with the King.
Matters of state were our preoccupation
- invariably the enemies of light   285

---

262   sacrifice my life: Octavio's assertion of loyalty and obedience to the monarch regardless of self-interest provides the moral context within which Don Pedro's actions can be judged.

279   When those dark messengers: a rhetorical flourish which is not characteristic of the language of the play in general but which is perfectly suited here both to the dramatic tale which Don Pedro is about to tell and to the role which he gives himself in it as the King's confidante, which in turn is designed to impress on Octavio his own hopeless position.

23

son siempre los poderosos,
voces de mujer oímos
cuyos ecos, menos roncos
por los artesones sacros,
nos repitieron "¡socorro!"   290
A las voces y al ruido
acudió, duque, el rey propio,
halló a Isabela en los brazos
de algún hombre poderoso;
mas quien al cielo se atreve,   295
sin duda es gigante o monstruo.
Mandó el rey que los prendiera;
quedé con el hombre solo;
llegué y quise desarmarlle;
pero pienso que el Demonio   300
en él tomó forma humana,
pues que, vuelto en humo y polvo,
se arrojó por los balcones,
entre los pies de esos olmos
que coronan, del palacio,   305
los chapiteles hermosos.
Hice prender la duquesa,
y en la presencia de todos
dice que es el duque Octavio
el que con mano de esposo   310
la gozó.

Octav.   ¿Qué dices?
D. Ped.   Digo
lo que al mundo es ya notorio
y que tan claro se sabe:
que Isabela por mil modos. . .
Octav.   Dejadme, no me digáis   315
tan gran traición de Isabela.
Mas si fué su amor cautela,
proseguid, ¿por qué calláis?
Mas si veneno me dais,
que a un firme corazón toca,   320
y así a decir me provoca,

---

295 assault the heavens: the allusion is to the Titans of Greek mythology, a
     race of giants who rebelled against the Olympian gods, were defeated
     and condemned to Tartarus. In the same way the 'handsome stranger',
     an intruder in the palace, offends the king.

Are men who wield great influence and power!
Without warning, we heard a woman's voice,
Its echo somewhat muffled and less harsh
In the great vastness of the royal chambers,
But calling out repeatedly for help.   290
The woman's cries and general confusion
Succeeded in attracting the attention
Of the King, and there – would you believe it? –
Was Isabela with a handsome stranger;
Though anyone who dares assault the heavens   295
Is better called a giant or a monster.
The King at once commanded their arrest,
And left me to apprehend the daring fellow.
I did my best, seeking to disarm him,
But I am quite convinced the very devil   300
Had in that person taken human form.
Enveloped in a cloud of smoke and dust,
He flung himself down from the balcony,
And landed at the foot of those great elms
Whose soaring majesty is equalled only   305
By the high towers of the royal palace.
The duchess was arrested on my orders,
And there and then, and overheard by others,
She claimed that Duke Octavio was the man
Who, pretending that he would marry her,   310
Enjoyed her favours.

Octav.   What?

. Ped.   I just repeat
A fact that's now become quite common knowledge;
Some tittle-tattle that the whole world knows;
For Isabela in one way or another. . .

Octav.   Enough, enough! I'll not hear any more   315
Of Isabela's wicked treachery!
But if this business does involve deception,
You'd better tell me more and not be silent,
Even though you are feeding me with poison
That's strong enough to make a stout heart break.   320
This is a matter that obliges me

---

00   the very devil: see 15, note. Don Pedro's description of Don Juan's
       escape is intended merely to impress upon Octavio the daring of the
       intruder. On the other hand, the diabolical implication is one which,
       taken in conjunction with other images in the play, raises Don Juan to
       a poetic, superhuman plane.

que imita a la comadreja,
que concibe por la oreja
para parir por la boca.
¿Será verdad que Isabela,   325
alma, se olvidó de mí
para darme muerte? Sí,
que el bien suena y el mal vuela.
Ya el pecho nada recela
juzgando si son antojos;   330
que, por darme más enojos,
al entendimiento entró,
y por la oreja escuchó
lo que acreditan los ojos.
Señor marqués, ¿es posible   335
que Isabela me ha engañado,
y que mi amor ha burlado?
¡Parece cosa imposible!
¡Oh, mujer! ¡Ley tan terrible
de honor, a quien me provoco   340
a emprender! Mas ya no toco
en tu honor esta cautela.
¿Anoche con Isabela
hombre en palacio?. . . Estoy loco.

D. Ped. Como es verdad que en los vientos   345
hay aves, en el mar peces,
que participan a veces
de todos cuatro elementos;
como en la gloria hay contentos,
lealtad en el buen amigo,   350
traición en el enemigo,
en la noche escuridad
y en el día claridad,
así es verdad lo que digo.

Octav. Marqués, yo os quiero creer.   355
Ya no hay cosa que me espante,

---

322   <u>To imitate the weasel</u>: Octavio is simply saying, in a rather obscure
conceit, that he is absorbing Don Pedro's unpleasant news through his
ears and that its effect is to force him to speak, just as the weasel,
having conceived through its ear, produced its off-spring through its
mouth. The story that the weasel gives birth through its mouth goes
back to classical times. It may be found, for example, in Ovid,
Metamorphosis, IX, 306-21.

339   honour's obligation!: the fact that Isabela's seduction is now public
knowledge means that her honour and reputation have been lost and can
only be restored if her seducer - Octavio himself as far as the world at

To imitate the weasel, who, it's said,
Conceives in some strange manner through its ear,
And then proceeds to give birth through its mouth.
Can it be true of Isabela that she,   325
My very soul, can have forgotten me,
In order to make certain of my death?
The sweetest dreams precede the blackest nightmares.
My heart will fear now no further harm,
Wondering whether this is true or false,   330
For to intensify my sense of anguish,
My fears serve to deepen understanding;
My ears provide the certain confirmation
Of all my eyes unwillingly observed.
Can it really be possible, my lord,   335
That Isabela's so abused my trust,
And made a mockery of my love for her?
How can I believe in such a cruel fate?
Oh, woman! Such is honour's obligation!
And I am now compelled to deal with it!   340
But why should your honour in any way
Concern me, when you are the one's deceived
Me? Discovered in someone else's arms
And in the palace! I daren't think of it!

D. Ped.   There's no one needs persuading that the sky's   345
The province of the birds, the sea of fish,
Though all of them partake in some degree
Of all the elements that make the world.
It's certain that the blessed are in Heaven,
That loyalty's the sure sign of friendship,   350
That treachery's the mark of enmity,
Darkness the very quality of night
And clarity the essence of the day.
As that is true, so is my story certain.

Octav.   Marquis, you have convinced me of the truth   355
Of this. There's nothing will now surprise me.

---

large is concerned – marries her. The literature of the Golden Age
contains many examples of women who have been seduced and
abandoned and who subsequently set out in pursuit of the seducer in
order to make him fulfill his obligation to her. Such is the predicament
of Rosaura at the beginning of Calderón's *La vida es sueño* and Dorotea
in Part I of *Don Quixote*. Later in *The Trickster* Isabela, Tisbea and
Aminta all set out in pursuit of Don Juan.

348   all the elements: the world was thought to be composed of the four
elements of earth, air, fire and water. For an interesting exposition of
this topic see E.M.W. Tillyard, *The Elizabethan World Picture* (London,
1952), especially pp. 55–60.

	que la mujer más constante	
	es, en efeto, mujer.	
	No me queda más que ver,	
	pues es patente mi agravio.	360
D. Ped.	Pues que sois prudente y sabio,	
	elegid el mejor medio.	
Octav.	Ausentarme es mi remedio.	
D. Ped.	Pues sea presto, duque Octavio.	
Octav.	Embarcarme quiero a España,	365
	y darle a mis males fin.	
D. Ped.	Por la puerta del jardín,	
	duque, esta prisión se engaña.	
Octav.	¡Ah, veleta! ¡Débil caña!	
	A más furor me provoco,	370
	y extrañas provincias toco	
	huyendo desta cautela.	
	¡Patria, adiós! ¿Con Isabela	
	hombre en palacio? ¡Estoy loco!	

*Vanse todos y sale Tisbea, pescadora, con una
caña de pescar en la mano*

Tisbea	Yo, de cuantas el mar,	375
	pies de jazmín y rosa,	
	en sus riberas besa	
	con fugitivas olas,	
	sola de amor esenta,	
	como en ventura sola,	380

---

376   sweet mixture of jasmine and rose: Tisbea is in social terms an ordinary
      fisher-girl and in that sense represents a third stratum of society in
      the play, the other two being the monarchy and the nobility. On the
      other hand, she belongs very much to the literary tradition of the
      pastoral novel, so popular in Spain in the sixteenth century. Thus, like
      the disdainful shepherdess, Tisbea glories in the torments of those
      admirers whose attentions she rejects. Like them too her language is
      highly poetic and courtly, much more the language of literature than of
      life. This long soliloquy contains elements – colourful imagery, involved
      syntax – which characterize the poetic movement known as *culteranismo*
      or *gongorismo*, through its association with the poet Luis de Góngora,
      which developed in Spain in the early part of the seventeenth century
      and which had subsequently a significant impact on both poetry and
      drama. The allusion to Tisbea's feet as 'sweet mixture of jasmine and
      rose' is, of course, one that evokes their colour – white-pink – though
      it also suggests scent, and is typical of *culteranismo* both in its
      idealization and in its sensuous character. As far as Tisbea's use of
      such language is concerned, Tirso clearly wished to draw attention to
      her pride. She considers herself to be superior to her friends and
      companions in the sense that she alone has resisted love and maintained

	The woman who is thought to be most constant	
	Is always in the end an ordinary	
	Woman. I need no further proof of this.	
	The degree of my injury's plain to see.	360
D. Ped.	Since you, sir, are a wise and prudent man,	
	It's best you think of some way out of this.	
Octav.	The only way's to get away at once.	
D. Ped.	In that case, Duke Octavio, don't delay.	
Octav.	I'll find a ship whose destination's Spain.	365
	Perhaps there my pain will find some remedy.	
D. Ped.	Best use the door that leads out from the garden,	
	And hurry if you want to escape these chains.	
Octav.	Oh, fickle weather-vane, oh, fragile reed!	
	I'm driven to this act of desperation,	370
	To spend my days in a land that's not my own,	
	As the consequence of your trickery!	
	I leave my country behind me! And you	
	With some other man! The thought drives me mad!	

They leave. Enter Tisbea, a fisher-girl carrying a fishing rod

Tisbea	Of all the girls who live along this shore,	375
	Whose feet, sweet mixture of jasmine and rose,	
	The waves gently kiss on golden sand,	
	Before attempting to escape and hide,	
	I alone am free from love's harsh tyranny,	
	And only I can boast I'm really happy!	380

---

her independence. Her high-flown language is thus a reflection of her feelings of superiority, for it distinguishes her from the others and gives her certain airs. It is worth drawing attention here too to the soliloquy as a form in Spanish Golden-Age drama. In the *Arte nuevo de hacer comedias* Lope de Vega had spoken of the restlessness of Spanish audiences and of the dramatist's need to retain their attention. In this respect the soliloquy poses problems, given the lack of action and incident that must accompany it, and Lope at one point in the *Arte nuevo* refers to the sonnet as a suitable form for the character who is alone on stage. Nevertheless, in practice Lope's plays often contain quite long soliloquies, as do the plays of other Golden-Age dramatists, notably those of Calderón. In this respect Spanish seventeenth-century drama is rather different from its English counterpart in which, on the whole, soliloquies are shorter and character is revealed through action. Tisbea's soliloquy of one hundred and forty one lines is not unlike an operatic aria. In practice, as the Theatre Clwyd workshop performance indicated, the speech works very well, not least because it falls into three clear sections — Tisbea in relation to her friends (375-434); description of Anfriso's love for her (435-481); description of the ship-wreck (482-516) —, each contrasting in mood and tone with the previous section.

tirana me reservo
de sus prisiones locas,
aquí donde el sol pisa
soñolientas las ondas,
alegrando zafiros   385
las que espantaba sombras.
Por la menuda arena,
(unas veces aljófar
y átomos otras veces
del sol que así la adora),   390
oyendo de las aves
las quejas amorosas,
y los combates dulces
del agua entre las rocas;
ya con la sutil caña   395
que al débil peso dobla
del necio pececillo
que el mar salado azota;
o ya con la atarraya
(que en sus moradas hondas   400
prenden cuantos habitan
aposentos de conchas),
segura me entretengo,
que en libertad se goza
el alma que amor áspid   405
no le ofende ponzoña.
En pequeñuelo esquife,
y en compañia de otras,
tal vez al mar le peino
la cabeza espumosa;   410
y cuando más perdidas
querellas de amor forman,
como de todo río,
envidia soy de todas.

---

383   the sun begins its daily journey: the allusion is to Phoebus, who daily
drives the chariot of the sun across the sky, rising at dawn out of the
sea. The poet Góngora describes dawn in somewhat similar fashion in
his great poem, Las soledades, written in 1613-1614. See the Soledad
primera, 179-181:
                    ... The Sun, emerging from its canopy
                        Of foam, took to its chariot, and its rays
                        Did strike the green obelisk of the cottage.
402   inside their shell: again these lines are reminiscent of a passage in
Góngora. See the Soledad segunda, 83-84:
                        Of no advantage to the lustful oyster
                        Is the bony armour of its shell...

For I can speak with pride of liberty,
And of my rejection of passion's bonds,
Here where the sun begins its daily journey,
Awakening the sleepy waves from slumber,
And showering the dawn with brightest sapphire 385
To banish the shadows of darkest night.
Whenever I walk on this pleasant sand,
Whose grains have the beauty of tiny pearls,
Or seem like particles of golden sun,
The object of its amorous advance, 390
I am compelled to listen to the birds'
Constant complaining of forsaken love,
And the gentle, persuasive dialogue
Of the water's embracing of the rocks.
Meanwhile, I am devoted to my fishing, 395
The slender rod bent double with the weight
Of foolish fish who gladly take my bait,
And then in desperation seek to escape;
Or, the rod discarding for a net,
I trap in the dark prison of its mesh 400
As many as I can of those who live,
They think, securely, inside their shell.
But I'm the only one who's truly free,
For only I enjoy the liberty
Of that happy person the serpent love 405
Has failed to infect with his fatal poison.
Trusting sometimes to a small, flimsy boat,
And in the company of other girls,
I venture out to sea, our boat a comb
To the ocean's flowing and foamy tresses. 410
The other girls, helpless victims of love,
Voice their constant and desperate complaints,
While I, since I can mock their hopeless plight,
Am the true envy of each and every one.

---

409 our boat a comb: although Tisbea's speech as a whole contains many
examples of *culteranismo*, this metaphor has a certain *conceptista*
quality, at least in its association of two otherwise quite disparate
things. *Conceptismo* was a feature of seventeenth-century prose style
and is often associated with Francisco de Quevedo y Villegas
(1580-1645), though its origins lay much further back in time. While
culteranismo appealed on the whole to the senses and *conceptismo* to the
intellect, it is true to say, nevertheless, that they often overlapped,
culteranismo having recourse to *conceptista* figures. Consequently,
examples of *conceptismo* are to be found in writers who are
predominantly *culterano*, while exponents of *culteranismo*, like Góngora
himself, often indulge in *conceptos*.

31

¡Dichosa yo mil veces,   415
amor, pues me perdonas,
si ya, por ser humilde,
no desprecias mi choza!
Obeliscos de paja
mi edificio coronan,   420
nidos, si no hay cigarras,
a tortolillas locas.
Mi honor conservo en pajas,
como fruta sabrosa,
vidrio guardado en ellas   425
para que no se rompa.
De cuantos pescadores
con fuego Tarragona
de piratas defiende
en la argentada costa,   430
desprecio soy y encanto;
a sus suspiros, sorda;
a sus ruegos, terrible;
a sus promesas, roca.
Anfriso, a quien el cielo   435
con mano poderosa,
prodigio en cuerpo y alma,
dotó de gracias todas,
medido en las palabras,
liberal en las obras,   440
sufrido en los desdenes,
modesto en las congojas,
mis pajizos umbrales,
que heladas noches ronda,
a pesar de los tiempos,   445
las mañanas remoza;
pues con los ramos verdes
que de los olmos corta,
mis pajas amanecen
ceñidas de lisonjas.   450

---

419   obelisk: a four-sided pillar which tapers to a point, usually monumental.
      The roof of Tisbea's cottage is presumably steep.
421   crickets: the sound of the cricket, which is produced by the friction of
      its forewings, is to be heard throughout the Spanish countryside
      during the hot summer months.
422   doves, whose silly and constant cooing: the dove is, of course,
      associated with Venus and thus with love. For this reason their
      presence is a source of annoyance to the disdainful Tisbea.
428   Tarragona: a seaport on the north-east coast of Spain, some sixty-five

Oh, blessed, Love, am I a thousand times   415
When you decide that I shan't be your slave,
Seeing I'm just an ordinary girl
Whose cottage isn't worth a second glance.
Thatch or humble straw's the only obelisk
That crowns my simple, unpretentious dwelling,   420
Making it a refuge not just for crickets
But for doves, whose silly and constant cooing
Drives me mad. But that straw protects my virtue,
A perfect fruit without the slightest blemish,
A piece of glass packed with the utmost care   425
To avoid the risk of damage on the journey.
To all the fishermen along the coast
Of Tarragona, where bright bonfires warn
Of pirates and help us to keep at bay
Those ships which navigate that silver shore,   430
I am an irresistible attraction;
But I reject them all, deaf to their sighs,
Unmoved by the fierce anguish of their cries,
To all their promises a piece of granite.
Amongst them is Anfriso, a young man   435
Who's favoured by the heavens in every way;
In soul and body Nature's prodigy,
Endowed with every possible attraction.
He uses words with utmost moderation;
His actions are so generous and kind;   440
He suffers my disdain without complaint;
His anguish really is quite moderate.
My cottage, this abode of humble straw,
He guards at night, although the nights be freezing,
And, through the different seasons of the year,   445
He brings to each morning a touch of Spring,
For always there are lovely green bouquets,
Cut from the branches of the towering elms,
And placed before my door to greet the day,
To surround me with Nature's flattery.   450

---

miles south of Barcelona. It was one of the earliest Roman settlements
in Spain. Evidence of Roman architecture may still be seen in the older
parts of the city.

429   pirates: the Mediterranean coastline was constantly threatened in the
sixteenth and seventeenth centuries. Raids by Moors from North Africa
were common, while the Turks posed a considerable threat to both
Charles V and Philip II up until their defeat in the Battle of Lepanto in
1571. The approaching danger was announced, as 428 suggests, by the
lighting of bonfires.

Ya con vigüelas dulces
y sutiles zampoñas
músicas me consagra;
y todo no me importa,
porque en tirano imperio   455
vivo, de amor señora;
que hallo gusto en sus penas
y en sus infiernos gloria.
Todas por él se mueren,
y yo, todas las horas,   460
le mato con desdenes:
de amor condición propia,
querer donde aborrecen,
despreciar donde adoran;
que si le alegran, muere,   465
y vive si le oprobian.
En tan alegre día
segura de lisonjas,
mis juveniles años
amor no los malogra;   470
que en edad tan florida,
amor, no es suerte poca
no ver entre estas redes
las tuyas amorosas.
Pero, necio discurso   475
que mi ejercicio estorbas,
en él no me diviertas
en cosa que no importa.
Quiero entregar la caña
al viento, y a la boca   480
del pececillo el cebo.
Pero al agua se arrojan
dos hombres de una nave,
antes que el mar la sorba,
que sobre el agua viene   485
y en un escollo aborda;

---

452   The soft guitar: the instrument referred to in the Spanish text is the
      vihuela, which was in fact an early form of the guitar. The second
      instrument, which I have translated as 'flute', is the *zampoña*, a rustic
      flute or shepherd's pipe.
486   Battered against the rocks: there is evidently a sudden storm at sea
      which drives the boat onto the rocks. This storm is also, of course, as

Sometimes as well he'll offer me sweet music,
The soft guitar, the shepherd's gentle flute,
Their music dedicated just to me.
Despite all this, I'm totally unmoved,
For I am ever mistress of my fate,   455
As far as love's concerned, it's queen and sovreign.
In fact, my greatest pleasure is his pain,
And in his suffering I find my heaven.
The other girls willingly die for him,
While I, at every opportunity,   460
Destroy his eager hopes with my disdain;
But isn't this the proper thing to do
In love's affairs? To love the man who hates
You; likewise, to despise the man who loves?
For if you favour him, you'll kill his love;   465
Despise him and he'll love you all the more.
This is the pleasant way I spend my days,
Assured of every kind of flattery.
No, I'll not waste the precious years of youth
Devoting all my time to love's pursuit.   470
When life's exciting and so full of fun,
It's truly not the greatest of misfortunes
That here amongst these nets of mine there's not
A sign of love's net, set to capture me.
But that's enough of all this foolish talk!   475
It's only interfering with my fishing;
And what's the point of squandering my time
On something that's not worth a second thought?
I'll cast out my line, see how far the wind
Carries it out to sea, so that the fish   480
Into its eager mouth will take my bait.
But what is that? My eyes perceive two men
Who are throwing themselves into the sea
Before the greedy waves swallow their boat.
It's being swept by the incoming tide,   485
Battered against the rocks and smashed to pieces.

---

was often the case in sixteenth and seventeenth-century literature, an
external manifestation of the emotional confusion which Don Juan's
arrival is about to unleash in Tisbea herself, for the girl who has
boasted of resisting love's storms and tempests is on the point of being
overwhelmed by them. This final section of the soliloquy is particularly
effective if it is spoken with a sense of horror and fascination as
Tisbea, rooted to the spot, observes the dramatic events.

como hermoso pavón,
hace las velas cola,
adonde los pilotos
todos los ojos pongan.   490
Las olas va escarbando;
y ya su orgullo y pompa
casi la desvanece.
Agua un costado toma. . .
Hundióse y dejó al viento   495
la gavia, que la escoja
para morada suya,
que un loco en gavias mora.

[Dentro] ¡Que me ahogo!
Un hombre al otro aguarda
que dice que se ahoga.   500
¡Gallarda cortesía!
En los hombros le toma.
Anquises le hace Eneas,
si el mar está hecho Troya.
Ya, nadando, las aguas   505
con valentía corta,
y en la playa no veo
quien le ampare y socorra.
Daré voces. ¡Tirseo,
Anfriso, Alfredo, hola!   510
Pescadores me miran,
¡plega a Dios que me oigan!
Mas milagrosamente
ya tierra los dos toman:
sin aliento el que nada,   515
con vida el que le estorba.

Saca en brazos Catalinón a Don Juan, mojados

---

487   some lovely peacock: Sebastián de Covarrubias, *Tesoro de la lengua
       castellana o española* (Madrid, 1611), makes the point that the peacock
       was often seen as a symbol of the proud and beautiful woman who is all
       too conscious of her beauty. For the writers of the Golden Age, with
       its strongly religious and moral character, physical beauty was, of
       course, something essentially fleeting and transcient and in that sense
       typical of wordly values. Thus, in Góngora's *Soledad primera*, 309–314,
       the peacock's dazzling beauty cannot save it from death. In Calderón's
       religious play, *No hay más fortuna que Dios*, the allegorical figure
       Beauty (Hermosura) falls into a pit and, when rescued by her
       companions, emerges as a skeleton, stripped of all her good looks. The

Stranded there, it's like some lovely peacock,
The sails in imitation of the tail,
Their beauty and dazzling brightness commanding
The sailors' eyes, ravishing their sight.   490
The movement of the waves plucks at its feathers;
It's loveliness and pride begin to fade,
And all its splendour's slowly stripped away.
The water's ripped a great hole in its side.
Now it's gone under; only its main sail   495
Remains above the waves, so that the wind
May choose, if it so wishes, to dwell there,
A madman locked and howling in a cage.
Cries for help off-stage
One of the men is struggling with the other
Whose head has disappeared beneath the waves.   500
What bravery and courage he displays!
He's trying to lift him onto his shoulders,
The one Aeneas to the other's Anchises,
As though the sea is suddenly Troy's wreckage.
He's striking out now for the shore, the water   505
Making way before this brave show of courage,
Though on the shore there's no one to be seen
Who can provide them with the help they need.
I'll call for help! See if they hear! Tirseo!
Anfriso! Alfredo! Hurry! Come at once!   510
The fishermen all turn in my direction.
I pray to God they will have heard my words!
By some miraculous stroke of luck the two
Swimmers have struggled to the shore at last.
The one who was swimming has now collapsed.   515
The other, clinging to his back, is still breathing.
Catalinón carries Don Juan from the water

---

irony of Tisbea's situation is that she does not associate the shipwreck
with her own fate, but the point would have been clear to a
contemporary audience.

503   The one Aeneas to the other's Anchises: Aeneas was a Trojan hero, son
of Anchises and Venus. After the destruction of Troy by the Greeks,
Aeneas rescued his father. For an account of the story see Virgil's
Aeneid, II, 705-710. The brave and courageous swimmer compared to
Aeneas is, of course, Don Juan who saves his servant, Catalinón, from
drowning (500).

515   The one who was swimming: as the result of his heroic efforts Don Juan
is totally exhausted and Catalinón finally drags him from the water
(516+).

37

Catal.   ¡Válgame la cananea,
          y qué salado está el mar!
          Aquí puede bien nadar
          el que salvarse desea,   520
          que allá dentro es desatino,
          donde la muerte se fragua;
          donde Dios juntó tanta agua,
          no juntara tanto vino.
          Agua salada: ¡estremada   525
          cosa para quien no pesca!
          Si es mala aun el agua fresca,
          ¿qué será el agua salada?
          ¡Oh, quién hallara una fragua
          de vino, aunque algo encendido!   530
          Si del agua que he bebido
          escapo yo, no más agua.
          Desde hoy abernuncio della,
          que la devoción me quita
          tanto, que aun agua bendita   535
          no pienso ver, por no vella.
          ¡Ah, señor! Helado y frío
          está. ¿Si estará ya muerto?
          Del mar fué este desconcierto,
          y mío este desvarío.   540
          ¡Mal haya aquel que primero
          pinos en la mar sembró,
          y que sus rumbos midió
          con quebradizo madero!
          ¡Maldito sea el vil sastre   545
          que cosió el mar que dibuja
          con astronómica aguja,
          causa de tanto desastre!

---

517   **Cana's wine!**: the Spanish text contains no reference to wine.
       Catalinón's words are '¡Válgame la cananea...!' In his footnote to this
       line in the Clásicos Castellanos edition Américo Castro observes that
       cananea is a corruption of *hacanea*, 'a nag', and that Catalinón, the
       gracioso or comic character of the play, is merely indulging in a
       ridiculous joke, alluding to himself, since he is bowed down by Don
       Juan's weight, as a beast of burden. In this case the line might be
       translated: 'He'd have me for his nag this master of mine!' On the
       other hand, the allusion to salt water in 518 suggests that there should
       be a contrast in 517. Christ's transformation of water into wine at Cana
       is the basis for my suggestion.

524   **If he'd used wine:** the *gracioso* of Golden-Age plays, like the fool of
       Elizabethan drama, is essentially a materialist, given to wine, women
       and song, even though he is fond of giving his master moral advice.

38

Catal.   Someone give me a swig of Cana's wine!
               All I can taste is the salt of bloody brine!
               This spot is shallow; it's alright to swim
               Here, and get the hang of how to save your skin.   520
               Out there it's deep, a bloody dangerous place,
               With death waiting to look you in the face.
               God's gone and put together all that water.
               If he'd used wine, I'd pray to Him forever!
               But the sea is all salt! That's a fine thing,   525
               I suppose, for someone who's keen on fishing.
               As for me, I hate water of any kind,
               So water full of salt's a sodding bind!
               Oh, can't someone give me a scalding pot
               Of wine? I'd drink it though it's boiling hot!   530
               If the water I've swallowed doesn't stop
               My breath, I'll never touch another drop.
               From this day forth I shall renounce the stuff!
               It's destroyed my reverence! I've had enough!
               I swear in future even holy water   535
               I shall ignore, and that's no laughing matter!
               Oh, master! Frozen stiff and cold as ice!
               A penny to a pound he's left this life!
               It's the sea's responsible for this lot.
               It's gone and put me in a real spot!   540
               I curse the wretch who had the silly notion
               To put trees in the middle of the ocean!
               Who could that fool be, measuring the sea
               With bits of flimsy wood chopped from a tree?
               Who's the fart, the madcap idiot tailor   545
               Who thought the sea's a pattern the sailor
               Could thread by using a needle and stars?
               For all the sea's disasters there's your cause!

Catalinon is a particularly fine. example of this traditional comic character.

541   I curse the wretch: Catalinón's attack on sea-faring parallels similar passages in other Golden-Age writers. It has been suggested that Tirso found his inspiration in two odes of Horace, notably *Ode I*, iii, though Lope de Vega's *Isidro* seems a more likely source of inspiration. There is also an extremely powerful attack on sea-faring, voyages of discovery and the ruthless exploitation of countries and peoples associated with them in Góngora's *Soledad primera*, 366–502. In the seventeenth century the theme, part of the more general theme of the increasing materialism and moral emptiness of the so-called civilized world, acquired an added force as a result of the discoveries of Columbus and Vasco da Gama.

547   needle: the sailor's needle is, of course, the compass.

	¡Maldito sea Jasón,	
	y Tifis maldito sea!	550
	Muerto está, no hay quien lo crea;	
	¡mísero Catalinón!	
	¿Qué he de hacer?	
Tisbea	Hombre, ¿qué tienes	
	en desventuras iguales?	
Catal.	Pescadora, muchos males,	555
	y falta de muchos bienes.	
	Veo, por librarme a mí,	
	sin vida a mi señor. Mira	
	si es verdad.	
Tisbea	No, que aun respira.	
Catal.	¿Por dónde? ¿Por aquí?	
Tisbea	Sí;	560
	pues ¿por dónde?	
Catal.	Bien podía	
	respirar por otra parte.	
Tisbea	Necio estás.	
Catal.	Quiero besarte	
	las manos de nieve fría.	
Tisbea	Ve a llamar los pescadores	565
	que en aquella choza están.	
Catal.	Y si los llamo, ¿vernán?	
Tisbea	Vendrán presto. No lo ignores.	
	¿Quién es este caballero?	
Catal.	Es hijo aqueste señor	570
	del camarero mayor	
	del rey, por quien ser espero	
	antes de seis días conde	
	en Sevilla, donde va,	

549   Jason: the leader of the Argonauts who in the ship *Argo* sailed to Colchis, a country at the eastern end of the Black Sea, in search of the Golden Fleece.

550   Typhys: pilot of the Argonauts.

571   high chamberlain: Don Juan's father, Don Diego Tenorio, holds a position of high office indeed, for the High Chamberlain attended the king in his quarters and was responsible for the many ceremonial activities that took place in the palace. Mention has been made earlier – see note to 26+ – of the influence acquired by those men close to the King during the reigns of Philip III and Philip IV. The High Chamberlain in 1620, a possible date for *The Trickster's* composition, was, interestingly enough, Pedro Girón, Duke of Osuna (see the Introduction). Clearly, Don Diego Tenorio, portrayed as a good and morally upright man in the play, has the qualities which Pedro Girón lacked and is to be seen as the ideal royal adviser. Tirso embodied Pedro Girón's deficiencies in Don Pedro Tenorio rather than in the High Chamberlain to the King of Castle, but the implications would have been

	As for that Jason, he can go to hell!	
	And that Typhys too, he can go as well!	550

As for that Jason, he can go to hell!
And that Typhys too, he can go as well!   550
My poor master's dead, no doubt at all!
Oh, Catalinón, you're a wretched mortal!
What am I going to do?

Tisbea   Man, what's the matter
With you? Can your trouble be as great as that?

Catal. Oh, fishermaid, a great surfeit of problems   555
Matched only by a total lack of fortune.
Through his efforts to save me, you can see
My master's done himself in! Look at him!
Tell me the truth!

Tisbea   I'd say your master's breathing.

Catal. Where's he breathing? Through here?

Tisbea   Of course through there!
How else would he be breathing?   560

Catal.   Who's to know?
That's not the only place the wind comes through!

Tisbea Don't be disgusting!

Catal.   How I'd like to kiss
Those hands of yours, as white as whitest snow.

Tisbea Just go and call the other fishermen.   565
You'll find them in that cottage over there!

Catal. If I call them, can I be sure they'll come?

Tisbea Of course they'll come! Tell them that I sent you.
But first tell me who's this fine gentleman.

Catal. Oh, this fine, handsome gentleman's the son 570
Of the most excellent high chamberlain
To the King. Through him I'm expecting
To be a count before six days are out,
In Seville, which city's his destination,

---

574 clear to a contemporary audience.
   Seville: together with Madrid, Seville was an extremely important city
   during the Golden Age, for it was there that the greatest impact of
   South American trade was felt. Consequently, in the course of the
   sixteenth century Seville became one of the largest cities in Europe and
   continued to enjoy considerable prosperity long after other centres of
   commerce had declined. By the time Tirso wrote *The Trickster* the
   economic situation of the country as a whole was very serious, a fall
   from greatness was accompanied by moral decline, and writers were
   portraying past greatness as present sleaziness. While Seville remained
   an important city, Tirso portrays it here as tawdry and immoral, a city
   of rakes and prostitutes and largely dissolute nobleman. It is a picture
   of the city also painted by Cervantes in his exemplary short stories,
   Rinconete y Cortadillo and *El celoso extremeño*. Even given that the
   town-country contrast, so common in Golden-Age literature, had a long
   tradition, the unfavourable picture of Seville clearly had a basis in
   reality.

	y adonde su alteza está,	575
	si a mi amistad corresponde.	
Tisbea	¿Cómo se llama?	
Catal.	Don Juan	
	Tenorio.	
Tisbea	Llama mi gente.	
Catal.	Ya voy.	

Coge en el regazo Tisbea a Don Juan

Tisbea	Mancebo excelente,	
	gallardo, noble y galán.	580
	Volved en vos, caballero.	
D. Juan	¿Dónde estoy?	
Tisbea	Ya podéis ver:	
	en brazos de una mujer.	
D. Juan	Vivo en vos, si en el mar muero.	
	Ya perdí todo el recelo,	585
	que me pudiera anegar,	
	pues del infierno del mar	
	salgo a vuestro claro cielo.	
	Un espantoso huracán	
	dió con mi nave al través,	590
	para arrojarme a esos pies	
	que abrigo y puerto me dan.	
	Y en vuestro divino oriente	
	renazco, y no hay que espantar,	
	pues veis que hay de amar a mar	595
	una letra solamente.	
Tisbea	Muy grande aliento tenéis	
	para venir sin aliento,	
	y tras de tanto tormento	
	muy gran contento ofrecéis.	600
	Pero si es tormento el mar	
	y son sus ondas crueles,	
	la fuerza de los cordeles,	
	pienso que os hace hablar.	
	Sin duda que habéis bebido	605
	del mar la oración pasada,	
	pues, por ser de agua salada,	

---

584   To die in the sea: this passage is particularly effective in performance
if spoken quietly, as though Don Juan is waking from a dream. The
language, especially the contrasts involving birth and death and the
allusions to woman's beauty as heavenly, is, of course, the language of
Courtly Love. In *The Trickster*, however, the traditional theme of love
as something that ennobles is used largely for ironic effect. On the one
hand, Don Juan himself is far removed from the traditional,

	And where his majesty's in residence,	575
	That is, if I've not lost his confidence!	
Tisbea	What name does he go by?	
Catal.	Don Juan Tenorio's	
	My master's name.	
Tisbea	Then go and call my friends.	
Catal.	I'm on my way!	

Tisbea places Don Juan's head in her lap

Tisbea	What a fine man this is!	
	Oh, what a noble, handsome, dashing fellow!	580
	You must recover your senses, sir! Speak up!	
D. Juan	Where am I?	
Tisbea	Can't you tell where you are, sir?	
	Don't you know when you're in a woman's arms?	
D. Juan	To die in the sea and be born again	
	To your beauty! And to set aside	585
	The fear of death that almost destroyed me!	
	For from the depths of the sea's darkest hell	
	I'm rescued by the beauty of your heaven!	
	A whirlwind, frightening in its sheer fury,	
	Set upon my ship and overturned it,	590
	In order to wash me up at your feet,	
	Making them a safe refuge from the storm,	
	And so in the light of your lovely dawn	
	I swear I'm born again and fear nothing.	
	To tell the truth, from ocean to devotion	595
	The distance must be reckoned very small.	
Tisbea	My goodness, sir, but you've a lot of breath	
	For someone who just now was almost breathless!	
	And after all the danger you've been through,	
	I can't believe that you can be so cheerful!	600
	But if the sea's an instrument of torture	
	Whose waves are full of hate and cruelty,	
	Then it will be their battering of you	
	That's forcing you to speak to me like this.	
	Apart from that, it's true you will have swallowed	605
	All those fine words on swallowing the water,	
	For since the ocean's water is so sharp,	

---

long-suffering courtly lover who gladly endures the torments of love,
while Tisbea, as her reply to him suggests – 597-620 –, is hardly the
kind of woman worthy of being placed on a pedestal. In a sense Tirso
treats the situation as mockingly as does Cervantes in the
Quixote-Dulcinea episodes of *Don Quixote*, though Don Juan, it has to
be said, is himself lacking in the virtues – devotion, selflessness,
fidelity – exemplified by Don Quixote.

	con tan grande sal ha sido.	
	Mucho habláis cuando no habláis,	
	y cuando muerto venís	610
	mucho al parecer sentís;	
	¡plega a Dios que no mintáis!	
	Parecéis caballo griego	
	que el mar a mis pies desagua,	
	pues venís formado de agua,	615
	y estáis preñado de fuego.	
	Y si mojado abrasáis,	
	estando enjuto, ¿qué haréis?	
	Mucho fuego prometéis;	
	¡plega a Dios que no mintáis!	620
D. Juan	A Dios, zagala, plugiera	
	que en el agua me anegara	
	para que cuerdo acabara	
	y loco en vos no muriera;	
	que el mar pudiera anegarme	625
	entre sus olas de plata	
	que sus límites desata;	
	mas no pudiera abrasarme.	
	Gran parte del sol mostráis,	
	pues que el sol os da licencia,	630
	pues sólo con la apariencia,	
	siendo de nieve abrasáis.	
Tisbea	Por más helado que estáis,	
	tanto fuego en vos tenéis,	
	que en este mío os ardéis.	635
	¡Plega a Dios que no mintáis!	

Salen Catalinón, Coridón y Anfriso, pescadores

Catal.	Ya vienen todos aquí.
Tisbea	Y ya está tu dueño vivo.
D. Juan	Con tu presencia recibo

---

613   <u>Trojan horse</u>: the wooden horse in which the Greeks concealed themselves in order to enter Troy. Allusions to Troy are frequent in relation to Tisbea. She has already spoken in 503 of Don Juan's rescue of Catalinón in terms of Aeneas carrying his father from the burning city. Suspecting now that Don Juan's flattery is merely intended to deceive her, she alludes once more to Troy in a manner which evokes not heroism but deception. While the image was a literary commonplace and its meaning clear, it does serve to indicate here that Tisbea is no fool, which in turn underlines the irony of her subsequent seduction.

615   <u>water</u>: Tisbea responds to Don Juan's conceits with conceits of her own which are both teasing and provocative. They are clearly more earthy than the flowery conceits which marked the opening of her soliloquy, for now her interest in Don Juan is increasingly sexual. Tisbea

44

	Your words are sharp too, sir, and full of wit.	
	You speak a lot when you can barely speak,	
	And though you seem half dead, it's pretty clear	610
	That there's a lot of life still left in you.	
	Please God you aren't a trickster and a liar!	

Your words are sharp too, sir, and full of wit.
You speak a lot when you can barely speak,
And though you seem half dead, it's pretty clear   610
That there's a lot of life still left in you.
Please God you aren't a trickster and a liar!
There's something tells me you're a Trojan horse
The sea's washed up here at my very feet.
And though you've gone and swallowed all that water,   615
When I touch you, you seem to be on fire!
So if you burn when you are soaking wet,
Heaven knows what you'll be up to when you're dry!
It's my opinion you've got lots of fire.
Please God you aren't a trickster and a liar!   620

D. Juan If only God, sweet fishergirl, had let
The ocean take away this precious life,
Had let me leave this life with all my senses,
He'd have spared me the madness of this passion.
The waves would have embraced me, swallowed me   625
Completely in their limitless expanse,
Ranging as far as any eye can see,
But even they would not have dared burn me.
Your beauty has the power of the sun,
Enjoying its supreme authority.   630
To gaze upon it is for any man,
Though it be white as snow, to be consumed.

Tisbea You're still as cold as ice itself, my lord,
And yet there's still sufficient spark in you
To catch fire from the flame that burns in me!   635
Please God you aren't a trickster and a liar!

Enter Catalinón, Córidon and Anfriso, fishermen

Catal. They came at once in answer to my call.

Tisbea And here's your master, as good as ever was.

D. Juan Your presence has restored to me the gift

---

evidently delights here in a teasing game whose dangers she does not
recognize. She is indeed 'playing with fire', and although the fire–love
image is a purely conventional one, it points to the danger that lies
ahead.

632 snow: her skin is as white as snow but to gaze upon it kindles the
fires of love in any man. This is a typical Gongoristic paradox.

635 flame: in the course of her soliloquy Tisbea has boasted of her coldness
and lack of feeling for her many suitors. Now the flame of love begins
to burn in her. Indeed, in performance touch should play an important
part, for from 616, where Tisbea refers to touching Don Juan, there
should be an increasing emphasis on physical contact between them. At
first – 579 – Tisbea simply places Don Juan's head in her lap. By 636
she is on the point of kissing him but is interrupted by the arrival of
the fishermen.

	el aliento que perdí.	640
Corid.	¿Qué nos mandas?	
Tisbea	Coridón,	
	Anfriso, amigos. . .	
Corid.	Todos	
	buscamos por varios modos	
	esta dichosa ocasión.	
	Di que nos mandas, Tisbea,	645
	que por labios de clavel	
	no lo habrás mandado a aquel	
	que idolatrarte desea,	
	apenas, cuando al momento,	
	sin cesar, en llano o sierra,	650
	surque el mar, tale la tierra,	
	pise el fuego, y pare el viento.	
Tisbea	[Ap.] ¡Oh, qué mal me parecían	
	estas lisonjas ayer,	
	y hoy echo en ellas de ver	655
	que sus labios no mentían!	
	Estando, amigos, pescando	
	sobre este peñasco, vi	
	hundirse una nave allí,	
	y entre las olas nadando	660
	dos hombres; y compasiva,	
	di voces, y nadie oyó;	
	y en tanta aflicción, llegó	
	libre de la furia esquiva	
	del mar, sin vida a la arena,	665
	déste en los hombres cargado,	
	un hidalgo ya anegado,	
	y envuelta en tan triste pena	
	a llamaros envié.	
Anfriso	Pues aquí todos estamos,	670
	manda que tu gusto hagamos,	
	lo que pensando no fué.	
Tisbea	Que a mi choza los llevemos	
	quiero, donde, agradecidos,	

---

644   <u>to serve you</u>: the notion of serving a lady with devotion, without expectation of reward, is central to the philosophy of Courtly Love and thus to the pastoral novel whose characters, far from being real shepherds and shepherdesses, owe much to the courtly love tradition. Tisbea's attitude to her suitors, as revealed in her soliloquy, is, as we have seen, in the tradition of the disdainful shepherdess of pastoral literature, but it would seem too that her suitors have something of the unrequited lovers of the pastoral novel.

	Of life that I considered lost forever.	640
Corid.	[To Tisbea] Your wish is our command.	
Tisbea	Thanks, Coridón,	

Anfriso, loyal friends. . .

Corid.   Each one of us
Looks only for the opportunity
And happy chance to serve you as he can.
Tell us, Tisbea, what you'd have us do,   645
For orders given by those lips of yours,
Sweet as the sweet carnation, are most precious
Gifts to the man who idolizes you.
No sooner given, your command's his will,
He'll set his mind to it without delay,   650
Though his task be to plough the sea, submerge
The land, to walk on fire or stop the wind.

Tisbea [Aside] Why, only yesterday such flattery
Seemed painful to me, more than I could bear!
But now I see there's more to it than that.   655
I fancy that their words proclaim the truth.
[Aloud] My friends, it's just that I was fishing here,
Sitting upon this rock, when suddenly
I saw a ship capsize far out to sea
And two men thrown into the water, fighting   660
For their lives. Moved by their sorry plight,
I called for help, but no one heard my cries.
Imagine my bewilderment! But then,
As though freed from the fury of the sea,
There landed at my feet upon the sand,   665
Borne on the shoulders of this valiant man,
This other handsome gentleman, half-dead.
It was a sight that filled my heart with pity,
And so I sent the servant off for help.

Anfriso And so we came in answer to your call.   670
Just tell us what you wish. It will be done.
Not often do we get a chance like this.

Tisbea My wish is that you take them to my cottage.
For there, in payment for the honour they

---

674 the honour: the fisherfolk are honoured by the mere presence of a
nobleman and by the opportunity of serving him. The corollary to this
is that the nobleman should respect them and not take advantage of his
superior social position. The theme of the individual's right to honour
and respect became the subject of many Golden-Age plays, amongst
which Lope de Vega's *Peribáñez y el Comendador de Ocaña* and
Fuenteovejuna, as well as Calderón's *El alcalde de Zalamea*, can be
singled out. In a sense these plays can be regarded as the dramatists'
advocacy of a greater democratic spirit in a society characterized by its
strict social divisions. Don Juan, of course, abuses nobleman and
peasant alike.

47

	reparemos sus vestidos,	675
	y allí los regalaremos;	
	que mi padre gusta mucho	
	desta debida piedad.	
Catal.	¡Estremada es su beldad!	
D. Juan	Escucha aparte.	
Catal.	Ya escucho.	680
D. Juan	Si te pregunta quién soy,	
	di que no sabes.	
Catal.	¡A mí...	
	quieres advertirme a mí	
	lo que he de hacer!	
D. Juan	Muerto voy	
	por la hermosa pescadora.	685
	Esta noche he de gozalla.	
Catal.	¿De qué suerte?	
D. Juan	Ven y calla.	
Corid.	Anfriso: dentro de una hora	
	los pescadores prevén	
	que canten y bailen.	
Anfriso	Vamos,	690
	y esta noche nos hagamos	
	rajas y palos también.	
D. Juan	Muerto soy.	
Tisbea	¿Cómo, si andáis?	
D. Juan	Ando en pena, como veis.	
Tisbea	Mucho habláis.	
D. Juan	Mucho entendéis.	695
Tisbea	¡Plega a Dios que no mintáis!	

Vanse todos y salen Don Gonzalo de Ulloa y
el Rey Don Alfonso de Castilla

Rey	¿Cómo os ha sucedido en la embajada,
	comendador mayor?
D. Gon.	Hallé en Lisboa

---

682   you don't know my name!: Catalinón has in fact already informed Tisbea
         – 570–576 – both of his master's name and position.
685   Has got me hooked!: this is my own free rendering of Don Juan's
         'Muerto voy/por la hermosa pescadora', 'I'm dying for the lovely
         fishergirl'. It seems perfectly appropriate to Don Juan's character.
693   I'm dying: there is a strong element of teasing and banter between Don
         Juan and Tisbea. Thus he utters 695 – 'You know what I desire' –
         with a laugh. On the other hand, Tisbea's suspicions and fears are
         genuine enough, as 696 suggests.

48

	Bestow on us, we'll mend their damaged clothes,	675
	And see if we can give them entertainment.	
	My father loves to give a helping hand.	
	It's something that will always warm his heart.	
Catal.	I swear this fishergirl's a real beauty!	
D. Juan	Come here, my friend! Listen!	
Catal.	I'm listening.	680
D. Juan	If anyone should ask you who I am,	
	Tell them that you don't know my name!	
Catal.	Me tell	
	Them that? No need for you to tell me that.	
	I know exactly what to say.	
D. Juan	The girl	
	Has got me hooked! Her beauty is outstanding	685
	Tonight I plan to have her for myself.	
Catal.	How will you do that?	
D. Juan	Come, and not a word!	
Corid.	Anfriso! In an hour from now our friends	
	The fishermen should be prepared to sing	
	And dance in honour of our guests.	
Anfriso	Let's go.	690
	Tonight's the night we'll all go celebrate,	
	Slices of lemon, grapes fresh from the vine!	
D. Juan	I'm dying, Tisbea!	
Tisbea	You're on your feet!	
D. Juan	But in the direst pain, as you can see.	
Tisbea	You've breath enough!	
D. Juan	You know what I desire!	695
Tisbea	Please God you aren't a trickster and a liar!	

*They exit. Enter Don Gonzalo de Ulloa and the King
Don Alfonso of Castile*

King	I trust your royal embassy went well,	
	My lord Commander?	
D. Gon.	In Lisbon I encountered	

696+   Don Alfonso of Castile: as has already been indicated, the king in
       question is Alfonso XI who died in 1350.

698   My lord Commander?: the reference is to the Grand Commander of the
       order of Calatrava – see Act II, 65-66 –, one of the semi-military,
       semi-religious orders which were of great importance in Spain in the
       Middle Ages. The order of Calatrava was founded in 1158, those of
       Alcántara and Santiago in 1166 and 1170. They lost much of their actual
       power at the end of the fifteenth century but continued to have great
       social prestige throughout the Golden Age. The position of grand
       Commander was second in rank to that of Grand Master.

	al rey don Juan, tu primo, previniendo	
	treinta naves de armada.	
Rey	¿Y para dónde?	700
D. Gon.	Para Goa me dijo; mas yo entiendo	

Rey   ¿Y para dónde?   700
D. Gon. Para Goa me dijo; mas yo entiendo
        que a otra empresa más fácil apercibe.
        A Ceuta o Tánger pienso que pretende
        cercar este verano.
Rey   Dios le ayude,
        y premie el celo de aumentar su gloria.   705
        ¿Qué es lo que concertasteis?
D. Gon.   Señor, pide
        a Serpa y Mora, y Olivencia y Toro;
        y por eso te vuelve a Villaverde,
        al Almendral, a Mértola y Herrera
        entre Castilla y Portugal.
Rey   Al punto   710
        se firmen los conciertos, don Gonzalo.
        Mas decidme primero cómo ha ido
        en el camino, que vendréis cansado
        y alcanzado también.
D. Gon.   Para serviros,
        nunca, señor, me canso.
Rey   ¿Es buena tierra   715
        Lisboa?
D. Gon.   La mayor ciudad de España;
        y si mandas que diga lo que he visto
        de lo exterior y célebre en un punto
        en tu presencia te pondré un retrato.
Rey   Yo gustaré de oíllo. Dadme silla.   720
D. Gon.   Es Lisboa una otava maravilla.

---

699   His majesty, your cousin John:the king in question is King John I, who was indeed a cousin of Alfonso XI, but he did not become king until 1385, thirty five years after Alfonso's death.

701   Goa: the capital of those territories acquired by Portugal in India, though it did not fall into Portuguese hands until the sixteenth century. This is yet another of the many anachronisms in the play.

703   Ceuta or Tangier: seaports on the coast of what is now Morocco from which Moorish raiders frequently invaded Spanish territory. John I is said by some historians to have captured Ceuta in 1415, the first part of Africa to be taken by any Spanish or Portuguese king.

707   Serpa, Mora, Toro: although these three towns, and those mentioned subsequently, existed and were located on the Spanish-Portuguese border, the exchange alluded to here has no historical basis.

717   The largest city: Lisbon was not a part of Spain during the reign of Alfonso XI. It did not become so until 1580 when Philip II of Spain acquired Portugal. In 1578 the young Portuguese king, Sebastian, had been killed in a foolish campaign in North Africa, leaving Philip in the direct line of succession.

	His majesty, your cousin John, busily	
	Preparing thirty ships.	
King	With what in mind?	700
D. Gon.	En route for Goa, I was told. I think,	

King   With what in mind? 700

D. Gon. En route for Goa, I was told. I think,
Though, they're intended for some easier task.
To lay seige to Ceuta or Tangier
This coming Summer.

King   May God assist his cause
And thus reward his servant's dedication. 705
What was the outcome of your conversations?

D. Gon. My lord, he asks for Serpa, Mora, Toro
And Olivenza, in return for which
he'll give you Villaverde, Almendral
Herrera and Mertola, districts each 710
Of them between Castile and Portugal.

King   Then have the contract signed. But tell me now
About your journey. You'll be tired and out
Of pocket, I'm quite sure.

D. Gon.   I never tire
In your service, your majesty.

King   What kind 715
Of place is Lisbon?

D. Gon.   In the whole of Spain
The largest city. If you wish to listen,
I'll set before your eyes a verbal picture
Of all the sights from which it draws its fame.

King   In readiness, Gonzalo, I'll sit down. 720

D. Gon. That city is undoubtedly the world's

---

721   That city: the ensuing description of Lisbon contains a great deal of accurate detail and suggests first-hand knowledge of the city. The point has been made by Blanca de los Ríos, *Tirso de Molina. Obras dramáticas completas* (Madrid, 1946-1958), II, 854a, that Tirso may have visited Galicia and Portugal in 1619, while it is certainly true that a number of his plays have a Portuguese setting and, as in the case of *Doña Beatriz de Silva*, point to a familiarity with Lisbon. The very different question of the relevance of this passage to the play as a whole is one that has been discussed by several critics. The emphasis on the religious character of Lisbon is very clear and suggests a deliberate contrast to the corrupt life of Seville and the immorality of Court life which is embodied there. Thus, the dramatist uses the Lisbon speech, significantly given to Don Gonzalo de Ulloa, a good and virtuous man, to attack the moral condition of Spain, exemplified in one of its principal cities, Seville, and, of course, in its most infamous son, Don Juan. See J.E. Varey, 'Social Criticism in *El burlador de Sevilla*', *Theatre Research International* and Robert Ter Horst, 'The *loa* of Lisbon and the Mythical Substructure of *El burlador de Sevilla*',

De las entrañas de España,
que son las tierras de Cuenca,
nace el caudaloso Tajo,
que media España atraviesa.   725
Entra en el mar Oceano,
en las sagradas riberas
de esta ciudad, por la parte
del sur; mas antes que pierda
su curso y su claro nombre,   730
hace un puerto entre dos sierras,
donde están de todo el orbe
barcas, naves, carabelas.
Hay galeras y saetías
tantas, que desde la tierra   735
parece una gran ciudad
adonde Neptuno reina.
A la parte del poniente
guardan del puerto dos fuerzas
de Cascaes y San Gian,   740
las más fuertes de la tierra.
Está, desta gran ciudad,
poco más de media legua,
Belén, convento del santo
conocido por la piedra,   745
y por el león de guarda,
donde los reyes y reinas
católicos y cristianos
tienen sus casas perpetuas.
Luego esta máquina insigne,   750
desde Alcántara comienza
una gran legua a tenderse
al convento de Jabregas.
En medio está el valle hermoso
coronado de tres cuestas,   755

Bulletin of Hispanic Studies, L (1973), 147-65. Varey argues that the
speech is also important 'as a bridge scene allowing for the passage of
time between Tisbea's coming upon the shipwrecked Don Juan and his
subsequent seduction of her. . .' (p.199). In practice the bridge
proves to be far too long and was finally cut in the Theatre Clwyd
performance.

724   The Tagus: this major river has its source in the mountains of Cuenca,
less than one hundred miles from Spain's east coast, flows in a
south-westerly direction across Spain and Portugal and enters the
Atlantic at Lisbon.

740   Cascais and Saint Julian: Cascais is situated some sixteen miles to the
west of Lisbon on the bay of Cascais. Saint Julian is the name of a fort

Eighth wonder. In the very heart of Spain,
That is to say the region known as Cuenca,
The Tagus has its source, that mighty river
Which in its course divides our land in two.   725
The point where finally it meets the sea
Is on the hallowed banks of this fine city,
But somewhat to the southern side of it.
And there, before it makes the sacrifice
Of both its name and its identity,   730
It forms a harbour set between two hills:
A port in which are found from all the world's
Great oceans ships and vessels of all kinds:
Galleons and caravels in such abundance
That from the shore this teeming harbour seems   735
To be a city, a great capital
Where Neptune proudly rules and holds his Court.
On Lisbon's western side, where the sun sets,
Two fortresses are built to give protection
To the harbour, Cascais and Saint Julian   740
By name, by far the strongest in the land.
Outside the city, half a mile away
Or more, there stands the convent of Belem,
In honour of our blessed Saint Jerome,
The saint whose trusted guardian was a lion,   745
Whose sinfulness was punished with a stone.
There nowadays the royal family,
True fountainhead of Catholic belief
And Christianity, is laid to rest.
Then, having left this wondrous place behind,   750
You must proceed at least another league,
And there beyond Alcántara's stream you'll find
Another convent, called this time *Jabregas*.
It fills the centre of a lovely valley
And is surrounded on all three sides by hills   755

<table>
<tr><td></td><td>some eight miles to the west of the city, constructed by Philip II.</td></tr>
<tr><td>743</td><td>Belem: the name of the Hieronymite convent built in the sixteenth century.</td></tr>
<tr><td>745</td><td>a lion: after Saint Jerome removed a thorn from the paw of a lion, the beast protected the monks of the convent.</td></tr>
<tr><td>746</td><td>punished with a stone: it was Saint Jerome's practice to atone for his sins by striking himself on the chest with a stone.</td></tr>
<tr><td>749</td><td>is laid to rest: a reference to the royal tombs situated in one of the monastery buildings.</td></tr>
<tr><td>752</td><td>Alcántara's stream: the stream separates Lisbon and the convent of Belem.</td></tr>
<tr><td>753</td><td>Jabregas: the Franciscan convent of Jabregas, founded in 1508.</td></tr>
</table>

que quedara corto Apeles
cuando pintarlas quisiera;
porque, miradas de lejos,
parecen piñas de perlas
que están pendientes del cielo,   760
en cuya grandeza inmensa
se ven diez Romas cifradas
en conventos y en iglesias,
en edificios y calles,
en solares y encomiendas,   765
en las letras y en las armas,
en la justicia tan recta,
y en una Misericordia
que está honrando su ribera,
y pudiera honrar a España   770
y aun enseñar a tenerla.
Y en lo que yo más alabo
desta máquina soberbia,
es que del mismo castillo
en distancia de seis leguas,   775
se ven sesenta lugares
que llega el mar a sus puertas,
uno de los cuales es
el convento de Odivelas,
en el cual vi por mis ojos   780
seiscientas y treinta celdas,
y entre monjas y beatas
pasan de mil y doscientas.
Tiene desde allí Lisboa,
en distancia muy pequeña,   785
mil y ciento y treinta quintas,
que en nuestra provincia Bética
llaman cortijos, y todas
con sus huertos y alamedas.
En medio de la ciudad   790
hay una plaza soberbia

---

756   Apeles: a Greek painter of the fourth century B.C.
770   Misericordia: completed in 1534, the 'Casa de Misericordia' ('House of Mercy') was a temple and hospital. In 1755 it was almost completely destroyed by an earthquake.
774   castle: the reference appears to be to the Saint George's Castle, an ancient Moorish citadel situated on a hill dominating the eastern part of Lisbon.
779   Odivelas: a Cistercian convent built in 1305, situated some five miles

Before whose dazzling beauty even Apelles,
Prince amongst painters, must admit defeat.
Looked at from far away this is a city
That seems a cluster of the finest pearls
Whose lovely beauty's balanced in the sky,   760
And in whose greatness even Rome itself
Could be contained at least a dozen times.
Beyond belief the number of its churches,
While convents too, and mansions and great houses
Adorn the streets that are themselves beyond   765
Compare, matched only by this city's fame
In learning, in the exercise of arms,
And in the application of true justice.
Her greatest building, though, is one that's called
Misericordia, source of inspiration   770
To true pity, and envy of all Spain.
Another feature of this city calls
For praise, in this case more than any other,
For from the battlements of its great castle
A distance of six leagues can be perceived,   775
And sixty towns scattered throughout the region,
Each one of them within the sea's embrace.
One of these has a special claim to fame:
This is the convent known as *Odivelas*,
For there I swear that my own eyes beheld   780
Six hundred cells and more, and all of them
Inhabited by nuns, at least twelve hundred,
Their lives to our blessed Lord devoted.
Within its boundaries Lisbon contains
Some fifteen hundred country villas, each   785
With its fine garden and its avenues
Of poplar trees, the kind of house that those
Of us familiar with the South of Spain,
The land of Andalusia, call *cortijos*,
The city has too at its very centre   790
A square whose splendour is beyond belief

---

northwest of Lisbon. It contained the remains of the famous Portuguese monarch, King Denis (1279–1325).

82   twelve hundred: the number seems to be an exaggeration, for evidence suggests that there were four hundred nuns at this convent in 1608 and six hundred in 1620, the approximate year of the play's composition.

89   'cortijos': the *Diccionario de Autoridades* defines *cortijo* as a farmhouse, the word being particularly associated with Andalusia.

que se llama del Rucio,
grande, hermosa y bien dispuesta,
que habrá cien años y aun más
que el mar bañaba su arena,   795
y ahora della a la mar
hay treinta mil casas hechas,
que, perdiendo el mar su curso,
se tendió a partes diversas.
Tiene una calle que llaman   800
rua Nova o calle Nueva,
donde se cifra el Oriente
en grandezas y riquezas;
tanto, que el rey me contó
que hay un mercader en ella   805
que, por no poder contarlo,
mide el dinero a fanegas.
El terrero, donde tiene
Portugal su casa regia,
tiene infinitos navíos,   810
varados siempre en la tierra,
de sólo cebada y trigo
de Francia y Ingalaterra.
Pues el palacio real,
que el Tajo sus manos besa,   815
es edificio de Ulises,
que basta para grandeza,
de quien toma la ciudad
nombre en la latina lengua,
llamándose Ulisbona.   820
cuyas armas son la esfera,
por pedestal de las llagas
que en la batalla sangrienta
al rey don Alfonso Enríquez
dió la Majestad Inmensa.   825

---

792   Rossío: the square, situated in the older part of the city, is still
      referred to by this name, though its official name is *Praça de Dom
      Pedro Quarto*.
802   the treasures of the East: an allusion to the riches brought to Lisbon
      from Portuguese territories in the East.
808   Terreiro: this is the *Terreiro do Paço*, the square in front of the royal
      palace which faces the Tagus. The square was destroyed by the
      earthquake of 1755 but was subsequently rebuilt and called the *Praça
      do Commercio*.
816   fashioned by Ulysses' hand: the story of the foundation of Lisbon by
      Ulysses has no basis.
820   Ulisbona: the ancient name of Lisbon was *Olisipiom*, which was also
      written as *Ulyssipo*, clearly deriving from the myth which stated that
      Ulysses had founded a city in Iberia.

And which is called *Rossío*, great in size,
A pleasure to the eye, and well arranged.
A hundred years ago, so it is said,
The ocean lapped that very spot where now   795
The square is to be found, and there as well
Some thirty thousand houses stand and force
The raging sea to turn its back on them
And vent its anger on some other shore.
This district of the city has a street   800
Called *Rua Nova*, in our language New
Street, where the treasures of the East in all
Their grandeur and wealth are now contained.
According to the King, a merchant there
Has such excessive wealth he cannot count   805
In coins, so is obliged to weigh his money
And measure it, apparently, in bushels.
Terreiro, as the place is called, is where
The royal family of Portugal
Resides, and from the house ships can be seen,   810
A great armada anchored in the port,
A fleet that bears great quantities of wheat
And barley all the way from France and England.
Such is the splendour of the royal palace,
The mighty Tagus comes to pay it homage,   815
For it was fashioned by Ulysses' hand,
A name whose very synonym is greatness
And after whom the city once was called,
For in the Latin language Lisbon bore
The celebrated name of *Ulisbona*.
The royal court of arms have for their base
A sphere in celebration of the wounds
Which in a battle fought against the Moors
The King Alfonso Enriquez gladly suffered
In order to proclaim God's glorious name.   825

---

824   King Alfonso Enríquez: the battle fought against the Moors took place at
Ourique in 1139. The Portuguese coat of arms, said here to be given to
the victorious king by God, consisted according to tradition of five
small shields which form a cross on a larger shield. In the battle King
Alfonso Enríquez received five wounds, corresponding to the five
wounds of Christ on the cross, which became the five shields of the
coat of arms. In another play, *Las quinas de Portugal*, Tirso has
Christ addressing King Alfonso in the following manner:
> This court of arms which Portugal receives
> From me, in token of my gratitude,
> Consists of five small shields, their colour blue,
> Their number corresponding to my wounds,
> And as a cross arranged. . .   (Act I.)

57

Tiene en su gran tarazana   —
diversas naves, y entre ellas,
las naves de la conquista,
tan grandes, que de la tierra
miradas, juzgan los hombres   830
que tocan en las estrellas.
Y lo que desta ciudad
te cuento por excelencia
es, que estando sus vecinos
comiendo, desde las mesas   835
ven los copos del pescado
que junto a sus puertas pescan,
que, bullendo entre las redes,
vienen a entrarse por ellas;
y sobre todo, el llegar   840
cada tarde a su ribera
más de mil barcos cargados
de mercancías diversas,
y de sustento ordinario:
pan, aceite, vino y leña,   845
frutas de infinita suerte,
nieve de Sierra de Estrella
que por las calles a gritos,
puestas sobre las cabezas,
las venden. Mas, ¿qué me canso?   850
porque es contar las estrellas
querer contar una parte
de la ciudad opulenta.
Ciento y treinta mil vecinos
tiene, gran señor, por cuenta,   855
y por no cansarte más,
un rey que tus manos besa.

Rey   Más estimo, don Gonzalo,
escuchar de vuestra lengua
esa relación sucinta,   860
que haber visto su grandeza.
¿Tenéis hijos?

D. Gon.   Gran señor,
una hija hermosa y bella,

---

846   Ice: for the purpose of cooling drinks. The Serra da Estrela is a mountain range situated some one hundred and thirty five miles northeast of Lisbon.

855   one hundred and thirty thousand people: the population of Lisbon in 1620 was indeed approximately this. See Oliveyra's *Livro das grandezas de Lisboa* (Lisbon, 1620).

58

The harbour too impresses in its size,
An anchorage for ships of different kinds,
And there you'll find the mighty 'men o'war',
So massive in their size that, looked at from
The land, they have the appearance of giants   830
That seem to reach up to the stars themselves.
Above all, what I found most pleasing there
Is that the citizens, in the course of
Their eating can, when seated at their tables,
Look out upon a fleet of fishing boats   835
And watch them fishing there so close to home
That, in their struggle to escape the nets,
The fish leap from the sea only to meet
Their end instead, stranded on the shore.
They have the opportunity to see   840
There too, arriving every evening,
More than a thousand vessels, fully laden
With every kind of rare and common goods:
Bread, oil, wine, wood, and such variety
Of fruit the mind can scarcely entertain.   845
Ice too brought from the Serra da Estrela,
And sold by women in the city's streets,
The nature of their wares loudly proclaimed
And borne in baskets balanced on their heads.
But why attempt to tell you any more?   850
To try to paint a picture of a fraction
Of Lisbon's opulence is just as vain
As if I were to try to count the stars.
It has, your majesty, a population
Of one hundred and thirty thousand people.   855
And to conclude, and tire you no further,
A King who through me pays you loyal homage.

King   I'm more than grateful to you, Don Gonzalo,
For that brief summary. It's almost better,
Coming from your own mouth, than if I'd gone   860
To Lisbon and observed it for myself.
Do you have any children?

D. Gon.   Yes, my lord,
A daughter blessed with such outstanding beauty,

---

859   that brief summary: although Don Gonzalo is presented in general as a
good and virtuous man, he is initially very conventional and extremely
boring, as the king's ironic comment suggests. Tirso seems to be
exposing in the course of the play not merely the corruption of the
Spanish court – though Don Gonzalo is an exception to this – but also
its stiffness and pomposity.

	Nature surpassed itself in the formation	
	And true perfection of her lovely face.	865
King	In that case it will be a privilege	
	For me to arrange her marriage.	
D. Gon.	If that, sir,	
	Is your wish, I'm happy to accept	
	On her behalf, as she'll be happy too.	
	But who, your majesty, is the lucky man?	870
King	Unfortunately, he's away at present,	
	But he's a native of Seville, his name	
	Don Juan Tenorio.	
D. Gon.	In that case I shall	
	Ensure that Doña Ana is informed.	
King	Then go at once, Gonzalo, inform your daughter,	875
	And let me know her wishes in this matter.	

They exit. Enter Don Juan and Catalinón

D. Juan	Quick as you can, get the two horses ready.	
	They'll guarantee a swift escape for us.	
Catal.	My name's Catalinón, that's true enough,	
	Master. It means a 'shit', but I'm no 'shit'.	880
	There's not a man could ever say to me:	
	'Catalinón, your name's appropriate'.	
	They gave me my name quite improperly.	
	They should have known there are no flies on me!	
D. Juan	The fishermen are having a fine time,	885
	So while they're wholly occupied with wine	
	And feasting, you will saddle up the horses.	
	Remember the success of this deception,	
	Depends upon the fleetness of their feet.	

---

colloquialism meaning 'excrement'. There is also the word, *catalicón*, a vulgar form of *diacatalicón* which means a purgative. The *gracioso* or comic character of Golden-Age plays is usually someone lacking in any kind of virtue, and his name often epitomises his failings. Thus, Clarín, the *gracioso* of Calderón's *La vida es sueño*, is a self-interested individual whose name – meaning 'bugle' or 'trumpet' – points to his willingness to inform on others, to betray confidences, in order to advance himself.

884   no flies on me!: there is no basis for this joke in the Spanish text, but it seems appropriate to the character.

887   saddle up the horses: the galloping horse suggests, of course, the unbridled nature of passion and may be related both to Don Juan and to Tisbea whose head is now ruled by her heart. As far as Don Juan is concerned, the swift movement of the horse links with other allusions to speed and impetuosity – as in 303 where Don Pedro describes his leap from the balcony – and combines with them to create an impression of a sweeping and irresistible force.

	en cuyo rostro divino	
	se esmeró naturaleza.	865
Rey	Pues yo os la quiero casar	
	de mi mano.	
D. Gon.	Como sea	
	tu gusto, digo, señor,	
	que yo lo acepto por ella.	
	Pero ¿quién es el esposo?	870
Rey	Aunque no está en esta tierra,	
	es de Sevilla, y se llama	
	don Juan Tenorio.	
D. Gon.	Las nuevas	
	voy a llevar a doña Ana.	

....

Rey	Id en buen hora, y volved,	
	Gonzalo, con la respuesta.	

Vanse y salen Don Juan Tenorio y Catalinón

D. Juan	Esas dos yeguas prevén,	
	pues acomodadas son.	
Catal.	Aunque soy Catalinón,	
	soy, señor, hombre de bien;	880
	que no se dijo por mí:	
	"Catalinón es el hombre";	
	que sabes que aquese nombre	
	me asienta al revés a mí.	
D. Juan	Mientras que los pescadores	885
	van de regocijo y fiesta,	
	tú las dos yeguas apresta,	
	que de sus pies voladores	
	sólo nuestro engaño fío.	

---

867   <u>to arrange her marriage</u>: in many Golden-Age plays the monarch is portrayed in an idealized light, the representative on earth of divine justice, the source of a country's health and harmony. In one sense Don Alfonso of Castile is precisely this, for he is constantly trying to patch up the havoc created by Don Juan. He is certainly more favourably portrayed than the King of Naples who prefers to close his eyes to problems in his court. On the other hand, it has to be said that Tirso would have been unwise to have presented his audience with an ostensibly unfavourable picture of the Spanish king. What he does very effectively is show us a man who is always a step behind events and who, in consequence, is ever looking for solutions and rarely finding them. Thus, when he arranges Ana's marriage to Don Juan, we know that Isabela's seduction makes the marriage impossible. The King will have to change his mind. In short, Tirso's portrayal of Alfonso is one that points to inefficiency and hasty pragmatism. The Crown is shown to be out of touch with events.

879   <u>My name's Catalinón</u>: the precise meaning of the name is difficult to ascertain, though it may well be derived from *catalina*, an Andalusian

Catal.	Your mind's made up, then, master, to deceive	890
	Tisbea?	
D. Juan	What do you expect of me?	
	Seduction is the habit of a lifetime.	
	If you already know it's in my nature,	
	Why ask the question?	
Catal.	What I know for sure,	
	Master, is that you are the scourge of women.	895
D. Juan	Oh, I can hardly wait to have Tisbea!	
	What a fine body of a girl!	
Catal.	A fine	
	Reward for all her hospitality!	
D. Juan	Don't be a bore! This was the way Aeneas	
	Acted towards the lovely Queen of Carthage.	900
Catal.	What sort of man is it that takes advantage	
	Of these poor women? But you'll pay the price	
	For it one day. I hope you'll rot in Hell!	
D. Juan	Plenty of time for me to pay that debt!	
	Whoever gave you your name was right.	905
	Catalinón, he's always got the runs!	
Catal.	You run your way. In matters of deceiving	
	Honest women I prefer to run away.	
	Here comes the wretched girl. I pity her!	
D. Juan	You just make sure the horses are prepared.	910
Catal.	Poor girl! Her loss is our benefit.	
	Such is the way we pay for board and lodge!	

Exit Catalinón. Enter Tisbea

Tisbea	I've hardly been away from you, and yet	
	It's just as if I'd left my soul behind.	
D. Juan	I fancy you are teasing me, Tisbea,	915
	And so I won't believe a word you say.	
Tisbea	Why won't you?	

---

904   Plenty of time for me to pay that debt!: the phrase '¡Qué largo me lo fiáis!' was, in the slightly different form of *Tan largo me lo fiáis*, the title of an earlier version of *The Trickster* (see the Introduction). It is used by Don Juan on a number of occasions in the play to express his scorn for the conventional fear of death and the day of reckoning. As a young man, he wishes only to enjoy the pleasures of life and forget what lies ahead, but in so doing he closes his eyes to the fact that the pleasures of the world are fleeting and pass quickly by. The themes of the brevity of human life and the importance of placing one's faith in those values that are spiritual and eternal were central to the literature of seventeenth-century Spain and were powerfully expressed in the work of such writers as Quevedo, Góngora and Calderón.

914   my soul: once again Tisbea expresses herself in the language of Courtly Love. See Octavio's allusion to his love for Isabela, 205, note.

Catal.	Al fin ¿pretendes gozar	890
	a Tisbea?	
D. Juan	Si burlar	
	es hábito antiguo mío,	
	¿qué me preguntas, sabiendo	
	mi condición?	
Catal.	Ya sé que eres	
	castigo de las mujeres.	895
D. Juan	Por Tisbea estoy muriendo,	
	que es buena moza.	
Catal.	¡Buen pago	
	a su hospedaje deseas!	
D. Juan	Necio, lo mismo hizo Eneas	
	con la reina de Cartago.	900
Catal.	Los que fingís y engañáis	
	las mujeres de esa suerte	
	lo pagaréis con la muerte.	
D. Juan	¡Qué largo me lo fiáis!	
	Catalinón con razón	905
	te llaman.	
Catal.	Tus pareceres	
	sigue, que en burlar mujeres	
	quiero ser Catalinón.	
	Ya viene la desdichada.	
D. Juan	Vete, y las yeguas prevén.	910
Catal.	¡Pobre mujer! Harto bien	
	te pagamos la posada.	

Sale Catalinón y entra Tisbea

Tisbea	El rato que sin ti estoy	
	estoy ajena de mí.	
D. Juan	Por lo que finges ansí,	915
	ningún crédito te doy.	
Tisbea	¿Por qué?	

---

895   the scourge of women: the literal translation of the Spanish phrase is 'the punishment of women', and it is a curious fact of the play that, as has already been suggested in Isabela's case, the women who suffer are all themselves guilty of wrongdoing. That Don Juan should be the instrument of their punishment and the punishment more serious than their offence is undoubtedly ironic, but irony and ambiguity are two of the play's most interesting features.

898   all her hospitality!: see 90, note. Again the servant is used to comment on his master's moral shortcomings.

899   Aeneas: after his flight from Troy he encountered Dido, the reputed founder of Carthage and its beautiful queen. She fell in love with him and committed suicide when he abandoned her. The story is recounted in Virgil's *Aeneid*, Book IV.

D. Juan	Porque, si me amaras,	
	mi alma favorecieras.	
Tisbea	Tuya soy.	
D. Juan	Pues di, ¿qué esperas,	
	o en qué, señora, reparas?	920
Tisbea	Reparo en que fué castigo	
	de amor el que he hallado en ti.	
D. Juan	Si vivo, mi bien, en ti	
	a cualquier cosa me obligo.	
	Aunque yo sepa perder	925
	en tu servicio la vida,	
	la diera por bien perdida,	
	y te prometo de ser	
	tu esposo.	
Tisbea	Soy desigual	
	a tu ser.	930
D. Juan	Amor es rey	
	que iguala con justa ley	
	la seda con el sayal.	
Tisbea	Casi te quiero creer;	
	mas sois los hombres traidores.	935
D. Juan	¿Posible es, mi bien, que ignores	
	mi amoroso proceder?	
	Hoy prendes con tus cabellos	
	mi alma.	
Tisbea	Yo a ti me allano	
	bajo la palabra y mano	940
	de esposo.	
D. Juan	Juro, ojos bellos,	
	que mirando me matáis,	
	de ser vuestro esposo.	

---

929   I'm unworthy: Tisbea is well aware of the fact that the social divide between herself and Don Juan is very great indeed. In the play as a whole the social hierarchy of monarchy, nobility and peasants is suggested very clearly, as well as the divisions between the classes. Thus Isabela and Octavio, Ana and Mota are suited to each other in terms of class and marriage prospects, for all of them are nobles. Similarly, Tisbea is suited to the fisherman, Anfriso, whom she rejects, and the peasants, Batricio and Aminta, are made for each other. In contrast, although she has pretensions and aspirations to higher things, Tisbea is totally unsuited to Don Juan and can only bring trouble upon herself in trying to surmount the class barriers. In Golden - Age literature in general the rigid, hierarchical nature of society and the social and moral disorder attendant on its disruption are common themes. One of the best examples of a member of the lower orders who attempts to rise socially and comes to grief is Pablos, the protagonist of Quevedo's picaresque novel of 1626, *Historia de la vida*

D. Juan	Because, if you really loved	
	Me, you would ease this anguish in my soul.	
Tisbea	I do love you.	
D. Juan	Then why wait any longer?	
	I think there must be something on your mind.	920
Tisbea	What makes me hesitate's the thought that my	
	Love for you is a punishment on me.	
D. Juan	How can that be when from this moment on	
	My life is dedicated to your cause?	
	Why, though my life be lost in your service,	925
	The loss is one that, given the reward,	
	Makes such a sacrifice appear quite small!	
	In any case, I've given you my word	
	That we'll be joined in marriage.	
Tisbea	I'm unworthy	
	Of your status.	
D. Juan	Love's a king supreme,	930
	According to whose law there's no distinction	
	Between the finest silk or roughest sackcloth.	
Tisbea	I'm tempted to believe your argument,	
	But it's a fact that men are cheats and liars.	
D. Juan	How can it be, my love, that you are deaf	935
	To pleas inspired by my true devotion?	
	Such is the beauty of your lovely hair,	
	It has ensnared my soul.	
Tisbea	And you, my lord,	
	Command me. I accept your word and hand	
	In holy matrimony.	
D. Juan	The perfection	940
	Of your eyes is such that they destroy	
	Me with their gaze. I swear we shall be married.	

---

del buscón. While the literature of the time examines these issues, it is nevertheless true to say that in reality the degree of social movement upwards was somewhat greater.

941   your eyes: Don Juan speaks to Tisbea in the manner of a courtly lover, for whom, as Otis Green observes – *Spain and the Western Tradition: The Castilian Mind in Literature from 'El Cid' to Calderón*. . . I, p.255-, '. . .love is born of beauty, and the eyes are the instruments of its communication'. See too Sebastián de Covarrubias, *Tesoro de la lengua castellana o española*, in which eyes are described as 'the most precious part of the body. . ., the windows where the soul reveals itself, providing us with evidence of its passions and affections. . ., the messengers of the heart, the advocates of what is concealed deeply in our hearts. . .' Needless to say, Don Juan is merely giving a performance, though a highly convincing one. Throughout the play the idea of individuals giving a performance, in particular the nobility, points to the facade and the superficiality of Court life.

Tisbea	Advierte,

Tisbea   Advierte,
mi bien, que hay Dios y que hay muerte.

D. Juan   ¡Qué largo me lo fiáis!
         ᵛ mientras Dios me dé vida,   945
         yo vuestro esclavo seré.
         Esta es mi mano y mi fe.

Tisbea   No seré en pagarte esquiva.

D. Juan   Ya en mí mismo no sosiego.

Tisbea   Ven, y será la cabaña   950
         del amor que me acompaña
         tálamo de nuestro fuego.
         Entre estas cañas te esconde
         hasta que tenga lugar.

D. Juan   ¿Por dónde tengo de entrar?   955

Tisbea   Ven y te diré por dónde.

D. Juan   Gloria al alma, mi bien, dais.

Tisbea   Esa voluntad te obligue,
         y si no, Dios te castigue.

D. Juan   ¡Qué largo me lo fiáis!   960

    Vanse y salen Coridón, Anfriso, Belisa y
    Músicos

Corid.   Ea, llamad a Tisbea,
         y los zagales llamad
         para que en la soledad
         el huésped la corte vea.

Anfriso   ¡Tisbea, Usindra, Atandria!   965
         No vi cosa más cruel.
         ¡Triste y mísero de aquel
         que en su fuego es salamandria!

---

947   And here's my hand: the motif of the hand, associated with a promise
solemnly given, occurs in various forms throughout the play. For the
most part the promise is made to Don Juan's female victims and is
broken. Later the hand motif is reintroduced in the case of the promise
made to the stone guest, and the promise is kept. The stone guest also
extends his hand to Don Juan in a gesture of goodwill and proceeds to
crush him, deceiving him as he has deceived others. The deceiver is
thus deceived, the 'burlador burlado', the title of the play turned on
its head.

954   an opportunity to enter: the literal meaning of Tisbea's words does not
conceal a powerful sexual quality, reinforced by 956. By the end of Act
I she is very different indeed from the woman who earlier gloated over
the sufferings of the men she delighted in rejecting. According to
Jung, *Psychology and Alchemy* (London, 1953), 72, a door symbolises
female virginity. There is a very interesting discussion of this topic in
relation to Spanish ballads and traditional poetry by J.M. Aguirre,
'Moraima y el prisionero: ensayo de interpretación', in *Studies of the
Spanish and Portuguese Ballad*, ed. N.D. Shergold (London, 1972),

Tisbea	Do not forget God's punishment for men
	Who break their promises is death.
D. Juan	I trust

Tisbea Do not forget God's punishment for men
        Who break their promises is death.
D. Juan   I trust
        Death's still a long way off, but while I've life   945
        My promise is I'll be your loyal slave.
        And here's my hand, in token of my faith.
Tisbea In payment of your faith my coldness melts.
D. Juan With your acceptance my heart's all ablaze.
Tisbea Our love we'll celebrate in this, my humble   950
        Cottage, and there we'll consummate our passion.
        My bedroom shall be our bridal chamber.
        But first wait here among the reeds, until
        You have an opportunity to enter.
D. Juan But how shall I get in and not be seen?   955
Tisbea I'll show you. Look! This is the best way in.
D. Juan Already it's as if my soul were blessed.
Tisbea Don't forget your obligation to me!
        If you forget it, may God take revenge!
D. Juan A debt I'm not obliged to pay as yet!   960
        They exit. Enter Coridón, Anfriso, Belisa and Musicians
Corid. Go call Tisbea and bid her come at once.
        Bid all our good companions hurry too,
        So that our honoured guest in this secluded
        Spot may feast his eyes on our company.
Anfriso Tisbea, Usindra, Atandria! Join us here!   965
        No other girl can match her cruelty!
        Pity the man who falls in love with her!
        For like the salamander, he'll dwell in fire.

53-72. Aguirre gives as a pertinent example the conversation between a
young girl and her lover in the ballad *El enamorado y la muerte*:
               'Open the door to me, my dove
               Open the door to me, my love.'
               'How can I open the door to you
               When circumstance forbids I do?
               My father's home, for goodness sake,
               And mother is still wide awake.'
In Act II of *The Trickster* Don Juan tells the Marquis of Mota that Doña
Ana's door will be open from eleven o'clock at night. He, of course,
intends entering it before Mota.
968   the salamander: a kind of lizard which, according to legend, was
capable of surviving in fire. Allusions of this kind abound in Golden
Age literature in relation to the fires of love. Cf. Don Alonso in Lope
de Vega's *El caballero de Olmedo*:
               ...... for if I were to find myself
               Where I would gaze forever on Inés,
               Then would my soul be like the salamander.   (Act II, 912-14)

	Antes que el baile empecemos	
	a Tisbea prevengamos.	970
Belisa	Vamos a llamarla.	
Corid.	Vamos.	
Belisa	A su cabaña lleguemos.	
Corid.	¿No ves que estará ocupada	
	con los huéspedes dichosos,	
	de quien hay mil envidiosos?	975
Anfriso	Siempre es Tisbea envidiada.	
Belisa	Cantad algo mientras viene,	
	porque queremos bailar.	
Anfriso	¿Cómo podrá descansar	
	cuidado que celos tiene?	980

Cantan :

A pescar salió la niña
tendiendo redes;
y, en lugar de peces,
las almas prende.

Sale Tisbea

Tisbea	¡Fuego, fuego, que me quemo,	985

que mi cabaña se abrasa!
Repicad a fuego, amigos,
que ya dan mis ojos agua.
Mi pobre edificio queda
hecho otro Troya en las llamas,   990
que después que faltan Troyas
quiere amor quemar cabañas.
Mas si amor abrasa peñas
con gran ira y fuerza extraña,
mal podrán de su rigor   995
reservarse humildes pajas.
¡Fuego, zagales, fuego, agua, agua!
¡Amor, clemencia, que se abrasa el alma!
¡Ay, choza, vil instrumento
de mi deshonra y mi infamia!   1000

---

985   **My cottage is ablaze**: some critics believe that Tisbea's cottage is not on fire and that the allusion is merely to her anger, passion and frustration. Thus Gerald L. Wade, *El burlador de Sevilla y convidado de piedra* (New York, 1969), 191, note to 986–1045: 'Tisbea's cry of *fuego* in 986, and repeated hereafter at intervals, has on occasion been mistakenly thought to be a call for aid for her burning cabin. This would indicate Don Juan's attempt at arson after her seduction. Rather, her cry is one of desperation at his deceit, now that he has fled, and her cabin is burning only figuratively as a result of her own intense fire of thwarted love. . .' The end of the Act is clearly much more

	My friends, we'll wait a moment to begin	
	The dance until Tisbea joins us here.	970
Belisa	We'll go and fetch her.	
Corid.	Yes, we'll go at once!	
Belisa	We'll find her in her cottage. Let's go there!	
Corid.	We'd better not! She'll be preoccupied	
	In entertaining our noble guests!	
	How envious we are of their good fortune!	975
Anfriso	Tisbea's always the one who's envied most.	
Belisa	Until she comes we'll entertain ourselves	
	In song, and straight away begin the dance.	
Anfriso	How can the lover rest whose heart is heavy	
	And torn in two by cruel jealousy?	980

They sing

'The fishergirl went out to fish,
But all the fish swam by in shoals,
When she returned, she had no fish,
Her net was full of lovers' souls.'

Enter Tisbea

Tisbea	Help me, my friends! My cottage is ablaze,	985
	Burning, and I too am consumed by flames!	
	Sound the alarm! Bring water too as quickly	
	As you can, for my tears are not enough	
	To quench these flames! My cottage has become	
	Another Troy, destroyed by flame and fire!	990
	As though, having burnt all the other Troys,	
	Love's flame consumes the humblest cottage too.	
	But if love's fire is such that its assault	
	Reduces to mere ash the hardest stone,	
	What chance of escape from its fierce ardour	995
	Can straw have, when fragility's its nature?	
	My friends, the fire spreads! Bring water quickly!	
	My soul's on fire too! It burns! Have pity!	
	My own cottage, the vile and treacherous source	
	Of my disgrace and infamous dishonour!	1000

---

dramatic if the fire is real. If it were, it would parallel the flames of
the torches in Act II, 579, and the fire that fills the chapel in Act III,
976. In purely practical terms, setting fire to Tisbea's cottage provides
Don Juan with a better opportunity to escape, for the blaze occupies
the fishermen's attention and thus creates a timely diversion.

990   Another Troy: cf. 613.
996   straw: Tisbea has alluded earlier to the straw roof of her cottage which
protects her unblemished virtue in the same way that straw protects
glass-ware. Don Juan's blazing passion has now consumed and
destroyed her honour just as the flames destroy the brittle roof of the
cottage.

¡Cueva de ladrones fiera,
que mis agravios ampara!
Rayos de ardientes estrellas
en tus cabelleras caigan,
porque abrasadas estén,   1005
si del viento mal peinadas.
¡Ah, falso huésped, que dejas
una mujer deshonrada!
Nube que del mar salió
para anegar mis entrañas.   1010
¡Fuego, fuego, zagales, agua, agua!
¡Amor, clemencia, que se abrasa el alma!
Yo soy la que hacía siempre
de los hombres burla tanta;
que siempre las que hacen burla,   1015
vienen a quedar burladas.
Engañóme el caballero
debajo de fe y palabra
de marido, y profanó
mi honestidad y mi cama.   1020
Gozóme al fin, y yo propia
le di a su rigor las alas
en dos yeguas que crié,
con que me burló y se escapa.
Seguilde todos, seguilde.   1025
Mas no importa que se vaya,
que en la presencia del rey
tengo de pedir venganza.
¡Fuego, fuego, zagales, agua, agua!
¡Amor, clemencia, que se abrasa el alma! 1030

Vase Tisbea

Corid.   Seguid al vil caballero.
Anfriso ¡Triste del que pena y calla!
Mas ¡vive el cielo! que en él,
me he de vengar desta ingrata.
Vamos tras ella nosotros.   1035
porque va desesperada,
y podrá ser que ella vaya
buscando mayor desgracia.

1009   A cloud emerging from the sea: reference has already been made to the
        four elements of which the world was thought to be composed. See 348,
        note. A cloud's natural element was, of course, air and not water, but
        Tisbea refers here to a cloud emerging from water. In short, this
        confusion of elements points to the confusion and chaos which Don Juan
        has brought into her previously peaceful life. The whole of Tisbea's

A lair and hiding-place for cruel thieves,
For those two architects of my offence.
Let blazing sparks, hot as the hottest star,
Fall on your head and set your hair on fire;
Let flames consume, destroy it totally,   1005
And the wind comb whatever ruin's left!
False guest, that you should act so treacherously
Towards a woman's hospitality!
A cloud emerging from the sea to drown
And overwhelm me, to destroy my being!   1010
My friends, the fire spreads! Bring water quickly!
My soul's on fire too. It burns. Have pity!
I am the one who always mocked all men
And took delight in all their suffering.
The truth is those who think they fool all others   1015
Are in the end the ones who fool themselves.
The nobleman's the source of my deception,
For he's betrayed the promise of his hand
In marriage, abused me, profaned my bed
And robbed me of my honesty and virtue.   1020
For he's the one's seduced me. I'm the one
Who's favoured his escape by giving him
The wings of horses to facilitate
His trickery and make a fool of me.
I beg you, follow him and track him down.   1025
The fact that he's escaped won't help him much.
I'll seek an audience with the King and beg him
To intervene and guarantee me vengeance.
My friends, the fire spreads! Bring water quickly!
My soul's on fire too. It burns. Have pity!   1030

Exit Tisbea

Corid.   We'll all pursue this treacherous nobleman.
Anfriso   Pity the man who loves in vain!
           But even so i swear that Heaven through him
           Gives me my vengeance for her faithlessness.
           We'd better go at once and look for her;   1035
           Her state of mind is desperate; we'd best
           Make sure she doesn't, in her desperation,
           Add further to the sum of her misfortunes.

---

speech, as well as its physical action, underline this idea, for
throughout the allusions to the contrasting elements of fire and water
mingle, while at the end of the act Tisbea herself, burning with
passion, wades into the sea.

1023   The wings of horses: presumably a reference to Pegasus, the winged
horse of Greek mythology.

Corid.	Tal fin la soberbia tiene.
	¡Su locura y confianza 1040
	paró en esto!

[Dice Tisbea dentro] ¡Fuego, fuego!

Anfriso	Al mar se arroja.
Corid.	Tisbea, detente y para.
Tisbea	¡Fuego, fuego, zagales, agua, agua!
	¡Amor, clemencia, que se abrasa el alma!

Corid.   How true it is: pride always comes before
           A fall. Such was her over-confidence,   1040
           Such is its consequence.
      Tisbea's cries off-stage: My soul's on fire!
Anfriso   She's in the water!
Corid.   Tisbea! Wait! Come back! Go out no further!
Tisbea   My friends, the fire spreads! Bring water quickly!
           My soul's on fire too! It burns! Have pity!

Salen el Rey Don Alonso y Don Diego Tenorio,
de barba

Rey	¿Qué me dices?
D.Diego	Señor, la verdad digo.

Por esta carta estoy del caso cierto,
que es de tu embajador y de mi hermano:
halláronle en la cuadra del rey mismo
con una hermosa dama de palacio.   5

Rey	¿Qué calidad?
D.Diego	Señor, es la duquesa

Isabela.

Rey	¿Isabela?
D.Diego	Por lo menos. . .
Rey	¡Atrevimiento temerario! ¿Y dónde

ahora está?

D.Diego	Señor, a vuestra alteza

no he de encubrille la verdad: anoche   10
a Sevilla llegó con un criado.
Ya conocéis, Tenorio, que os estimo,
y al rey informaré del caso luego,
casando a ese rapaz con Isabela,
volviendo a su sosiego al duque Octavio,   15
que inocente padece; y luego al punto
haced que don Juan salga desterrado.

D.Diego	¿Adónde, mi señor?
Rey	Mi enojo vea

en el destierro de Sevilla; salga
a Lebrija esta noche, y agradezca   20
sólo al merecimiento de su padre. . .
Pero, decid, don Diego, ¿qué diremos
a Gonzalo de Ulloa, sin que erremos?
Caséle con su hija, y no sé cómo
lo puedo ahora remediar.

D.Diego	Pues mira, 25

gran señor, qué mandas que yo haga

---

1   Don Diego: in the earlier version of the play entitled *Tan largo me lo*
fiáis – see Introduction – Don Juan's father is called Don Juan Tenorio,
viejo. In this respect see Act II, 669 of *The Trickster* where Gaseno
clearly thinks that the father's name is also Don Juan Tenorio.

3   your ambassador: of Don Alfonso of Castile, sent by him to Naples. Don
Diego, we recall, is High Chamberlain to King Alfonso.

7   Isabela!: it is not clear how the King of Castile would have known quite
so well a particular lady of the Court of Naples. In reality, as has been

74

ACT II

Enter the King, Don Alfonso and Don Diego Tenorio,
bearded

King	What are you saying?
D.Diego	Nothing but the truth,

My lord. This letter makes the matter clear.
It's signed by your ambassador, my brother.
They found him in the King's own royal chamber,
And with him there a lady of the Court.   5

King	What rank was she?
D.Diego	None other than the Duchess

Isabela!

King	The Duchess Isabela?

What bare-faced boldness! Where's the rascal now?

D.Diego	Your majesty, I am an honest man.

I'll not conceal the truth from you. Last night   10
He reached Seville, accompanied by his servant.

King	You know, Tenorio, I esteem you highly.

I'll see the King of Naples is informed
Of this. The rogue must marry Isabela.
We must restore Octavio's peace of mind.   15
He suffers in all innocence. As well
As that, Don Juan is exiled from this moment!

D.Diego	Where shall he go, your majesty?
King	My anger's

Such, that he's now banished from Seville.
Lebrija'll be his home, and he can thank   20
His father that his sentence is so light. . .
But now, Don Diego, what are we to say
To Don Gonzalo de Ulloa when I've
Arranged his daughter's marriage to your son?
What are we now to do?

D.Diego	My only wish, 25

Your majesty, whatever you command,

---

stated previously, there were no political links between Castile and
Naples at the time of the play's action. Even if there had been, King
Alfonso would have been unlikely to respond to Isabela's plight in this
way. Tirso invented and heightened relationships for greater dramatic
effect.

20   Lebrija: the town of Lebrija is situated some thirty-five miles south of
Seville and was mentioned by Roman writers.

```
             que esté bien al honor de esta señora,
             hija de un padre tal.
                                Un medio tomo,
             con que absolvello del enojo entiendo:
             mayordomo mayor pretendo hacelle.          30
        Sale un Criado
Criado       Un caballero llega de camino,
             y dice, señor, que es el duque Octavio.
Rey          ¿El duque Octavio?
Criado                           Sí, señor.
Rey                                      Sin duda
             que supo de don Juan el desatino,
             y que viene, incitado a la venganza,       35
             a pedir que le otorgue desafío.
D.Diego      Gran señor, en tus heroicas manos
             está mi vida, que mi vida propia
             es la vida de un hijo inobediente;
             que, aunque mozo, gallardo y valeroso,     40
             y le llaman los mozos de su tiempo
             el Héctor de Sevilla, porque ha hecho
             tantas y tan extrañas mocedades,
             la razón puede mucho. No permitas
             el desafío, si es posible.
Rey                                Basta.              45
             Ya os entiendo, Tenorio: honor de padre.
             Entre el duque.
D.Diego                      Señor, dame esas plantas.
             ¿Cómo podré pagar mercedes tantas?
        Sale el Duque Octavio, de camino
Octav.       A esos pies, gran señor, un peregrino,
             mísero y desterrado, ofrece el labio,      50
             juzgando por más fácil el camino
             en vuestra gran presencia.
Rey                                     Duque Octavio. . .
Octav.       Huyendo vengo el fiero desatino
```

---

30   <u>major-domo</u>: Don Gonzalo de Ulloa is, as we have seen, the Grand Commander of the order of Calatrava. See Act I, 698. The position of major-domo involved living in the palace, assuming responsibility for the palace keys at night, arranging official functions, attending the king at ceremonies in public, and commanding the palace guard. Clearly, King Alfonso sees the promotion of Don Gonzalo in terms of a sop to offended pride. Once more he is seen to be a step behind events as they occur, attempting to behave pragmatically in order to resolve them but in the process revealing himself to be a monarch who is somewhat hasty and inefficient. See Act I, 867, note.

42   <u>the Hector of Seville</u>: in Homer's *Iliad* Hector, son of Priam and Hecuba,

	Is that the lady's honour be considered.	
	Her father is a worthy man.	
King	My plan	
	To overcome his wrath should prove sufficient.	
	I'll make him major-domo of the palace.	30

A servant enters

Servant	A nobleman's arrived, your majesty,	
	From Italy. His name is Duke Octavio.	
King	The Duke Octavio?	
Servant	Yes, your majesty.	
King	No doubt he's learned of Don Juan's treachery	
	And comes inflamed with thoughts of vengeance, bent	35
	On seeking my permission for a duel.	
D.Diego	Your majesty, my life is in your hands,	
	A father's name and reputation tied	
	Inexorably to a disobedient	
	Son, young, handsome and bold, who by his friends	40
	Throughout the length and breadth of this our city	
	Is called the Hector of Seville, because	
	His deeds appear to defy the mortal.	
	But reason can achieve great things, my lord.	
	I beg of you, forbid they fight a duel.	45
King	I understand, Tenorio, what a father's	
	Honour means to him. Bid the Duke come in.	
D.Diego	Your majesty, I am forever grateful.	

Enter Duke Octavio, dressed as a traveller

Octav.	I kneel before you, your great majesty,	
	And pay you homage, the misery of exile,	50
	My long and tedious journey now transformed	
	By your noble presence.	
King	Duke Octavio. . .	
Octav.	A woman's senseless folly and the actions	

---

is portrayed as the Trojan hero during the seige of Troy. This kind of heroism is evidently not that for which Don Juan is best known in Seville, but Don Diego, though aware of his son's shortcomings, is anxious that the King should see him in the most favourable light possible.

47   Honour: the implication seems to be that a duel at Octavio's request would require an accusation against Don Juan which would make his seduction of and treachery towards Isabela public knowledge, thereby dragging the Tenorio name through the mud.

48+   dressed as a traveller: Octavio is probably wearing the traditional costume of coloured cloth, a hat with plumes and boots with spurs.

	de una mujer, el no pensado agravio
	de un caballero que la causa ha sido 55
	de que así a vuestros pies haya venido.
Rey	Ya, duque Octavio, sé vuestra inocencia.
	Yo al rey escribiré que os restituya
	en vuestro estado, puesto que el ausencia
	que hicisteis algún daño os atribuya. 60
	Yo os casaré en Sevilla con licencia
	y también con perdón y gracia suya,
	que puesto que Isabela un ángel sea,
	mirando la que os doy, ha de ser fea.
	Comendador mayor de Calatrava 65
	es Gonzalo de Ulloa, un caballero
	a quien el moro por temor alaba,
	que siempre es el cobarde lisonjero.
	Este tiene una hija en quien bastaba
	en dote la virtud, que considero, 70
	después de la beldad, que es maravilla;
	y es sol de las estrellas de Sevilla.
	Esta quiero que sea vuestra esposa.
Octav.	Cuando este viaje le emprendiera
	a sólo esto, mi suerte era dichosa 75
	sabiendo yo que vuestro gusto fuera.
Rey	Hospedaréis al duque, sin que cosa
	en su regalo falte.
Octav.	Quien espera
	en vos, señor, saldrá de premios lleno.
	Primero Alfonso sois, siendo el onceno. 80

Vanse el Rey y Don Diego, y sale Ripio

Ripio	¿Qué ha sucedido?
Octav.	Que he dado
	el trabajo recebido,

---

67   Whose reputation terrifies the Moors: since the action of the play is set
in the first half of the fourteenth century, the Reconquest of Spain by
the Christians still had more than a century left for its completion. The
orders of Calatrava, Alcántara and Santiago, all founded in the twelfth
century, had, as has been stated – Act I, 698, note –, both a military
and religious character and were responsible for defence at important
points along the frontier between the Christian and Moorish territories,
wherever that happened to be at any given time between the second
half of the twelfth century and the final defeat of the Moors in 1492.

72   she is the sun: just as the world was thought to consist of the four
elements – see Act I, 348, note–, so everything had its alloted place in
the great chain of being, the sun reigning supreme amongst the
planets. The medieval and post-medieval habit of thinking in terms of

	Of a nobleman are the cause of my	
	Departure and the reason why I now	55
	Appear before you and implore your help.	
King	I know, Octavio, you are innocent.	
	Your king shall be informed of this; his favour	
	You shall enjoy once more, lest it be thought	
	Your absence is the proof of your guilt.	60
	A marriage in Seville I shall arrange	
	For you, with his permission and agreement,	
	To a lady who in her beauty far	
	Exceeds Isabela. Her father's Don	
	Gonzalo de Ulloa, the commander	65
	Of Calatrava, nobleman and soldier,	
	Whose reputation terrifies the Moors	
	And out of fear generates their praise.	
	His daughter's virtue is itself sufficient	
	As a dowry, matched only by her beauty	70
	Which is itself a second miracle.	
	Amongst Seville's bright stars she is the sun,	
	The lovely bride that I intend for you.	
Octav.	Were this, your majesty, the only purpose	
	Of my journey, I would be happy indeed	75
	In the knowledge that this is your pleasure.	
King	[To Don Diego]	
	Accommodate the Duke and make quite sure	
	He's not deprived of anything.	
Octav.	How wise	
	Are we who place our faith in King Alfonso,	
	Eleventh in line but first in generosity!	80

Exit the King and Don Diego. Enter Ripio

Ripio	What did he say?
Octav.	The troubles that have plagued
	Me, Ripio, are now nothing when compared

---

correspondences between man and the world in which he lived led too to analogies and images of the kind we have here: the supreme beauty of Don Gonzalo's daughter expressed in terms of the sun, the supreme planet.

80   **Eleventh in line but first in generosity:** from the moment of his arrival at Alfonso's court, Octavio is all humility and gratitude. His difficulties are, as we have seen, considerable, involving not only the loss of Isabela but also the disfavour of his king, and it is therefore understandable that he should express himself as he does. On the other hand, it is clear that Tirso's ironic portrayal of Octavio, evident in Act I, continues here. His earlier distress over Isabela's treachery vanishes with the promise of a new bride, even though he has not set eyes on her. Self-interest appears to motivate him as much as it does all the other characters of the play.

79

conforme me ha sucedido,
desde hoy por bien empleado.
Hablé al rey, vióme y honróme.   85
César con el César fuí,
pues vi, peleé y vencí;
y hace que esposa tome
de su mano, y se prefiere
a desenojar al rey   90
en la fulminada ley.

Ripio   Con razón el nombre adquiere
de generoso en Castilla.
Al fin, ¿te llegó a ofrecer
mujer?

Octav.   Sí, amigo, mujer   95
de Sevilla, que Sevilla
da, si averiguallo quieres,
porque de oíllo te asombres,
si fuertes y airosos hombres,
también gallardas mujeres.   100
Un manto tapado, un brío,
donde un puro sol se esconde,
si no es en Sevilla, ¿adónde
se admite? El contento mío
es tal que ya me consuela   105
en mi mal.

Salen Don Juan y Catalinón

Catal.   Señor: detente,
que aqui está el duque, inocente
Sagitario de Isabela,
aunque mejor le diré
Capricornio.

D. Juan   Disimula.   110

Catal.   Cuando le vende la adula.

---

87   **I came, I saw, and even conquered too!**: Tirso's mockery of a man capable of uttering such absurdities in the full flush of his own success, yet blind to that absurdity, is very clear here.

105   **my anguish has become my joy!**: no sooner are Octavio's fortunes transformed for the better than he is confronted by the author of his original misfortune, though he is as yet unaware of Don Juan's part in it. Nevertheless, the apparently episodic and loose structure of the play is often, as in this case, used for ironic effect. Don Juan's casual appearance already sets before us the prospect of Octavio's losing the bride he has not yet seen, of the bubble of self-congratulatory complacency about to be pricked. In the light of this possibility Octavio's fulsome praise of Don Juan renders him even more comic, while Don Juan's blatant flattery of Octavio ensures that we warm to the rogue.

80

	To the good fortune I've been favoured with	
	Today. I'd say the wheel has come full-circle.	
	The audience with the King has honoured me,	85
	Caesar favoured by yet another Ceasar;	
	I came, I saw, and even conquered too!	
	The King has chosen to arrange my marriage	
	By his own hand, and promised he will speak	
	On my behalf to our King in Naples.	90
	The law that exiles me will be repealed.	
Ripio	My word, my lord! He's famous in Castile	
	For generosity. It's well deserved!	
	Do you mean to say he offered you a wife	
	As well?	
Octav.	He did, Ripio. He told me she	95
	Is from Seville, and as I understand	
	It – and if you wish, you can confirm this truth	
	If you have little faith in this assertion –,	
	Seville boasts of its strong and handsome men	
	And also of the beauty of its women.	100
	A veil conceals a face, a lively spirit,	
	Hiding the dazzling beauty of the sun!	
	Where else but in Seville can that be true?	
	In short, the happiness confered on me	
	Is such, my anguish has become my joy!	105

Enter Don Juan and Catalinon

Catal.	Hold your horses, master! Look who's here!
	The Duke himself, in all his innocence,
	The Sagittarius to your Isabela,
	Though I'd prefer to call him Capricorn!
D. Juan	You hold your tongue! Pretend that nothing's happened!
Catal.	Flatter him well, before you turn the knife!

---

108 Sagittarius: the ninth sign of the zodiac. The constellation is portrayed as a centaur shooting an arrow. The classical story relates to Chiron, the wise centaur, who was accidentally wounded by Heracles and subsequently placed by Zeus among the stars as Sagittarius. Catalinón refers to Octavio as Sagittarius because he has been wounded by Isabela's treachery and exiled on account of her.

109 Capricorn!: the tenth sign of the zodiac. In classical mythology Capricorn was in fact the god Pan who changed himself into a goat through fear of the giant, Typhon. As a constellation Capricorn was represented with goat's feet and horns. For the seventeenth century horns suggested infidelity and cuckoldry, and for Catalinón, therefore, Octavio is not only a Sagittarius, a man betrayed, but a Capricorn, a cuckold.

D. Juan	Como a Nápoles dejé	
	por enviarme a llamar	
	con tanta priesa mi rey,	
	y como su gusto es ley,	115
	no tuve, Octavio, lugar	
	de despedirme de vos	
	de ningún modo.	
Octav.	Por eso,	
	don Juan, amigo os confieso:	
	que hoy nos juntamos los dos	120
	en Sevilla.	
D. Juan	¡Quién pensara,	
	duque, que en Sevilla os viera	
	para que en ella os sirviera,	
	como yo lo deseaba!	
	¿Vos Puzol, vos la ribera	125
	dejáis? Mas aunque es lugar	
	Nápoles tan excelente,	
	por Sevilla solamente	
	se puede, amigo, dejar.	
Octav.	Si en Nápoles os oyera	130
	y no en la parte que estoy,	
	del crédito que ahora os doy	
	sospecho que me riera.	
	Mas llegándola a habitar	
	es, por lo mucho que alcanza,	135
	corta cualquiera alabanza	
	que a Sevilla queréis dar.	
	¿Quién es el que viene allí?	
D. Juan	El que viene es el marqués	
	de la Mota. Descortés	140
	es fuerza ser.	
Octav.	Si de mí	
	algo hubiereis menester,	
	aquí espada y brazo está.	
Catal.	[Ap.] Y si importa gozará	
	en su nombre otra mujer;	145
	que tiene buena opinión.	

---

121   A coincidence, Octavio: a good example of Don Juan's ironic mocking tone and of the way in which, during the first half of the play in particular, he makes the audience a sympathetic party to his mockery of others.

125   Pozzuoli: a town near Naples, distinguished for its beautiful sandy bay.

144   In that case you won't mind if your name: the asides of Catalinón provide an additional mocking, deflating element in the play, here in relation to Octavio's chivalrous offer to Don Juan. Golden-Age literature

D. Juan	Octavio, my apologies! I left	
	Naples with what must seem unseemly haste.	
	The King's orders, you understand, so blame	
	Him for my not taking my leave of you.	115
	He sent for me quite unexpectedly.	
	I couldn't disobey but neither could	
	I say goodbye to you. You will forgive	
	My disrespect now won't you?	
Octav.	There's no need	
	To forgive when now we renew our friendship	120
	In Seville.	
D. Juan	A coincidence, Octavio,	
	Beyond belief! Who would have guessed I'd see	
	You once again and in Seville, where I	
	Can serve you, place myself at your disposal.	
	How could you bring yourself to leave Pozzuoli,	125
	That sandy shore? And Naples too? The world	
	Acclaims it as a city unsurpassed,	
	Except by Seville, which, to tell the truth,	
	Cannot be matched by any other place.	
Octav.	If we were still in Naples, my dear friend,	130
	And not in Seville, I would hardly give	
	The slightest credence to such lavish praise.	
	It's much more likely that I'd laugh at it.	
	But now I've had a chance to see the place,	
	I'd even say that such extravagance	135
	As yours falls short of any approbation	
	That this most beautiful of cities merits.	
	But who's this man that now approaches us?	
D. Juan	His name's the marquis of Mota, a friend	
	Of mine. You'll understand that if I speak	140
	To him, it's no discourtesy to you.	
Octav.	My sword's at your disposal if you need	
	It. Your wish, Don Juan, is my command.	
Catal.	*[Aside]* In that case you won't mind if your name	
	Will help my master, give him half a chance,	145
	To fool some other girl - with your permission!	

---

abounds in such mockery, often realized through the juxtaposition of opposites. Thus, Sancho Panza's earthy good sense constantly pierces Don Quixote's inspiring idealism, while in the drama especially the down-to-earth, sometimes crude observations of the *graciosos* explode all manner of high-flown rhetoric on matters such as love and honour. In a sense it is a pointer to the growing disillusionment of the seventeenth century, of a much more sceptical attitude to the high ideals of the Renaissance. And it is certainly an indication of the greater complexity of the age.

D. Juan	De vos estoy satisfecho.	
Catal.	Si fuere de algún provecho,	
	señores, Catalinón,	
	vuarcedes continuamente	150
	me hallarán para servillos.	
Ripio	¿Y dónde?	
Catal.	En los Pajarillos,	
	tabernáculo excelente.	

*Vanse Octavio y Ripio, y sale el Marqués
de la Mota*

Mota	Todo hoy os ando buscando,	
	y no os he podido hallar.	155
	¿Vos, don Juan, en el lugar,	
	y vuestro amigo penando	
	en vuestra ausencia?	
D. Juan	¡Por Dios,	
	amigo, que me debéis	
	esa merced que me hacéis!	160
Catal.	*[Ap.]* Como no le entreguéis vos	
	moza o cosa que lo valga,	
	bien podéis fiaros dél;	
	que en cuanto en esto es cruel,	
	tiene condición hidalga.	165
D. Juan	¿Qué hay de Sevilla?	
Mota	Está ya	
	toda esta corte mudada.	
D. Juan	¿Mujeres?	
Mota	Cosa juzgada.	
D. Juan	¿Inés?	
Mota	A Vejel se va.	

---

153   'The Duck and Drake'!: this is a free rendering of the Spanish text in which the name of the inn is given as 'Pajarillos', 'Little Birds'. The two servants here imitate mockingly the earlier exchanges between Don Juan and Octavio, a common device in Golden Age drama aimed in part, no doubt, at raising a laugh amongst the servants in the audience who would have been situated in the standing area immediately in front of the stage.

159   A gesture of friendship: just as Don Juan has mocked Octavio with affirmations of loyalty and friendship, so he now mocks Mota, once more carrying with him the sympathies of the spectator. Mota, like Don Juan, represents the Spanish nobility but is shown by Tirso to have little nobility about him. Throughout Act II he is presented as an individual distinguished above all by a double standard of sexual morality, as Catalinón observes in 165.

168   Any worthwhile women?: the women alluded to in the ensuing conversation are, of course, prostitutes, and the picture of Seville which emerges is of an extremely corrupt and immoral place. At the

84

D. Juan	Glad to have seen you once again, Octavio!	
Catal.	If any of you gentlemen would like	
	To have me at your disposal, I'd be glad	
	To wait on you. You'll find me always ready	150
	And willing to provide the best of service.	
Ripio	I need a lackey! Where would you serve me?	
Catal.	'The Duck and Drake'! A very fine hostelry!	

Exit Octavio and Ripio. Enter the Marquis of Mota

Mota	My friend, I've spent the whole day scouring	
	The city looking for you! Here and there,	155
	Up and down, in and out, and not a scrap	
	Of care or concern for a dear friend	
	Who's broken-hearted because he can't find	
	You!	
D. Juan	A gesture of friendship matching my	
	Affection for you! How can you complain?	160
Catal.	*[Aside]* As long as you don't offer him something	
	Valuable, such as your best girl-friend,	
	You can be sure he's a gentleman.	
	But when it comes to girls, it's something else!	
	He just behaves like all these gentlemen!	165
D. Juan	What news in Seville since I went away?	
Mota	The place has changed. Barely recognizable.	
D. Juan	Any worthwhile women?	
Mota	Not much to shout	
	About.	
D. Juan	What about Inés? She still here?	
Mota	She's gone. To Vejel.	

---

time of the play's composition Seville was – see Act I, 574, note – one of Spain's most important cities and felt the greatest impact of South American trade. Reference has been made to the portrayal of Sevillian 'low-life' in such writers as Cervantes, and this picture is clearly reinforced by contemporary accounts of a more factual nature. Thus, an apparent contemporary of Tirso, the *licenciado* Porras de la Cámara, writing to the Archbishop of Seville, draw attention to the city's immorality, its adulterers, murderers, swindlers, idlers, usurers, its 300 gambling houses and its 3000 brothels. See *Revista de Archivos Bibliotecas y Museos*, IV (1900), 550-54. The point has been made already that the description of Seville, with its evident criticism of the Spanish Court, contrasts with the earlier praise of Lisbon – see Act I, 721, note.

169 Vejel: this is Vejel de la Frontera, a city in the province of Cadiz, but in the Spanish text there is also a joke which cannot be suggested in English, for Vejel brings to mind the Spanish word for old age, 'vejez', which Inés is quickly travelling towards.

D. Juan	Buen lugar para vivir	170
	la que tan dama nació.	
Mota	El tiempo la desterró	
	a Vejel.	
D. Juan	Irá a morir.	
	¿Constanza?	
Mota	Es lástima vella	
	lampiña de frente y ceja.	175
	Llámale el portugués vieja,	
	y ella imagina que bella.	
D. Juan	Sí, que velha en portugués	
	suena vieja en castellano.	
	¿Y Teodora?	
Mota	Este verano	180
	se escapó del mal francés	
	por un río de sudores;	
	y está tan tierna y reciente,	
	que anteayer me arrojó un diente	
	envuelto entre muchas flores.	185
D. Juan	¿Julia, la del Candilejo?	
Mota	Ya con sus afeites lucha.	
D. Juan	¿Véndese siempre por trucha?	
Mota	Ya se da por abadejo.	
D. Juan	El barrio de Cantarranas,	190
	¿tiene buena población?	
Mota	Ranas las más dellas son.	
D. Juan	¿Y viven las dos hermanas?	
Mota	Y la mona de Tolú	
	de su madre Celestina	195
	que les enseña dotrina.	
D. Juan	¡Oh, vieja de Bercebú!	
	¿Cómo la mayor está?	

---

176   Her hair's dropped out: no doubt her loss of hair is a symptom o
venereal disease.
179   In Portuguese: the Portuguese word for 'old' is *velha*, the Spanish fo
'pretty' *bella*. As in the case of 169, the joke cannot be translated.
182   She sweated over that: sweating was one of the traditional treatment
for venereal disease. In Cervantes's short story, *El casamient*
engañoso, the protagonist, Campuzano, emerges from the Hospital de l
Resurrección in Valladolid where he has been treated for syphilis an
made to sweat profusely twice a day for twenty days.
186   flowers: the literal translation of the Spanish here is 'wrapped in man
flowers'. It is not clear whether the flowers are real or whether th
word *flores* is being used in the sense of 'compliment'.
187   Lamp Street?: the street was apparently known by this name from a
early as 1492, the name deriving from a story connected with Pedro

| D. Juan | A fine place to live | 170 |

D. Juan   A fine place to live   170
For a woman of such distinguished birth.

Mota   It's time that marched her there, and not before
Time!

D. Juan   Sounds as if her only future bed–
Fellow is death! And any news of Constance?

Mota   I'm sorry to say she's a sorry sight.   175
Her hair's dropped out, her eyebrows too. A chap
I knew – a Portuguese – called her a hag.
She thought the poor fellow'd called her pretty!

D. Juan   In Portuguese the Spanish word for pretty
Does mean old! A nice mistake! How's Theodora?   180

Mota   A narrow escape this summer from the pox.
She sweated over that and now she's cured,
A tender piece of ham, so appetising!
She gave me a nice present yesterday:
A tooth of hers she's cut quite recently,   185
And with it a beautiful bunch of flowers.

D. Juan   What about Julia, she lives in Lamp Street?

Mota   Gets on your wick! She's just a painted tart!

D. Juan   And passing herself off as tasty trout?

Mota   A piece of cod gone off! Just have a sniff?   190

D. Juan   The district Cantarranas. What's that like?

Mota   As you'd expect! It means the Singing Frogs,
It's full of them.

D. Juan   Are those two sisters still
Around?

Mota   Yes, and the monkey from Tolú,
The old procuress teaching them her tricks.   195

D. Juan   Yes, that's the one! Truly a hag from Hell.
The elder of the girls, what's she like now?

(the Cruel), King of Castile from 1350 to 1369. Seeing Pedro killing a
man in a duel, an old woman, overcome by fright, dropped a lamp from
her window.

189   tasty trout?: the allusions to these women as trout, cod and frogs, in
descending order of tastiness, are common enough in the literature of
the Golden Age.

191   Cantarranas: the meaning of the name is 'the singing frogs'. It has
been suggested that the district was so called on account of an area of
swampy ground which contained many frogs. Santiago Montoto, *Las
calles de Sevilla* (Seville, 1940), p.245, suggests that the name was
applied not to a district but to a street, now named Gravina, and that
the name derived from the fact that the street contained the outlet
drains for the city.

194   Tolú: a town on the coast of Colombia from which monkeys were
dispatched to Europe.

Mota	Blanca, sin blanca ninguna;	
	tiene un santo a quien ayuna.	200
D. Juan	¿Agora en vigilias da?	
Mota	Es firme y santa mujer.	
D. Juan	¿Y esotra?	
Mota	Mejor principio	
	tiene; no desecha ripio.	
D. Juan	Buen albañir quiere ser.	205
	Marqués: ¿qué hay de perros muertos?	
Mota	Yo y don Pedro de Esquivel	
	dimos anoche un cruel,	
	y esta noche tengo ciertos	
	otros dos.	
D. Juan	Iré con vos,	210
	que también recorreré	
	cierto nido que dejé	
	en güevos para los dos.	
	¿Qué hay de terrero?	
Mota	No muero	
	en terrero, que en-terrado	215
	me tiene mayor cuidado.	
D. Juan	¿Cómo?	
Mota	Un imposible quiero.	
D. Juan	Pues ¿no os corresponde?	
Mota	Sí,	
	me favorece y estima.	
D. Juan	¿Quién es?	
Mota	Doña Ana, mi prima,	220
	que es recién llegada aquí.	
D. Juan	Pues ¿dónde ha estado?	
Mota	En Lisboa,	
	con su padre en la embajada.	
D. Juan	¿Es hermosa?	
Mota	Es estremada,	
	porque en doña Ana de Ulloa	225
	se estremó naturaleza.	
D. Juan	¿Tan bella es esa mujer?	

---

198   If you mean Penny: the Spanish line reads: 'Blanca, sin blanca
ninguna'. There is a play on words, *Blanca* being the name of the girl,
sin blanca meaning 'without a penny'. To retain the joke in English
requires changing the girl's name.

Mota	If you mean Penny, she's quite penniless!
	But pure with it! A good and honest man
	Suffers on her behalf.
D. Juan	And she abstains 200
	On his account?
Mota	Oh, she's become a true
	And constant woman. No chance there for you!
D. Juan	The other one?
Mota	Now she's more promising.
	Show her a good hand and she'll come up trumps!
D. Juan	That sounds more like it! But what about the tarts 205
	You've tricked, done business with and left them empty-
	Handed?
Mota	Last night Pedro Esquivel and I
	Plucked all the feathers from a lovely bird.
	Two more are certain to be plucked tonight.
D. Juan	In that case you won't mind if I come too. 210
	There's a little love-nest I'd like to find.
	A little plot I'd like to hatch. What about
	Courting ladies at their windows from
	The terrace below?
Mota	Don't mention below.
	Below ground's where I'll find myself quite soon. 215
	Believe me. I'm a sick man, doomed to die.
D. Juan	But what is your affliction?
Mota	Hopeless love!
D. Juan	You mean she doesn't favour you at all?
Mota	She does! She loves me, thinks the world of me.
D. Juan	Who is she?
Mota	She's my cousin, Doña Ana! 220
	It's only recently she's come to live
	Here in Seville.
D. Juan	Where was she?
Mota	Lived in Lisbon
	With her father. He was ambassador.
D. Juan	Good looking girl?
Mota	No, more than that. Outstanding!
	When nature fashioned Ana de Ulloa, 225
	It must have been amazed by its achievement.
D. Juan	No woman is as beautiful as that!

---

207   Pedro Esquivel: Gerald E. Wade, *El burlador de Sevilla y convidado de piedra* (New York, 1969), p.197, observes that the Esquivel family 'was well known in Sevilla' and cites various works of reference as evidence. He concludes: 'Although we cannot identify exactly the Pedro Esquivel of our text, we do not doubt his reality as a person of Tirso's time. .'

	¡Vive Dios que la he de ver!	
Mota	Veréis la mayor belleza	
	que los ojos del rey ven.	230
D. Juan	Casaos, pues es estremada.	
Mota	El rey la tiene casada,	
	y no se sabe con quién.	
D. Juan	¿No os favorece?	
Mota	Y me escribe.	
Catal.	[Ap.] No prosigas, que te engaña	235
	el gran burlador de España.	
D. Juan	Quien tan satisfecho vive	
	de su amor, ¿desdichas teme?	
	Sacalda, solicitalda,	
	escribilda y engañalda,	240
	y el mundo se abrase y queme.	
Mota	Agora estoy aguardando	
	la postrer resolución.	
D. Juan	Pues no perdáis la ocasíon,	
	que aqui estoy aguardando.	245
Mota	Ya vuelvo.	

Vanse el Marqués y el Criado

Catal.	Señor Cuadrado	
	o señor Redondo, adiós,	
Criado	Adiós.	
D. Juan	Pues solos los dos,	
	amigo, habemos quedado,	
	síguele el paso al marqués,	250
	que en el palacio se entró.	

Vase Catalinón. Habla por una reja una Mujer

Mujer	Ce, ¿a quién digo?	
D. Juan	¿Quién llamó?	
Mujer	Pues sois prudente y cortés	

---

232   I can't. The King has just arranged her marriage: the King has, in fact, arranged a marriage for Doña Ana on two occasions: firstly, in Act I he informs her father, Don Gonzalo, that she shall be married to Don Juan; secondly, in Act II, having been informed of Don Juan's seduction of Isabela, Alfonso banishes him from Seville and promises Ana to Octavio. Mota's words indicate that neither marriage has been announced publicly.

235   If he says any more: Don Juan has skilfully elicited from Mota all the information he requires. As well as being a man of extremely dubious morality, Mota is portrayed by Tirso as being highly gullible. If he is so well acquainted with Don Juan's inclinations, the very last thing he should do is offer him information about his own beloved. No doubt Mota's feelings for Ana blind him to the danger. At all events Tirso exploits fully the comic and ironic possibilities of the situation.

	You prove it to me! I'll have to see her!
Mota	See her and you will see the greatest beauty
	Any king could hope to cast his eyes on. 230
D. Juan	Well, why not marry her if she's so pretty?
Mota	I can't. The King has just arranged her marriage.
	But no one knows who she's supposed to marry.
D. Juan	And yet she loves you?
Mota	Writes me daily too!
Catal.	[Aside] If he says any more, it serves him right!
	Spain's greatest trickster's got her in his sights!
D. Juan	A man can have such faith in a woman's
	Love and fear still some terrible misfortune?
	You ought to show her off, be more forthcoming,
	Bombard her with your letters, lead her up 240
	The garden-path and stuff the world's opinion.
Mota	The only reason why I'm here's to find
	Out what decision's taken on the girl.
D. Juan	Then don't waste time! Go and find out! I'll wait
	Here for you. Come and tell me what they've done! 245
Mota	Alright! You wait for me! I'll be back soon.

Mota and his servant exit

Catal.	Farewell then, Mister Square or Mister Round.
Servant	Farewell.
D. Juan	Well since we're on our own again,
	My friend, here's what you have to do for me.
	Just keep an eye on Mota! Follow him 250
	Closely. Go after him into the palace!

Exit Catalinón. A woman calls to Don Juan through the bars of her window

Woman	You there! Who are you?
D. Juan	Did someone call me?
Woman	You seem a good and honest gentleman,

---

247   Mister Square or Mister Round: Mota's servant is evidently known by one of these names, in Spanish *Señor Cuadrado* and *Señor Redondo* respectively. There is an element of joke here, which may have to do with the physical shape of the actor who played the part. An actor with the name of Juan Quadrado died in 1636, but there is no evidence that such a person had a role in *The Trickster*. It is a well-known fact that Tirso liked to tease friends by introducing their names into his plays and it seems quite possible that it may be the case here. A certain Fray Alonso Redondo is, for instance, said to have been a friend of Tirso's, though there is not other information about him.

251+   through the bars of her window: the *reja* or iron framework which traditionally covered the windows of Spanish houses on the outside, protecting the house against intruders. It was also here that lovers would meet, the man speaking to the woman through the bars.

	y su amigo, dalde luego	
	al marqués este papel;	255
	mirad que consiste en él	
	de una señora el sosiego.	
D. Juan	Digo que se lo daré:	
	soy su amigo y caballero.	
Mujer	Basta, señor forastero.	260
	Adiós.	
Vase		
D. Juan	Ya la voz se fué.	

¿No parece encantamiento
esto que agora ha pasado?
A mí el papel ha llegado
por la estafeta del viento. 265
Sin duda que es de la dama
que el marqués me ha encarecido:
venturoso en esto he sido.
Sevilla a voces me llama
el Burlador, y el mayor 270
gusto que en mí puede haber
es burlar una mujer
y dejalla sin honor.
¡Vive Dios, que le he de abrir,
pues salí de la plazuela! 275
Mas, ¿si hubiese otra cautela?. . .
Gana me da de reír.
Ya está abierto el tal papel;
y que es suyo es cosa llana,
porque firma doña Ana. 280
Dice así: "Mi padre infiel
en secreto me ha casado
sin poderme resistir;
no sé si podré vivir,
porque la muerte me ha dado. 285

---

258   I give my word, madam: another example of a promise made by Don
Juan which he has no intention of keeping. See Act I, 90, note; 947,
note. On this occasion the lady places her trust in Don Juan, having
seen that he is a friend of Mota. Don Juan abuses both that trust and
Mota's friendship. He refers to himself in 259 as a 'gentleman', a
'caballero', the implication being that he possess all the qualities of
chivalry, valour and honour associated with such a person. What Tirso
is showing us very clearly is that in the society of his day, notably in
the Spanish Court, the old values have lost their meaning. A.A.
Parker, *The Approach to the Spanish Drama of the Golden Age*,
Diamante, VI (London, 1957), p.13, observes: 'Because Don Juan is the

	A friend of the Marquis. Give him this letter!	
	I beg of you, please place it in his hands!	255
	The only other thing I need to say,	
	My friend, is a lady's life depends on it.	
D. Juan	I give my word, madam. You have my promise.	
	In me you find both friend and gentleman	
	Combined.	
Woman	My thanks, sir. I appreciate	260
	Your kindness. Fare you well!	

The woman withdraws

D. Juan	She's disappeared.	
	Was that a vision, a fantastic dream	
	That seemed so magical but also real?	
	I swear this letter reached me as though it	
	Were transported by the wind or air!	265
	I wonder if the woman is the one	
	Whose beauty our friend Mota's just been praising	
	To the skies! If so, it's a piece of luck	
	I'll not despise! Not for nothing am I	
	Labelled the greatest trickster of Seville.	270
	My very favourite pastime, my delight's	
	To trick a woman, steal away her honour,	
	Deprive her of her treasured reputation.	
	As for this letter, now I've left the square,	
	I'm sorry, but I'll have to open it.	275
	Could be there's yet another trick in this	
	For me. Already it gives me good cause	
	To laugh. Let's have a look. At least I know	
	That Ana de Ulloa is the sender.	
	Here, clearly written, is her signature.	280
	And this is what it says: 'My love, my father	
	Has betrayed me. Secretly he's arranged	
	That I be married. It's impossible	
	For me to disobey. I have no say	
	In it. I don't know how I'll go on living.	285

---

negation of "caballerosidad" in every respect, he disrupts all social ties, and society itself will fall apart and disappear if his anarchism is allowed to prevail.'

282 Has betrayed me: the fact is, of course, that Ana is deceiving her father by conducting a secret affair with Mota which compromises both her own honour and that of the family. Since Mota is a nobleman, there is presumably no obstacle to his marriage to Ana and Don Gonzalo would not oppose it. As in the case of Isabela and Octavio, the lovers appear to enjoy the vicarious thrill of a secret courtship and in that sense behave both recklessly and dishonourably.

Si estimas, como es razón,
mi amor y mi voluntad,
y si tu amor fué verdad,
muéstralo en esta ocasión.
Por que veas que te estimo,   290
ven esta noche a la puerta,
que estará a las once abierta,
donde tu esperanza, primo,
goces, y el fin de tu amor.
Traerás, mi gloria, por señas   295
de Leonorilla y las dueñas,
una capa de color.
Mi amor todo de ti fío,
y adiós." ¡Desdichado amante!
¿Hay suceso semejante?   300
Ya de la burla me río.
Gozárela, ¡vive Dios!,
con el engaño y cautela
que en Nápoles a Isabela.

Sale Catalinón

Catal.	Ya el marqués viene.
D. Juan	Los dos 305

aquesta noche tenemos
que hacer.

Catal.	¿Hay engaño nuevo?
D. Juan	Estremado.
Catal.	No lo apruebo.

Tú pretendes que escapemos
una vez, señor, burlados;   310
que el que vive de burlar
burlado habrá de escapar
pagando tantos pecados
de una vez.

---

292   You'll find the door already open: see Act I, 954, note. The sexual
      implications of Ana's message are very clear. It is hardly surprising that
      Don Juan should react to the content of the letter with such relish and
      anticipation.
297   A cloak – crimson: at night men generally wore coloured clothing but
      Mota's crimson cloak is to be for the purposes of identification. Red is
      also a colour associated with passion and in that sense can be linked to
      other distinctive metaphors of passion in the play, notably fire.
301   This trick delights: the word *burla*, 'trick', links with the title of the
      play, *El burlador de Sevilla, The Trickster of Seville*, and underlines
      the point that it is not only the seduction and the enjoyment of a
      woman which appeal to Don Juan but the cunning and ingenuity with

I'm certain this will bring about my death.
If you, as I am sure you do, esteem
My love and know my will, I beg of you,
In honour of our love, do what I ask.
I'll prove to you the depth of my affection.   290
Come to my door at eleven o'clock tonight.
You'll find the door already open. Come
Inside and there, cousin, your love for me
And all your deepest hopes will be fulfilled.
My maids will need to know you by your dress.   295
So for their benefit it's best you wear
A cloak – crimson would be most suitable.
My love, my fate's entirely in your hands.
Farewell.' Farewell to love's appropriate,
I think, given these happy circumstances!   300
This trick delights me even as I think
Of how I'll see it through! I'll have this girl
With all the ingenuity with which
The Duchess Isabela succumbed in Naples!

   Enter Catalinón

Catal.   Here comes the Marquis, master!
D. Juan   Both of us   305
Have pressing business to attend to, designed
To occupy us half the night!
Catal.   Executors
Of some new trick!
D. Juan   The best of all! You'll see!
Catal.   Not me! I don't approve of it. Besides,
The way you're going you are bound to get   310
Your fingers burnt, and mine. I'm telling you,
The man who spends his time deceiving others
Is in the end deceived and comes off second
Best. Live now and pay later! On the day
Of reckoning!

---

which the seduction is achieved. Thus, Daniel Rogers observes of him
in *Tirso de Molina. El burlador de Sevilla*. Critical Guides to Spanish
Texts (London, 1977), p.36: '. . . the truly distinctive thing about
him is that he adopts the pretence for fun . . . not just for the
fulfilment of his physical desires, but for the malicious pleasure of
deceit. . .'

313   Is in the end deceived: this piece of advice from Catalinón encapsulates
one of the central themes of the play, the idea of the *burlador burlado*,
'the trickster tricked'. The notion of poetic justice, of man reaping the
harvest of his deeds and actions, is deeply embedded in the literature
of the Golden Age, reflecting, of course, the predominantly religious
character of the time.

D. Juan	¿Predicador	
	te vuelves, impertinente?	315
Catal.	La razón hace al valiente.	
D. Juan	Y al cobarde hace el temor.	
	El que se pone a servir	
	voluntad no ha de tener,	
	y todo ha de ser hacer,	320
	y nada de ser decir.	
	Sirviendo, jugando estás,	
	y si quieres ganar luego,	
	haz siempre, porque en el juego,	
	quien más hace gana más.	325
Catal.	Y también quien hace y dice	
	pierde por la mayor parte.	
D. Juan	Esta vez quiero avisarte,	
	porque otra vez no te avise.	
Catal.	Digo que de aquí adelante	330
	lo que me mandas haré,	
	y a tu lado forzaré	
	un tigre y un elefante.	
	Guárdese de mí un prior,	
	que si me mandas que calle	335
	y le fuerce, he de forzalle	
	sin réplica, mi señor.	
D. Juan	Calla, que viene el marqués.	
Catal.	Pues, ¿ha de ser el forzado?	

Sale el Marqués de la Mota

D. Juan	Para vos, marqués, me han dado	340
	un recaudo harto cortés	
	por esa reja, sin ver	
	el que me lo daba allí;	
	sólo en la voz conocí	
	que me lo daba mujer.	345
	Dícete al fin que a las doce	
	vayas secreto a la puerta	
	(que estará a las once abierta),	
	donde tu esperanza goce	
	la posesión de tu amor;	350

---

315   a boring preacher: the play is indeed a dramatic sermon, though a highly entertaining one. The moral lesson, often in the form of warnings or advice, is placed in the mouths of many characters and is given more and more emphasis as the action unfolds, though in this respect Catalinón undoubtedly has pride of place.

337   and not a word I'll speak!: the point has been made previously that although the servants in Golden-Age plays give moral advice, they are

D. Juan	You are a boring preacher,	315
	And you've become too forward for a servant!	
Catal.	Wisdom and reason make a brave man, sir!	
D. Juan	And fear makes a coward! Some men, fool,	
	Are born to serve, not born for bravery!	
	A servant has no will to call his own!	320
	Does everything he's told and bites his tongue!	
	A servant's like a man who's playing cards.	
	To profit from the game he has to work,	
	The more he works the more he always wins.	
	You work and shut your mouth you'll be a winner!	325
Catal.	Wise words, master! Many's the man who's lost	
	At cards through opening his mouth too soon!	
D. Juan	Make sure you learn the lesson. Don't forget	
	It. I don't want to have to teach you more!	
Catal.	I promise, master. Seen and never heard	330
	I'll be! Obedient to your every word,	
	That's me! At your side my loyalty	
	Will force an elephant or fierce tiger	
	To its knees. And as for any blabbing preacher,	
	He'd best look out! Give me the order, sir,	335
	To shut him up, I'll do it silently,	
	To good effect, and not a word I'll speak!	
D. Juan	Be silent! The Marquis is coming back!	
Catal.	Is he the one whose mouth I have to shut?	

Enter the Marquis of Mota

D. Juan	A message for you, Marquis, that someone's	340
	Just this minute asked me to give to you.	
	The message was delivered through this window,	
	And though the speaker wasn't visible,	
	The voice was unmistakably a woman's;	
	Of that there's not the slightest doubt at all.	345
	She asks that you at twelve o'clock tonight	
	Proceed with all discretion to her door	
	(She says she'll leave it open from eleven),	
	Where all your fondest hopes and steadfast love	
	Will have their just reward and satisfaction.	350

---

not themselves particularly moral characters and are more often than
not motivated by self-interest. What seems to make Catalinón a distictive
comic character is the fact that, as here, he has the capacity to
ridicule his own shortcomings.

348   open from eleven: by revealing this piece of information Don Juan is
clearly delighting in advance in what he believes will be Mota's helpless
rage when he learns of Ana's seduction.

	y que llevases por señas	
	de Leonorilla y las dueñas	
	una capa de color.	
Mota	¿Qué dices?	
D. Juan	Que este recaudo	
	de una ventana me dieron,	355
	sin ver quién.	
Mota	Con él pusieron	
	sosiego en tanto cuidado.	
	¡Ay amigo! Sólo en ti	
	mi esperanza renaciera.	
	Dame esos pies.	
D. Juan	Considera	360
	que no está tu prima en mí.	
	Eres tú quien ha de ser	
	quien la tiene de gozar,	
	¿y me llegas a abrazar	
	los pies?	
Mota	Es tal el placer,	365
	que me ha sacado de mí.	
	¡Oh sol!, apresura el paso.	
D. Juan	Ya el sol camina al ocaso.	
Mota	Vamos, amigos, de aquí,	
	y de noche nos pondremos.	370
	¡Loco voy!	
D. Juan	[Ap.] Bien se conoce;	
	mas yo bien sé que a las doce	
	harás mayores estremos.	
Mota	¡Ay, prima del alma, prima,	
	que quieres premiar mi fe!	375
Catal.	[Ap.] ¡Vive Cristo, que no dé	
	una blanca por su prima!	

Vase el Marqués y sale Don Diego

D. Dieg.	¿Don Juan?	
Catal.	Tu padre te llama.	
D. Juan	¿Qué manda vueseñoría?	
D. Diego	Verte más cuerdo quería,	380
	más bueno y con mejor fama.	
	¿Es posible que procuras	
	todas las horas mi muerte?	
D. Juan	¿Por qué vienes desa suerte?	

---

356 Oh, my friend!: Mota behaves towards Don Juan just as Octavio did
     previously – see Act II, 120. Once more the gullibility of someone who

98

	To avoid confusion and make recognition	
	By the maids more certain, ensure you wear	
	A crimson cloak.	
Mota	Are you quite sure?	
D. Juan	As sure	
	As I'm your loyal friend! The message came	
	From that window, and every word was clear,	355
	But not the speaker.	
Mota	Oh, my friend! The message	
	Has given me new hope where there was none!	
	What proof of friendship! You, my dear friend,	
	Bear all responsibility for my	
	Rebirth! How can I show my gratitude?	360
D. Juan	Remeber, friend, I'm not your lovely cousin!	
	Your obligation, as I understand	
	It, is to show your love for her, not me!	
	I fancy your embraces would be better	
	Spent on your lover!	
Mota	Oh, my pleasure's such,	365
	I'm quite beside myself! How can I wait!	
	Oh, sun, I beg of you, quicken your pace!	
D. Juan	The sun's already sinking in the west.	
Mota	Let's go quickly! We must prepare ourselves	
	And dress in preparation for tonight.	370
	I'm quite beside myself!	
D. Juan	[Aside] That's pretty plain	
	To anyone. At twelve o'clock tonight	
	It's not beside himself, more out of his mind	
	He'll be!	
Mota	Oh, cousin dear to my soul!	
	That you reward me for my loyalty!	375
Catal.	[Aside] By God, look at the way this fellow prances!	
	Who'd give a farthing for his cousin's chances?	

Exit the Marquis. Enter Don Diego

D. Diego	Don Juan! Where are you?	
Catal.	It's your old father!	
D. Juan	I'm here, my lord. Command me as you wish!	
D. Diego	I wish you were a bit more sensible,	380
	More honest, and a better reputation!	
	I can't believe your every deed's designed	
	Deliberately with my death in mind!	
D. Juan	Oh, father! What is it makes you so angry?	

is himself fond of deceiving others becomes a source of comic irony.

370   And dress in preparation: see 297, note.

D. Diego	Por tu trato y tus locuras.	385
	Al fin el rey me ha mandado	
	que te eche de la ciudad,	
	porque está de una maldad	
	con justa causa indignado.	
	Que, aunque me lo has encubierto,	390
	ya en Sevilla el rey lo sabe,	
	cuyo delito es tan grave,	
	que a decírtelo no acierto.	
	¿En el palacio real	
	traición y con un amigo?	395
	Traidor, Dios te dé el castigo	
	que pide delito igual.	
	Mira que, aunque al parecer	
	Dios te consiente y aguarda,	
	su castigo no se tarda,	400
	y que castigo ha de haber	
	para los que profanáis	
	su nombre, que es jüez fuerte	
	Dios en la muerte.	
D. Juan	¿En la muerte?	
	¿Tan largo me lo fiáis?	405
	De aquí allá hay gran jornada.	
D. Diego	Breve te ha de parecer.	
D. Juan	Y la que tengo de hacer,	
	pues a su alteza le agrada,	
	agora, ¿es larga también?	410
D. Diego	Hasta que el injusto agravio	
	satisfaga el duque Octavio,	
	y apaciguados estén	
	en Nápoles de Isabela	
	los sucesos que has causado,	415
	en Lebrija retirado	

---

393 Force myself to speak!: for someone who can barely force himself to
speak, Don Diego has plenty to say. The effect, even given that Don
Diego is a good man, is comic, contributing further to the ironic tone
that suffuses the play as a whole. In a sense the irascible old man is
the 'babbling preacher' alluded to by Catalinón in Act II, 334.

396 A punishment appropriate to your crime!: see A.A. Parker, *The
Approach to the Spanish Drama of the Golden Age*: '. . . in literature
it was, in seventeenth-century Spain, considered fitting that
wrongdoing should not go unpunished and that virtue should not remain
unrewarded . . . . The most severe punishment is damnation,
consignment to hell. This is rare, but it occurs in two famous plays by
Tirso de Molina, *El burlador de Sevilla* and *El condenado por
desconfiado*. It indicates, of course, that the evil in question has been

D. Diego	Your own stupidity! Tomfoolery!	385
	The King's just told me he's commanded you	
	Be exiled from the city, thrown right out	
	On account of a certain misdemeanour	
	Of yours that with good cause has angered him.	
	Although you hid the truth from me, the King	390
	Has been informed of it here in Seville.	
	A crime so serious, hideously offensive,	
	That I can barely force myself to speak!	
	Such terrible behaviour in the palace!	
	Such treachery, committed in the name	395
	Of friendship! Traitor! May God seek of you	
	A punishment appropriate to your crime!	
	And take note now that though it seems that God	
	Gives you permission for the things you do,	
	The day of judgement's never far behind.	400
	The one thing that is absolutely sure	
	Is punishment for those who take His name	
	In vain. There's no judge more severe than God	
	In matters after death!	
D. Juan	Why speak of death?	
	Plenty of time for me to pay that debt!	405
	In any case, who's ready for it yet?	
D. Diego	My boy, the journey's shorter than you think.	
D. Juan	And what about this journey I'm to make	
	To save my skin and satisfy the King?	
	You'll tell me next that journey has no end!	410
D. Diego	Until you satisfy the grave offence	
	Against Octavio, who is a Duke no less,	
	And give sufficient time for all the scandal	
	To die down in Naples over that affair	
	With Isabela, the King's command is this:	415
	You're exiled to Lebrija where you'll pay	

---

so great and so deliberate that there are no extenuating circumstances to redeem it . . .' (p. 7). Don Juan's greatest offence is his presumption that God's mercy can be taken for granted and will be available to him whenever he wishes to repent and it is for this that he is finally punished. Theologians and moralists of the Golden Age often preached of the perils of procrastination in relation to repentance. See, for example, Fray Luis de Granada, *Guía de los pecadores* (1556).

406   who's ready for it yet?: Don Juan exemplifies in a sense the Renaissance zest for life and enjoyment of life's pleasures which by the seventeenth century had given way to Baroque *desengaño*, the sense of the transience of worldly things which is communicated to Don Juan by so many of the characters and embodied finally in the figure of the stone man.

416   Lebrija: see Act II, 20, note.

	por tu traición y cautela,	
	quiere el rey que estés agora:	
	pena a tu maldad ligera.	
Catal.	*[Aparte.]* Si el caso también supiera	420
	de la pobre pescadora,	
	más se enojara el buen viejo.	
D.Diego	Pues no te vence castigo	
	con cuanto hago y cuanto digo,	
	a Dios tu castigo dejo.	

Vase

Catal.	Fuese el viejo enternecido.	
D. Juan	Luego las lágrimas copia,	
	condición de viejo propia.	
	Vamos, pues ha anochecido,	
	a buscar al marqués.	
Catal.	Vamos,	430
	y al fin gozarás su dama.	
D. Juan	Ha de ser burla de fama.	
Catal.	Ruego al cielo que salgamos	
	della en paz.	
D. Juan	¡Catalinón,	
	en fin!	
Catal.	Y tú, señor, eres	435
	langosta de las mujeres,	
	y con público pregón,	
	porque de ti se guardara	
	cuando a noticia viniera	
	de la que doncella fuera,	440
	fuera bien se pregonara:	
	"Guárdense todos de un hombre	
	que a las mujeres engaña,	
	y es el burlador de España,"	
D. Juan	Tú me has dado gentil nombre.	445

*Sale el Marqués, de noche, con Músicos, y
pasea el tablado, y se entran cantando*

Músic.	El que un bien gozar espera,	
	cuanto espera desespera.	

---

422   choleric!: choler was, with melancholy, phlegm and blood, one of the humours or liquid substances in the body, created in the liver and acting as the body's life-giving moisture. A choleric man was someone in whom choler, a hot and dry humour, gained ascendancy over the others, be it a temporary or permanent ascendancy.

425   I recommend your punishment to God!: in his advice on the writing of plays Lope de Vega had indicated that mid-way through the action of a play some crucial incident should occur, or a key moment should be reached, from which the remainder of the action springs. Don Diego's

	For all your cunning and your treachery.	
	The King thinks such a punishment is just.	
	As far as I'm concerned, it's far too light!	
Catal.	*[Aside]* If only the old man knew how his son	420
	Had fooled the fishergirl, I'm sure that trick	
	Would let you see him even more choleric!	
D. Diego	In that case, seeing that my good advice	
	And prudent admonition are quite useless,	
	I recommend your punishment to God!	425

Exit Don Diego

Catal.	Look what you've done! The old man's left in tears!	
D. Juan	Don't tell me you're about to join him too,	
	Though tears are quite appropriate to dotage!	
	Come on! It's dark already! I must find	
	The Marquis.	
Catal.	Yes. Come on! Let's go and seek	430
	An opportunity to fool his girl!	
D. Juan	And this, you'll see, will be the best trick yet!	
Catal.	Please God, I pray that you watch over me	
	And save your servant from catastrophe!	
D. Juan	True to your name, a man who runs away!	435
Catal.	And you, master, a locust to all women!	
	There ought to be a public proclamation,	
	A timely warning of your destination	
	Delivered to all virgins everywhere:	
	'Beware this locust and this plague embodied	440
	In a man! Take the greatest care with him,	
	Or he will rob you of your treasured harvest.	
	This man deceives all women as he will,	
	He is, no less, the trickster of Seville'.	
D. Juan	Congratulations! What a fine description!	445

*Enter the Marquis, with musicians. He is dressed for
the night. He crosses the stage. They exit singing*

Musicians	*[Sing]*
	'For him who's waiting in anticipation,
	Passing time's a source of desperation.'

---

abandonment of his son to the judgement of God constitutes that
moment, and the second half of the play moves inevitably into the more
sinister area of Don Juan's confrontation with the supernatural.

432   the best trick yet!: see Act II, 301, note.
436   a locust to all woman!: this is clearly an evocation of those locusts and
       plagues which, according to the Old Testament, were sent by God to
       punish the sins of nations and tribes. Similarly, each of Don Juan's
       victims is in some way guilty of wrongdoing and Don Juan the
       instrument of retribution.

D. Juan	¿Qué es esto?
Catal.	Música es.
Mota	Parece que habla conmigo
	el poeta. ¿Quién va?
D. Juan	Amigo.	450
Mota	¿Es don Juan?
D. Juan	¿Es el marqués?
Mota	¿Quién puede ser sino yo?
D. Juan	Luego que la capa vi,
	que érades vos conocí.
Mota	Cantad, pues don Juan llegó.	455
Músic.	*Cantan*
	El que un bien gozar espera,
	cuanto espera desespera.
D. Juan	¿Qué casa es la que miráis?
Mota	De don Gonzalo de Ulloa.
D. Juan	¿Dónde iremos?
Mota	A Lisboa.	460
D. Juan.	¿Cómo, si en Sevilla estáis?
Mota	Pues ¿aqueso os maravilla?
	¿No vive, con gusto igual,
	lo peor de Portugal
	en lo mejor de Castilla?	465
D. Juan	¿Dónde viven?
Mota	En la calle
	de la Sierpe, donde ves,
	a Adán vuelto en portugués;
	que en aqueste amargo valle
	con bocados solicitan	470
	mil Evas que, aunque dorados,
	en efecto, son bocados
	con que el dinero nos quitan.
Catal.	Ir de noche no quisiera
	por esa calle cruel,	475
	pues lo que de día es miel
	entonces lo dan en cera.

---

460   Destination Lisbon!: the meaning of the phrase is clarified in the following lines. There was not in fact a district or street in Seville known as Lisbon, nor does it seem that Portuguese prostitutes were sufficiently abundant in the city to give Portugal a bad name.

467   Serpent Street: Santiago Montoto, *Las calles de Sevilla*. . ., p.424, notes that the street now known as *Sierpes* was indeed called *La calle de la Sierpe* at an earlier date. It acquired this name because it contained an inn which had hanging on its frontage the jawbone of a serpent. In the fifteenth century the street was also known as the *Calle*

D. Juan	What is that racket?
Catal.	Only music, master!
Mota	As though the muse addresses me, creating
	Poetry of inspiration! Who goes there? 450
D. Juan	A friend!
Mota	Are you Don Juan?
D. Juan	Are you Mota?
Mota	Who else could it possibly be but I?
D. Juan	Of course! As soon as I saw your crimson
	Cape, I knew it was you and no mistake.
Mota	Musicians, sing! My friend Don Juan's arrived! 455
Musicians	*[Sing]*
	'For him who's waiting in anticipation,
	Passing time's a source of desperation'.
D. Juan	Tell me, what house is this that takes your fancy?
Mota	The house of Don Gonzalo de Ulloa.
D. Juan	Where are we going?
Mota	Destination Lisbon! 460
D. Juan	How can that be when we're here in Seville?
Mota	I am surprised that that surprises you!
	Is it not possible the very worst
	Of Portugal may live quite happily
	Here in Castille, the best that Spain can offer? 465
D. Juan	And where would that be?
Mota	It's a street they call
	Serpent Street. Walk through there and you will see
	Adam transformed into a Portuguese.
	That street's a dark and sinful alleyway
	Where lurk a thousand Eves who offer pleasure, 470
	Invite us to enjoy the taste of lips
	That promise honey but, as we partake,
	Serve merely to divest us of our money.
Catal.	I'll tell you one thing. You won't find me there
	After dark! No, the place is far too dangerous! 475
	Go there by day, they shower you with honey.
	Go there by night, they shower you with shit!

---

  de los Espaderos after the swordsmiths who lived there. At no stage,
  however, was the street noted for its prostitutes.

468 Adam transformed into a Portuguese: the reputation of Portuguese men
  was that they were extremely amorous and prone, therefore, to be
  tempted by modern-day Eves.

477 they shower you with shit!: under cover of darkness chamber-pots were
  emptied from bedroom windows into the street below, to the obvious
  discomfort of passers-by.

	Una noche, por mi mal,	
	la vi sobre mí vertida,	
	y hallé que era corrompida	480
	la cera de Portugal.	
D. Juan	Mientras a la calle vais,	
	yo dar un perro quisiera.	
Mota	Pues cerca de aquí me espera	
	un bravo.	
D. Juan	Si me dejáis,	485
	señor marqués, vos veréis	
	cómo de mí no se escapa.	
Mota	Vamos, y poneos mi capa,	
	para que mejor lo deis.	
D. Juan	Bien habéis dicho. Venid,	490
	y me enseñaréis la casa.	
Mota	Mientras el suceso pasa,	
	la voz y el habla fingid.	
	¿Veis aquella celosía?	
D. Juan	Ya la veo.	
Mota	Pues llegad	495
	y decid: "Beatriz", y entrad.	
D. Juan	¿Qué mujer?	
Mota	Rosada y fría.	
Catal	Será mujer cantimplora.	
Mota	En Gradas os aguardamos.	
D. Juan	Adiós, marqués.	
Catal.	¿Dónde vamos?	500
D. Juan	Calla, necio, calla agora;	
	adonde la burla mía	
	ejecute.	
Catal.	No se escapa	
	nadie de ti.	
D. Juan	El trueque adoro.	
Catal.	Echaste la capa al toro.	505
D. Juan	No, el toro me echó la capa.	

Vanse Don Juan y Catalinón

---

483 a trick that's much more daring: Mota is planning a trick of his own
here and Don Juan, as a means of obtaining Mota's cloak for the
planned seduction of Ana, offers to trick another girl, Beatrix, whom
Mota has also had in his sights.

498 water-bottle: the water-bottle referred to here is that which was used
in the summer to keep water cool. It was often made of porous clay
rather than metal and was thus reddish in colour, a fact which allows
for the joke about a pink and cold woman.

106

It happened to me once, trust my bad luck!
Came down on me from up above, as though
Heaven sent. But if you want to know the truth,   480
That dung from Portugal was far from heavenly!

D. Juan   Mota, while you are visiting that place,
My own plan's for a trick that's much more daring.

Mota   There's one not far from here I've had in mind.
It's far from easy.

D. Juan   I'll do it for you,   485
Marquis. Let me do it and you'll be sure
The trick will give us double satisfaction.

Mota   Done! Tell you what! You'd better take my cape.
Wear it and it will guarantee success.

D. Juan   An excellent idea! All I need now   490
Is to know the house. You'd better show me where
It is.

Mota   Another thing. Use all your cunning.
Put on another voice! Disguise your speech!
You see that window? That one over there?

D. Juan   I see the one.

Mota   Well go right up to it,   495
Call out the name of Beatrix and go
Inside.

D. Juan   What sort of girl?

Mota   She's pink and cold.

Catal.   More like a water-bottle than a woman!

Mota   Afterwards go to Gradas. We'll be there.

D. Juan   Farewell, Marquis.

Catal.   Where are we going now?   500

D. Juan   Shut up, you fool! Just try to hold your tongue!
Where else but where I'll have the chance to play
My trick.

Catal.   There's no one in the world escapes
From you, master!

D. Juan   Oh, how I love deception!

Catal.   A neat pass of the cape to fool the bull   505
Back there!

D. Juan   He's given me his cape instead!

Exit Don Juan and Catalinón

---

499   Gradas: the allusion is to an area around the Cathedral, raised above
street-level to a height of some four feet, ringed on its outer edge by
strong chains.

505   the bull: a mocking reference to Mota, whom Don Juan will deceive with
his own cloak. Mota doubtless thinks of himself as a bull in a sexual
sense, but Catalinón's thoughts are much more focused on the bull's
horns, synonymous with cuckoldry.

Mota	La mujer ha de pensar que soy él.
Músic.	¡Qué gentil perro!
Mota	Esto es acertar por yerro.
Músic.	Todo este mundo es errar. 510
	Cantan
	El que un bien gozar espera, cuanto espera desespera.
	Vanse, y dice Doña Ana dentro
Ana	¡Falso!, no eres el marqués, que me has engañado.
D. Juan	Digo. que lo soy.
Ana	¡Fiero enemigo, 515 mientes, mientes!
	Sale Don Gonzalo con la espada desnuda
D. Gon.	La voz es de doña Ana la que siento.
Ana	*[Dentro.]* ¿No hay quien mate este traidor, homicida de mi honor?
D. Gon.	¿Hay tan grande atrevimiento? 520 muerto honor, dijo, ¡ay de mí!, y es su lengua tan liviana que aquí sirve de campana.
Ana	Matalde.
	Salen Don Juan y Catalinón con las espadas desnudas
D. Juan	¿Quién está aqui?
D. Gon.	La barbacana caída 525 de la torre de mi honor, echaste en tierra, traidor, donde era alcaide la vida.
D. Juan	Déjame pasar.
D. Gon.	¿Pasar? Por la punta desta espada. 530
D. Juan	Morirás.
D. Gon.	No importa nada.
D. Juan	Mira que te he de matar.

---

513   You traitor!: Don Juan does not in fact seduce Ana, a fact which he
himself acknowledges in Act III, 962-65. Her father, Don Gonzalo,
evidently believes that she has been seduced, for he refers in 521 to
'honour lost' and in 523 to 'all our shame'.

527   its central fortress: not only has Don Juan found his way into Don

Iota	The girl is bound to think, when she sees me, I'm him.
Musicians	Oh, what a wonderful deception!
Iota	This is to take advantage of confusion!
Musicians	What makes the world go round but men's delusions? 510
	[They sing]
	'For him who's waiting in anticipation,
	Passing time's a source of desperation.'

They exit. Doña Ana's voice, off-stage

Ana	You traitor! Pretending to be the Marquis! Trying to trick me!
D. Juan	Won't you believe me? I am the Marquis!
Ana	Nothing but a liar! 515 Your every word a lie!

Enter Don Gonzalo. Sword drawn

D. Gon.	My daughter's voice! I'm sure it's hers!
Ana	[Off-stage] Is there no one who'll kill This traitor on my behalf, this treacherous Assassin of my honour? Will no one help?
D. Gon.	What man could be so bold and arrogant? 520 Did she not speak of honour lost, of honour Murdered? Her tongue, voicing such things aloud, Is like a bell, proclaiming all our shame!
Ana	Kill him!

Enter Don Juan and Catalinón, with swords drawn

D. Juan	Who's there? Reveal yourself! Speak up!
D. Gon.	You, sir, have broken through the strong defences 525 Of my honour and made your treacherous Assault upon its central fortress where My life itself was sovereign.
D. Juan	Let me pass. You block my path.
D. Gon.	If you, sir, wish to pass, You'll have to find your way past this sharp steel. 530
D. Juan	Stand in my way, you'll die.
D. Gon.	To me it matters Not!
D. Juan	In that case, fool, you will have to die!

Gonzalo's house and his daughter's bedroom, he has also, as Gonzalo sees it, made an assault on his honour at that point where honour needs to be most staunchly defended – Ana herself. Golden-Age drama is full of fathers, husbands and brothers who see their women-folk as vulnerable and in need of constant watchfulness. See Act I. 153, note.

D. Gon.	¡Muere, traidor!
D. Juan	Desta suerte
	muero.
Catal.	Si escapo de aquesta,
	no más burlas, no más fiesta. 535
D. Gon.	¡Ay, que me has dado la muerte!
D. Juan	Tú la vida te quitaste.
D. Gon.	¿De qué la vida servía?
D. Juan	Huye.

Vanse Don Juan y Catalinón

D. Gon.	Aguarda que es sangría,
	con que el valor aumentaste. 540
	Muerto soy; no hay quien aguarde.
	Seguiráte mi furor;
	que es traidor, y el que es traidor
	es traidor porque es cobarde.

Entran muerto a Don Gonzalo, y salen el Marqués
de la Mota y Músicos

Mota	Presto las doce darán, 545
	y mucho don Juan se tarda:
	¡fiera prisión del que aguarda!

Salen Don Juan y Catalinón

D. Juan.	¿Es el marqués?
Mota	¿Es don Juan?
D. Juan	Yo soy; tomad vuestra capa.
Mota	¿Y el perro?
D. Juan	Funesto ha sido. 550
	Al fin, marqués, muerto ha habido.
Catal.	Señor, del muerto te escapa.
Mota	¿Búrlaste, amigo? ¿Qué haré?
Catal.	[*Aparte.*] También vos sois el burlado.
D. Juan	Cara la burla ha costado. 555
Mota	Yo, don Juan, lo pagaré,
	porque estará la mujer
	quejosa de mí.
D. Juan	Las doce
	darán.
Mota	Como mi bien goce,
	nunca llegue a amanecer. 560
D. Juan	Adiós, marqués.

---

540   <u>serves only to increase my fury</u>: in earlier centuries blood-letting was considered to be a remedy for specific ills. Don Gonzalo is suggesting here that his outrage has been insufficient and that the loss of blood is therefore a cure for his deficiency in that regard.

. Gon.	You die like this!
. Juan	A death that any man
	Would welcome!
:atal.	I'm dying to save my skin!
	From hereon in I shall renounce this trickster's 535
	Tricks!
. Gon.	Traitor! You've mortally wounded me!
). Juan	You, sir, have brought upon yourself your death.
). Gon.	What use was life to me to end like this?
). Juan	Come on! Quickly!

Exit Don Juan and Catalinón

). Gon.	Each drop of precious blood
	That's lost serves only to increase my fury. 540
	I am dying; no one can help me now.
	But you, traitor, will not escape my vengeance.
	Treachery's the province of the man who runs,
	The coward who's afraid to stand his ground.

The body of Don Gonzalo is taken away. Enter the Marquis of Mota and musicians

Mota	It's almost twelve! It's just about to strike! 545
	No sign of Don Juan! Why is he so late?
	How hard it is on him who has to wait!

Don Juan and Catalinón enter

D. Juan	Psst! Marquis! Is that you?
Mota	Is that Don Juan?
D. Juan	Of course it's me! Here! Take your blessed cape!
Mota	And what about the trick?
D. Juan	A pretty deadly
	Trick, Marquis, as things turned out in the end.
Catal.	Master, forget the trick. Quickly. Let's go.
Mota	Are you joking, my friend? What shall I do?
Catal.	*[Aside]* Acknowledge that the real joke's on you!
D. Juan	A pretty price we had to pay for that! 555
Mota	Leave it to me, Don Juan. I'll settle up
	And pay the debt, for I'm the one the girl
	You've fooled will want to get.
D. Juan	The clock strikes twelve.
Mota	If I strike lucky, let the night be endless,
	Keep dawn at bay, prolong my happiness! 560
D. Juan	Farewell, Marquis.

---

545   It's almost twelve!: an excellent example of the way in which the
dialogue of Golden-Age drama locates the action. Here, is addition, the
allusion to the time prepares us for Mota's reaction when he discovers
what has happened, though even here there is, as we soon learn, an
unexpected twist to events.

111

Catal.	Muy buen lance
	el desdichado hallará.
D. Juan	Huyamos.
Catal.	Señor, no habrá
	aguilita que me alcance.

Vanse D. Juan y Catalinón

Mota	Vosotros os podéis ir	565
	todos a casa, que yo	
	he de ir solo.	
Criados	Dios crió	
	las noches para dormir.	

Vanse y queda el Marqués de la Mota
[Dentro.] ¿Vióse desdicha mayor,
y vióse mayor desgracia?   570

Mota	¡Válgame Dios! Voces siento	
	en la plaza del Alcázar.	
	¿Qué puede ser a estas horas?	
	Un hielo el pecho me arraiga.	
	Desde aquí parece todo	575
	una Troya que se abrasa,	
	porque tantas luces juntas	
	hacen gigantes de llamas.	
	Un grande escuadrón de hachas	
	se acerca a mí; ¿porqué anda	580
	el fuego emulando estrellas,	
	dividiéndose en escuadras?	
	Quiero saber la ocasión.	

Sale Don Diego Tenorio y la Guardia con
hachas

D. Diego	¿Qué gente?	
Mota	Gente que aguarda	
	saber de aqueste ruïdo	585
	el alboroto y la causa.	
D. Diego	Prendeldo.	
Mota	¿Prenderme a mí?	

[Mete mano a la espada.]

D. Diego	Volved la espada a la vaina,	
	que la mayor valentía	
	es no tratar de las armas.	590

---

576   **a Troy consumed by flames**: the square is ablaze with flaming torches as Don Tenorio and the guards hunt for the murderer of Don Gonzalo. While Mota uses the Trojan metaphor simply to suggest that the whole city seems to be on fire, it does also link this episode to the ending of Act I. In both instances Don Juan has, in a manner reminiscent of the Trojan horse, succeeded in entering the abode of a lady, deceiving her in relation to his identity and his intentions.

Catal.	Farewell, and lots of fun!
	Oh, what a treat awaits this simpleton!
D. Juan	Let's go!
Catal.	Oh, master, I can guarantee
	There's not an eagle can keep up with me.

Exit Don Juan and Catalinón

Mota	All of you can go now! Back to your homes!	565
	Such is the nature of my task, I must	
	Go on alone!	
Servants	God in his wisdom made	
	The night so we can sleep away our cares.	

The servants leave. Mota is alone

Voices off	Whoever saw a deed as black as this?	
	Whoever such a crime as this shall witness?	570
Mota	May God protect me! Voices raised and shouting	
	There in the middle of the castle square?	
	What can it be at this hour of the night?	
	A sudden fear turns my heart to ice.	
	And there, before my eyes, the whole world seems	575
	To be ablaze, a Troy consumed by flames	
	That leap up to the sky, a blaze of torches	
	That giant-like assaults the very heavens!	
	A regiment of flares, a mighty army	
	Approaching, step by step, as though their fire	580
	Envied and sought to emulate the stars.	
	In serried ranks the blazing flames advance.	
	What can the explanation be for this?	

Enter Don Diego Tenorio and guards bearing torches

D. Diego	Who goes there?	
Mota	Someone who would like to know	
	The cause of this disturbance, and the reason	585
	Why there's such confusion.	
D. Diego	Arrest this man!	
Mota	Arrest me? Why arrest me? I've done nothing!	

[Mota attempts to draw his sword]

D. Diego	Don't be a fool! Don't try to draw your sword!	
	Much more courageous to resist the foolish	
	Urge to try to overcome such odds!	590

---

578   giant-like: another reference to the Titans of Greek mythology who rebelled against the gods. See Act I, 295, note.

581   sought to emulate the stars: the flames of the torches leap towards the sky, as though they are attempting to be stars. Of the four elements – see Act I, 348, note – both air and fire had a natural tendency to move upwards towards their source, the source of fire being the sun and the stars.

Mota	¿Cómo al marqués de la Mota hablan ansí?
D.Diego	Dad la espada, que el rey os manda prender.
Mota	¡Vive Dios!

Salen el Rey y acompañamiento

Rey	En toda España no ha de caber, ni tampoco en Italia, si va a Italia.	595
D.Diego	Señor, aquí está el marqués.	
Mota	¿Vuestra alteza a mí me manda prender?	
Rey	Llevalde y ponelde la cabeza en una escarpia. ¿En mi presencia te pones?	600
Mota	¡Ah, glorias de amor tiranas, siempre en el pasar ligeras, como en el vivir pesadas! Bien dijo un sabio que había entre la boca y la taza peligro; mas el enojo del rey me admira y espanta. No sé por lo que voy preso.	605
D.Diego	¿Quién mejor sabrá la causa que vueseñoría?	610
Mota	¿Yo?	
D.Diego	Vamos.	
Mota	¡Confusión extraña!	
Rey	Fulmínesele el proceso al marqués luego, y mañana le cortarán la cabeza. Y al comendador, con cuanta solenidad y grandeza se da a las personas sacras y reales, el entierro se haga; en bronce y piedras varias un sepulcro con un bulto le ofrezcan, donde en mosaicas labores, góticas letras	615 620

---

599 Take him away!: it is not so much a question of the King acting hastily
here. His conviction that Mota is the murderer of Don Gonzalo springs
from the fact that someone has glimpsed a figure in a red cloak

114

Mota	I am the Marquis of Mota! You dare To speak to me like this?
D.Diego	Give me your sword. At once, Marquis! His majesty's command!
Mota	In God's name!

Enter the King and his attendants

King	In the whole of Spain no hiding Place for him! If he makes for Italy, 595 He'll find there's no security for him There either.
D.Diego	Your majesty, the Marquis!
Mota	Your highness, I am told you order my Arrest.
King	Take him away! Display his head On an iron spike! Do you dare to show 600 Yourself to me, his royal majesty?
Mota	Oh, how love's pleasure soon becomes its chains! Oh, how love's estasy's as swift in passing As in our lives it is our constant pain! How wisely spoke the wise-man who declared 605 That many is the slip 'tween cup and lip! As for the anger of the King, its cause Is both a source of fright and mystery. What crime is it makes me his prisoner?
D.Diego	I fancy you, my lord, will know the answer 610 To that question.
Mota	I, sir, am totally Bemused.
D.Diego	I'm sure!
Mota	And hopelessly confused.
King	End his confusion, hurry up his trial, Tomorrow morning this fine fellow'll lose His head! The Commander's a different matter. 615 A man of his nobility and worth Deserves a burial that in all its pomp And ceremony's worthy of a royal Personage. See to it and make his funeral Appropriate to his person. A sepulchre 620 Of bronze and stone shall be his resting place, And there a fine statue in his memory Shall be placed, and on it an inscription

---

escaping from the scene of the crime.

615   **The Commander's a different matter:** on Don Gonzalo de Ulloa's standing, see Act I, 698, note.

115

	den lenguas a sus venganzas.	
	Y entierro, bulto y sepulcro	625
	quiero que a mi costa se haga.	
	¿Dónde doña Ana se fué?	
D. Diego	Fuese al sagrado, doña Ana,	
	de mi señora la reina.	
Rey	Ha de sentir esta falta	630
	Castilla; tal capitán	
	ha de llorar Calatrava.	

Vanse todos
Sale Batricio, desposado con Aminta; Gaseno,
viejo; Belisa y Pastores músicos
Cantan

	Lindo sale el sol de abril	
	con trébol y torongil,	
	y aunque le sirva de estrella,	635
	Aminta sale más bella.	
Batric.	Sobre esta alfombra florida,	
	adonde, en campos de escarcha,	
	el sol sin aliento marcha	
	con su luz recién nacida,	640
	os sentad, pues nos convida	
	al tálamo el sitio hermoso.	
Aminta	Cantalde a mi dulce esposo	
	favores de mil en mil.	

Cantan

	Lindo sale el sol de abril	645
	con trébol y torongil,	
	y aunque le sirva de estrella,	
	Aminta sale más bella.	
Gaseno	Muy bien lo habéis solfeado;	
	no hay más sones en el kiries.	650

---

628   She's taken sanctuary: the reason for Ana's seeking sanctuary is not
specifically stated. She has obviously fled in the general confusion that
follows her cries for help - 517 - and is presumably unaware of her
father's death. Conscious of the dishonour she may have brought upon
the family name, she appears to be afraid that Don Gonzalo will take
vengeance on her. Her desperate seeking for a safe place to hide
parallels the behaviour of many dishonoured women in Golden Age
plays.

632   Calatrava: see Act I, 698, note.

633   April's sun is warm and bright: there are several songs in the course
of the play, as there are in Golden-Age drama in general. Theatre
companies of the time generally included both musicians and singers. In
The Trickster most of the songs are ironic, contrasting with what is
actually happening. In this particular case, though, the song's purpose

	Boldly written, announcing to the world	
	His vengeance. The cost of burial, tomb	625
	And statue the royal treasury shall meet.	
	But what about the whereabouts of Ana?	
D.Diego	She's taken sanctuary, your majesty,	
	In the safety of the Queen's royal chapel.	
King	This loss is one, my friend, that all Castile	630
	Will surely feel. This man, this great Commander	
	The whole of Calatrava now shall weep.	

Exit all
Enter Batricio, betrothed to Aminta; Gaseno, an old
man; Belisa and shepherd musicians

Musicians	[Sing]	
	'April's sun is warm and bright,	
	With orange flower and lovely clover.	
	Aminta to the sun's a star,	635
	But she is warm and bright all over'.	
Batric.	Upon this lovely carpet, green and full	
	Of flowers, but white still with the hoary frost,	
	And where the sun steps out, still bleary-eyed	
	But warming slowly to his daily task,	640
	Sit you all down! The beauty of the place	
	Invites us all to make this spot our bed.	
Aminta	I beg you all, bestow your songs and favours	
	On Batricio. To him I'll soon be wed.	
Musicians	[Sing]	
	'April's sun is warm and bright,	645
	With orange flower and lovely clover.	
	Aminta to the sun's a star,	
	But she is warm and bright all over'.	
Gaseno	A fine song, lads, a joy to all our ears.	
	Much better than the choir we have in church!	650

---

is to establish an idyllic mood and to contrast the beauty and harmony
of the countryside with the corruption of the Court, whose values have
been embodied in the scene just ended. Praise of the countryside and
of country people is an important topic in Golden-Age literature in
general. While the town-country contrast had its origins in classical
literature, Horace's *Beatus ille* being a notable influence, the
seventeenth century was itself marked by a growing awareness of the
hollowness of urban life - a feeling which grew throughout the period
as towns and cities grew and became more corrupt in all kinds of ways.
In the drama country people are often shown to be morally superior to
sophisticated courtiers, as Calderón's *El alcalde de Zalamea* and Lope de
Vega's *Peribáñez* both suggest, though the matter is not quite as
simple in *The Trickster*. For a general study of the theme see Noël
Salomon, *Recherches sur le thème paysan dans la 'comedia' au temps de
Lope de Vega* (Bordeaux, 1965).

117

Batric.	Cuando con sus labios tiries	
	vuelve en púrpura los labios	
	saldrán, aunque vergonzosas,	
	afrentando el sol de abril.	
Aminta	Batricio, yo lo agradezco;	655
	falso y lisonjero estás;	
	mas si tus rayos me das,	
	por ti ser luna merezco;	
	tú eres el sol por quien crezco	
	después de salir menguante.	660
	Para que el alba te cante	
	la salva en tono sutil,	

Cantan

lindo sale el sol, etc.

Sale Catalinón, de camino

Catal.	Señores, el desposorio	
	huéspedes ha de tener.	665
Gaseno	A todo el mundo ha de ser	
	este contento notorio.	
	¿Quién viene?	
Catal.	Don Juan Tenorio.	
Gaseno	¿El viejo?	
Catal.	No ese don Juan.	
Belisa	Será su hijo galán.	670
Batric.	Téngolo por mal agüero,	
	que galán y caballero	
	quitan gusto y celos dan.	
	Pues ¿quién noticia les dió	
	de mis bodas?	
Catal.	De camino	675
	pasa a Lebrija.	
Batric.	Imagino	
	que el demonio le envió.	
	Mas, ¿de qué me aflijo yo?	
	Vengan a mis dulces bodas	
	del mundo las gentes todas.	680
	Mas, con todo, un caballero	
	en mis bodas, ¡mal agüero!	

---

657 the bright sun in my blue heaven: see Act II, 72, note. As the sun rules supreme amongst the planets, so Batricio reigns supreme in Aminta's life.

662 add its harmony: The relationship of Aminta and Batricio is here presented as harmonious and it is also placed within the context of Nature's harmony, of which the singing of the birds is one example. For the seventeenth century the perfect music of the spheres, evidence

Batric.	The sun, Aminta, wakes and fills its lips
	And cheeks with brightest red, a dazzling hue;
	And yet, no sooner does it dare peep out,
	It's all ablush with shame, for it sees you!
Aminta	Batricio, your words are very pleasing, 655
	Though I believe that you are teasing me.
	Still, you are the bright sun in my blue heaven,
	So I to your sun will be your moon.
	As your warmth and brightness shines on me,
	So my light glows and shines out silvery. 660
	Let the dawn greet you! Let its gentle music
	Add its harmony to your majesty.
Musicians	*[Sing]*
	'April's sun is warm and bright, etc.,. . .'
	Enter Catalinón, dressed as a traveller
Catal.	Ah, gentlemen, this wedding's to be honoured
	Further by another special guest. 665
Gaseno	My friend, the whole world has our invitation,
	So everyone may share our celebration!
	Who is the newcomer?
Catal.	Don Juan Tenorio.
Gaseno	The old one would that be?
Catal.	The other one.
Belisa	He means his son. He has the reputation 670
	Of a rake.
Batric.	I don't like the sound of that!
	A man who's rich and has that reputation
	Gives every cause for fear and suspicion.
	But how was it he got the information
	About our marriage?
Catal.	Just in passing, heading 675
	For Lebrija.
Batric.	I wouldn't put it past
	Him that the devil sent him straight to us.
	Still, what's the point of worrying about
	It? Let the whole world come! Let everyone
	Attend the celebration of our wedding! 680
	Though seeing this nobleman close to my dear
	Betrothed still gives me cause for utmost fear!

---

of divine perfection, was reflected imperfectly in the earthly world, and
the music of Nature was one example of it.

668   Don Juan Tenorio: Gaseno assumes that Catalinón is alluding to the
father, not the son. In the earlier version of *The Trickster* - see Act
II, 1, note - our Don Diego Tenorio was indeed called Don Juan
Tenorio, *viejo.*

119

Gaseno	Venga el Coloso de Rodas,	
	venga el Papa, el Preste Juan	
	y don Alfonso el Onceno	685
	con su corte, que en Gaseno	
	ánimo y valor verán.	
	Montes en casa hay de pan,	
	Guadalquivides de vino,	
	Babilonias de tocino,	690
	y entre ejércitos cobardes	
	de aves, para que las lardes,	
	el pollo y el palomino.	
	Venga tan gran caballero	
	a ser hoy en Dos Hermanas	695
	honra destas viejas canas.	
Belisa	El hijo del camarero	
	mayor. . .	
Batric.	[Ap.] Todo es mal agüero	
	para mí, pues le han de dar	
	junto a mi esposa lugar.	700
	Aun no gozo, y ya los cielos	
	me están condenando a celos.	
	Amor, sufrir y callar.	

Sale Don Juan Tenorio

D. Juan	Pasando acaso he sabido	
	que hay bodas en el lugar,	705
	y dellas quise gozar,	
	pues tan venturoso he sido.	
Gaseno	Vueseñoría ha venido	
	a honrallas y engrandecellas.	
Batric.	Yo, que soy el dueño dellas,	710
	digo entre mí que vengáis	
	en hora mala.	

---

683   **We shall invite:** given the initial idealization of country life, elements of doubt begin to intrude. Gaseno is seen to be foolishly over-proud and anxious that the nobility itself should be astonished by the feast that he has arranged. He lacks the dignity of a man like Pedro Crespo in Calderón's *El alcalde de Zalamea*. The implication is that in reality the peasants, though less deliberately malicious, are as flawed as the nobility.

689   **Guadalquivirs:** the Guadalquivir is one of Spain's longest rivers. It flows two hundred and twenty five miles in a south-westerly direction across the plains of Andalusia, through Seville, and enters the sea some fifty miles south of the city.

690   **Babylons of ham:** amongst other things the city of Babylon was famous in ancient times for its luxury. Subsequently any place distinguished by material wealth and comfort came to be referred to as Babylon.

Gaseno	We shall invite the Colossus of Rhodes
	Itself. Why not the Pope? The Emperor
	Of Ethiopia? Alfonso the Eleventh 685
	And all his courtiers? For in Gaseno
	They shall discover spirit and true valour.
	Mountains of bread we'll put upon their plates;
	Guadalquivirs of wine shall pour into
	Their mouths; Great Babylons of ham delight 690
	Their palates; and their stomachs shall be filled
	With flocks of succulent and timid birds,
	Chickens and tender doves fit for a King.
	Go tell this honourable gentleman
	He's welcome here, for here in Dos Hermanas 695
	His presence honours this grey head of mine.
Belisa	He's son of the high chancellor!
Batric.	*[Aside]* That means
	They'll seat him at the table next to my
	Sweetheart! And nothing could be worse than that!
	I'm thinking everything is going badly. 700
	My happiness has turned to misery!
	The heavens condemn me to this jealousy!
	To love's to suffer in silent agony!

Enter Don Juan Tenorio

D. Juan	A happy chance, my friends, to learn in passing
	There's a wedding here! To be sure, a stroke 705
	Of luck, an opportunity for pleasure
	And revelry that's quite unexpected.
Gaseno	The arrival of your noble lordship serves
	To add distinction to our humble feast.
Batric.	*[Aside]* To think that all this here's supposed to be 710
	For me, designed to honour my good name!
	I curse the day that this fine fellow came!

---

695   Dos Hermanas: the town is to the south-east of Seville and is approximately half-way between the city and Lebrija, to which Don Juan has been banished by the King.

696   His presence honours: the peasant wedding is undoubtedly graced by the presence of a nobleman, especially by a nobleman who is the son of the High Chancellor. At the same time, however, Gaseno is shown to be a man who equates honour with nobility of birth and, as Don Juan's subsequent behaviour proves, is quite misguided in making that assumption.

711   to honour my good name!: like many peasants in Golden-Age drama, Batricio has a keen sense of his own good name and reputation. On the other hand, he does nothing to assert himself and to protect Aminta, and is therefore very different both from Lope's Peribáñez and Calderón's Pedro Crespo. He is presented by Tirso as a rather passive individual who is only too ready to think the worst of his bride.

Gaseno	¿No dais
	lugar a este caballero?
D. Juan	Con vuestra licencia quiero
	sentarme aquí.

Siéntase junto a la novia

Batric.	Si os sentáis	715
	delante de mí, señor,	
	seréis de aquesa manera	
	el novio.	
D. Juan	Cuando lo fuera,	
	no escogiera lo peor.	
Gaseno	¡Que es el novio!	
D. Juan	De mi error	720
	e ignorancia perdón pido.	
Catal.	*[Ap.]* ¡Desventurado marido!	
D. Juan	*[Ap. a* Catal.*]* Corrido está.	
Catal.	*[Ap.]* No lo ignoro;	
	mas si tiene de ser toro,	
	¿qué mucho que esté corrido?	725
	No daré por su mujer	
	ni por su honor un cornado.	
	¡Desdichado tú, que has dado	
	en manos de Lucifer!	
D. Juan	¿Posible es que vengo a ser,	730
	señora, tan venturoso?	
	Envidia tengo al esposo.	
Aminta	Parecéisme lisonjero.	
Batric.	Bien dije que es mal agüero	
	en bodas un poderoso.	735
Gaseno	Ea, vamos a almorzar,	
	por que pueda descansar	
	un rato su señoría.	

Tómale Don Juan la mano a la novia

D. Juan	¿Por qué la escondéis?	
Aminta	Es mía.	
Gaseno	Vamos.	
Belisa	Volved a cantar.	740
D. Juan	¿Qué dices tú?	

---

718   bridegroom: the situation of Aminta and Batricio is that they have taken their marriage vows before witnesses but the marriage has not yet been consummated. This is clearly what is meant by Catalinón's remark in 722.

724   playing the bull: once more, as in the earlier situation concerning Mota – see 505, note –, the allusions to the bull have to do with cuckoldry.

Gaseno	Make way there for our noble guest to sit.	
D. Juan	With your permission I should like to sit	
	Here.	

He takes his seat next to the bride

Batric.	If you sit there, sir, and take you place	715
	Before I do, it's just as if you've stepped	
	Into my shoes, taking my place as well	
	As bridegroom!	
D. Juan	My fine fellow, were I bridegroom	
	To this bride, who would dare condemn my choice?	
Gaseno	This is the bridegroom, sir!	
D. Juan	And for my error	720
	And sheer discourtesy, I beg forgiveness!	
Catal.	*[Aside]* A wretched fellow and before he's married!	
D. Juan	*[Aside]* The fellow's flummoxed and confused!	
Catal.	No wonder,	
	Master, playing the bull to your passes!	
	Are you surprised you've got him in a spin?	725
	[Aside] As for the girl, I wouldn't give a toss	
	For her virtue, nor for her suitor's honour!	
	Unfortunate the man whose fate it is	
	To fall into Lucifer's grasping hands!	
D. Juan	I can hardly believe that fortune smiles	730
	On me, oh lovely lady, with such favour!	
	Though envy of your husband moves me greatly.	
Aminta	I fancy, sir, you aim to flatter me.	
Batric.	And I was right to think a nobleman	
	Darkens a happy wedding with ill omen.	735
Gaseno	Come, then, let us begin the wedding-feast	
	And bid our gracious lord to take his ease	
	And join with us in our festivities.	

Don Juan takes Aminta's hand

D. Juan	But why remove your hand?	
Aminta	Because it's mine.	
Gaseno	Let's go!	
Belisa	And let the song begin again!	740
D. Juan	What's your impression?	

---

33 <u>you aim to flatter me</u>: although Aminta is dazzled by Don Juan's social position and the attention which he showers upon her, she distrusts him from the beginning and never leads him on. In the sense that she offers no encouragement, she is to be distinguished from the noblewomen who indulge in secret affairs. She is also totally unlike Tisbea. In general, it can be said of her that she is probably the least blameworthy character in the play of those who suffer at Don Juan's hands.

123

Catal.	¿Yo? que temo
	muerte vil destos villanos.
D. Juan	Buenos ojos, blancas manos,
	en ellos me abraso y quemo.
Catal.	¡Almagrar y echar a extremo! 745
	Con ésta cuatro serán.
D. Juan	Ven, que mirándome están.
Batric.	En mis bodas, caballero,
	¡mal agüero!
Gaseno	Cantad.
Batric.	Muero.
Catal.	Canten, que ellos llorarán. 750

*Vanse todos, con que da fin la segunda
jornada*

---

744   her beauty burns: although Aminta's hands are as white as snow, her
beauty burns Don Juan. See Act I, 632, note.

124

Catal.	Me? I'm scared to death	
	These country fellows have our own deaths planned.	
D. Juan	What lovely eyes she has! Her hands like snow!	
	Already her beauty burns into my soul!	
Catal.	You mark them out like sheep, master, before	745
	You turn them out. With her the total's four.	
D. Juan	Come! They can't stop staring. I wonder why?	
Batric.	This nobleman's presence at my wedding's	
	A bad omen!	
Gaseno	Begin the song!	
Batric.	I die!	
Catal.	All those who sing will soon be forced to cry.	750

Exit all

---

746   <u>the total's four</u>: Catalinón's total consists of Isabela, Tisbea, Ana and Aminta. <u>Clearly</u> he is alluding only to those seductions or attempted seductions that take place during the action of the play, for the list of Don Juan's conquests is very much longer than that. His uncle, Don Pedro, refers in Act I, 80, to 'a Spanish lady of distinction' seduced by him, he himself alludes to his habit of seduction – Act I, 892 – and in Seville with his companion, Mota, he embarks on a new round of seductions.

Sale Batricio, pensativo

Batric.   Celos, reloj de cuidados,
que a todas las horas dais
tormentos con que matáis,
aunque dais desconcertados;
celos, del vivir desprecios,   5
con que ignorancias hacéis,
pues todo lo que tenéis
de ricos, tenéis de necios;
dejadme de atormentar,
pues es cosa tan sabida   10
que, cuando amor me da vida,
la muerte me queréis dar.
¿Qué me queréis, caballero,
que me atormentáis ansí?
Bien dije cuando le vi   15
en mis bodas, "¡mal agüero!"
¿No es bueno que se sentó
a cenar con mi mujer,
y a mí en el plato meter
la mano no me dejó?   20
Pues cada vez que quería
metella la desviaba,
diciendo a cuanto tomaba:
"¡Grosería, grosería!"
Pues llegándome a quejar   25
a algunos, me respondían
y con risa me decían:
"No tenéis de qué os quejar;
eso no es cosa que importe;
no tenéis de qué temer;   30
callad, que debe de ser
uso de allá de la corte."
¡Buen uso, trato estremado!
Más no se usara en Sodoma:
que otro con la novia coma,   35
y que ayune el desposado.
Pues el otro bellacón

---

34   <u>Sodom!</u>: a city on the shore of the Dead Sea, destroyed by God on
account of the excessive wickedness of its people. See *Genesis* xix.

37   <u>this utter rogue</u>: it is, of course, Don Juan's roguishness which carries
the audience with him and ensures that it laughs at the deception of

Enter Batricio, pensive

Batric.　Jealousy, the timepiece of all our cares,
　　　　You strike at every hour of the day,
　　　　Not pleasing and harmonious sounds but discords
　　　　That pierce and assault our very souls.
　　　　Jealousy, you despise all happiness　　　　　　　5
　　　　And life, and in your ignorance of it
　　　　Make everything its opposite, transforming
　　　　All our joy to pain, delight to anguish.
　　　　I beg of you, spare me this awful torment!
　　　　As everyone knows well, love gives new meaning　10
　　　　To my existence, while you, despising
　　　　Pleasure, conspire to bring about my death!
　　　　As for you, nobleman, what do you want
　　　　Of me that you should come and plague me so?
　　　　The moment I set eyes on him arriving　　　　　15
　　　　At my wedding, I thought it ominous!
　　　　What else could it be when he sat himself
　　　　Right next to my dear bride at our wedding
　　　　Feast and, would you believe it, tried to stop
　　　　Me eating from the plate in front of me!　　　　20
　　　　For every time I reached for food he knocked
　　　　Away my hand, and every time I tried
　　　　To grab the smallest morsel, he complained:
　　　　'Who's ever seen gluttony as this?'
　　　　I did protest, of course, to all the others,　　25
　　　　But, far from helping me, they only laughed
　　　　At me, answering my grief with their mirth:
　　　　'You have no cause for worry or complaint.
　　　　You take the matter far too seriously.
　　　　Why be afraid when there's no cause to fear?　　30
　　　　Just hold your tongue and be assured that this
　　　　Is probably the custom of the Court'.
　　　　Custom indeed! Oh, yes! You wouldn't find
　　　　A custom more refined than that in Sodom!
　　　　That he should sit down by the bride and eat,　35
　　　　And I, the bridegroom, am denied my meat!
　　　　Imagine! This fellow, this utter rogue,

---

men like Batricio. Almost every word uttered by Batricio here, though
critical of Don Juan, backfires on Batricio himself. Needless to say, for
a sophisticated city audience watching the play, the foolish country
bumpkin was a ready source of humour.

a cuanto comer quería:
"¿Esto no come?", decía;
"No tenéis, señor, razón";   40
y de delante al momento
me lo quitaba. Corrido
estó; bien sé yo que ha sido
culebra y no casamiento.
Ya no se puede sufrir   45
ni entre cristianos pasar;
y acabando de cenar
con los dos, ¿mas que a dormir
se ha de ir también, si porfía,
con nosotros, y ha de ser,   50
el llegar yo a mi mujer,
"grosería, grosería?"
Ya viene, no me resisto.
Aquí me quiero esconder;
pero ya no puede ser,   55
que imagino que me ha visto.

    Sale Don Juan Tenorio

D. Juan   Batricio.
Batric.   Su señoría
       ¿qué manda?
D. Juan   Haceros saber. . .
Batric.   *[Ap.]* ¿Mas que ha de venir a ser
       alguna desdicha mía?   60
D. Juan   Que ha muchos días Batricio,
       que a Aminta el alma le di
       y he gozado. . .
Batric.   ¿Su honor?
D. Juan   Sí.
Batric.   *[Ap.]* Manifiesto y claro indicio
       de lo que he llegado a ver;   65
       que si bien no le quisiera
       nunca a su casa viniera.
       Al fin, al fin es mujer.
D. Juan   Al fin, Aminta celosa,
       o quizá desesperada   70
       de verse de mí olvidada
       y de ajeno dueño esposa,

---

63   Her honour?: highly conscious of his own good name, Batricio is quick
      to suspect the worst of Aminta. In this respect – as 1. 68 confirms –
      he is remarkably like Duke Octavio, suspecting the worst of Isabela. In

No sooner do I try to grab some food,
Chastises me. 'You can't eat that', he says,
'You need to learn how to behave yourself!'   40
And there and then the food in front of me
Is gone, snatched right away, and there am I
Left open-mouthed, and made to look a fool!
Call this a wedding? It's a cruel joke,
An insult of the kind no man can bear   45
And still deserve respect from all his friends.
I'm sure when this nobleman has finished
Supper, and I and my fair bride are off
To bed, he's going to insist on coming
With us! And when I take her in my arms,   50
Drawing her close to me, he'll be there too,
Complaining that my love's indecency!
Talk of the devil, here the devil comes!
I'd better hide myself. I can't abide
Him! No, I can't do that! I've missed my chance.   55
Worse luck the fellow's caught a glimpse of me!

Enter Don Juan

D. Juan   Batricio!
Batric.   Oh, your lordship, there you are!
What would you have me do?
D. Juan   I'd have you know. . .
Batric.   *[Aside]* It's bound to be bad news! It can't be good,
He wouldn't want to see me otherwise!   60
D. Juan   For some days now, Batricio, Aminta has
Possessed my soul. I am her prisoner.
And as for her I have possessed. . .
Batric.   Her honour?
D. Juan   What else?
Batric.   *[Aside]* What more proof could I need of what
I have become, of everything I feared?   65
It's obvious too she loves him just as much.
Why else would she invite him to her house?
But then, what else could I expect of woman?
D. Juan   The truth of the matter is simply this.
Aminta, torn by jealousy and fear   70
Of seeing herself rejected and abandoned
By me, through marriage to another man,

---

short, the peasant's attempt to ape the nobleman in matters of honour
exposes him to precisely the same agonies and, given his
pretentiousness, renders those agonies comic.

	esta carta me escribió	
	enviándome a llamar,	
	y yo prometí gozar	75
	lo que el alma prometió.	
	Esto pasa de esta suerte.	
	Dad a vuestra vida un medio;	
	que le daré sin remedio	
	a quien lo impida, la muerte.	80
Batric.	Si tú en mi eleción lo pones,	
	tu gusto pretendo hacer,	
	que el honor y la mujer	
	son males en opiniones.	
	La mujer en opinión	85
	siempre más pierde que gana,	
	que son como la campana,	
	que se estima por el són.	
	Y así es cosa averiguada	
	que opinión viene a perder,	90
	cuando cualquiera mujer	
	suena a campana quebrada.	
	No quiero, pues me reduces	
	el bien que mi amor ordena,	
	mujer entra mala y buena,	95
	que es moneda entre dos luces.	
	Gózala, señor, mil años,	
	que yo quiero resistir,	
	desengañar y morir,	
	y no vivir con engaños.	100

Vase Batricio

D. Juan Con el honor le vencí,
         porque siempre los villanos

---

73   this letter: Batricio presumably cannot read. We may imagine Don Juan,
     sure in that knowledge, waving the letter in front of the bemused
     peasant's face. But if Batricio cannot read, it is even more probable
     that Aminta cannot write. His utter belief in Don Juan's assertion that
     she is the author of the letter is thus even more comic.

80   I shall kill him!: Don Juan's threat runs the risk of alienating an
     audience which throughout the scene delights in Batricio's confusion. It
     is important therefore that this phrase be delivered in a light-hearted
     and flippant manner, contrasting with the solemnity of Batricio's reply.

85   gossip: characters in the drama of the Golden Age are frequently
     concerned with the dangers of any gossip attaching to them, for to be
     talked about in a derogatory sense is tantamount to dishonour. Honour
     can thus be seen to have little to do with virtue and integrity and
     everything to do with the way the individual is perceived by others.
     Batricio, as we have seen, regards honour in this second sense, and is
     quick to abandon Aminta to Don Juan rather than have her, and thus
     himself, talked about. He is a complete contrast to Calderón's Pedro

	Wrote me this letter. It's an invitation,	
	A plea to call on her, and in reply	
	To it I merely promised that I would,	75
	In recognition of our heart's desires.	
	Such is the situation, my dear friend.	
	Accept it! Nothing else that you can do!	
	You see, if any man thinks that he can win	
	Her heart, he'd better know that I shall kill him!	80
Batric.	Since it's a choice I have to make, my lord,	

Batric.   Since it's a choice I have to make, my lord,
            I choose to do what you suggest I should.
            Honour and woman have a lot in common:
            They both go hand in hand on people's tongues,
            Are bad companions when it comes to gossip,   85
            And any woman, given a bad name,
            Is bound to lose much more than she can gain.
            A woman's not much different from a bell:
            Its quality is good if it rings well.
            So it's a fact you have to take as proven   90
            That any woman's name, taken in vain
            By others, is a bell that's cracked, no less!
            As far as love's concerned, you've ruined it
            For me, destroyed it's glitter, leaving me
            A girl who, since her worth is now uncertain,   95
            Is like a coin in the dim light of evening.
            You have her for eternity, my lord.
            I'd rather give her up, accept the truth
            For what it is and die resigned to it
            Than be the butt of other people's jibes.   100
      Exit Batricio
D. Juan   I've overcome this fellow through his honour!
            Easy enough, of course, for all these rustics

Crespo, the proud peasant of *El alcalde de Zalamea* for whom honour is a spiritual thing, 'offspring of the soul', the province of God and not of man. Yet even when a man like Crespo knows what true honour is, he cannot isolate himself from other people's more worldly concept of honour. The same is seen to be true of the peasant Peribáñez in the play of the same name, for despite the fact that he knows his wife to be innocent of any affair with the overlord of the village, he is embarrassed by the fact that the latter's attentions to her should have become public knowledge.

102   these rustics: an expression of scorn towards peasants who have regard for their honour is often to be found in Golden-Age plays in the mouths of those who consider themselves superior. In *El alcalde de Zalamea* the Sergeant feels nothing but contempt for Pedro Crespo:

> I've heard it said this country fellow thinks
> Himself the finest fellow ever lived.
> He's so puffed up with pride and self-presumption,
> He has the manner of a nobleman. (Act I, 168-71)

             tıenen su honor en las manos,
             y siempre miran por sí.
             Que por tantas falsedades,   105
             es bien que se entienda y crea,
             que el honor se fué al aldea
             huyendo de las ciudades.
             Pero antes de hacer el daño
             le pretendo reparar: 110
             a su padre voy a hablar
             para autorizar mi engaño.
             Bien lo supe negociar:
             gozarla esta noche espero.
             La noche camina, y quiero   115
             su viejo padre llamar.
             Estrellas que me alumbráis,
             dadme en este engaño suerte,
             si el galardón en la muerte
             tan largo me lo guardáis.   120
        Vase. Salen Aminta y Belisa
Belisa   Mira que vendrá tu esposo:
             entra a desnudarte, Aminta.
Aminta   De estas infelices bodas
             no sé que siento, Belisa.
             Todo hoy mi Batricio ha estado   125
             bañado en melancolía,
             todo es confusión y celos;
             ¡mirad qué grande desdicha!
             Di, ¿qué caballero es éste
             que de mi esposo me priva?   130
             La desvergüenza en España
             se ha hecho caballería.
             Déjame, que estoy sin seso,
             déjame, que estoy corrida.
             ¡Mal hubiese el caballero   135
             que mis contentos me priva!
Belisa   Calla, que pienso que viene,
             que nadie en la casa pisa
             de un desposado, tan recio.

---

107   night approaches: see Act I, 10, note, for a comment on the way in
       which the dialogue locates time and place. A brief consideration of the
       play is sufficient to reveal that there is considerable movement in space
       and time, but the observer is always kept informed through the
       dialogue of any change of scene.
132   no different from nobility: Aminta's observation is a pointer to her own
       perceptiveness and to one of the key issues of the play. On the

```
                    Hold their honour near to their hearts,
                    As though they hold it dear as life itself.
                    The truth is that the prevalence of cunning          105
                    And deceit has obliged honour to seek
                    A safer refuge in the countryside,
                    Forsaking all the ills of city-life.
                    But coming to this piece of trickery,
                    I'll cloak it in respectability.                     110
                    I'll seek the father of the girl and let
                    Him give permission for her own deception.
                    What better way than that to set it up
                    And guarantee my pleasure for tonight?
                    The night approaches quickly now, it's time        115
                    I went to find the old man's whereabouts,
                    Oh, stars, you who illuminate my path,
                    Assist me carry out this cunning trick.
                    Though death may be my ultimate reward,
                    I'm sure there's time enough to pay that debt!      120
        Exit Don Juan. Enter Aminta and Belisa
Belisa              Your husband will be here quite soon, Aminta.
                    You'd better go inside and get undressed.
Aminta              The wedding's turned out badly. I don't know
                    Belisa, whether I feel sad or happy.
                    The whole day long Batricio had a face              125
                    As long as this: a proper misery!
                    Confusion in his heart, and jealousy!
                    Oh, what a fine mess it's turned out to be!
                    Tell me, who is this nobleman who's turned
                    Up here and turned my man away from me?             130
                    As far as I can see, plain roguery
                    In Spain's no different from nobility.
                    You'd better leave me for a while, Belisa.
                    I'm all confused, and thoroughly ashamed.
                    That nobleman! A curse upon his head!               135
                    He's driven my Batricio from our bed!
Belisa              Listen! It sounds as if Batricio's coming.
                    Who else would dare to make his presence known
                    By boldly entering the bridegroom's home?
```

---

question of the morality of the Spanish nobility as it is presented to us
in the play, see Act II, 258, note.

36   from our bed!: the marriage is still to be consummated, see Act II, 718,
        note. Don Juan's comment, Act III, 61, indicates that a few days have
        passed since he first set eyes on Aminta. The action of Act III is not
        therefore an unbroken continuation of the ending of Act II, for several
        days have elapsed.

Aminta	Queda adiós, Belisa mía.	140
Belisa	Desenójale en los brazos.	
Aminta	¡Plega a los cielos que sirvan	
	mis suspiros de requiebros,	
	mis lágrimas de caricias!	

Salen Don Juan, Catalinón y Gaseno

D. Juan	Gaseno, quedad con Dios.	145
Gaseno	Acompañaros querría,	
	por dalle desta ventura	
	el parabién a mi hija.	
D. Juan	Tiempo mañana nos queda.	
Gaseno	Bien decís: el alma mía	150
	en la muchacha os ofrezco	

Vase

D. Juan	Mi esposa decid.	
	[A Catal.] Ensilla,	
	Catalinón.	
Catal.	¿Para cuándo?	
D. Juan	Para el alba, que de risa	
	muerta, ha de salir mañana,	155
	de este engaño.	
Catal.	Allá, en Lebrija,	
	señor, nos está aguardando	
	otra boda. Por tu vida,	
	que despaches presto en ésta.	
D. Juan	La burla más escogida	160
	de todas ha de ser ésta.	
Catal.	Que saliésemos querría	
	de todas bien.	
D. Juan	Si es mi padre	
	el dueño de la justicia,	
	y es la privanza del rey,	165
	¿qué temes?	
Catal.	De los que privan	
	suele Dios tomar venganza,	
	si delitos no castigan;	
	y se suelen en el juego	
	perder también los que miran.	170

---

150   I offer you: although, in reaching an agreement with Don Juan, Gaseno shows himself to be unduly ambitious, he has no real reason to believe that Don Juan will seduce and abandon his daughter.

157   another wedding in Lebrija: which wedding is this? In Act II, 14, the King of Castile informs Don Juan's father that the young man is to marry Isabela and immediately banishes him to Lebrija. When Isabela arrives at Tarragona in Act III, she is on her way to Seville where her marriage to Don Juan is presumably to take place. The latter is not

Aminta	Oh, Belisa! Quickly! You'd better go!	140
Belisa	Embrace him! Let your kisses soothe his sadness!	
Aminta	I pray to Heaven above, please grant me this:	
	That all my sighs be pure flattery,	
	And every tear of mine a sweet carress!	

Enter Don Juan, Catalinón and Gaseno

D. Juan	Gaseno, God be with you! I'll take my leave.	145
Gaseno	My greatest wish, my lord, is to present	
	My daughter with the news of her good fortune.	
	I beg you grant a father this small favour.	
D. Juan	Oh, time enough to tell her that tomorrow!	
Gaseno	Well, I suppose you're right. I offer you	150
	My soul itself in the gift of my daughter.	

Exit Gaseno

D. Juan	You mean, of course, in the gift of my bride!	
	[To Catalinón] Catalinón, the horses! Get them ready!	
Catal.	When for, master?	
D. Juan	The crack of dawn, for when	
	The sun peeps out and sees what I have done,	155
	It's sure to split its sides with laughter.	
Catal.	Then,	
	My lord, another wedding in Lebrija	
	Waiting for you. Take my advice, you'd better	
	See to it this one is consummated quick!	
D. Juan	Not only consummated, but a trick	160
	That in its artistry is consumate.	
Catal.	Let's hope we get away with it! That's all	
	I want to do!	
D. Juan	Catalinón, my father,	
	As you know, is chief justice in the land	
	And very influential with the king.	165
	Why be afraid?	
Catal.	Because, master, there's God	
	To think about, and his vengeance always	
	Gets those who think they've got away with it.	
	And don't forget that when it comes to gambling,	
	It's often those who watch who end up losing.	170

---

actually informed in the lines of the play of the proposed marriage to Isabela. Presumably lines have been lost in which he is told both of the marriage and of its celebration at Lebrija.

64   chief justice: what we know of Don Diego Tenorio is that he is High Chamberlain to the King - see Act I, 571, note. In Act II, after the murder of Don Gonzalo, it is Don Diego who commands the guards to arrest the Marquis of Mota in the name of the King and who throughout Act III is concerned that justice shall be done. See Act III, 240.

	Yo he sido mirón del tuyo,	
	y por mirón no querría	
	que me cogiese algún rayo	
	y me trocase en ceniza.	
D. Juan	Vete, ensilla, que mañana	175
	he de dormir en Sevilla.	
Catal.	¿En Sevilla?	
D. Juan	Sí.	
Catal.	¿Qué dices?	
	Mira lo que has hecho, y mira	
	que hasta la muerte, señor,	
	es corta la mayor vida,	180
	y que hay tras la muerte infierno.	
D. Juan	Si tan largo me lo fías,	
	vengan engaños.	
Catal.	Señor. . .	
D. Juan	Vete, que ya me amohinas	
	con tus temores estraños.	185
Catal.	Fuerza al turco, fuerza al scita,	
	al persa y al garamante,	
	al gallego, al troglodita,	
	al alemán y al japón,	
	al sastre con la agujita	190
	de oro en la mano, imitando	
	contino a la Blanca niña.	

Vase Catalinón

D. Juan	La noche en negro silencio	
	se estiende, y ya las cabrillas	
	entre racimos de estrellas	195
	el polo más alto pisan.	
	Yo quiero poner mi engaño	
	por obra. El amor me guía	

---

177   You must be mad!: the rashness of Don Juan's action has to be measured against the fact that any flouting of a royal edict of banishment constituted a capital offence. In addition, he is prepared to ignore the marriage which the King has arranged for him. It is little wonder that Catalinón reacts as he does, for his master's actions increasingly defy both earthly and heavenly authority.

186   Admire the Turk: in Act II, 332-37, Catalinón promises Don Juan that he will perform heroic and extraordinary deeds. He vows now that he intends to leave such reckless endeavours to Don Juan, listing in the process nations and people renowned for their ferocity. The Turks, for example, were a constant menace in the Mediterranean in the sixteenth century and were renowned for their cruelty and savagery before that. Similarly, the Scythians, an ancient and nomadic people dwelling on the

136

	Now, as for me, I've been a regular watcher	
	Of your game, and I don't aim on that	
	Account to be the target for any bolt,	
	Heaven-sent or not, that turns my bones to dust.	

D. Juan   Just get a move on! Saddle up! My plan's   175
         To spend tomorrow night back in Seville.

Catal.   Seville?

D. Juan   Of course!

Catal.   You can't! You must be mad!
         Remember what you've done there, and remember
         Too that, though we think our life may last
         Forever, it's over, gone, you're up the spout,   180
         And then the fires of hell to think about!

D. Juan   All in good time, my friend, I'll meet that debt.
         Plenty of fun in store as yet. . .

Catal.   But master. . .

D. Juan   Get moving! You've become a tedious fellow,
         Extremely boring, and irrationally   185
         Fearful.

Catal.   Admire the Turk, sir, and the Scythian!
         Admire the Lybian, Persian and Galician!
         The fierce caveman, the courageous German.
         The Japanese with their reputation;
         Admire, if you want, sir, the old tailor,   190
         His needle fashioning the well-known story.
         Such bravery, master, but not for me!

Exit Catalinón

D. Juan   The night, enveloped in darkest shadow, spreads
         Its silence. The bright Pleiades, adorned
         With starry clusters, treads the highest point   195
         Of heaven. Now comes the hour when I must seize
         The opportunity to exercise
         My cunning; when I, guided by the power

---

north shore of the Black Sea about 100 B.C., were wildly feared. The reference to the old tailor 'fashioning the well-known story' is presumably to the well-known ballad which begins 'How white and beautiful you are, my love' which recounts the story of a young woman's adultery while her husband is away and his subsequent vengeance. Clearly, the situation of the ballad has a relevance to Don Juan, for his seduction of various women will, in Catalinón's view, lead to trouble. In short, Catalinón is not anxious to face avenging husbands or lovers.

94   The bright Pleiades: in Greek mythology the seven daughters of Atlas and Pleione. They killed themselves through grief over the death of their sisters, the Hyades, and were set by Jupiter as a group of stars in the heavens.

137

```
                a mi inclinación, de quien
                no hay hombre que se resista.                    200
                Quiero llegar a la cama.
                ¡Aminta!
        Sale Aminta como que está acostada
Aminta          ¿Quién llama a Aminta?
                ¿Es mi Batricio?
D. Juan                         No soy
                tu Batricio.
Aminta                      Pues ¿quién?
D. Juan                                 Mira
                de espacio, Aminta, quién soy.                   205
Aminta          ¡Ay de mí! ¡yo soy perdida!
                ¿En mi aposento a estas horas?
D. Juan         Estas son las horas mías.
Aminta          Volveos, que daré voces.
                No excedáis la cortesía                          210
                que a mi Batricio se debe.
                Ved que hay romanas Emilias
                en Dos-Hermanas también,
                y hay Lucrecias vengativas.
D. Juan         Escúchame dos palabras,                          215
                y esconde de las mejillas
                en el corazón la grana,
                por ti más preciosa y rica.
Aminta          Vete, que vendrá mi esposo.
D. Juan         Yo lo soy; ¿de qué te admiras?                   220
Aminta          ¿Desde cuándo?
D. Juan                         Desde agora.
Aminta          ¿Quién lo ha tratado?
D. Juan                                 Mi dicha.
Aminta          ¿Y quién nos casó?
```

202+   Aminta appears . . .: it seems very likely that Aminta emerges here
        from an area at the back of the stage which in the Golden-Age theatre
        was known as the 'discovery space' or inner stage. This was situated
        below the gallery which ran across the back of the stage, and between
        the two doors through which entrances and exits were made. The
        'discovery space', curtained off, was ideally suited to suggesting an
        inner room, such as a bedroom, or even a prison cell, as is the case in
        the opening scenes of Calderón's *La vida es sueño* where the
        man-beast, Segismundo, chained and attired in animal skins, is revealed
        to us in his dark prison-tower.
208   my special hours: another reference which has the effect of investing
        Don Juan with daemonic significance. See Act I, 15, note.
209   call for help: the point here is that if Aminta calls out, the presence of

	Of love, pursue its irresistible	
	Attraction, faithful to my inclination.	200
	I approach Aminta's bed. I'll call her name.	
	Aminta!	

Aminta appears, as though she has been sleeping

Aminta   Who calls Aminta? Is that you,
Batricio? Is it you?

D. Juan   I assure you,
Aminta, I'm not your sweet Batricio.

Aminta   Who are you?

D. Juan   Look, observe, Aminta! Don't   205
You recognize me?

Aminta   You! And in my bedroom
At this late hour! My reputation's ruined!

D. Juan   These late hours are my special hours.

Aminta   Leave me alone! Don't make me call for help!
You dare to throw aside your obligation,   210
Your debt and loyalty to my Batricio!
Remember that in Dos Hermanas too,
No less than in the world of ancient Rome,
Lucretias and Emilias may be found
Who will extract their vengeance!

D. Juan   Let me speak!   215
No need to be afraid! The blush of your
Cheeks, made lovlier still through being yours,
Is better buried deep within your heart.

Aminta   Go quickly! My husband will soon be here!

D. Juan   I am your husband. Why this strange surprise?   220

Aminta   Since when are you my husband?

D. Juan   From today!

Aminta   And who's arranged the marriage?

D. Juan   My good fortune.

Aminta   Who's wedded you to me?

---

a stranger in her bedroom will become public knowledge and will lead to her dishonour. A similar situation occurs in Act II of Lope de Vega's *Peribáñez* when Casilda, startled by the appearance of the Comendador in her bedroom, refrains from calling for assistance. See Act III, 85, note, of *The Trickster*.

12   Dos Hermanas: see Act II, 695, note.

14   Lucretias and Emilias: Lucretia, wife of Collatinus, was violated by the Roman Emperor, Sextus Tarquinius, and committed suicide. In literature she is often mentioned as the epitome of wifely fidelity. The reference to Emilia is less clear since there were several Roman Emilias. The wife of Scipio Africanus was especially renowned for her fortitude in adversity.

20   your husband: see Act II, 718, note.

139

D. Juan	Tus ojos.
Aminta	¿Con qué poder?
D. Juan	Con la vista.
Aminta	¿Sábelo Batricio?
D. Juan	Sí, 225

que te olvida.

Aminta	¿Que me olvida?
D. Juan	Sí, que yo te adoro.
Aminta	¿Cómo?
D. Juan	Con mis dos brazos.
Aminta	Desvía.
D. Juan	¿Cómo puedo, si es verdad

que muero?

Aminta	¡Qué gran mentira! 230
D. Juan	Aminta, escucha y sabrás,

si quieres que te lo diga,
la verdad, que las mujeres
sois de verdades amigas.
Yo soy noble caballero,   235
cabeza de la familia
de los Tenorios, antiguos
ganadores de Sevilla.
Mi padre, después del rey,
se reverencia y estima,   240
y en la corte, de sus labios
pende la muerte o la vida.
Corriendo el camino acaso,
llegué a verte, que amor guía
tal vez las cosas de suerte,   245
que él mismo dellas se olvida.
Vite, adoréte, abraséme
tanto, que tu amor me anima
a que contigo me case;
mira qué acción tan precisa.   250

---

224   Why, sight: in Act I Don Juan observes that Tisbea's eyes destroy him
         with their gaze. See 941, note, on the way in which love and the power
         of love are communicated through the eyes. In Aminta's case, as in
         Tisbea's, Don Juan is, of course, putting on his stock performance.
229   away from you: on absence from the loved one, see Act I, 205, note.
231   A lie: as indicated previously, Aminta is probably the most moral
         character in the play, and certainly the one who least deserves to be

D. Juan	Your eyes, so bright!
Aminta	Who's given you authority?
D. Juan	Why, sight,

Of course!

Aminta	Batricio hasn't!
D. Juan	But he knows. 225

And wishes to forget you!

Aminta	Forget me?
D. Juan	Since I adore and worship you!
Aminta	But how?
D. Juan	With these two arms of mine!
Aminta	You stay away

From me!

D. Juan	How can I when, away from you,

I die?

Aminta	Because I know your every word's 230

A lie.

D. Juan	Aminta, listen and you'll know

I speak the truth, for women are the friends
Of truth and thus are able to distinguish
Clearly between the man whose only wish
Is to deceive, and he who tells the truth.   235
I am a nobleman, heir to the great
Tenorio family, the ancient founders
Of Seville. My father, second in fame
And reputation only to the King,
Is in the Court Chief Justice, on whose word   240
There hangs the life or death of every man.
And so it happened, as I was passing by,
My eyes beheld you, guided by the hand
Of love, whose influence so rules our lives
By chance, that love itself, more often than not, 245
Forgets the lovers conquered by its glance.
I saw you, I adored you, you inflamed
My passions so, that love for you ordained
That I should seek your hand in marriage,
Transforming adoration into action.   250

---

disgraced. On the other hand, while mistrusting Don Juan, she is also flattered by his intentions, naturally enough in the light of her inexperience and social position.

237   the ancient founders: various historical sources suggest that the Tenorio family, some of whom were stewards of the dukes of Osuna, had been involved in the conquest of Seville if not in its founding.

240   Chief Justice: see Act III, 164, note.

	Y aunque lo mormure el reino,	
	y aunque el rey lo contradiga,	
	y aunque mi padre enojado	
	con amenazas lo impida,	
	tu esposo tengo de ser.	255
	¿Qué dices?	
Aminta	No sé qué diga,	
	que se encubren tus verdades	
	con retóricas mentiras.	
	Porque si estoy desposada,	
	como es cosa conocida,	260
	con Batricio, el matrimonio	
	no se absuelve aunque él desista.	
D. Juan	En no siendo consumado,	
	por engaño o por malicia	
	puede anularse.	
Aminta	En Batricio	265
	puede anularse.	
D. Juan	Ahora bien: dame esa mano,	
	y esta voluntad confirma	
	con ella.	
Aminta	¿Que no me engañas?	
D. Juan	Mío el engaño sería.	270
Aminta	Pues jura que cumplirás	
	la palabra prometida.	
D. Juan	Juro a esta mano, señora,	
	infierno de nieve fría,	
	de cumplirte la palabra.	275
Aminta	Jura a Dios que te maldiga	
	si no la cumples.	
D. Juan	Si acaso	
	la palabra y la fe mía	
	te faltaré, ruego a Dios	
	que a traición y alevosía	280
	me dé muerte un hombre. . .	
	([Ap.] muerto: que, vivo, ¡Dios no	
	permita!)	

---

251   <u>the kingdom disapprove</u>: Don Juan's suggestion here is that opposition
to the marriage would be on grounds of social inequality. He
conveniently omits to mention his flouting of the arranged marriage to
Isabela as another reason for the King's disapproval, were he to be
aware of it.

255   <u>I give my word</u>: yet another example of a promise made.

263   <u>unconsummated</u>: how does Don Juan know this? Batricio does not speak
about this aspect of his marriage to Aminta in the earlier conversation
with Don Juan. Either Don Juan is guessing, and hoping for the

142

	And even though the kingdom disapprove	
	It and the King express his opposition	
	To our union, or my father's anger	
	Threaten to bring about our separation,	
	I give my word that I shall be your husband.	255
	Give me your answer!	
Aminta	How shall I answer?	
	I suspect that words which all seem truthful	
	Are just a pretty covering for lies.	
	In any case, if, as the whole world knows,	
	My marriage vows now tie me to Batricio,	260
	He's still my husband, that's a sure fact,	
	And nothing you can do destroys that pact.	
D. Juan	A marriage which remains unconsummated	
	Whether the cause be malice or deceit,	
	Is clearly a marriage null and void.	265
Aminta	Batricio's without malice or deceit.	
D. Juan	Come now. Enough of that. Give me your hand	
	And with it confirmation of your oath	
	And promise.	
Aminta	You promise you won't deceive	
	Me!	
D. Juan	Deceive you is to deceive myself!	270
Aminta	Then swear to me you'll never break your word,	
	And promise that our marriage is assured.	
D. Juan	I swear, my dearest, by this lovely hand,	
	White as the whitest snow yet full of fire,	
	That I, as you command, will keep my word.	275
Aminta	Then swear to God, for if you break that vow,	
	Your punishment is His to take.	
D. Juan	I swear	
	That if somehow I fail to keep my word	
	To you, all given in good faith, then God	
	Repay my treachery and bring about	280
	My death at someone else's hands. . . *[Aside]* Provided	
	That someone is already dead himself!	

---

confirmation which Aminta gives in 266, or the matter is common
knowledge.

270 Deceive you is to deceive myself!: Don Juan's words, taken at face
value by Aminta, are not as straightforward in meaning as they seem.
Put in a different way, the meaning could well be 'To seduce you is to
be the seducer myself', and in that sense Don Juan really does keep
his word. Clearly, the whole of his oath is ironic, the promise which he
vows to keep being the promise which he has made to himself that the
deception of Aminta will be his finest trick.

Aminta	Pues con ese juramento
	soy tu esposa.
D. Juan	El alma mía
	entre los brazos te ofrezco.
Aminta	Tuya es el alma y la vida.
D. Juan	¡Ay, Aminta de mis ojos!
	Mañana sobre virillas
	de tersa plata estrellada
	con clavos de oro de Tíbar,
	pondrás los hermosos pies,
	y en prisión de gargantillas
	la alabastrina garganta,
	y los dedos en sortijas,
	en cuyo engaste parezcan
	trasparentes perlas finas.
Aminta	A tu voluntad, esposo,
	la mía desde hoy se inclina:
	tuya soy.
D. Juan	[Ap.] ¡Qué mal conoces
	al Burlador de Sevilla!

Líneas 285, 290, 295, 300

Vanse. Salen Isabela y Fabio, de camino

Isabela	¡Que me robase el dueño,
	la prenda que estimaba y más quería!
	¡Oh, riguroso empeño.
	de la verdad! ¡Oh, máscara del día!
	¡Noche al fin, tenebrosa
	antípoda del sol, del sueño esposa!
Fabio	¿De qué sirve, Isabela,
	la tristeza en el alma y en los ojos,
	si amor todo es cautela,
	y en campos de desdenes causa enojos,

Líneas 305, 310

---

295   the whiteness of your skin: Don Juan addresses the peasant girl in
       language with which she is totally unfamiliar and offers her presents
       beyond her wildest dreams. It is little wonder that she should be
       overwhelmed by such an experience. In relation to language, the
       difference between Aminta and Don Juan in this respect is a pointer to
       the social gulf that separates them. Golden-Age dramatists frequently
       used the language of a play in order to make this point. Lope de
       Vega's *Peribáñez* is a particularly good example, for in the encounters
       of noblemen and peasants the different way in which they speak
       constantly underlines the theme of the unnaturalness of the overlapping
       of two very different social layers.

305   your darkness: several kinds of darkness are suggested here. First,
       the sea and the land are enveloped in darkness, for the weather is
       rough and the sun is hidden by dark clouds. Secondly, Isabela's life in

Aminta	Then I accept your vow and give my word I'll be your wife.
D. Juan	Within these arms of mine I offer you as well my very soul.
Aminta	And I to you my soul and life itself.
D. Juan	Aminta! As dear to me as life, as breath! Tomorrow you shall walk in shoes of pure And polished silver, whose beauty is enhanced By clasps and buttons of the finest gold From Africa. Your throat, whiter than The purest alabaster, shall be encased In necklaces, imprisoning its flesh, And on your fingers dazzling rings whose beauty Is eclipsed by the whiteness of your skin.
Aminta	From this day forth my will, oh dearest husband, Inclines to yours. Your wish is my command! Do with me as you will!
D. Juan	[Aside] Of that she can Be absolutely sure! I'll keep that promise And prove I am the trickster of Seville!

Line numbers: 285, 290, 295, 300

Exit both. Enter Isabela and Fabio dressed as travellers

Isabela	That he should rob me of the only master Of my soul; of the man I dearly love! That lies should cruelly masquerade as truth, And night assume the appearance of day! Oh, night, your darkness banishes the light, Obliterates the sun and allies you With sleep!
Fabio	But what's the point of all this weeping, Isabela? Of all these sighs and tears? I tell you, love's a maze, a cunning game That's full of tricks, disdain and cruel lies,

Line numbers: 305, 310

---

general has been darkened by the events that have overtaken her, and the loss of her name and reputation is equivalent to the obliteration of the sun. The correlation of man and the natural world, microcosm and macrocosm, is, of course, highly characteristic of seventeenth-century literature. Again the reader is referred to E.M.W. Tillyard. See Act I, 348, note.

307 With sleep!: if night is associated with sleep, sleep is also associated with death. Isabela's dishonour is for her a kind of death, and she will not truly live again until her honour is restored by marriage to the man who has seduced her and deprived her of her good name.
all this weeping: this passage is similar in its ironic tone and its deflation of Isabela's weighty sentiments to Ripio's response to Octavio's complaints in Act I, 191-242. It is another good example of the juxtaposition of serious and comic elements in the drama of the Golden Age.

	si el que se ríe agora	
	en breve espacio desventuras llora?	
	El mar está alterado	
	y en grave temporal, riesgo se corre.	
	El abrigo han tomado	315
	las galeras, duquesa, de la torre	
	que esta playa corona.	

Isabela   ¿Dónde estamos ahora?
Fabio   En Tarragona.
          De aquí a poco espacio
          daremos en Valencia, ciudad bella,   320
          del mismo sol palacio.
          Divertiráste algunos días en ella,
          y después a Sevilla,
          irás a ver la octava maravilla.
          Que si a Octavio perdiste,
          más galán es don Juan, y de Tenorio
          solar. ¿De qué estás triste?
          Conde dicen que es ya don Juan Tenorio;
          el rey con él te casa,
          y el padre es la privanza de su casa.   330

Isabela   No nace mi tristeza
          de ser esposa de don Juan, que el mundo
          conoce su nobleza;
          en la esparcida voz mi agravio fundo,
          que esta opinión perdida   335
          es de llorar mientras tuviere vida.

Fabio   Allí una pescadora
          tiernamente suspira y se lamenta,
          y dulcemente llora.
          Acá viene, sin duda, y verte intenta.   340
          Mientras llamo tu gente,
          lamentaréis las dos más dulcemente.

Vase Fabio y sale Tisbea

---

317   towers: these would have been watchtowers, erected to warn of invasion
       by sea, especially by Turks and Moors. See Act I, 429, note.
324   Eighth wonder of the world: while Fabio applies the description to
       Seville, Don Gonzalo de Ulloa has previously spoken of Lisbon in
       exactly the same way. See Act I, 722. This suggests quite clearly that
       there is a deliberate intention in the play to compare and contrast the
       two cities.
335   blackening my reputation: that is to say, Isabela is still the subject of
       common gossip. Even though her marriage to Don Juan will provide her

	And in the end gets on your wick! Show me	
	The lover whose happy sighs won't soon become	
	His anguished cries! Look at the sea, how rough	
	It is! The waves whipped up! A real tempest!	
	The ships are making for the greater safety	315
	Of the harbour, lowering their anchor	
	Where those great towers overlook the shore.	
Isabela	What is this place?	
Fabio	This place is Tarragona,	
	Duchess. A few days' travelling, we'll reach	
	Valencia, the most beautiful of cities,	320
	Aboae and palace of the sun itself.	
	Spend a few days there, take in all the sights,	
	And then our journey's onward to Seville,	
	Eighth wonder of the world in all its glory.	
	As for Octavio, you may well have lost	325
	Him, but Don Juan's an even better catch,	
	So snatch him while you can! Don't be so sad!	
	That's madness when Don Juan's to be a count!	
	The King himself has called the marriage banns,	
	And Don Juan's father is his right-hand man!	330
Isabela	It's not the marriage to Don Juan that makes	
	Me sad. The whole world knows of his most noble	
	Birth and origins. I would gladly be	
	His wife on that account, but sadly they	
	Pursue me, blackening my reputation,	335
	And in lost honour there is no salvation.	
Fabio	My lady, look! A fishergirl approaches.	
	Like you she fills the air with anguished sighs.	
	Like you her tears fill her lovely eyes.	
	No doubt she wants to have a word with you.	340
	I'll disappear, fetch the others. Better	
	For you two if you bare your souls together!	

Exit Fabio. Enter Tisbea

---

with status, it will not prevent people from continuing to talk about her earlier disgrace.

343   I curse you: see Catalinon's similar attack on the sea and the invention of ships in Act I, 541. Tisbea's language here is as full of elaborate conceits as when we first saw her in Act I. Thus, the ocean contains not only water but fire – in the sense that it deposited the passionate Don Juan literally on her doorstep. His subsequent behaviour brought her grief, expressed in tears which not merely wet her cheeks but burn them, such is her shame. Once more the character of Tisbea's language can be described as Gongoresque. See Act I, 376, note.

Tisbea	Robusto mar de España,	
	ondas de fuego, fugitivas ondas,	
	Troya de mi cabaña,	345
	que ya el fuego, por mares y por ondas,	
	en sus abismos fragua,	
	y el mar forma, por las llamas, agua.	
	¡Maldito el leño sea	
	que a tu amargo cristal halló carrera,	350
	antojo de Medea,	
	tu cáñamo primero o primer lino,	
	aspado de los vientos	
	para telas de engaños e instrumentos!	
Isabela	¿Por qué del mar te quejas	355
	tan tiernamente, hermosa pescadora?	
Tisbea	Al mar formo mil quejas.	
	¡Dichosa vos, que en su tormento, agora	
	dél os estáis riendo!	
Isabela	También quejas del mar estoy haciendo.	360
	¿De dónde sois?	
Tisbea	De aquellas	
	cabañas que miráis del viento heridas	
	tan vitorioso entre ellas,	
	cuyas pobre paredes desparcidas	
	van en pedazos graves,	365
	dando en mil grietas nidos a las aves.	
	En sus pajas me dieron	
	corazón de fortísimo diamante;	
	mas las obras me hicieron,	
	deste monstruo que ves tan arrogante,	370
	ablandarme de suerte,	
	que al sol la cera es más robusta y fuerte.	
	¿Sois vos la Europa hermosa?	
	¿Que esos toros os llevan?	
Isabela	A Sevilla	
	llévanme a ser esposa	375
	contra mi voluntad.	

---

351   Medea's grief: in Greek legend Medea helped Jason obtain the Golden
Fleece and fled with him to Thessaly. He subsequently abandoned her
for Creusa, the daughter of the King of Corinth, and Medea,
overwhelmed by grief and hatred, took vengeance by murdering her
children.

372   melts hardest wax: a contemporary audience, well-versed in classical
legend, would have thought immediately of Icarus, whose father
Daedalus constructed wings held together by wax in order to escape
from Crete. In the course of the flight Icarus ventured too near the

isbea	I curse you, cruel sea, for your waves,
	As full of blazing fire as of foam,
	Destroyed my little cottage, burnt my home 345
	As if it were as great as ancient Troy!
	Who would have thought that from your salty deep
	Flames would emerge and tears scald my cheeks?
	I curse the wood that, made into a boat,
	Made your bitter surface its abode, 350
	In imitation of Medea's grief.
	That canvas, that great sweep of sail and cloth
	Nailed to a wooden cross, is but a spider's
	Web in which all our dearest hopes are lost!
sabela	Sweet fishergirl, tell me why you complain 355
	So bitterly, and of the sea's treachery!
isbea	Of the sea I complain a thousand fold,
	While you, though buffeted by its assaults,
	Can happily afford to laugh at it.
sabela	But I, like you, have good cause for complaint. 360
	Where are you from?
isbea	You see that cottage there?
	That tiny cabin was my home where now
	The wind alone proclaims its victory.
	Its poor walls reduced to dust or full
	Of holes, where once I took my happy rest, 365
	Are now a ruin where only birds can nest.
	There in its straw I lived a happy life,
	My heart as hard as diamond to all
	Men's sighs, until the sea in all its fury,
	This fierce monster, conspired to bring 370
	About my ruin, softening my heart
	As quickly as the sun melts hardest wax.
	My friend, are you the beautiful Europa,
	Borne by bulls to your cruel destiny?
Isabela	Seville's my destination. My destiny 375
	A marriage now imposed on me against
	My will.

---

sun, the wax melted, and the boy plunged to his death in the sea. In
Renaissance and post-Renaissance literature the fate of Icarus became a
metaphor for excessive pride and confidence and in this context
Tisbea's allusion is appropriately ironic.

373   the beautiful Europa: according to legend, Europa, virgin of Tyre, was
abducted by Jupiter in the form of a bull. A version of the legend has
it that Jupiter abandoned Europa on the coast of Tarragona. Tisbea's
allusion to bulls may also have something to do with the fact that large
boats arriving at Spanish destinations were pulled into the shore by
oxen. Isabela has, of course, arrived by boat from Italy.

Tisbea	Si mi mancilla	
	a lástima os provoca,	
	y si injurias del mar os tienen loca,	
	en vuestra compañía,	
	para serviros como humilde esclava	380
	me llevad; que querría,	
	si el dolor o la afrenta no me acaba,	
	pedir al rey justicia	
	de un engaño cruel, de una malicia.	
	Del agua derrotado,	385
	a esta tierra llegó don Juan Tenorio,	
	difunto y anegado:	
	amparéle, hospedéle en tan notorio	
	peligro, y el vil güésped	
	víbora fué a mi planta en tierno césped.	390
	Con palabra de esposo,	
	la que de esta costa burla hacía,	
	se rindió al engañoso:	
	¡Mal haya la mujer que en hombres fía!	
	Fuese al fin y dejóme:	395
	mira si es justo que venganza tome.	
Isabela	¡Calla, mujer maldita!	
	Vete de mi presencia, que me has muerto.	
	Mas si el dolor te incita,	
	no tienes culpa tú, prosigue el cuento.	400
Tisbea	La dicha fuera mía.	
Isabela	¡Mal haya la mujer que en hombres fía!	
	¿Quién tiene de ir contigo?	
Tisbea	Un pescador, Anfriso; un pobre padre	
	de mis males testigo.	405
Isabela	[Ap.] No hay venganza que a mi mal tanto	
	Ven en mi compañía. [le cuadre.	
Tisbea	¡Mal haya la mujer que en hombres fía!	

*Vanse Tisbea y Isabela. Salen Don Juan
y Catalinón*

Catal.	Todo en mal estado está.	
D. Juan	¿Cómo?	
Catal.	Que Octavio ha sabido	410
	la traición de Italia ya,	

---

390   a viper: there are many legends concerning the viper. The female was
said, for example, to conceive through its mouth, and in the very act
of conception to bite off the male's head. On giving birth, the female
herself suffered an equally horrible fate, for her offspring simply tore
their way through her breast. Acts of such ingratitude clearly led to
the association of the viper with any ungrateful or treacherous person.

Tisbea	Then if my plight moves you to feel
	Some pity for me, and the sea's injustice
	Is the source of your anguish, I beg you
	Take me with you. I'll be your loyal servant. 380
	My greatest wish, if only my anguish
	And dishonour allow me to survive,
	Is to obtain the justice of the King
	As punishment for such a vile deception.
	Don Juan Tenorio, spewed up by the waves, 385
	Set foot upon this shore, a man more dead
	Than living from the water still inside him.
	I cared for him, provided him with shelter
	Until he was much better, when he showed
	His gratitude, a viper at my feet! 390
	Believing his promise he'd be my husband,
	I, the girl whose pleasure was deceiving
	Others, was cruelly deceived by him!
	More fool the woman who puts her faith and trust
	In men! Finally he abandoned me. 395
	Surely there's justice in my claim for vengeance!
Isabela	I want to hear no more! A curse on you!
	Leave me alone! Your every word destroys
	Me! But no! No! For grief incites your anguish.
	The fault's not yours! Continue your story! 400
Tisbea	If only the story ended happily!
Isabela	More fool the woman who puts her faith and trust
	In men! And who are your two companions?
Tisbea	A fisherman, Anfriso, and a poor
	Father, both witnesses to my offence. 405
Isabela	[Aside] No vengeance is too great as punishment
	For this man's crimes! [Aloud] Let's go together then!
Tisbea	More fool the woman who puts her faith in men!

Exit Tisbea and Isabela. Enter Don Juan and Catalinón

Catal.	I fancy things are going from bad to worse!
D. Juan	Explain yourself!
Catal.	Well, first of all, Octavio 410
	Knows what really happened in Italy.

---

394   faith and trust: Tisbea's pronouncement about men can be compared
with the observations in the play made by men about women - by the
King of Naples, for example, Act I, 153-56, and by Octavio, Act I,
357-59.

398-9   destroys/Me!: Isabela's marriage to Don Juan will not, as she has
observed, prevent people from talking about her seduction. How much
more her peace of mind is endangered should Tisbea's fate also become
known!

151

<pre>
                    y el de la Mota ofendido
                    de ti justas quejas da,
                    y dice, que fué el recaudo,
                    que de su prima le diste   415
                    fingido y disimulado,
                    y con su capa emprendiste
                    la traición que le ha infamado.
                    Dice que viene Isabela
                    a que seas su marido,   420
                    y dicen. . .
D. Juan   ¡Calla!
Catal.   Una muela
                    en la boca me has rompido.
D. Juan   Hablador, ¿quién te revela
                    tantos disparates juntos?
Catal.   ¡Disparate, disparate!   425
                    Verdades son.
D. Juan   No pregunto
                    si lo son. Cuando me mate
                    Otavio: ¿estoy yo difunto?
                    ¿No tengo manos también?
                    ¿Dónde me tienes posada?   430
Catal.   En la calle, oculta.
D. Juan   Bien
Catal.   La iglesia es tierra sagrada.
D. Juan   Di que de día me den
                    en ella la muerte. ¿Viste
                    al novio de Dos-Hermanas?   435
Catal.   También le vi ansiado y triste.
D. Juan   Aminta, estas dos semanas,
                    no ha de caer en el chiste.
Catal.   Tan bien engañada está,
                    que se llama doña Aminta.   440
D. Juan   ¡Graciosa burla será!
Catal.   Graciosa burla y sucinta,
                    mas siempre la llorará.
          Descúbrese un sepulcro de Don Gonzalo
          de Ulloa
D. Juan   ¿Qué sepulcro es éste?
</pre>

---

422   broken a precious tooth: Don Juan, driven to distraction by Catalinón'
      prattling, suddenly loses control, hits him across the face and break
      one of his teeth. This is a finely observed moment on Tirso's part, fo
      Don Juan's bravado is suddenly seen to be pierced by real doubt an
      uncertainty. He recovers quickly his former coolness, but the loss o

	Then Mota, your friend so grievously	
	Offended by you, bitterly complains	
	Of treachery. His claim is that the message	
	Which his cousin gave you, you passed to him	415
	In quite a different form, its meaning changed.	
	On top of that you took his cloak and tricked	
	His girl-friend, on account of which he stands	
	Accused himself. And then there's Isabela.	
	I've heard it said you'll have to marry her!	420
	The story has it too. . .	

. Juan   Shut up!

atal.   You've gone
And broken a precious tooth! You have a look!

. Juan   You idle chatterbox! Who filled your head
With all that silly nonsense? Talk some sense!

atal.   But master, how can it be nonsense when   425
It's common-sense and every word's the truth?

. Juan   Why should I care? If Octavio ever dares
To raise his hands against me, do I not
Have these hands for my defence? Stop your chatter
And show me where you've found us board and lodge.

atal.   It's down this street, a dark and quiet place.

. Juan   It suits me well.

atal.   This church is hallowed ground.

. Juan   Which means, my friend, that if I'm ever found
In it, I'm safe and sound! No need to worry!
Have you seen the bridegroom from Dos Hermanas?   435

atal.   I saw him too. A sad and sorry sight!

. Juan   Aminta's not exactly bright! It's two
Weeks on. She doesn't believe she's been deceived.

atal.   You've tricked her good and proper, ain't yer?
She even calls herself Lady Aminta!   440

. Juan   A real good laugh! Brings tears to my eyes!

atal.   No doubt, master! A sharp and cunning trick!
When she finds out, she'll laugh herself quite sick!

They come across the tomb of Don Gonzalo de Ulloa

. Juan   Whose tomb is this?

---

  control is illuminating.

2   hallowed ground: the scene is actually taking place in a church, though
this is not made clear at the very beginning of the scene. While Don
Juan remains within the sanctuary of its walls, Catalinón has been
searching for board and lodge, which he has now found - 431.

Catal.	<div align="center">Aquí</div>
	don Gonzalo está enterrado. 445
D. Juan	Este es al que muerte di.
	¡Gran sepulcro le han labrado!
Catal.	Ordenólo el rey ansí.
	¿Cómo dice este letrero?
D. Juan	"Aquí aguarda del Señor, 450
	el más leal caballero,
	la venganza de un traidor."
	Del mote reírme quiero.
	¿Y habéisos vos de vengar,
	buen viejo, barbas de piedra? 455
Catal.	No se las podrás pelar,
	que en barbas muy fuertes medra.
D. Juan	Aquesta noche a cenar
	os aguardo en mi posada.
	Allí el desafío haremos, 460
	si la venganza os agrada;
	aunque mal reñir podremos,
	si es de piedra vuestra espada.
Catal.	Ya, señor, ha anochecido;
	vámonos a recoger. 465
D. Juan	Larga esta venganza ha sido.
	Si es que vos la habéis de hacer,
	importa no estar dormido,
	que si a la muerte aguardáis
	la venganza, la esperanza 470
	agora es bien que perdáis,
	pues vuestros enojo y venganza
	tan largo me lo fiáis.

Vanse y ponen la mesa dos Criados *

C. 1.*	Quiero apercebir la cena,
	que vendrá a cenar don Juan. 475
C. 2.*	Puestas las mesas están.
	¡Qué flema tiene si empieza!
	Ya tarda como solía,
	mi señor; no me contenta;
	la bebida se calienta 480
	y la comida se enfría.

---

455   your beard's hard and stony: Don Juan's pulling of the statue's beard
suggests that the figure of Don Gonzalo de Ulloa is not standing but
prone, as is often the case in Spanish churches. Given that the tomb
is, in Don Juan's words, a 'splendid monument', it would probably be
quite high, the stone figure placed on a large block of marble. In order
to pull the beard Don Juan might well have to climb onto the block

atal.	Whose tomb? I though you'd know.
	This tomb belongs to your old friend, Gonzalo! 445
. Juan	What? The very same Gonzalo I sent
	Packing! For him this splendid monument?
atal.	They say they built it at the King's command.
	They've put some lettering here. See what it says!
. Juan	'Here lies buried a noble gentleman, 450
	A loyal subject of the realm, whom God
	Has promised vengeance on an evil traitor'.
	Well isn't that a laugh? Foolish old man!
	You really intend to avenge yourself on me?
	You can't move! Even your beard's hard and stony! 455
atal.	No point in pulling it! He only stares!
	It's not the sort of beard that needs much care!
. Juan	[To the statue] Tonight, my friend, a special invitation.
	Have dinner with me! A special celebration
	Where I'm staying! There you can challenge me 460
	If you want, see if you can take your vengeance.
	Though I can't see you making me atone,
	Not when that sword of yours is made of stone.
atal.	Look, master, it's as black as night in here.
	We ought to get back to our place I'm sure. 465
. Juan	[To the statue] Your vengeance is a long time coming, sir!
	If you intend to take it, best be sure
	You aren't as still and sleepy as you seem.
	A man in your state can only dream
	Of vengeance and wait in hope till doomsday. 470
	A forlorn hope you'd just as well forget!
	Plenty of time for me to pay that debt!
	They leave. Two servants lay the table
irst	I'd better get a move on, warm his supper.
ervant	If it's not done, I'm sure to come a cropper.
econd	The table's laid. There's nothing else to do. 475
ervant	Don Juan's a cool one. You can be quite sure
	He'll take his time, as usual, even though
	The wine, instead of being cool, is hot,
	And what was quite a supper's gone to pot!

---

itself. The pulling of a man's beard was, of course, an insult, and had been from ancient times. There are frequent references to it in the medieval Spanish epic, the *Poema de Mío Cid*. As far as staging is concerned, a Golden-Age production in a public theatre would probably have the statue located in the 'discovery space'.

72+   lay the table: the scene changes here to the inn in which Catalinón has found a room.

Mas, ¿quién a don Juan ordena
esta desorden?

Entran Don Juan y Catalinón

D. Juan   ¿Cerraste?

Catal.   Ya cerré como mandaste.

D. Juan   ¡Hola! Tráigenme la cena.   485

C. 2.°   Ya está aquí.

D. Juan   Catalinón,
siéntate.

Catal.   Yo soy amigo
de cenar de espacio.

D. Juan   Digo
que te sientes.

Catal.   La razón
haré.

C. 1.°   También es camino   490
éste, si come con él.

D. Juan   Siéntate.

Un golpe dentro

Catal.   Golpe es aquél.

D. Juan   Que llamaron imagino;
mira quién es.

C. 1.°   Voy volando.

Catal.   ¿Si es la justicia, señor?   495

D. Juan   Sea, no tengas temor.

Vuelve el Criado, huyendo

       ¿Quién es? ¿De qué estás temblando?

Catal.   De algún mal da testimonio.

D. Juan   Mal mi cólera resisto.
Habla, responde, ¿qué has visto?   500
¿Asombróte algún demonio?
Ve tú, y mira aquella puerta:
¡presto, acaba!

Catal.   ¿Yo?

D. Juan   Tú, pues.
Acaba, menea los pies.

Catal.   A mi agüela hallaron muerta   505
como racimo colgada,
y desde entonces se suena

---

492   to share his food and drink: clearly, the servants are surprised by the
            fact that Catalinón should be ordered to share his master's table.

493+   *A mighty knock is heard:* the door which figures so prominently in this
            episode would have been, in a seventeenth-century production, one of

Anyway, who can order our Don Juan,   480
The very architect of all disorder?
Enter Don Juan and Catalinón
D. Juan Make sure you've shut the door!
Catal.   It's shut, master,
And bolted! Exactly as you ordered.
D. Juan Hey, you two! Have you got my dinner ready?
Second Servant Of course, sir! Here it is!
D. Juan   Catalinón!   485
Sit down! Pacing around! What is the matter?
Catal.   Truth is, master, I don't want to get fatter!
Besides, I like to take my time if you
Don't mind.
D. Juan   Sit down I said! Do what you're told!
Catal.   Alright! If you say so! I'm not so bold   490
As to disobey an order!
First Servant   This one
Travels with him to share his food and drink!
D. Juan Sit!
A mighty knock is heard
Catal.   Shit! What's that?
D. Juan   I fancy someone's knock.
See who it is!
First Servant   At once.
Catal.   Bit of a shock
If it's the law. . . you know. . . a raid!   495
D. Juan What if it is? No need to be afraid!
The servant returns running
Who's there? You look as if you've seen a ghost!
Catal.   Perhaps it is, my lord! A sign we'll roast
In Hell!
D. Juan   Come on, man! Tell us what you saw!
I'm losing patience! Out with it, before   500
I force it out of you! An evil spirit
Was it? Here, you! You go and open it!
And get a move on!
Catal.   Me?
D. Juan   Of course! Who else?
Your mouth is quick enough! Why not your feet?
Catal.   I had a grandmother. They found her dead,   505
Just hanging like a bunch of grapes they said
She was, and ever since, the story goes,

---

the two doors at the back of the stage. These were sometimes actual
doors, sometimes just a curtain. In the latter case the loud knock would
have to be made off-stage.

	que anda siempre su alma en pena.	
	Tanto golpe no me agrada.	
D. Juan	Acaba.	
Catal.	Señor, si sabes	510
	que soy un Catalinón. . .	
D. Juan	Acaba.	
Catal.	¡Fuerte ocasión!	
D. Juan	¿No vas?	
Catal.	¿Quién tiene las llaves	
	de la puerta?	
C. 2.º	Con la aldaba	
	está cerrada no más.	515
D. Juan	¿Qué tienes? ¿Por qué no vas?	
Catal.	Hoy Catalinón acaba.	
	¿Mas si las forzadas vienen	
	a vengarse de los dos?	

Llega Catalinón a la puerta, y viene corriendo; cae y levantase

D. Juan	¿Qué es eso?	
Catal.	¡Válgame Dios!	
	¡Que me matan, que me tienen!	
D. Juan	¿Quién te tiene, quién te mata?	
	¿Qué has visto?	
Catal.	Señor, yo allí	
	vide cuando. . . luego fuí. . .	
	¿Quién me ase, quién me arrebata?	525
	Llegué, cuando después ciego. . .	
	cuando vile, ¡juro a Dios!. . .	
	Habló y dijo, ¿quién sois vos?. . .	
	respondió, y respondí luego. . .	
	topé y vide. . .	
D. Juan	¿A quién?	
Catal.	No sé.	530
D. Juan	¡Cómo el vino desatina!	
	Dame la vela, gallina,	
	y yo a quien llama veré.	

---

508   full of pain and woe: if Catalinón's grandmother had indeed committed suicide, a mortal sin in the eyes of the Church, her soul would, of course, be damned. In typical *gracioso* fashion, Catalinón invents an absurd story in order to delay having to answer the door. He is less

	Her spirit wanders, full of pain and woe.	
	That knock! I'm scared it might be granny's soul!	
D. Juan	Stop prattling on!	
Catal.	But master! If you know	510
	That I'm the greatest coward ever lived. . .	
D. Juan	I said shut up!	
Catal.	Oh, what a mess this is!	
D. Juan	Are you defying me?	
Catal.	Who's got the key?	
	The bloody door's locked!	
Second Servant	Only with the bolt,	
	My friend! You are a dolt if you can't open	515
	It!	
D. Juan	So get a move on! You can't sit there	
	All night!	
Catal.	Oh, poor Catalinón's all finished!	
	What if the visitors are women you	
	Raped, come to take their vengeance on us two?	

*Catalinón goes to the door, comes running back, falls
down, gets up again*

D. Juan	So what's the verdict?	
Catal.	God help me! I thought	520
	I was going to die! I thought they'd got	
	Me!	
D. Juan	Who got you? Why were you going to die?	
	What did you see?	
Catal.	Oh, master! There was I. . .	
	My goodness!. . . Oh, my word!. . . What did I see?	
	Who's trying to grab me, get hold of me?	525
	I got there, had a look. . . I must be blind!	
	There, I see. . . suddenly. . . Oh, God be kind	
	To me. . . It spoke and 'Who are you?' it said.	
	I answered, God knows what, and bumped into. . .	
D. Juan	Who?	
Catal.	I don't know! I haven't got a clue!	530
D. Juan	Good God! The wine has driven him insane!	
	Give me the candle! A coward through and through!	
	I'll go myself and see who's at the door.	

---

concerned with his own dignity than with saving his skin in the event
of the visitor's being the stone guest.

514   locked: we can well imagine Catalinón's fumbling with the door.
Throughout the scene his physical actions combine with his absurd
babbling to suggest very vividly a fearful state of mind.

Toma Don Juan la vela y llega a la puerta.
Sale al encuentro Don Gonzalo, en la forma que
estaba en el sepulcro, y Don Juan se retira atrás
turbado, empuñando la espada, y en la otra la
vela, y Don Gonzalo hacia el, con pasos menudos,
y al compas Don Juan, retirandose hasta
estar en medio del teatro

D. Juan	¿Quién va?
D. Gon.	Yo soy.
D. Juan	¿Quién sois vos?

D. Gon.   Soy el caballero honrado   535
            que a cenar has convidado.

D. Juan   Cena habrá para los dos,
            y si vienen más contigo,
            para todos cena habrá.
            Ya puesta la mesa está.   540
            Siéntate.

Catal.   ¡Dios sea conmigo!
            ¡San Panuncio, San Antón!
            Pues ¿los muertos comen, di?
            Por señas dice que sí.

D. Juan   Siéntate, Catalinón.   545

Catal.   No, señor, yo lo recibo
            por cenado.

D. Juan   Es desconcierto:
            ¡qué temor tienes a un muerto!
            ¿Qué hicieras estando vivo?
            Necio y villano temor.   550

Catal.   Cena con tu convidado,
            que yo, señor, ya he cenado.

D. Juan   ¿He de enojarme?

---

532   the candle: again it is worth reminding ourselves that in the seventeenth-century public theatres the play would be performed in broad daylight. As we have seen previously, nocturnal episodes are suggested very often by the dialogue, which is usually the immediate spur to the audience's imagination. The suspension of disbelief was achieved as well, however, by the fact that the actors acted in these scenes as though it were in fact night – groping and stumbling, feeling their way around, as at the very beginning of Act I, or, as here, making use of appropriate props.

533+   a slow, measured step: the literal translation of the Spanish here is 'with small steps'. Whether 'small' or 'measured', the movement of the statue suggests the stiff, automaton-like advance of a non-human figure. How, in fact, would this have been done in a seventeenth-century production? On the one hand an actor could have played the part of the statue, perhaps wearing a mask or having had his face painted, and dressed in the same clothes as the recumbent

*Don Juan takes the candle and goes to the door. Don
Gonzalo enters in the form of the stone statue above
the tomb. Don Juan steps back, disturbed, his sword
in one hand, the candle in the other. Don Gonzalo
advances towards him with a slow, measured step.
Don Juan retreats to centre stage*

D. Juan   Who are you?

D. Gon.   Who am I? The honourable
Gentleman who's come to dine with you!   535
You haven't forgotten the invitation!

D. Juan   Of course not! For this occasion there's food
Enough for both of us, and more should any
Of your friends express the wish to join us.
As you can see, the table's set and ready.   540
So take a seat!

Catal.   Oh God above protect
Me! And Saint Panuncio! And Saint Anthony!
I'll ask him a question. Do dead men eat?
Good lord! He nods his head and says they do!

D. Juan   Catalinón! You'll join us. Take a seat!   545

Catal.   Oh, thank you, master! I'd rather not! I'm full
Already!

D. Juan   Full of what? Plain foolishness?
Scared as a rabbit of a man who's dead?
I wonder what you'd do were he alive!
Still, such a fear befits a common fool!   550

Catal.   You eat, sir, with your guest! I've got a rule
That having eaten once, I ought to rest.

D. Juan   You're asking me to lose my temper!

---

figure in the church. On the other hand, the actor might have worn a
suit of armour, and it is interesting to note in this respect that
stage-directions in the earlier version of the play, *Tan largo me lo
fidis*, suggest this. Another possibility is that an actual automaton was
used. Golden - Age stage-designers and technicians often showed
themselves to be capable of quite ingenious effects, and it is certainly a
fact that the better-off acting companies could have afforded an
automatom. For interesting observations on the subject, see J.E. Varey,
*Historia de los títeres en España (desde sus orígenes hasta mediados del
siglo XVIII)* (Madrid, 1957), in particular pp. 24-90.

542   Panuncio: Catalinón's comic corruption of Pafnucio. The corruption or
mispronunciation of names by comic characters is a common feature of
Golden-Age drama. *Panuncio* presumably suggests both *pan*, 'bread',
and *anuncio* 'I proclaim' or 'I announce'.

544   He nods his head: again the indication that the actor should adopt the
movements and gestures of a non-human is quite clear.

Catal.	Señor,

Catal.   Señor,
              ¡vive Dios que güelo mal!
D. Juan   Llega, que aguardando estoy.   555
Catal.   Yo pienso que muerto soy,
              y está muerto mi arrabal.

Tiemblan los Criados

D. Juan   Y vosotros, ¿qué decís?
              ¿Qué hacéis? ¡Necio temblar!
Catal.   Nunca quisiera cenar   560
              con gente de otro país.
              ¿Yo, señor, con convidado
              de piedra?
D. Juan   ¡Necio temer!
              Si es piedra, ¿qué te ha de hacer?
Catal.   Dejarme descalabrado.   565
D. Juan   Háblale con cortesía.
Catal.   ¿Está bueno? ¿Es buena tierra
              la otra vida? ¿Es llano o sierra?
              ¿Prémiase allá la poesía?
C. 1.°   A todo dice que sí,   570
              con la cabeza.
Catal.   ¿Hay allá
              muchas tabernas? Sí habrá,
              si Noé reside allí.
D. Juan   ¡Hola! dadnos de beber.
Catal.   Señor muerto, ¿allá se bebe   575
              con nieve?

Baja la cabeza

                      Así, que hay nieve:
              buen país.
D. Juan   Si oír cantar
              queréis, cantarán.

Baja la cabeza

C. 2.°   Sí, dijo.
D. Juan   Cantad.
Catal.   Tiene el seor muerto
              buen gusto.
C. 1.°   Es noble, por cierto,   580
              y amigo de regocijo.

---

554   the awful smell: a moment to delight the servants and soldiers, the
         equivalent of the 'groundlings' in the Elizabethan theatre, who would
         have been standing close to the stage. At the same time, the physical
         manifestation of fear in Catalinón is well observed on the part of the
         dramatist. We can compare the incident with another in *Don Quijote*,

Catal.	Well,
	Sir, you'll have to excuse the awful smell.
D. Juan	Stop dithering! Come over here and sit! 555
Catal.	The way I'm smelling sir, I must be dead.
	Or otherwise I've accidentally shit
	Myself!

The two servants are shaking with fear

D. Juan	What's wrong with you? Come. Answer me!
	Don't tell me you both suffer from weak knees!
Catal.	I can't say, master, I'm exactly pleased 560
	To dine with anyone from overseas.
	It's even worse to eat with this one here!
	A guest who's turned to stone!
D. Juan	A foolish fear!
	A man of stone, what can he do to you?
Catal.	Oh, only split my poor head wide open. 565
D. Juan	So when you speak to him, just be polite.
Catal.	Yes, well, let's see then. . . Oh, feeling alright
	Are you, mate? Often wondered what it's like
	Down there. . . you know. . . whether its flat or hilly. . .
	And whether or not they've got any poetry. . . 570
	Know what I mean. . .?
First Servant	Looks like he's keen to agree
	With everything, the way he nods his head.
Catal.	Got many taverns, have you? Course you have,
	Seeing old Noah lives there.
D. Juan	Bring some wine
	At once!
Catal.	Pretty refined as well, I expect, 575
	Mr Dead Man. . . you know. . . ice in your drinks
	Down there!

The statue nods its head

	Hell of a fancy place, I'd think!
D. Juan	You give the word, my friend, we'll have a song.

The statue nods its head

Second Servant	He fancies hearing one.
D. Juan	All of you sing
	To him!
Catal.	You can't go wrong with him! Such taste! 580
First Servant	All noblemen enjoy a bit of fun.

Part I, ch. 20, when Sancho Panza, terrified by hammering sounds
during the night, reacts in identical fashion.

574   old Noah: according to Genesis, ix, 20–21, Noah was the first man to
discover wine.

Cantan dentro
Si de mi amor aguardáis,
señora, de aquesta suerte
el galardón en la muerte,
¡qué largo me lo fiáis!   585

Catal.   O es sin duda veraniego
el seor muerto, o debe ser
hombre de poco comer.
Temblando al plato me llego.
Poco beben por allá;   590

Bebe

yo beberé por los dos.
Brindis de piedra ¡por Dios!
menos temor tengo ya.
Cantan
Si ese plazo me convida
para que gozaros pueda,
pues larga vida me queda,
dejad que pase la vida.
Si de mi amor aguardáis,
señora, de aquesta suerte
el galardón en la muerte,   600
¡qué largo me lo fiáis!

Catal.   ¿Con cuál de tantas mujeres
como has burlado, señor,
hablan?

D. Juan   De todas me río,
amigo, en esta ocasión.   605
En Nápoles a Isabela. . .

Catal.   Esa, señor, ya no es hoy
burlada, porque se casa
contigo, como es razón.
Burlaste a la pescadora   610
que del mar te redimió,
pagándole el hospedaje
en moneda de rigor.
Burlaste a doña Ana. . .

D. Juan   Calla,

581+   Singing: on songs in Golden-Age plays, see Act II, 633, note. It is
also worth making the point that songs were used very dramatically in
the religious plays, the *autos sacramentales*, of the Golden Age. A
chorus sung off-stage often acted, for example, as a further stimulus
to the character who is about to transgress, while another chorus
sought to deter him from his course of action. Although Tirso's *El*

[Singing off-stage]
'The lady's foolishly deceived in love,
She waits for vengeance sent down from above.
Death to the faithless lover is her prayer,
But he enjoys himself without a care.'   585

Catal. I wonder if this fellow's on a diet.
        Perhaps he isn't eating 'cos it's hot,
        Or maybe he's the sort don't eat a lot.
        I'll have a go at eating, though my hand's
        Still shaking. Seems he doesn't fancy drinking   590
        Either. Perhaps I'd better sink the lot!

    Catalinón drinks

        Ah, well, me old stone feller, here's to you!
        I'm feeling better now, give you your due!
        [Singing off-stage]
        'The time you've got on earth's a tidy span.
        Enjoy as many women as you can.   595
        And since most of your life's in front of you,
        Eat, drink, make merry as you're passing through.
        The lady's foolishly deceived in love,
        She waits for vengeance sent down from above.
        Death to the faithless lover is her prayer,   600
        But he enjoys himself without a care.'

Catal. Hey, master, of all those women you've gone through,
        Which one d'you think the song's referring to?

D. Juan How do I know? They're all the same to me,
        My friend. A good laugh, even though I fancy   605
        Them! Remember Naples and Isabela?

Catal. Of course I do! But. . . you didn't fool her,
        Did you? Not now she's fixed it that you marry
        Her! She'll get her own back, make you feel sorry.
        The fishergirl. . . oh, yes, you took her in,   610
        After she'd helped you out and saved your skin.
        Offered you lodging too. A sorry sight
        She was! Oh, yes, you paid her back alright!
        And then there was Dona Ana. . .

D. Juan   Don't speak

---

condenado por desconfiado is not a genuine *auto sacramental*, a similar
if not identical use of song may be noted in it, a very good example
occuring in Act III where the devil's exhortation to the criminal Enrico
to escape from the prison is answered by a chorus which advises him
not to yield to temptation. In this example in *The Trickster* the two
opposing strands – the exhortation to pleasure, the warning of
retribution – are neatly combined.

	que hay parte aquí que lastó	615
	por ella, y vengarse aguarda.	
Catal.	Hombre es de mucho valor,	
	que él es piedra, tú eres carne:	
	no es buena resolución.	

*Hace señas que se quite la mesa y queden
solos*

D. Juan	¡Hola! quitad esa mesa,	620
	que hace señas que los dos	
	nos quedemos, y se vayan	
	los demás.	
Catal.	¡Malo, por Dios!	
	No te quedes, porque hay muerto	
	que mata de un mojicón	625
	a un gigante.	
D. Juan	Salíos todos.	
	¡A ser yo Catalinón. . .!	
	Vete, que viene.	

*Vanse, y quedan los dos solos, y hace señas
que cierre la puerta*

D. Juan	La puerta	
	ya está cerrada. Ya estoy	
	aguardando. Di, ¿qué quieres,	630
	sombra o fantasma o visión?	
	Si andas en pena o si aguardas	
	alguna satisfación	
	para tu remedio, dilo,	
	que mi palabra te doy	635
	de hacer lo que me ordenares.	
	¿Estás gozando de Dios?	
	¿Dite la muerte en pecado?	
	Habla, que suspenso estoy.	

Habla paso, como cosa del otro mundo

D. Gon.	¿Cumplirásme una palabra	640
	como caballero?	

---

621   all his gestures: see Act III, 533 and 544, notes.
633   your soul's in torment: it has to be borne in mind that Don Gonzalo
      died suddenly, without confession, and was not therefore absolved of
      his sins. For that reason his soul is still in purgatory. A comparison
      may be made with Hamlet's father, poisoned in his sleep, whose ghost
      haunts the castle battlements at night. When Hamlet has the opportunity
      to avenge his father's death, he draws back from killing the murderer,
      Claudius, precisely because Claudius is at that moment praying, and to
      kill him in a state of grace would merely be to guarantee his soul a
      place in heaven.

	So loudly! This fellow's resolved to keep	615
	His word and take his vengeance if he can.	
Catal.	I'm not surprised. Just look at him! A man	
	Of stone, and you of ordinary flesh.	
	I tell you straight, you're in a proper mess!	

The statue indicates that the table should be cleared
and that he and Don Juan should be left alone

D. Juan	You there! Make sure the table's cleared quickly!	620
	If I interpret all his gestures rightly,	
	He wants to be alone with me. You'd better	
	Leave us.	
Catal.	Oh, master! I'm scared stiff for you!	
	Don't stay with him all on your own! One blow	
	From a man of stone's enough to finish	625
	Off a giant!	
D. Juan	Come on! All of you out!	
	I'm no Catalinón! No cause to doubt	
	My nerve! Away now! Our guest approaches.	

The others leave. The two men are alone. The statue
indicates that the door be closed

D. Juan	Well now, sir. The door's firmly shut behind	
	You and here you have me at your disposal,	630
	Eager and willing to please. What would you	
	Ask of me? Ghost, phantom, fantastic vision,	
	Can it be your soul's in torment or do	
	You seek from me some kind of satisfaction	
	To ease your suffering? I beg you say	635
	What's on your mind. You have my word and promise	
	I shall obey whatever you command.	
	Do you enjoy the grace of God, my friend,	
	Or could it be you died in mortal sin?	
	I'm eager to know, sir. Give me your answer.	640

The statue speaks slowly, like something from another
world

| D. Gon. | One thing I ask of you. Give me your word | |
| | As a gentleman. | |

640+ **The statue speaks slowly:** the first occasion on which the statue
speaks. Clearly, the stage-direction calls for a voice that will
distinguish the stone-guest from the human characters of the play and
at the same time evoke the horrors of the other world. Dan Rogers,
Tirso de Molina, El burlador de Sevilla. . . p.23, notes that the
stage-direction 'seems to call for some kind of hollow whisper. If so, it
would have had to be a good "stage whisper": his words are so
important that they must be heard all over the house'. Indeed they
must. Moreover, a hollow whisper would need to be done in a way
which did not merely provoke laughter.

D. Juan	Honor
	tengo, y las palabras cumplo,
	porque caballero soy.
D. Gon.	Dame esa mano, no temas.
D. Juan	¿Eso dices? ¿Yo temor? 545
	Si fueras el mismo infierno
	la mano te diera yo.

Dale la mano

D. Gon.	Bajo esta palabra y mano,
	mañana a las diez estoy
	para cenar aguardando. 650
	¿Irás?
D. Juan	Empresa mayor
	entendí que me pedías.
	Mañana tu güésped soy.
	¿Dónde he de ir?
D. Gon.	A mi capilla.
D. Juan	¿Iré solo? 655
D. Gon.	No, los dos;
	y cúmpleme la palabra
	como la he cumplído yo.
D. Juan	Digo que la cumpliré;
	que soy Tenorio.
D. Gon.	Yo soy
	Ulloa.
D. Juan	Yo iré sin falta. 660
D. Gon.	Yo lo creo. Adiós.

Va a la puerta

D. Juan	Adiós.
	Aguarda, iréte alumbrando.
D. Gon.	No alumbres, que en gracia estoy.

*Vase muy poco, mirando a Don Juan,
y Don Juan a él, hasta que desaparece, y
queda Don Juan con pavor*

D. Juan	¡Válgame Dios! todo el cuerpo
	se ha bañado de un sudor, 665
	y dentro de las entrañas
	se me hiela el corazón.
	Cuando me tomó la mano,
	de suerte me la apretó,
	que un infierno parecía: 670
	jamás vide tal calor.

---

644   <u>your hand</u>: this is the first occasion in the play on which Don Juan offers his hand as a token of keeping his promise, and actually keeps it.

D. Juan   I, sir, am a man
                 Of honour who always keeps his word faithfully.
D. Gon. Then give me your hand! Don't be afraid!
D. Juan Afraid of you? I'm not some silly maid.   645
         My friend, I tell you I'd give you my hand
         Were you the burning fires of Hell itself.
    Don Juan holds out his hand
D. Gon. I accept it as I accept your word.
         Promise me this. Tomorrow night at ten
         You'll dine with me. Now can you guarantee   650
         You'll come and join me?
D. Juan   Of course! I guarantee
         It! I must admit I thought your plans
         For me were somewhat more ambitious. Where
         Shall I find you?
D. Gon.   Come straight to the chapel.
D. Juan Should I come alone?
D. Gon.   No. The two of you.   655
         And don't forget! Be sure you keep your word
         To me, my friend, as I kept mine to you.
D. Juan My word's my bond, sir! Do you think I make
         A promise – I a Tenorio – I'll not keep?
D. Gon. And I, sir, an Ulloa!
D. Juan   I shall be there,   660
         Without fail!
D. Gon.   I believe you. Fare you well!
    He goes to the door
D. Juan Wait a moment! I'll light the way in case
         You fall.
D. Gon.   My way is lit, sir, by God's grace.
    *The statue withdraws very slowly, observing Don Juan,
    as he observed it. It disappears, leaving Don Juan in
    a state of fear*
D. Juan Oh, God assist me! The whole of my body's
         Suddenly bathed in sweat. And deep inside   665
         Here, it's as if my heart's been stilled and frozen
         Into a solid block of ice. The moment
         He took my hand and held it in his grip,
         So hard, so like a vice, I had a vision,
         A sudden premonition of the agony   670
         Of Hell, as though the hand itself burned me.

---

50   You'll dine with me: on the motif of the double-invitation, see the
      Introduction.

169

Un aliento respiraba,
organizando la voz,
tan frío, que parecía
infernal respiración.   675
Pero todas son ideas
que da la imaginación:
el temor y temer muertos
es más villano temor;
que si un cuerpo noble, vivo,   680
con potencias y razón
y con alma, no se teme,
¿quién cuerpos muertos temió?
Mañana iré a la capilla
donde convidado soy,   685
por que se admire y espante
Sevilla de mi valor.

Vase
Salen el Rey y Don Diego Tenorio y
acompañamiento

Rey   ¿Llegó al fin Isabela?
D.Diego   Y disgustada.
Rey   Pues ¿no ha tomado bien el casamiento?
D.Diego   Siente, señor, el nombre de infamada.   690
Rey   De otra causa procede su tormento.
               ¿Dónde está?
D.Diego   En el convento está alojada
               de las Descalzas.
Rey   Salga del convento
               luego al punto, que quiero que en palacio
               asista con la reina más de espacio.
D.Diego   Si ha de ser con don Juan el desposorio,
               manda, señor, que tu presencia vea.
Rey   Véame, y galán salga, que notorio
               quiero que este placer al mundo sea.

---

674   And deathly sound: see 640+ above, note. This line gives a much
       clearer indication of the way in which the actor playing the stone-guest
       is required to speak. Evidently the voice must have a hoarse quality,
       lacking the resonance and intonation of the voice of a living person.
679   the mark of pure cowardice!: to act in a cowardly manner was, of
       course, to act dishonourably, and Don Juan is never willing to let
       himself down in the eyes of the world or, in the last resort, the other
       world. A somewhat similar situation occurs in the final Act of Lope de
       Vega's *El caballero de Olmedo* when the protagonist, Alonso, warned by
       a ghostly figure of impending doom, refuses to heed the warning on the
       basis that to do so would be to compromise his name and reputation.

And yet his breath and voice contained the coldness
Of some frozen wasteland, the icy blast
And deathly sound of some forbidden place,
As if, a mortal man, I gazed upon   675
The face of Hell!. . . But this is pure fancy,
Imagination's silly trickery!
To be afraid is bad enough. To fear
Dead men's worse: the mark of pure cowardice!
Have I been known to fear any man,   680
Though he be noble, strong, endowed with reason,
In full possession of his faculties?
Then why this fear of a man who's dead?
Tomorrow I shall appear in the chapel
And fulfil my obligation to my host.   685
The city of Seville shall be amazed
By Don Juan's confrontation with this ghost.

*Exit Don Juan. Enter the King, Don Diego Tenorio and
their retinue*

King   So Isabela's here at last?

D. Diego   Against
Her will, I fear.

King   Not displeased with the marriage?

D. Diego   The loss of her good name distresses her.   690

King   Perhaps her anguish has another cause.
Where is she now?

D. Diego   Lodged, I think, in the convent
Of the Descalzas.

King   Have the lady brought
To the palace as quickly as you can.
Here she can be of service to the Queen.   695

D. Diego   My lord, if her marriage is to Don Juan,
Command him to present himself before
You.

King   Indeed I shall. We'll have this nobleman
Appear here at Court, and as a measure

---

90   The loss of her good name: see Act III, 335, note.
93   the Descalzas: there seem to have been twenty-one or so convents in
Seville at or around the time of the play's composition but none of them
was known by this name. It is possible that the allusion is to the
Convento de las Descalzas Franciscas in Madrid, whose founder was
Princess Juana, the daughter of Charles V, and which was opened in
1559. This convent may have been chosen by Tirso simply because it
would be well known to a Madrid audience watching the play who, like
the dramatists of the Golden Age, would have been indifferent to
geographical and historical accuracy. The convent in question was one
where distinguished people often stayed and it was frequently visited
by both Philip III and Philip IV.

	Conde será desde hoy don Juan Tenorio	700
	de Lebrija; él la mande y la posea,
	que si Isabela a un duque corresponde,
	ya que ha perdido un duque, gane un conde.
D.Diego	Todos por la merced tus pies besamos.
Rey	Merecéis mi favor tan dignamente,	705
	que si aquí los servicios ponderamos,
	me quedo atrás con el favor presente.
	Paréceme, don Diego, que hoy hagamos
	las bodas de doña Ana juntamente.
D.Diego	¿Con Octavio?
Rey	No es bien que el duque Octavio	710
	sea el restaurador de aqueste agravio.
	Doña Ana con la reina me ha pedido
	que perdone al marqués, porque doña Ana,
	ya que el padre murió, quiere marido;
	porque si le perdió, con él le gana.	715
	Iréis con poca gente y sin ruido
	luego a hablalle a la fuerza de Triana;
	por su satisfacción y por su abono
	de su agraviada prima, le perdono.
D.Diego	Ya he visto lo que tanto deseaba.	720
Rey	Que esta noche han de ser, podéis decille,
	los desposorios.
D.Diego	Todo en bien se acaba.
	Fácil será al marqués el persuadille,
	que de su prima amartelado estaba.
Rey	También podéis a Octavio prevenille.	725
	Desdichado es el duque con mujeres;
	son todas opinión y pareceres.
	Hanme dicho que está muy enojado
	con don Juan.
D.Diego	No me espanto si ha sabido
	de don Juan el delito averiguado,	730
	que la causa de tanto daño ha sido.
	El duque viene.

---

717   the castle of Triana: a Moorish castle situated across the river from
Seville. It served as a prison but was also used by the dreaded
Inquisition. The building is no longer in existence.

723   Be put right: the various marriages, arranged or otherwise, signify the
restitution of harmony and order. Throughout the play Don Juan
constantly denies the importance of marriage as a social institution, for
in following his impulses and desires he represents the anarchic force

	Of my good faith, the world shall know my pleasure's	
	This: that Don Juan now become Count of Lebrija.	
	If Isabela's worthy of a duke	
	And he is lost to her, a count should be	
	Sufficient compensation.	

D. Diego   Your majesty
Honours me greatly.

King   Your loyal service   705
Deserves such favour, Don Diego. I hardly
Think this recompense or adequate reward
For your life-long sacrifice towards
Your king. I fancy too that Doña Ana
Should be married.

D. Diego   To Octavio?

King   I think not.   710
It's not appropriate that he should be
The saviour of her good name when she herself,
Assisted by the queen, has intervened
With me and sought forgiveness for the Marquis.
Her father's death requires that she be married.   715
His loss to her shall now become her gain.
Proceed at once to the castle of Triana;
Inform the Marquis that the restoration
Of Ana's name's the source of his salvation.

D. Diego   And as for me, your majesty, the true   720
Fulfilment of my hopes.

King   The marriages
Will be performed tonight.

D. Dieg.   And all injustice
Be put right. The Marquis is sure to agree
To that. He loves his cousin dearly.

King   Inform Octavio too of our intention.   725
As far as women are concerned, the duke's
Been out of luck. And so he thinks all women
Superficial and fit for common gossip.
They tell me he's quite furious with Don Juan.

D. Dieg.   He'll know about the trick my son has played   730
On him, the source of all his great misfortune.
Why, here he comes!

---

of sexuality outside marriage. The King, the representative of God on earth and the source of society's well-being, attempts to restore order where Don Juan disrupts it. Even so, as has been pointed out, King Alfonso is always a step behind events as they occur, is ever trying to patch things up, and is certainly not the idealized monarch that is to be found in many Golden-Age plays.

Rey	No dejéis mi lado.
	que en el delito sois comprehendido.
	Sale el Duque Octavio
Octav.	Los pies, invicto rey, me dé tu alteza.
Rey	Alzad, duque, y cubrid vuestra cabeza. 735
	¿Qué pedís?
Octav.	Vengo a pediros,
	postrado ante vuestras plantas,
	una merced, cosa justa,
	digna de serme otorgada.
Rey	Duque, como justa sea, 740
	digo que os doy mi palabra
	de otorgárosla. Pedid.
Octav.	Ya sabes, señor, por cartas
	de tu embajador, y el mundo
	por la lengua de la fama 745
	sabe, que don Juan Tenorio,
	con española arrogancia,
	en Nápoles una noche,
	para mí noche tan mala,
	con mi nombre profanó 750
	el sagrado de una dama.
Rey	No pases más adelante.
	Ya supe vuestra desgracia.
	En efeto: ¿qué pedís?
Octav.	Licencia que en la campaña 755
	defienda como es traidor.
D.Diego	Eso no. Su sangre clara
	es tan honrada. . .
Rey	¡Don Diego!
D.Diego	Señor.
Octav.	¿Quién eres que hablas
	en la presencia del rey 760
	de esa suerte?
D.Diego	Soy quien calla
	porque me lo manda el rey;
	que si no, con esta espada
	te respondiera.
Octav.	Eres viejo.
D.Diego	Ya he sido mozo en Italia, 765
	a vuestro pesar, un tiempo;

---

751 Go no further: Octavio does not realize that Don Diego is Don Juan's father. Presumably, the King wishes to spare the old man further pain and for that reason cuts Octavio short.

King	Then you shall stay with me,
	For you too share responsibility.

Enter Duke Octavio

Octav.	Great majesty, I humbly kneel before	
	You.	
King	Arise, Octavio, and replace your hat.	735
	What would you ask of me?	
Octav.	Your majesty,	
	I ask one favour only that you, in your	
	Great mercy and in answer to the justice	
	Of my petition, must consider worthy	
	Of your approval.	
King	Should your case prove just	740
	Octavio, you have my word that I as king	
	Must give you satisfaction. State your case.	
Octav.	My lord, you'll know from your ambassador	
	In Italy, as surely as the whole	
	World knows through common gossip and malicious	745
	Tongues, that Don Juan Tenorio has recently,	
	And with true Spanish arrogance, betrayed	
	A certain lady. In Naples one dark night	
	The fellow took advantage of my name	
	To take advantage of this same lady,	750
	Depriving her of honour.	
King	Go no further,	
	Octavio. The details of your great misfortune	
	Are known to me already, so it's best	
	You simply state the nature of your request.	
Octav.	Permission of your majesty to challenge	755
	Him! Confront him with his treachery	
	And make him pay for it!	
D. Diego	My lord, his blood	
	Is noble! I beg of you!	
King	Don Diego!	
D. Diego	Your majesty!	
Octav.	Who is this person dares	
	To speak like this, and in the royal presence?	760
D. Diego	A man, sir, loyal to the king who therefore	
	Holds his tongue. Were it not so, this sword of mine	
	Would answer for me.	
Octav.	Come now! Fury ill	
	Becomes old age!	
D. Diego	I'll have you know, my youth	
	Was spent in Italy, and there the man	765

175

	ya conocieron mi espada	
	en Nápoles y Milán.	
Octav.	Tienes ya la sangre helada.	
	No vale fuí, sino soy.	770
D.Diego	Pues fuí y soy.	

Empuña

Rey
                    Tened; basta;
bueno está. Callad, don Diego,
que a mi persona se guarda
poco respeto. Y vos, duque,
después que las bodas se hagan,   775
más de espacio hablaréis.
Gentilhombre de mi cámara
es don Juan, y hechura mía;
y de aqueste tronco rama:
mirad por él.

Octav.
                  Yo lo haré,   780
gran señor, como lo mandas.

Rey   Venid conmigo, don Diego.

D.Diego *[Ap.]* ¡Ay, hijo! ¡qué mal me pagas
el amor que te he tenido!

Rey   Duque.

Octav.   Gran señor.

Rey   Mañana   785
vuestras bodas se han de hacer.

Octav. Háganse, pues tú lo mandas.

*Vanse el Rey y Don Diego, y salen Gaseno y
Aminta*

Gaseno Este señor nos dirá
dónde está don Juan Tenorio.
Señor, ¿si está por acá   790
un don Juan a quien notorio
ya su apellido será?

Octav. Don Juan Tenorio diréis.

---

767 Naples and Milan: as has been indicated previously, only Sicily belonged
to Spain at the time of the play's action. See Act I, 20+, note. During
the Golden Age, of course, Spain had much greater influence in Italy,
and many Spanish writers spent part of their youth or early manhood
there. The most notable example is, perhaps, Cervantes whose
short-story, *El licenciado vidriera*, clearly recalls his own experience of
various Italian cities which he visited when serving in the Spanish
army.

	Who dared to cross me had good cause to regret	
	His folly. In Naples and Milan, sir,	
	This sword became a by-word for my bravery.	
Octav.	But now you're old, sir, and your blood runs cold.	
	You have to say 'I am', sir, not 'I was'.	770
D.Diego	I am, sir, what I was!	

He seeks to draw his sword

King   Enough! No cause
For all this squabbling! You, Don Diego,
Show scant respect for me, and in my presence!
And as for you, Octavio, once your marriage
Has been arranged, you'll need to speak   775
With me of this at greater length. For now,
I'll have you know Don Juan's a nobleman,
An honoured member of my Court and under
My protection: a branch of this great tree.
You shall not harm him.

Octav.   Your majesty,   780
I promise to obey your every word.

King   Don Diego, come with me!
D.Diego   *[Aside]*   This boy of mine!
A fine way to repay a father's love
When he has put concern for him above
All else!

King   Octavio!
Octav.   Yes, my lord?
King   Tomorrow   785
Your marriage to the lady shall take place.
Octav.   Obedience is, sire, my greatest solace.

Exit the King and Don Diego. Enter Gaseno and Aminta

Gaseno   Ah, this kind gentleman will likely know
The whereabouts of Don Juan Tenorio.
Excuse me, sir! I'm looking for a certain   790
Fellow, his name's Don Juan. You ought to know
Him, seeing he's well known around these parts.

Octav.   You'll be referring to Don Juan Tenorio.

---

779   a branch of this great tree: the reference is not to the King himself
       but to Don Diego.
786   Your marriage: there is some confusion here. The King, having
       promised Octavio that he will marry Doña Ana, has subsequently stated
       that she, at her own request, is to marry Mota, while Isabela is, as we
       have seen, on her way to her marriage to Don Juan. To whom,
       therefore, is Octavio to be married? The confusion is clearly not the
       King's but the dramatist's. He is already looking forward to the series
       of marriages with which the play ends.

Aminta	Sí, señor; ese don Juan.	
Octav.	Aquí está: ¿qué le queréis?	795
Aminta	Es mi esposo ese galán.	
Octav.	¿Cómo?	
Aminta	Pues, ¿no lo sabéis	
	siendo del alcázar vos?	
Octav.	No me ha dicho don Juan nada.	
Gaseno	¿Es posible?	
Octav.	Sí, por Dios.	800
Gaseno	Doña Aminta es muy honrada.	
	Cuando se casen los dos,	
	que cristiana vieja es	
	hasta los güesos, y tiene	
	de la hacienda el interés,	805

....

	más bien que un conde, un marqués.	
	Casóse don Juan con ella,	
	y quitósela a Batricio.	
Aminta	Decid cómo fué doncella	
	a su poder.	
Gaseno	No es juicio	810
	esto, ni aquesta querella.	
Octav.	[Ap.] Esta es burla de don Juan,	
	y para venganza mía	
	éstos diciéndola están.	
	¿Qué pedís, al fin?	
Gaseno	Querría,	815
	porque los días se van,	
	que se hiciese el casamiento,	
	o querellarme ante el rey.	
Octav.	Digo que es justo ese intento.	
Gaseno	Y razón y justa ley.	820
Octav.	[Ap.] Medida a mi pensamiento	
	ha venido la ocasión.	
	En el alcázar tenéis	
	bodas.	
Aminta	¿Si las mías son?	
Octav.	[Ap.] Quiero, para que acertemos,	825
	valerme de una invención.	

---

801   Doña Aminta's: we can well imagine how a Madrid audience of the
      seventeenth century would roar with laughter at Gaseno's claim, moreso
      if he were to make it in a broad rural accent.

801   ancient Christian stock: that is to say, without any Moorish or Jewish
      blood, a matter of concern in the Spain of the Golden Age when,

Aminta	Yes, that's the one! The very Don Juan we're looking
	For.
Octav.	Look no further! What do you want of him? 795
Aminta	I need to find him, sir, seeing he's my husband.
Octav.	He's what?
Aminta	Oh, yes, sir! Nothing could be truer!
	And you a courtier should know that for sure.
Octav.	Don Juan has told me nothing! Not a word!
Gaseno	I can't believe that!
Octav.	Heavens above, it's easy 800
	To believe;
Gaseno	The fact is Doña Aminta's
	Honourable. And when she marries him
	She honours him, being herself of pure
	And ancient Christian stock. He can be sure
	Too her fortune's quite considerable. 805
	My land, you see! I'm like a count or marquis
	On his estates! That's why Don Juan Tenorio
	Pinched my daughter from her betrothed Batricio.
Aminta	You tell him she was a virgin before
	He took her from him!
Gaseno	That's no argument 810
	On which to base the righting of this wrong.
Octav.	*[Aside]* Another of his tricks! This fellow's song
	And dance gives me the chance to get Don Juan
	Hoist well and truly on his own petard!
	Then tell me, sir, what you intend to do. 815
Gaseno	Time's marching on, sir, I want him to keep
	His promise to my daughter and marry her.
	If not, the King shall hear about the traitor.
Octav.	Your case, my friend's entirely reasonable.
Gaseno	For reason's on my side and justice too. 820
Octav.	*[Aside]* Who would have dreamt that mere destiny
	Could offer me this opportunity?
	Today, of course, the palace celebrates
	A wedding.
Aminta	Looks as if he's fixed the date
	Then, don't it?
Octav.	*[Aside]* Now, I think, we'll nail our man. 825
	He shan't escape the cunning of this plan!

---

especially during the reign of Philip II and a feared Inquisition, religious orthodoxy became an obsession.

807 On his estates!: peasant pride in property and status is also a marked feature of Calderón's *El alcalde de Zalamea* and its protagonst, Pedro Crespo. See Act III, 102, note.

	Venid donde os vestiréis, señora, a lo cortesano, y a un cuarto del rey saldréis conmigo.	
Aminta	Vos de la mano a don Juan me llevaréis.	830
Octav.	Que de esta suerte es cautela.	
Gaseno	El arbitrio me consuela.	
Octav.	[Ap.] Estos venganza me dan de aqueste traidor don Juan y el agravio de Isabela.	835

Vanse
Salen Don Juan y Catalinón

Catal.	¿Cómo el rey te recibió?	
D. Juan	Con más amor que mi padre.	
Catal.	¿Viste a Isabela?	
D. Juan	También.	
Catal.	¿Cómo viene?	
D. Juan	Como un ángel.	840
Catal.	¿Recibióte bien?	
D. Juan	El rostro bañado de leche y sangre, como la rosa que al alba revienta la verde cárcel.	
Catal.	Al fin, ¿esta noche son las bodas?	845
D. Juan	Sin falta.	
Catal.	Si antes hubieran sido, no hubieras, señor, engañado a tantas; pero tú tomas esposa, señor, con cargas muy grandes.	850
D. Juan	Di: ¿comienzas a ser necio?	
Catal.	Y podrás muy bien casarte mañana, que hoy es mal día.	
D. Juan	Pues ¿qué día es hoy?	
Catal.	Es martes.	
D. Juan	Mil embusteros y locos dan en esos disparates. Sólo aquel llamo mal día, aciago y detestable, en que no tengo dineros; que lo demás es donaire.	855 860

836+   *Enter Don Juan*: as the two men enter, they are, to judge from 861, in
the process of getting ready to leave the inn, yet by 873 they are

180

	You shall in that case now accompany me	
	From here, assume the garments of a courtly	
	Lady, and at the court appear with me	
	As my companion.	
Aminta	You mean you'll take me	830
	With you and present me to my Don Juan?	
Octav.	The best plan I can think of, don't you see?	
Gaseno	I do agree, sir! You make an old man happy!	
Octav.	[Aside] These two offer me the opportunity	
	For vengeance on Don Juan. He'll pay as well	835
	For his offence against my Isabel.	

They leave. Enter Don Juan and Catalinón

Catal.	How did his majesty take to you, master?	
D. Juan	Oh, much more lovingly than my own father!	
Catal.	What about Isabela? See her, did you?	
D. Juan	Of course!	
Catal.	How is she then?	
D. Juan	She's like an angel.	840
Catal.	I bet she gave you hell!	
D. Juan	A face like heaven	
	Itself, my friend. The white of milk tinged pink,	
	As when at dawn the lovely rose emerges	
	From the leafy prison of its green cell.	
Catal.	Ah, well! The wedding's fixed for tonight then,	845
	Master?	
D. Juan	Without fail.	
Catal.	It's quite clear to me,	
	If you'd got hitched before, you'd not be lumbered	
	With all those women you deceived. But now,	
	Taking a wife's a very different matter,	
	And you with those responsibilities!	850
D. Juan	Don't start to play the fool again with me!	
Catal.	Marry tomorrow's my advice to you!	
	Marry today you're sure to be sorry!	
D. Juan	What day is it today?	
Catal.	You know it's Tuesday!	
D. Juan	Don't be a fool! A silly superstition,	855
	A piece of nonsense fit for fools and madmen!	
	As far as I'm concerned, the only day	
	I'd call unfortunate's the day I'm short	
	Of ready money. As for all the rest,	
	A sheer waste of time and best forgotten.	860

---

outside the church – a fine example of the fluidity of movement in the
drama of the Golden Age.

854   You know it's Tuesday!: in Spain Tuesday is associated with bad luck.

Catal.	Vamos, si te has de vestir,
	que te aguardan, y ya es tarde.
D. Juan	Otro negocio tenemos
	que hacer, aunque nos aguarden.
Catal.	¿Cuál es?
D. Juan	Cenar con el muerto. 865
Catal.	Necedad de necedades.
D. Juan	¿No ves que di mi palabra?
Catal.	Y cuando se la quebrantes,
	¿qué importa? ¿Has de pedirte
	una figura de jaspe 870
	la palabra?
D. Juan	Podrá el muerto
	llamarme a voces infame.
Catal.	Ya está cerrada la iglesia.
D. Juan	Llama.
Catal.	¿Qué importa que llame?
	¿quién tiene de abrir, que están 875
	durmiendo los sacristanes?
D. Juan	Llama a este postigo.
Catal.	Abierto
	está.
D. Juan	Pues entra.
Catal.	Entre un fraile
	con su hisopo y estola.
D. Juan	Sígueme y calla.
Catal.	¿Que calle? 880
D. Juan	Sí.
Catal.	Dios en paz
	destos convites me saque.
	Entran por una puerta y salen por otra
	¡Qué escura que está la iglesia,
	señor para ser tan grande!
	¡Ay de mí! ¡Tenme, señor, 885
	porque de la capa me asen!
	Sale Don Gonzalo como de antes, y
	encuéntrase con ellos
D. Juan	¿Quién va?
D. Gon.	Yo soy.

882   *from the opposite side of the stage*:   a fine example of the use of the two back-stage doors in a Golden-Age theatre. *They exit* in this stage-direction means, of course, that Don Juan and his servant leave the stage by one of the doors which represents the postern. In other words they enter the church whose interior at this moment is behind the back-stage area. When the two men reappear through the door at the opposite side of the stage, they are in fact inside the church,

Catal.	Alright then, master. Time for getting dressed.
	They're waiting for you and you're late already.
D. Juan	We've other business to attend to first,
	My friend. They'll have to wait until we're ready.
Catal.	What other business?
D. Juan	Dinner with the dead, 865
	Of course!
Catal.	You must be off your bloody head!
D. Juan	You know I gave the man my solemn word!
Catal.	You better break it while you can then, master!
	I'm sure he won't mind! In any case,
	How can a man of stone start arguing 870
	With you if you don't keep his silly bargain?
D. Juan	No dead man shall call me, Don Juan, a coward.
Catal.	Anyway, looks as if the church is locked.
D. Juan	Then knock them up!
Catal.	But what's the point in knocking,
	Master? Who's going to open up? Flat out 875
	They'll be, those sacristans, tucked up in bed.
D. Juan	Try the postern!
Catal.	Oh, Lord above! It's open.
D. Juan	In you go then!
Catal.	What? Me in there? A priest's
	What you need, sprinkling his holy water!
D. Juan	Out of my way! And stop your silly chatter! 880
Catal.	I will, I will! I pray God save this sinner!
	Deliver him safely from this dinner!

They exit and enter from the opposite side of the stage

	Oh, master! Have you ever seen a church
	As big as this and yet as black as pitch?
	Oh, God! Where are you? Answer! It's no joke 885
	In here! I swear that someone grabbed my cloak!

Enter Don Gonzalo as before. He stands before them

D. Juan	Who's there?
D. Gon.	Your host.

---

which is now represented by the stage itself. We have here a very good
example indeed of the freedom of movement and changes of location that
are characteristic of Golden-Age drama.

884   as black as pitch?: once more the reader should recall that in the
seventeenth-century public theatres the action on the stage took place
in the afternoon and that most theatres, including those in Madrid,
were not covered.

Catal.	¡Muerto estoy!	
D. Gon.	El muerto soy, no te espantes.	
	No entendí que me cumplieras	
	la palabra, según haces	890
	de todos burla,	
D. Juan	¿Me tienes	
	en opinión de cobarde?	
D. Gon.	Sí, que aquella noche huíste	
	de mí cuando me mataste.	
D. Juan	Huí de ser conocido;	895
	mas ya me tienes delante.	
	Di presto lo que me quieres.	
D. Gon.	Quiero a cenar convidarte.	
Catal.	Aquí escusamos la cena,	
	que toda ha de ser fiambre,	900
	pues no parece cocina.	
D. Juan	Cenemos.	
D. Gon.	Para cenar	
	es menester que levantes	
	esa tumba.	
D. Juan	Y si te importa,	
	levantaré esos pilares.	905
D. Gon.	Valiente estás.	
D. Juan	Tengo brío	
	y corazón en las carnes.	
Catal.	Mesa de Guinea es ésta.	
	Pues ¿no hay por allá quien lave?	
D. Gon.	Siéntate.	
D. Juan	¿Adónde?	
Catal.	Con sillas	910
	vienen ya dos negros pajes.	

Entran dos enlutados con dos sillas

	¿También acá se usan lutos	
	y bayeticas de Flandes?	
D. Gon.	Siéntate tú.	
Catal.	Yo, señor,	
	he merendado esta tarde.	915
D. Gon.	No repliques.	

---

904   move the stone: food for the dead was apparently kept beneath the
stone placed over the tomb in the floor of the church.

Catal.	Oh, Christ! The bloody ghost!
D. Gon.	The dead man! There's no need to be afraid
	Of me. I am surprised, my friend, to see
	You've kept your promise, seeing how remiss 890
	You've been, so often breaking it with others.
D. Juan	You aren't accusing me of cowardice!
D. Gon.	Was it not fear made you seek safety
	In flight the night you chose to murder me?
D. Juan	Not fear of you! Merely the fear of being 895
	Identified! But now I stand before
	You! Call that a sign of fear, do you?
	Just tell me quickly what you ask of me.
D. Gon.	Merely that you agree to dine with me.
Catal.	Master, you'd better think of some excuse. 900
	Tell him you like hot food. It's all cold here.
	Ask him where he does his cooking, seeing
	There's no sign of any bloody kitchen!
D. Juan	We shall eat with you, sir.
D. Gon.	Then move the stone
	That covers the tomb.
D. Juan	Just give the word, I'll move 905
	These pillars too.
D. Gon.	How brave you are, my friend!
D. Juan	To the very marrow, if you need proof.
Catal.	The table looks as if it's from the coast
	Of Guinea! Black as toast that's burnt! Maybe
	He hasn't got a servant.
D. Gon.	Take a seat. 910
D. Juan	Where?
Catal.	There, master! Two servants black as pitch
	And bringing chairs.

Enter two figures in black with chairs

	Must be the case down there
	They're all in mourning, draped in flanelling
	From Flanders.
D. Gon.	Take a seat!
Catal.	Don't need to eat
	Again, sir, if you don't mind. I've had my dinner. 915
	More than enough! I went and stuffed. . .
D. Gon.	Will you
	Shut up!

---

909 Of Guinea!: black servants were transported to Spain from Guinea.
914 From Flanders: the kind of material described here was particularly associated with Flanders. It was used especially to cover coffins.

Catal.	No replico.
	Dios en paz de esto me saque.
	¿Qué plato es éste, señor?
D. Gon.	Este plato es de alacranes
	y víboras.
Catal.	¡Gentil plato!	920
D. Gon.	Estos son nuestros manjares.
	¿No comes tú?
D. Juan	Comeré,
	si me dieses áspid y áspides
	cuantos el infierno tiene.
D. Gon.	También quiero que te canten.	925
Catal.	¿Qué vino beben acá?
D. Gon.	Pruébalo.
Catal.	Hiel y vinagre
	es este vino.
D. Gon.	Este vino
	esprimen nuestros lagares.
	Cantan
	Adviertan los que de Dios	930
	juzgan los castigos grandes,
	que no hay plazo que no llegue
	ni deuda que no se pague.
Catal.	¡Malo es esto, vive Cristo!
	que he entendido este romance,	935
	y que con nosotros habla.
D. Juan	Un hielo el pecho me parte.
	Cantan
	Mientras en el mundo viva,
	no es justo que diga nadie:
	¡qué largo me lo fiáis!	940
	siendo tan breve el cobrarse.
Catal.	¿De qué es este guisadillo?
D. Gon.	De uñas.
Catal.	De uñas de sastre
	será, si es guisado de uñas.

---

928   Rioja: in the Spanish text Catalinon words are, literally: 'This wine is gall and vinegar.' I have taken the liberty of introducing the allusion to Rioja in order to up-date the lines and, indeed, to make them more comic.

930+ *[Singing off-stage]*:the song that follows is precisely in the tradition of the *auto sacramental* alluded to previously. See Act III, 581+ note.

945   tailor's . . .: clearly an allusion to the greed of tailors. In the literature of the Golden Age the professions provided a rich vein of

Catal.	I am shut up, sir. Well and truly. . .
	Oh, God! Please save me! What nice dish is this,
	Sir?
D. Gon.	A plain dish for you. It's only snake
	And roasted scorpion!
Catal.	Oh, a fine concoction! 920
D. Gon.	Typical of the food the dead must eat.
	Won't you try some?
D. Juan	Of course! I've said I will.
	Pile snakes and scorpions on my plate, I'd still
	Devour them, all the snakes that Hell contains.
D. Gon.	I'll have them sing a song to entertain 925
	You.
Catal.	Drink real vintage stuff down there, do you?
D. Gon.	Taste it and you shall see.
Catal.	Oh, yes. A fine
	Rioja, an exquisite blend of gall and vinegar.
	Bit on the sharp side really to caress
	The palate.
D. Gon.	Made by our finest presses. 930
	[Singing off-stage]
	'Let all men know God's punishment is great.
	Take note all men who live below and wait,
	For everyone the day of judgement's set,
	And no one can escape the final debt.'
Catal.	In God's name that's a song to make us fear. 935
	The meaning of its every word is clear
	Enough. Look how it speaks to both of us.
D. Juan	My blood freezes and feels as cold as ice.
	[Singing off-stage]
	'As long as man lives out his total span,
	Let him avoid this boast, as best he can: 940
	"Plenty of time to pay the final debt".
	No sooner said, the payment must be met.'
Catal.	This stew here. What ingredients does it have?
D. Gon.	Mainly fingernails.
Catal.	By the way they jab
	And grab at me, they're obviously some tailor's 945
	Nails.

---

satire. Thus, Francisco de Quevedo in his highly satirical work, *Los sueños*, portrays professional men condemned to Hell for their sins or called to account for them on the Day of Judgement. In the *Sueño de las calaveras* a tailor is shown attempting to justify himself: '"What could I steal if I was always dying of hunger myself?" And the others told him, seeing that he denied having been a thief, that it really was the limit to despise his own profession.'

D. Juan	Ya he cenado; haz que levanten la mesa.	945
D. Gon.	Dame esa mano; no temas, la mano dame.	
D. Juan	¿Eso dices? ¿Yo temor? ¡Que me abraso! ¡No me abrases con tu fuego!	
D. Gon.	Este es poco para el fuego que buscaste. Las maravillas de Dios son, don Juan, investigables, y así quiere que tus culpas a manos de un muerto pagues, y si pagas desta suerte, esta es justicia de Dios: "quien tal hace, que tal pague".	950 955
D. Juan	¡Que me abraso, no me aprietes! Con la daga he de matarte. Mas ¡ay! que me canso en vano de tirar golpes al aire. A tu hija no ofendí, que vió mis engaños antes.	960
D. Gon.	No importa, que ya pusiste tu intento.	965
D. Juan	Deja que llame quien me confiese y absuelva.	
D. Gon.	No hay lugar; ya acuerdas tarde.	
D. Juan	¡Que me quemo! ¡Que me abraso! ¡Muerto soy!	970

Cae muerto

Catal.	No hay quien se escape, que aquí tengo de morir también por acompañarte.	
D. Gon.	Esta es justicia de Dios: "quien tal hace que tal pague".	

Húndese el sepulcro con Don Juan y Don Gonzalo, con mucho ruido, y sale Catalinón arrastrando

---

964   She has her honour: see Act II, 513, note.
968   No time, my friend!: the point is made for the benefit of a
contemporary audience that Don Juan has had time to change his ways
and has been warned of the dangers of not doing so. He has assumed
unwisely that he can confess his sins at the very last moment and is
therefore guilty of presumption. A contrast can be made in that sense
with Enrico, the sinner of *El condenado por desconfiado* who, though

D. Juan	All finished then. Shall we clear the table?	
D. Gon.	Give me your hand! No need to be afraid.	
	Don't be afraid, my friend. Give me your hand!	
D. Juan	I fear nothing. Your hand's on fire,	
	It's burning me. . .	
D. Gon.	But nothing, my dear friend,	950
	Compared with all the agony that lies	
	Ahead of you. God's workings are, Don Juan,	
	Intelligible to each and everyone.	
	I am the man through whom you meet your doom,	
	Your life the sacrifice for all your sins.	955
	God gives man life that he can call his own,	
	But he must reap the harvest he has sown.	
D. Juan	Your hand burns! Let me go! Before this knife	
	Of mine puts paid again to your life.	
	The blow strikes home. It hits its target square.	960
	But nothing! Nothing! Where it falls, it falls	
	On empty air! Your daughter. . . I did not	
	Seduce her. . . There was no offence against	
	Her. . . She has her honour. . . She saw the trick	
	In time!	
D. Gon.	Nothing excuses your intention.	965
	Her seduction was firmly in your mind.	
D. Juan	Give me confession! Grant me absolution!	
D. Gon.	No time, my friend! No time! Your time runs out.	
D. Juan	My body is on fire! Your flames destroy	
	Me!	

Don Juan falls dead

Catal.	There's no escape for me either. My fate's	970
	Bound to be his, and death my ultimate	
	Reward for being the servant and companion	
	Of Don Juan.	
D. Gon.	His fate provides the lesson	
	You should heed, for each man reaps the harvest	
	Of his deeds.	

The tomb sinks with much noise. Don Juan and Don Gonzalo
disappear with it. Catalinón drags himself to safety.

---

more evil than Don Juan, undergoes a conversion, confesses in time, and is saved.

974+ The tomb sinks: this is the only mechanical effect called for in the play. The trapdoor in the stage itself, a characteristic feature of the public theatre of the seventeenth-century, would have been used to allow the tomb to sink below stage-level. The noise alluded to in the stage-direction would probably have been produced by exploding thunderflashes.

Catal.	¡Válgame Dios! ¿Qué es aquesto?	975
	Toda la capilla se arde,	
	y con el muerto he quedado	
	para que le vele y guarde.	
	Arrastrando como pueda	
	iré a avisar a su padre.	980
	¡San Jorge, San Agnus Dei,	
	sacadme en paz a la calle!	

Vase
Salen el Rey, Don Diego y acompañamiento

D. Diego	Ya el marqués, señor, espera	
	besar vuestros pies reales.	
Rey	Entre luego y avisad	985
	al conde, porque no aguarde.	

Salen Batricio y Gaseno

Batric.	¿Dónde, señor, se permite	
	desenvolturas tan grandes,	
	que tus criados afrenten	
	a los hombres miserables?	990
Rey	¿Qué dices?	
Batric.	Don Juan Tenorio,	
	alevoso y detestable,	
	la noche del casamiento,	
	antes que le consumase,	
	a mi mujer me quitó;	995
	testigos tengo delante.	

Salen Tisbea y Isabela y acompañamiento

Tisbea	Si vuestra alteza, señor,	
	de don Juan Tenorio no hace	
	justicia, a Dios y a los hombres,	1000
	mientras viva, he de quejarme.	
	Derrotado le echó el mar;	
	dile vida y hospedaje,	
	y pagóme esta amistad	
	con mentirme y engañarme	
	con nombre de mi marido.	1005
Rey	¿Qué dices?	
Isabela	Dice verdades.	

Salen Aminta y el Duque Octavio

Aminta	¿Adónde mi esposo está?	
Rey	¿Quién es?	
Aminta	Pues ¿aun no lo sabe?	
	El señor don Juan Tenorio,	
	con quien vengo a desposarme,	1010

190

Catal.	Heavens above! What's going on? 975
	The chapel's full of smoke and flames. Don Juan's
	A gonner by the look of things, and here
	Am I, him dead, left to look after him.
	I'll creep away from here as best I can.
	I'll have to break the news to his old man. 980
	I pray to you Saint George, the Holy Lamb,
	Please get me out of such a bloody jam.

Exit Catalinón. Enter the King, Don Diego, attendants

D.Diego	The Marquis is outside, your majesty.
	He seeks an audience with you urgently.
King	Then bid him enter. I'll see the Count Don Juan 985
	As well. No need for him to wait out there.

Enter Batricio and Gaseno

Batric.	Oh where on earth, your majesty, are such
	Atrocities, such hideous deeds as these
	Permitted, when such men as you protect
	And favour take advantage of your loyal 990
	Subjects?
King	Which men? Explain.
Batric.	Don Juan Tenorio,
	Resorting to the vilest treachery,
	On the night of my wedding and before
	Its consummation, took my bride from me,
	Deprived her of her pure chastity. 995
	I have witnesses to prove it to you.

Enter Tisbea, Isabela and companions

Tisbea	Oh, your majesty, I bring to you
	This earnest plea. Punish Don Juan Tenorio,
	For otherwise both God and all the world
	Shall know, as long as I have breath, of his 1000
	Offence. This traitor, washed up by the sea,
	I cared for, took into my house, restored
	To life again. The hospitality
	That I gave him he cruelly abused,
	And promsing to be my husband, tricked 1005
	Me.
King	Another complainant?
Isabela	She tells the truth.

Enter Aminta and Duke Octavio

Aminta	Where is my husband?
King	And who would he be?
Aminta	Who would he be? I thought your majesty
	Would surely know that he's Don Juan Tenorio
	Who's promised faithfully to marry me. 1010

191

	I'm sure a man of such nobility	
	Is bound to act towards me honourably.	
	Will your majesty arrange the marriage?	

Enter the Marquis of Mota

Mota	It's time, your majesty, that certain facts	
	Should see the light of day. On that account	1015
	I'm forced to say the crime of which I stood	
	Accused was never mine. Don Juan Tenorio's	
	The man to blame for that, for he abused	
	My friendship and used for his advantage	
	My good name. These two witnesses will speak	1020
	On my behalf.	

King	Enough. Such shamelessness	
	Condemns itself. Arrest him. Have him put	
	To death.	

D. Diego	I've served you long, your majesty.	
	You'll honour me by punishing this son	
	Of mine, for then perhaps the Heavens will spare	1025
	A poor father, forgive him for the birth	
	Of such a worthless child.	

King	It shall be done.	
	Let no one think that noblemen can take	
	Advantage of the King.	

Enter Catalinón

Catal.	My lords, my lords,	
	I've come as quickly as I can to bring	1030
	You news of the most strange and terrible thing	
	The world has ever witnessed. Believe me,	
	It's all true, cross my heart and hope to die	
	Right here, struck down by God upon this spot.	
	My news involves Don Juan who, having robbed	1035
	The good Commander of precious life and honour,	
	Encountered his statue, upon which he	
	Pulled his beard, insulting him further,	
	And there and then invited him to dinner.	
	Oh what a stupid, idiotic thing	1040
	To go and offer him that invitation!	
	Anyway, so as not to bore you more,	
	The man of stone turned up and asked if we	
	Would like to sup with him. To be polite	

---

not only Don Juan, but Mota, Duke Octavio, and even Don Pedro
Tenorio. Ideally, of course, the nobility should be setting an example
for others to follow, but this was far from the case in Tirso's lifetime.
See Act I, 26+, note.

```
                    porque me debe el honor,
                    y es noble y no ha de negarme.
                    Manda que nos desposemos.
        Sale el Marqués de la Mota
Mota        Pues es tiempo, gran señor,
            que a luz verdades se saquen,                    1015
            sabrás que don Juan Tenorio
            la culpa que me imputaste
            tuvo él, pues como amigo,
            pudo el crüel engañarme;
            de que tengo dos testigos.                        1020
Rey         ¿Hay desvergüenza tan grande?
            Prendelde y matalde luego.
D.Diego     En premio de mis servicios
            haz que le prendan y pague
            sus culpas, porque del cielo                      1025
            rayos contra mí no bajen,
            si es mi hijo tan malo.
Rey         ¡Esto mis privados hacen!
        Sale Catalinón
Catal.      Señores, todos oíd
            el suceso más notable                            1030
            que en el mundo ha sucedido,
            y en oyéndome, matadme.
            Don Juan, del Comendador
            haciendo burla, una tarde,
            después de haberle quitado                        1035
            las dos prendas que más valen,
            tirando al bulto de piedra
            la barba por ultrajarle,
            a cenar le convidó:
            ¡nunca fuera a convidarle!                        1040
            Fué el bulto y convidóle;
            y agora porque no os canse,
            acabando de cenar,
            entre mil presagios graves,
```

1029   Advantage of the King: the moral and political point is made very
        clearly for the benefit of a contemporary audience. Throughout the play
        criticism has been made of the irresponsible behaviour of noblemen –

	de la mano le tomó,	1045
	y le aprieta hasta quitalle	
	la vida, diciendo: "Dios	
	me manda que así te mate,	
	castigando tus delitos.	
	Quien tal hace que tal pague."	1050

Rey
Catal. ¿Qué dices?
           Lo que es verdad,
diciendo antes que acabase,
que a doña Ana no debía
honor, que le oyeron antes
del engaño.

Mota   Por las nuevas   1055
mil albricias pienso darte.

Rey ¡Justo castigo del cielo!
Y agora es bien que se casen
todos, pues la causa es muerta,
vida de tantos desastres.   1060

Octav. Pues ha enviudado Isabela,
quiero con ella casarme.

Mota Yo con mi prima.

Batric.   Y nosotros
con las nuestras, porque acabe
El Convidado de piedra.   1065

Rey Y el sepulcro se traslade
en San Francisco en Madrid,
para memoria más grande.

1060   <u>Let order reign again</u>: see Act III, 723, note.

1067   <u>San Francisco's church</u>: San Francisco in Madrid became a church in the fifteenth century, having been founded as a hermitage two centuries earlier. It was renovated in 1617 – around the time of the play's composition – and rebuilt in 1761.

	We went and, when we'd finished, he commands 1045
	Don Juan give him his hand, which he then grips
	And squeezes till my master has no breath
	At all left in him, and the stone man says:
	'Death is God's punishment. Let each man heed
	The sinner reaps the harvest of his deeds' 1050
King	What are you saying?
Catal.	Just the honest truth,
	Your majesty. Oh, and there's one thing more.
	I heard my master say that Doña Ana
	Didn't lose her honour. They spotted him
	Before he could seduce her.
Mota	Oh, thank you, sir, 1055
	For news like this I willingly embrace
	You.
King	How justly God punishes Don Juan!
	But now, my friends, let marriage make amends
	For all the wrongs inflicted by this man,
	Their cause is dead. Let order reign again. 1060
Octav.	Now Isabela has no husband, I,
	Your majesty, can hope to satisfy
	Her need.
Mota	And I, your majesty, shall marry
	Doña Ana.
Batric.	All of us, as this play ends,
	Shall marry our girl-friends.
King	My last command 1065
	Is this. The tomb of Don Gonzalo shall
	be moved, from here to San Francisco's church.
	Madrid shall be his final resting-place.